W9-BZJ-008

PAUL N. MILIUKOV

The
Russian Revolution

Volume 3

The Agony of the
Provisional Government

Edited, Translated, and with an
Introduction by
G. M. Hamburg

WITHDRAWN

Academic International Press
1987

CoIRes
DK
265
.M49313
v.3

THE RUSSIAN SERIES / Volume 44/3

Paul N. Miliukov, *The Russian Revolution*, Volume 3: *The Agony of the Provisional Government*. Translation of *Istoriia vtoroi russkoi revoliutsii*, Volume 1, Part 3 (Sofia, 1921).

English translation and special contents of this book Copyright©1987 by Academic International Press.

All rights reserved. The reproduction or utilization of this work in any form or by any electronic, mechanical, or other means, now known or hereafter invented, including xerography, photocopying, and recording, or in any information storage and retrieval system, by any individual, institution or library, is forbidden under law without the prior written permission of the publisher.

ISBN 0-87569-096-3

Composition by Sandra Parker
Title page by King & Queen Press

Printed in the United States of America

A list of Academic International Press publications is found at the end of this volume.

ACADEMIC INTERNATIONAL PRESS
POB 1111 Gulf Breeze FL 32561

CONTENTS

MILIUKOV AND THE COMING OF THE OCTOBER REVOLUTION

More than thirty years before the October Revolution of 1917 the Russian Minister of Internal Affairs Dmitry Tolstoy worried that if the tsarist regime should fall, a Marxist government would replace it.[1] The minister was not far wrong.

When the tsarist administration was swept away in February and March 1917, it left an eight-month political vacuum in which its opponents struggled to create a new regime.[2] The honor of building a new government first fell to P.N. Miliukov and his liberal Constitutional Democratic (Kadet) party.[3] The Kadets dominated the Provisional Government during the first phase of its existence (March to early May). They advocated a strong Provisional Government that would ensure a disciplined Russian war effort, while simultaneously protecting the civil rights of all Russians and non-Russians under its dominion. The Kadets preferred to avoid "dangerous social experiments" during wartime, and they believed that the proper forum for considering such reforms was a nationally-elected Constituent Assembly—a kind of constitutional convention—that would meet as soon as circumstances permitted.

The Kadets did not long enjoy their control over the Provisional Government, for they were quickly forced to share power in a coalition with moderate socialists of the Socialist Revolutionary (SR) and Menshevik parties.[4] In the early revolutionary days the moderate socialists dominated the Executive Committee of the Petrograd Soviet and then the Central Executive Committee of the All-Russia Congress of Soviets. The moderate socialists and the organizations they represented were not unwilling to support a Kadet-controlled "bourgeois" government, but they made it clear that their support was contingent on Kadet sponsorship of genuinely "democratic" and pro-revolutionary policies. Their criticisms of the Kadets, more sweeping as time passed, led to tension between the Soviets and the Provisional Government and forced the liberals to share power in the coalition cabinets of May, July and September.

In retrospect, the policies advocated by the moderate socialists seem full of ambiguities and contradictions. On one hand, they disapproved of any systematic attempt to win the war in the field for the sake of territorial spoils. They thought the causes for which Russia fought—excepting always self-defense—were morally dubious, and they hoped that Russia could extricate itself from the Great War by means of a "democratic peace" without annexations and war indemnities imposed on the losers. This military stance made them nervous about increased discipline in the army and about turning over much authority to the generals. On the other hand, socialist leaders, notably A.F. Kerensky and I.G. Tsereteli, helped organize the Russian offensive of summer 1917 and advocated certain measures to bolster army discipline after the collapse of this offensive. The moderate socialists also issued ambiguous signals on the implementation of social reforms. For example, they worked to prepare the groundwork for the distribution of noble estates to the peasantry, but refused to sanction actual land seizures before the Constituent Assembly.

The most fateful of their contradictions was their attitude toward taking power. The Mensheviks regarded the overthrow of tsarism as an act in a "bourgeois revolution," and they therefore tended to see bourgeois government as proper and historically legitimate under the circumstances. Yet, as democrats, they felt obliged to restrain the worst, most undemocratic impulses of the bourgeoisie, to protect the interests of the nascent proletariat. These views led certain Mensheviks to participate in coalition cabinets with the bourgeoisie, yet forced them to repudiate any attempt by socialists to rule Russia alone. The Mensheviks acted as midwives at the birth of a bourgeois order, not as parents of a socialist order. The SRs, as the historian Radkey has shown, tended all too readily to accept the Menshevik conception of the revolution, and thus to fall into the same political contradictions as the Mensheviks.[5] In the case of the SRs, this error was compounded by leaders who had ceased to be revolutionaries except in name, and who felt almost comfortable in the penumbra of liberal giants such as Miliukov. Thus, the presence of moderate socialists in the cabinet moved the Provisional Government to the left, but certainly not to socialism.

The events of October 1917 demonstrated that Russia had tired of the Provisional Government, of its sempiternal contradictions and moderation. The future belonged to a more radical and consistent political faction—the Bolshevik party, led by Vladimir Ilich Lenin. As Dmitry Tolstoy had predicted, Russia would have its Marxist regime after all.

In *Istoriia vtoroi russkoi revoliutsii* (History of the Second Russian Revolution), largely composed in 1918 and published in three installments between 1921 and 1924, P.N. Miliukov tried to explain the failure of the Provisional Government and the triumph of Bolshevism. The present volume is a translation of the third installment of this history, and is the final volume to appear in print under the English title, *The Russian Revolution*.[6] As in the preceding two volumes of his history,

Miliukov organized his narrative around a single abstract principle—*gosudarstvennost*, or the "principle of the state."[7] He intended to show that the Constitutional Democrats, with their program of a strong government and pragmatic liberalism, were the true defenders of the "principle of the state," while other political parties either failed to understand this principle or were inimical to it. These other political factions were responsible for the collapse of the Provisional Government and for the "tragedy" of October 1917.

The third volume traces events from the suppression of the Kornilov movement in late August and early September 1917 to the defeat of anti-Bolshevik resistance in early November 1917. Miliukov gave this volume the interesting subtitle "*Agoniia vlasti*." In Russian "*agoniia*" can mean simply "agony" in the sense of physical and moral suffering, or "death throes"—a final, desperate battle to hang onto life. The word can also carry from the Greek the connotation of "deliberate struggle," "confrontation," "fight." Miliukov linked "*agoniia*" with the genitive form of the word "*vlast*," which concretely denotes "the government," but which also can have a more abstract meaning such as "power" or "authority." Thus, the subtitle of the volume actually suggests a final, painful, titanic struggle of the government, indeed of the principle of genuine political authority (gosudarstvennost), against a terrible nemesis. Miliukov wished his readers to understand that after the Kornilov affair the very concept of statehood was imperiled, and that with the triumph of Bolshevism this principle suffered defeat.

For practical purposes Miliukov's interpretation of this period of revolutionary crisis consists of two interlocking arguments. The first is that after the Kornilov affair Kerensky's government was isolated politically, internally divided, and incompetent to rule. The second is that by means of excellent leadership, unscrupulousness, and demagoguery the Bolshevik party won significant support among the politically unenlightened workers and soldiers of Petrograd and Moscow. The impotence of the Kerensky government, combined with the Bolsheviks' leadership and mass support, made it possible for the Bolsheviks to seize power in October and November 1917. The purpose of this essay is to review Miliukov's arguments, to examine their persuasiveness in the light of current scholarship, and to place them in the context of Miliukov's evolution as a historian and politician.

In Miliukov's opinion, the key to Kerensky's political ascendancy in the summer of 1917 had been his attempt to define a political position somewhere between the moderate socialists, who dominated the Petrograd Soviet and the Executive Committee of the All-Russia Soviets, and the right wing, represented by the Kadets and the army high command. Until the Kornilov crisis Kerensky was useful to both moderate left and right. Moderate leftists viewed him as one of their own, a democrat who cherished the great achievements of the early revolution, who despised the tsarist order, and who would resist any attempt by the Kadets to restore the old regime. Yet Kerensky, they knew, was comfortable working with "bourgeois" politicians and would not challenge the pious notion that the revolution was after all "bourgeois." The Kadets, for their part, saw Kerensky as one of the few popular revolutionaries who might be made to understand the need for a strong government, a disciplined army and domestic restraint. They thought Kerensky might be persuaded to rein in popular emotions, to teach the fool Ivan how to reason.

Miliukov argued that the Kornilov affair destroyed the tacit agreement of moderate left and right about Kerensky. To the left anyone who had dealt with Kornilov was suspicious, and there were some who felt that Kerensky had been plotting with Kornilov behind the back of the Soviet. Worse yet, Kerensky's demand that his cabinet resign and entrust him full power to fight Kornilov suggested that Kerensky himself harbored dictatorial intentions. Kerensky's plan to form a five-man "directory" to rule Russia did not dissipate this distrust. Both the Mensheviks and the SRs condemned the "directory" as not in the interests of the revolution. Furthermore, the Kornilov affair cast into doubt any cooperation with the Kadet party, which had seemed to align itself with the rebellious general's camp. Therefore, Kerensky's utility as a link to the Kadets was destroyed for the moderate left. For the Kadets Kerensky was the man who had frustrated plans for a strong government and a revitalized army. He was both a symptom and a cause of the impotence of coalition government, a government that seemed all too often to lean to the left. As Miliukov put it: "For both groups he (Kerensky) ceased to be the lesser evil, for now both groups regarded as harmful the continued existence of the fictional system of the 'coalition.' . . . Thus the alliance was broken at both ends."

The difficulty was, of course, that neither the moderate left nor the right had the wherewithal to impose a new government. The Mensheviks still did not wish to govern themselves, for how could socialists preside over a bourgeois revolution? Moreover, the popular influence of the Mensheviks was fast waning. They had been defeated badly by the more radical Bolsheviks in Petrograd municipal elections, and in early September the Bolsheviks took control of the presidium of the Petrograd Soviet. The Menshevik Tsereteli, at one time the leading figure in the Petrograd Soviet, publicly lamented: "It is obvious that the banner of the revolution, which for six months we held in our hands, is now being transferred to other hands." The Kadets, badly compromised in the eyes of the Soviet by their ideological proximity to Kornilov, to say nothing of their ill-concealed preference for a Kornilov victory, had fallen out of grace even with the most moderate socialists. The Kadets social base of support in Petrograd was simply too narrow for them to form a government. Yet if neither group could govern on its own, what was the alternative to a continued coalition?

This question haunted the politics of the moderate left and the right until the October Revolution. There were two attempts—both unsuccessful—to work out a new basis for government. The first was at the so-called Democratic Conference in mid-September. The pretension of this conference was that, as a representative agency of the Russian democracy, the conference was superior to the Provisional Government and had the right to dictate the government's composition and direction. Miliukov and the Kadets bitterly criticized the conference's presumption of sovereign authority and refused to participate in it. Unfortunately, the Democratic Conference was divided so badly that it could not agree on the shape of a government. It found itself in the self-contradictory position of narrowly approving the principle of a coalition with the bourgeoisie, while rejecting any coalition with the leading "bourgeois" party—the Kadets. The failure of the Democratic Conference prompted the moderate socialists to create a second body, the so-called Soviet of the Republic or Pre-Parliament, which they hoped would be more successful in guiding the Provisional Government.

The Pre-Parliament, which met from October 7-25, suffered the same debilities as its predecessor. In Chapters V and VI Miliukov treated the Pre-Parliament's efforts to hammer out a common position on the problems of defense and foreign policy, critical issues to be faced by any future government. The Pre-Parliament did not formulate any position on the army question. The chairman of the Left SRs, Shteinberg-Karelin, observed: "The basic tragedy of the revolution is that having commenced under common slogans, its defenders soon split into various factions. If the revolution was necessary to the propertied elements in order to clear the road for their military successes, for the democracy it was the first step toward ending the war. And since these goals were diametrically opposed, there was no way of bringing about unity." In other words, a wartime coalition government between propertied elements and the democracy was, in principle, nonsense. When the Pre-Parliament got around to debating foreign policy, there was precious little time left to either moderate left or right. The last arguments were made to an auditorium of scarcely one hundred people. Life had passed the Pre-Parliament by, and the real decisions would be made in the streets.

Throughout this period of futile agonizing over the practical and theoretical bases of a coalition government, Kerensky continued to preside over the Provisional Government. In late September he even announced a new cabinet, divided equally between socialist nonentities and those "bourgeois" politicians who had had nothing to do with the Kornilovites. Not only was the new cabinet politically isolated, it was internally divided.

Miliukov observed that between Foreign Minister Tereshchenko and War Minister Verkhovsky there was little love lost. After pursuing a foreign policy that, in Miliukov's opinion, was based on the disastrous principles of the Zimmerwald Conference, Tereshchenko suddenly had a change of heart. In a newspaper interview he confessed that the results of past policy were the opposite of what the government intended: "We have spoken in favor of peace, but our actions have created conditions that prolonged the war. We have striven to reduce casualties, but consequently have increased bloodshed. We have worked for a democratic peace, but instead we have brought nearer the triumph of German imperialism. Such misunderstandings are not permissible." Tereshchenko hinted that the government would have to be more resolute in prosecuting the war if it wished to win peace. At the Pre-Parliament he condemned the moderate left for trying to impose the notorious "Instruction" on the Soviet delegate to the upcoming Paris Conference of the Allies. Tereshchenko's new tone was countered by Verkhovsky, who declared in a public forum that Russia could not long afford to continue to fight the war. Verkhovsky hoped to win approval for a contradictory policy that would promise soldiers a quick peace settlement, yet end "anarchy" and indiscipline in the army so as to facilitate a military victory in the field. Miliukov suggested that Verkhovsky's pessimism was the product of leftist sympathies and of the strange ambition to promote himself as military dictator, as a Kornilov of the left. To Tereshchenko the basis for Verkhovsky's pessimism was as murky as Verkhovsky's ambition was transparent. Prompted by the Foreign Minister, even Kerensky came to regard Verkhovsky as a liability and political competitor. On the eve of the Bolshevik Revolution Kerensky, facing a dangerous split in his cabinet, forced the War Minister out of office.

The disagreement between Verkhovsky and Tereshchenko was the most dramatic example of the government's internal division, but it was not the only one. Indeed, the chronic problem for cabinet members was to find a matter on which they could agree and on which they could persuade Kerensky to act. As Miliukov noted: "In his eternal indecisiveness, in his constant vacillations between pressures from the left and right and his searches for an equilibrium, Kerensky gradually arrived at a condition in which it was genuine torture for him to make a concrete decision. He instinctively avoided these torturous moments as only he could." By the end Kerensky had become aloof and inaccessible even to his closest associates. He still managed a Napoleonic pose, but it was the sad pose of Napoleon at Elba. Unsurprisingly, Kerensky spent much of October thinking about a grand tour of Russia. According to Miliukov, Kerensky did not seem to understand what was happening in the provinces, and was mystified utterly by the revolutionary process in the capital itself.

In the last month of its existence Kerensky's government was buffeted by forces that it was incompetent to control. Finland was moving toward independence, and the Provisional Government did little to stop this process. In negotiations with Finnish liberals, Petrograd quickly consented to the principle of Finnish self-determination in domestic policy. The Provisional Government did reserve the rights to quarter troops in Finland and to determine foreign policy, but these "rights" would have been difficult to exercise against an uncooperative Finnish public. In the Ukraine the separatist movement tested its muscle at Petrograd's expense. There was an attempt to build a specifically Ukrainian army and to "Ukrainize" the Black Sea Fleet. These initiatives were blocked temporarily, but by mid-October the Ukrainian Central Rada had made clear its desire for a separate Ukraine. On the eve of the October Revolution the Rada was in open conflict with the Petrograd government. In addition, Miliukov indicated there was a growing number of peasant disorders and land redistributions occurring in September and October. "Democratic" labor organizations such as the railroad union (Vikzhel) struck against the government with impunity, and Tsentroflot even dictated to the Navy Minister where it would locate its offices in the capital. A government that cannot distribute office space might as well hang out a sign: "Abandon hope, all ye who enter here."

As the Provisional Government shuffled off its mortal coil, the Bolshevik party prepared the advent of a new, historically unprecedented regime. Having won control over the Petrograd Soviet in the wake of the Kornilov affair, the Bolsheviks placed unrelenting pressure on the national government. In September they denounced the Provisional Government's cabinet as a "government of civil war," more bourgeois and less democratic than its predecessors. They worked hard to sabotage the Democratic Conference's efforts to find a compromise on the issue of a coalition. Led by Trotsky, they walked out of the Pre-Parliament, which they called a "new piece of stage setting" behind which "murderous work against the people would be done." Finally, in October they established the Military Revolutionary Committee, the engine of the forthcoming revolution. At every step Miliukov juxtaposed the Bolsheviks' decisiveness, clarity of vision and unity to the Provisional Government's blindness and incapacity for leadership.

Given the Bolsheviks' strength and the government's weakness, one is surprised to learn that the moderate left and the right shared the opinion that the Bolsheviks could not seize and retain state power. Tsereteli, who understood that the banner of the revolution was being transferred into other hands, thought that "the enemies of the revolution impatiently await the transfer of power to the Soviet of Workers' and Soldiers' Deputies in order to deal the revolution a decisive defeat." Kerensky was openly contemptuous of the Bolsheviks, and in mid-October smugly contented himself with the government's military readiness to put down an insurrection. As late as October 23 the cabinet refused to authorize the arrest of the Military Revolutionary Committee. Meanwhile, the Kadets suspected that if the Bolsheviks should succeed in winning power, the attempt to impose the Bolshevik program on Russia would open the eyes of the people to Bolshevik "deceptions" and would reopen the political doors to the liberal party.

It was in answer to the skepticism about Bolshevik prospects to rule that Lenin wrote the pamphlet "Can the Bolsheviks Retain State Power?" Miliukov treated this pamphlet as the key to understanding Bolshevism, as the ideological expression of the final stage of the Russian Revolution. Lenin explained that his party had wide enough support among proletarians and poor peasants to win power, destroy the old state apparatus, build a new popular government, expropriate the rich, and institute revolutionary changes in society. In one revealing passage the Bolshevik leader observed that these changes would provoke a civil war, but he added: "A revolution is the sharpest, the most violent, the most desperate class struggle and civil war. Not a single revolution has succeeded without civil war." He counselled his followers not to be afraid of this prospect, but to welcome it, for civil war would demonstrate the hidden appeal of socialism to the oppressed. "For each ten thousand of publicly-known socialists there will appear a million new fighters, who until that time will have been politically asleep." "Here, where the last unskilled worker, or unemployed person, every cook, every ruined peasant can see—not from the newspapers, but with his own eyes—that the proletarian government is not grovelling before wealth, but is aiding the poor, . . . that it is taking surplus products from parasites and is aiding the hungry, that it uses force to install the homeless in the apartments of the rich, that it forces the rich to pay for milk, but does not give them a single drop of milk until the children of the poor are fed, that the land is being transferred to the laboring peasants, the factories and banks are under the control of workers, that swift and serious punishment awaits the millionaires who conceal their wealth—when he sees and feels this, *then* no force of the capitalists and the kulaks . . . will be able to defeat the popular revolution, but, on the contrary, the revolution will conquer the entire world, for in all nations the socialist revolution is at hand."

Miliukov admitted the rhetorical power of Lenin's appeal to the masses. "Can the Bolsheviks Retain State Power?" was "demagoguery . . . and very effective demagoguery." Given the anarchy in the army, the moral exhaustion of the people, peasant land hunger, the proletariat's understandable desire for a better life, the evident weakness of the Provisional Government, widespread popular resentment of the rich—be they landlords, factory owners, war profiteers, or simply successful merchants, the Bolshevik promises had considerable allure. Miliukov sadly confided that "the logic of events was on Lenin's side."

Having gone so far toward recognition of the ideological force of Bolshevism, Miliukov characteristically could not resist mentioning two additional "traits" of Bolshevism. First, Lenin's credentials as a socialist were dubious. Lenin was really "a centralist and statist—and he counted first and foremost on measures of direct state compulsion." Lenin was completely alien to the anarchist strain of socialism and also to the communal strain, which in Europe traced its lineage to Fourier and in Russia to Herzen and the Populists. Second, Lenin was, if anything, a tool of German imperialism. At various points in his book Miliukov mentioned the German attitude toward events in Russia. He asserted that the Germans stood behind the separatist movements in the Ukraine and elsewhere, that the Germans supplied the content of the Russian pro-peace declarations in September and October 1917, that the Germans were happy to take advantage of the demoralized Russian armed forces to seize strategic territories. In a passage about German financing of the Bolshevik party, Miliukov alleged that the German Ministry of Foreign Affairs arranged a transfer of weapons and money to Trotsky and Antonov-Ovseenko in September 1917, and that Lenin himself received money from an intermediary in the German banking industry. In addition, when describing Bolshevik harassment of an oppositional women's organization in Moscow, Miliukov reported testimony from a witness that Bolshevik forces left behind "something of their own"—a German mark. These passages were meant to suggest that Bolshevik policy, if not made in Berlin, certainly carried out German designs. Miliukov wanted his readers to identify Bolshevism with treason to Russia, with the destruction of *gosudarstvennost*. In the showdown between the Bolsheviks and the Provisional Government all the actors played true to form. According to Miliukov, Kerensky pretended at first that there was no danger to the government, then he began to see dangers that were not there: for example, he came to suspect of treachery Colonel Polkovnikov, the head of the Petrograd military district. Ultimately, Kerensky's only concern was to justify his own conduct before the moderate left and posterity. As for the moderate left, they could not even arrange a vote of confidence for the beleaguered Provisional Government at the beginning of the actual insurrection. Their plan was to arrange an exclusively socialist government which would involve the Bolsheviks as junior partners. No socialist group took to the barricades against the Bolshevik Red Guards. For these moderate socialists "revolution" had become synonymous with passing (or not passing) resolutions.

Meanwhile, the Bolsheviks moved methodically toward power. The only question was whether the Bolsheviks really intended to seize power *before* the Second All-Russia Congress of Soviets, so as to present it with a *fait accompli*. Miliukov thought it not unlikely that Trotsky's original plan was to win control and legitimacy at the Congress of Soviets, not before; perhaps this original plan was abandoned when it became evident just how easily the Bolshevik insurrection would succeed. In any case, the Bolsheviks capitalized on the ambiguity of the situation. While seizing telephone exchanges and bridges, their agents talked with the moderate socialists about an exclusively socialist government. The "parliamentary" activity did no harm; indeed, it paralyzed the gullible moderate socialists while the Red Guards did what must be done in true revolutions.

As victors, Miliukov contended, the Bolsheviks were arrogant, unceremonious and ruthless. The only heroes of the October Revolution came from the defenders of the Winter Palace—the "bourgeois" ministers and the members of the Women's Batallion. The former were rewarded with arrest and were nearly lynched by an unruly crowd; the latter suffered verbal and physical abuse at the hands of Bolshevik captors.[8]

After the Bolsheviks took power in Petrograd, they faced immediate challenges in the army and in Moscow. Miliukov showed that the anti-Bolshevik activity of Kerensky and General Krasnov near Petrograd was doomed to failure. The common soldiers were indifferent to the fate of Kerensky, and the high command had been poisoned against anti-Bolshevik crusades through Kerensky's promotion of political generals such as Cheremisov. Miliukov compared the collapse of the tsarist government in February with the collapse of the Provisional Government in October. He concluded that both governments fell because they lacked the support of the army. As to events in Moscow, Miliukov celebrated the efforts of patriots there to resist Petrograd's example. However, he noted that the leadership of the anti-Bolshevik forces was poor, and that the morale of the resistance was weakened by misunderstandings among its members, by jealousies and political shortsightedness.

With the fall of the Moscow resistance "the Bolsheviks' victory was complete and final. Their victory in Moscow assured their triumph in the rest of Russia." This was hard for Miliukov to accept. In the bitter concluding paragraph of his book, a paragraph obviously added in 1924, he wrote: "The Party of Popular Liberty was then [1917] predicting that the Bolsheviks' victory would entail the loss of the war and partition of Russia. But no one, including that party, foresaw that the Bolshevik regime would last many years and would lead Russia to the destruction of all its national goals—political, economic, and cultural—goals that were the product of centuries."

Most contemporary scholars of the October Revolution accept in general terms Miliukov's contention that the last Kerensky cabinet was politically isolated. In the October 1917 crisis, as the journalist A.S. Izgoev put it, the government collapsed "beneath the weight of universal disgust."[9] Yet there are many aspects of Miliukov's interpretation that beg for modification or correction in the light of accumulated evidence.

First, Miliukov's picture of the 1917 political constellation did not accurately portray the nature of the fundamental political demarcations in Russian society. Miliukov's attention focused almost exclusively on the Petrograd elites—the propertied members of "census society" (tsenzovoe obshchestvo) and the intelligentsia—who constituted the leadership of the Kadets and the socialist parties. But by September 1917 the mood of the Russian populace had shifted sharply to the left, so that the Petrograd elites, the Bolshevik party excepted, were almost entirely isolated *vis-`a-vis* the nation as a whole. To spend so many pages recording the differences between the Central Executive Committee and Kerensky, or between the factions of the Democratic Conference and Pre-Parliament, was to miss the central drama of the post-Kornilov period. The great Menshevik chronicler N.N. Sukhanov underlined this point in the sixth volume of his classic *Zapiski o revoliutsii* (Notes on the Revolution): "He who shall write the history . . . of the post-Kornilov period must devote the bulk of his attention to the processes occurring among the masses. All the rest was ephemeral, transitory, and ultimately inconsequential . . . That is, to be more precise, all the rest was nothing more than a stage set, the background against which the revolution developed."[10] Miliukov's conceit was that the "stage set" was the play itself.

Second, Miliukov is not altogether convincing in his explanation of the divisions within the Petrograd elites. The main point of conflict in September and October was not the presence of Kerensky in the government, however distasteful various politicians found him. Nor was the crucial issue whether to include the Kadets in a coalition, for there was already so much popular hostility toward the Kadets as to bias any sensible politician against including them in the cabinet. The two most important issues were: (1) whether or not Russia should continue to fight the Germans; and (2) what form a socialist government might take in Russia.

The question of the war had been raised in the first days of the February Revolution, but was not posed point-blank until the Kornilov affair. The debate cut across normal factional lines. For example, the Bolsheviks, Left SRs, Menshevik-Internationalists, the left-wing Kadets and even War Minister Verkhovsky demanded a swift end to the war; meanwhile, with various equivocations, the Right SRs, the Potresov and Plekhanov groups of Mensheviks, the right-wing Kadets and the rest of Kerensky's cabinet favored continued fighting. Given the at best tenuous hold of the army command over frontline troops, the growth of pro-peace sentiment among soldiers, the more than occasional difficulties with desertion, and the terrible problems of food supply at the front, it is clear that a swift peace was desperately needed. Martov once had said: "Either the revolution will end the war, or the war will end the revolution."[11] It was now time for the revolutionaries to put an end to the war, or to face extinction themselves.

The debate over socialist rule began immediately after the Kornilov affair. On August 31 the Bolshevik Kamenev called on the Petrograd Soviet to renounce the politics of compromise and to demand a national government of "representatives of the revolutionary proletariat and peasantry."[12] The Soviet's passage of the Bolshevik-sponsored resolution on this question later that evening transformed the political climate, for subsequently the government and the moderate socialists were on the defensive. It is true that Kerensky made a successful last-ditch effort to rescue the idea of a liberal-leftist coalition, and that for a time the moderate socialists even supported this idea, *faute de mieux*. Nevertheless, after August 31 shrewd politicians understood that Russia would soon have a socialist regime, and the only issue was what form this new regime would take. Would it be based on the Soviet or on the Constituent Assembly? Would it be a one-party (Bolshevik) government or a multiparty government with representatives from all the major socialist factions? The radicalized masses could in all probability have been brought, at least temporarily, to support any form of socialist rule. Which form would prevail had as much to do with tactical considerations as with matters of political principle.

Recent scholarship has emphasized that the Bolshevik party was itself divided on the form socialist rule might take.[13] Zinoviev and Kamenev preferred a multi-party socialist government to one-party rule by the Bolsheviks, partly because of the dangers of civil war that one-party rule entailed. Even Lenin, who pressed so hard for a Bolshevik government to be installed before the Second Congress of Soviets, had wondered at moments whether it might make sense to collaborate with the moderate socialists. In an article written in early September he suggested that the Bolsheviks might be willing to live with an exclusively socialist regime led by SRs and Mensheviks.[14] He backed away from this plan because he preferred exclusively Bolshevik rule (though this preference was never a matter of doctrine for him) and because he saw that the moderate socialists were more comfortable with the "bourgeoisie" than with the Bolsheviks as allies.

The moderate socialists were very slow to accept the idea of an exclusively socialist government, even though individual socialists long had advocated such a political course. At the Central Executive Committee caucus of October 23 Sukhanov told his colleagues: "The old Menshevik-SR bloc must immediately resolve on complete liquidation of the [Kerensky] government, must proclaim the dictatorship of the democracy, announce their readiness to create a government from amongst the Soviet parties and swiftly promulgate the democratic program in its entirety." Sukhanov had the impression that "many of them evidently felt that I was speaking the truth, even if my plan could not be put into practice."[15] When the moderate socialists refused to give Kerensky a vote of confidence on October 24, they placed their hope precisely in a multi-party socialist government, although they were still unsure how it could be installed.

Miliukov's description of the internal divisions in Kerensky's cabinet is correct in the main, but his interpretation of Verkhovsky's political role is misleading.[16] Verkhovsky was not a partisan leftist; indeed, he had little interest in politics, if one means by that the ability to make fine distinctions between various political tendencies. Verkhovsky was a professional soldier whose loyalty was to his troops and to the government he served. Propelled into prominence when he refused to follow Kornilov in August, Verkhovsky found himself at the age of thirty in the awkward position of the chief military officer of the (soon-to-be-proclaimed) republic. His first impulse was to try to restore discipline in

army by purging the officer corps of Kornilovites, while simultaneously building institutional safegurds against "anarchy" among the soldiers. This latter program involved a strengthening of military courts,
the restoration to officers of the right to punish disobedient troops, and
the creation of punishment regiments.[17] As Verkhovsky studied the difficulties facing the army, he became convinced that his original program would be insufficient to save the army. On October 20 he told a
joint committee of the Pre-Parliament that Russia should sue for immediate peace. "The question is not whether to permit the realization of
German designs, rather the question is whether the Russian state can be
preserved . . . Only by an immediate move toward peace can this goal
be attained. The continuation of the war until spring will mean a deterioration of the situation and the intensification of anarchy, especially if
the harvest is poor."[18]   The Soviet historian V.S. Startsev has credited
Verkhovsky with "admirable clarity of vision on military questions,"
and with making a proposal that might greatly have complicated the
Bolshevik plan to take power.[19] In turning down Verkhovsky's plan,
the "Provisional Government rejected the last, albeit quite illusory
chance to save itself."[20] Miliukov's adamant support of the war prevented
him from acknowledging Verkhovsky's statesmanship in time of crisis.

To Miliukov's assertion that the Kerensky government was incompetent to control the revolutionary forces across the Russian lands, almost
all scholars have assented. The evidence is overwhelming that Kerensky
was out of his depth in the revolutionary sea. Kerensky's famous statement to the British ambassador, Buchanan, about the Bolsheviks, "I desire only that they [the Bolsheviks] come out onto the streets, and then
I shall crush them," forever will remain testimony to the prime minister's inability to cope with the greatest threat to his regime. [21] As Buchanan noted, "he [Kerensky] was a man of words and not of action. He
had his chances and never seized them. He thought more of saving the
revolution than of saving his country, and he ended by losing both."[22]
We need to add only one caveat: Miliukov could have done no better. A
Kadet regime that would have continued the war, delayed the solution of
the nationalities and agrarian questions, opposed factory committees and
strikes—such a regime would have been swept away just as quickly as
Kerensky's government. Only those who would swim with the tide,
rather than against it, could survive.

The most glaring weakness of Miliukov's history is his treatment of
the Bolsheviks. Before Chapter VII ("The Bolsheviks Prepare") Miliukov barely mentioned the Bolshevik party. He reduced Bolshevik ideology to the pamphlet "Can the Bolsheviks Retain State Power?"—obviously
an important document, but by no means a sufficient guide to Leninist

thinking on the subject of the coming revolution. Miliukov seemed to treat the Bolsheviks as a monolithic party, as mere followers of Lenin and Trotsky. The bitter disagreements over one-party rule versus multiparty socialist government received no attention at all from Miliukov. His commentary on the link between the Bolsheviks and the German government did nothing to illuminate the causes of the Bolshevik triumph, for nowhere did Miliukov suggest that German financial support was a necessary prerequisite for the October Revolution. Rather, as the passage on the German money demonstrates, he placed the real and putative evidence of a Bolshevik-German link at the service of his own *a priori* convictions about the destruction of *gosudarstvennost.*

Most disappointing of all is Miliukov's failure to explain the nexus between popular discontent and the Bolshevik success in October. As the winter of 1917 approached, the Russian economy was in disastrous condition. In Petrograd runaway inflation prevailed. If the cost of living had more than tripled between 1914 and January 1917, between January and October 1917 the cost of living jumped to fourteen times the prewar level.[23] Even taking into account enormous increases in workers' salaries, real wage levels fell rapidly for factory workers in the revolutionary year. The whole country suffered from a paralysis of rail traffic, so that precious food remained on freight cars, and spoiled before reaching its destination. Devastating shortages of fuel threatened to halt factory production. Strike activity in the country at large increased significantly in September and October 1917.[24] In response to the deterioration of the economic climate, many businesses laid off workers or shut their doors. Unemployment spread, and "the bony hand of Tsar Hunger" gripped the populace. One might have thought that, even in an economic crisis, the frontline army would have been relatively well fed. That was not the case; there were countless quartermasters who could not supply troops with proper rations. Indeed, hunger in the trenches was one of the reasons behind Minister Verkhovsky's plea for immediate peace.[25]

The disintegration of the economy played no small role in the workers' and soldiers' determination to be rid of the Kerensky government and also of coalition rule. Factory committees organized themselves to fight against falling real wages and to find fuel for production. Workers came to believe that the bourgeoisie was deliberately sabotaging the economy through artificial shortages.[26] In the workers' eyes any government with bourgeois cabinet members became automatically suspect. It was no wonder that in the great industrial centers and in the army the Bolsheviks found a ready-made constituency. The party's problem was to channel the masses' energy against the *Kerenshchina* into organizations that could overturn the regime at the proper time.

The Bolsheviks' task was easier than one might have suspected, because nearly all the organizational tools for an uprising had long existed. Various military units stood ready to move against the Provisional Government should the need arise. The Latvian Sharpshooters and the Kronstadt sailors could be counted upon as disciplined fighting units.[27] The Red Guards could be used either to defend Smolny or to move against vulnerable points in the capital.[28] The Bolsheviks had a majority not only in the Petrograd Soviet but also in several others.[29] They and their Left SR allies also had an effective majority at the impending Second Congress of Soviets. All they really required for a seizure of power was a means of holding the support of the Petrograd garrison. This means was provided by the Military Revolutionary Committee, which was founded on October 9 (not, as Miliukov would have it, on October 16) ostensibly to evaluate the defense needs of Petrograd.[30] The Military Revolutionary Committee orchestrated the revolution beginning on October 22. The public justification for the uprising was not articulated until later, on October 24, when Kerensky belatedly ordered the closing of the Bolshevik press and the arrest of the Bolshevik leaders. Then the Bolsheviks could claim to be acting in defense of Soviet power—a convenient pretext for open action.[31] The long and successful preparation for the revolution made the actual events of October 25 seem quite unextraordinary—"dry and businesslike," as one observer put it.[32]

Thus, Miliukov's analysis of the Bolshevik Revolution dealt almost exclusively with the politics of the doomed Provisional Government and the moderate socialists in the Central Executive Committee of the Soviet. He was superficial in discussing problems that, at least to current historians, seem more important: the radicalization of the masses; the extent of mass support for the Bolsheviks; and the Bolsheviks' ideology, especially in regard to the question of what form socialist rule ought to take. At the very heart of Miliukov's history of October 1917 there is a curious incomprehension, one is tempted to say ignorance, of the motive power behind events. How do we account for such incomprehension in a politician and intellectual otherwise known for acuity and political understanding?

It is not difficult to account for Miliukov's incomprehension of the masses. He was in this respect a descendant of the liberal statists of the 1840s and 1850s, thinkers who virtually excluded the masses from the category of conscious historical agents. The sharpest dismissal of the masses' independence as agents came from the Moscow University professor T.N. Granovsky, a moderate Westernizer and early liberal: "The masses, like the Scandinavian Thor, are senselessly cruel and unthinkingly good. They stagnate under the weight of historical and natural conditions, from which only the individual is freed by thought. The process of history consists of this decomposition of the masses by thought. Its task is [to create] the morally enlightened individual, independent of determining conditions, and a society corresponding to the demands of such an individual."[33]

Granovsky's disciple, the liberal historian B.N. Chicherin, adapted Granovsky's view of the masses to Russian history. According to Chicherin, the chief characteristic of the Russian people was passivity. "The Russian man does not gladly leave that private sphere into which his birth and environment have placed him. He loves to wander around by the hour, but he does not love concerted activity . . . . In general, he does not move untiringly forward, but does everything haphazardly, by chance, accidentally and lazily. He does not know how to create from inside himself an intellectually multi-faceted world and does not tear himself easily away from the influence of his surroundings. In him the force of custom and tradition is astonishing; it is amazing how he uncomplainingly and humbly submits himself to the sovereign dominion that he recognized on one occasion long ago."[34] The passivity of the Russian people, Chicherin thought, made it relatively easy for the Russian state to consolidate power. In fact, Chicherin argued that not the people but "the government always has led our development and forward movement. Given their passivity, the Russian people were in no condition to develop by their own efforts . . . ."[35] For Chicherin episodes such as the eighteenth-century peasant uprising led by Pugachev were exceptions to the historical rule, exceptions that warned statesmen against arbitrariness and reaction. Even the most docile of peoples could be provoked by desperation into taking up arms.

Chicherin's doctrines of the dominant role of the state and the general passivity of the Russian populace influenced all subsequent liberal statists, including Miliukov. Of course, Miliukov did not slavishly follow Chicherin. For example, Miliukov was more critical of the Russian autocracy than was Chicherin. Furthermore, in historical studies largely completed before 1904 Miliukov complained about previous historians who had ignored popular history. Miliukov's three-volume *Ocherki po istorii russkoi kultury* (Essays on the History of Russian Culture, 1897-1909) pretended to be a history "without proper names, without events, without military defeats and wars, without diplomatic intrigues"—a true "life of the popular masses."[36] Nevertheless, at the same moment Miliukov spoke of the importance of popular history, he argued that "given the lack of consciousness and the elemental nature [stikhinost] of the masses, with which heretofore social evolution always and everywhere has occurred, only individuals—the official or moral leaders of the masses—have accomplished socially rational acts."[37] Moreover, the masses were often obstacles to progressive developments, for their stagnation interfered with the "isolated acts of individuals." Miliukov hoped that the masses would play a more positive role in the future, but hopes for such progress were contingent on the spread of consciousness—a process with definite limits.[38]

By 1917 Miliukov had grown, if anything, more skeptical of the notion that the masses would soon play an independent positive role in Russian history. The masses might well take part in a revolution against the existing order, or even generate a wave of destruction. But neither prospect was inevitable. Rational statesmanship, he then supposed, could prevent a social revolution, or, at any rate, channel the energy of the masses in constructive directions. If the masses did explode uncontrollably, it would not be the fault of rational statesmen; rather it would be because the masses had succumbed to the irrational "demagoguery" of the Bolsheviks and other socialist parties. Thus, the masses would figure in the revolutionary equation only to the extent that revolutionary parties made them a factor. This view, consistent at root with the liberal statism of the nineteenth century, granted primacy to elitist politics over the popular movement as a motive force of change. The *Primat der elitären Politik* informed Miliukov's historical narrative.

Perhaps the SR leader Chernov was right when he wrote: "[Miliukov's] chief weakness was a complete lack of feeling for popular, mass psychology. He was too much a man of the study, hence a doctrinaire. The studious side of his nature had been moderated by the long schooling of parliamentary life and struggle . . . that peculiar little world which, in Russia more than elsewhere, was isolated, protected against the pressure of the street."[39]

Miliukov's understanding of Bolshevism as an ideology and mass movement was more complex than his history of the revolution would suggest. It is likely that when he planned and wrote the first draft of this history in 1918 he still expected that the Bolsheviks would be driven quickly from power. The "Bolshevik phase" of the Russian Revolution would be short, and the Bolsheviks would not deserve further attention. It soon became apparent, however, that the Bolsheviks would retain state power for a more or less protracted period. Therefore, in two major works Miliukov returned to the question of the nature of Bolshevism.

In *Bolshevism. An International Danger* (1920) Miliukov appealed to world opinion, asking "civilized" nations to pursue anti-Bolshevik politics. He argued that Bolshevism had two aspects—one domestic, the other international. The domestic, or specifically Russian aspect of Bolshevism consisted of those features of the ideology that made it heir to the revolutionary tradition of Stenka Razin and Pugachev.[40] Just what these features were Miliukov did not specify. Internationally, Bolshevism was an offshoot of Georges Sorel's revolutionary syndicalism. Miliukov thought the key to syndicalist thought lay in the notion of an elite that would guide the masses to revolution. Revolutionary syndicalists tried to persuade the working class that it had no obligations toward party, nation and state. Within the working class itself syndicalists organized a "conscious minority" who were to engage the class enemy in "direct action." This "direct action" by the conscious minority would capture the attention and imagination of the entire class, and thus lead the class into combat. Ultimately, this combat would catapult the active minority into power. In Miliukov's view, government by minority was "the last word of syndicalism, which it has in common with Bolshevism, not only in theory, but in practice."[41] Miliukov thought that the syndicalist-Bolshevik world view was narrow, exclusively class-oriented, and undemocratic. He could not refrain from adding that German imperialists used this undemocratic movement to destabilize Russia.

In his two-volume book *Rossiia na perelome* [Russia at the Turning Point] (1927) Miliukov reviewed the problem of Bolshevik ideology, this time distinguishing Leninism from syndicalism and from other varieties of Marxism. Miliukov argued that Lenin had been preoccupied from the beginning with political questions, to the exclusion of economic ones. While Mensheviks worried about the level of Russian economic development and the economic program of socialism, Lenin thought only of the seizure of power.[42] This political orientation, Miliukov believed, separated Lenin even from the syndicalists, who also had taken seriously economic issues. Lenin's discovery was that in a revolutionary situation all his predecessors had wished too soon to destroy completely the state.[43] Lenin understood that the state could be turned into an instrument of proletarian class domination. Miliukov asserted that Lenin's idea of the proletarian dictatorship went much further than anything Marx had had in mind. "Of course, Marx was not without responsibility for Lenin's construction . . . . But Marx never thought of narrowing the state to an exclusively oppressive class organization, nor of building socialism while by-passing democracy, nor did he mean by 'dictatorship of the proletariat' the organized violence of an oligarchical minority against an entire people, nor, in particular, did Marx wish violently to introduce socialism without society having reached the proper state of economic development."[44] In practice, if ever there was a conflict between Lenin's theoretical views and the advancement of the revolution, he chose to advance the revolution. His guiding principle, according to Miliukov, was *salus revolutionis—suprema lex.*[45]

In *Rossiia na perelome* Miliukov came close to admitting that something like the Bolshevik Revolution had been inevitable in Russia. Once the Romanov monarchy had been overthrown and Russia had embarked on the revolutionary path, it was inevitable that the revolution would become more extreme. "Revolution is a complex and prolonged process: the gradual change of temper in broad social strata. Time is needed for this process to commence and to pass through all its natural phases. Until the process is complete, the revolution *must* follow its inevitable course and cannot stop in the middle. A revolutionary fire must utterly consume everything that has remained intact from the overthrown order—not only all institutions but all the old habits of thought [perezhitki psikhologii]."[46] This general law of revolutions explained why the Russian Revolution had an extremist phase, but not why that phase should have been Bolshevik-led. Miliukov then added to his explanation the claim that four peculiarities of Russian history accounted for the appearance of Bolshevism: (1) the indigenous anarchism of the masses; (2) the decline in influence of the ruling classes; (3) the theoretical maximalism of the revolutionary intelligentsia; and (4) the separatist ambitions of the nationalities. "The result of the interaction of these factors was Russian Bolshevism—a specifically Russian development, that grew up on the national soil and could not have occurred in this form anywhere else but Russia."[47]

Study of Milukov's various attempts to define Bolshevism and explain the October Revolution suggests that the present volume of *History of the Second Russian Revolution* was only a trial sketch, rough and unsuccessful. In it Miliukov acknowledged the force of Bolshevik ideology, but classified Bolshevism as demagoguery. He saw Bolshevism in large part as a tool of German imperialism. In his second sketch Miliukov depicted Bolshevism as a variant of European syndicalism. This analysis suggested that there was perhaps more to Bolshevik ideology than demagoguery. Yet this depiction still highlighted the foreignness of Bolshevism to Russia, and raised again the German exploitation of Bolshevik extremism. Only with Miliukov's third major work, *Rossiia na perelome*, do we find a relatively nuanced treatment of Bolshevism. Miliukov now grounded Bolshevism firmly on Russian soil and came close to seeing it as the logical result of the Russian Revolution and of Russian history.

This last insight is a signal achievement in liberal historiography, one that opened the way for future, nonpolemical and nonpartisan scholarly work. Regarded on its own, in isolation from the rest of Miliukov's work, the present volume can be said to illustrate the defective vision of Russian liberalism. Regarded as the first sketch in a series intended to delineate a devilishly complicated historical problem, the present volume is of profound interest. Studying it, we look at the canvas of an artist whose ambition was to limn the features of intent Clio as she sowed the greatest revolution of our time. If the image on the canvas seems imperfect, we should perhaps not be too hard on the artist. Not every artist is blessed with perfect vision, and sometimes, after the most scrupulous surveillance of past events, even the sharpest of eyes may cloud over.

G.M. Hamburg

University of Notre Dame

The Russian Revolution

Volume 3

CHAPTER I

THE GOVERNMENT'S SECOND CRISIS

Having joined battle with Kornilov and the "Kornilovshchina,"[1] A. F. Kerensky not only missed the last chance to restore national unity and to reestablish a credible and strong revolutionary government, he also, once and for all, undermined the basis of his own personal influence. The longer he stayed in power, the more personal was the nature of his government, and with its preservation or destruction rode the fate of all non-utopian "achievements of the revolution." Moreover, this government depended on a very complicated and fragile system of balancing between contending forces. In order to maintain equilibrium, Kerensky constantly had to lean now to the left now to the right, and he demonstrated in this act a dexterity, a flexibility that was sometimes truly Byzantine. But, little by little, all his skill as a politician was devoted to this balancing act. It was for this reason that Kerensky's government, regardless even of his psychological traits, acquired such a personal and peculiar character. In order to maintain any semblance of support from the social and political groups on which Kerensky depended, Kerensky had to offer them something positive. The Bolsheviks, the advocates of "a soldiers', workers', and peasants' Soviet republic," were promising a great deal, even if they were not delivering on the promises: an immediate peace to the soldiers; all land to the peasants; all power over factories to the workers; and to everyone—direct political dominion and access to all levers of the state through the assistance of the organized "conscious" minority. One could not compete with the Bolsheviks, thanks to the absolute slogans they used, thanks to the ignorance of the masses upon which these slogans played, and thanks to the genuine unsavoriness of the tactics, from foreign bribes to armed robberies, which they had at their disposal.

Against the Bolsheviks' anarchical hooliganism all remaining political factions should have made a friendly alliance; indeed, that was the basis for the idea of the coalition government. But the alliance never came off because the more moderate currents of Russian socialism were still too profoundly permeated by elements of the same utopianism and the same abstract ideology. They felt more closely linked to the anarcho-communism advanced by Lenin than they did to social reformers of the "bourgeois" stripe, not to mention the "bourgeoisie" itself. And when they were forced to choose between a mysterious social experiment that threatened in the future to lead to dictatorship and to the restoration of autocracy, and support for the public forces and strata which they [the socialists] suspected of being hidden "counter-revolutionaries" capable of immediately restoring the old regime, then, despite all their hesitations, the sympathies of the moderate socialists—if not their active support—inclined to the mysterious social experiment. It would be better to let the Russian Revolution speak its "new word," even if this word was unfortunate, than to return at once to the old regime. If the Leninists said: "Better Wilhelm than the Kadets," the moderate socialists said: "Better Lenin than Kornilov . . . and the Kadets."

Tsereteli[2] had invented for Kerensky a combination in which a "democratic," and not merely a socialist platform (in its latest version—the platform of August 14)[3] was supported by "democratic" elements—that is, not merely by socialists, but also by those "bourgeois" elements who had rejected their class prejudices. It was for this reason that Tsereteli had called upon the "bourgeoisie" to renounce its class position, and he threatened by violence only those who, because of the deepening of class antagonisms, "fell away from the revolution."   However, this whole artificial construction long ago had developed profound structural flaws to the left and to the right.   On the left it possessed the trust neither of the socialist masses nor of the "democratic" elements in the narrow sense of that term.   On the right it could not have broad support.   The Moscow Conference[4] had demonstrated once and for all that the "bourgeoisie" would not follow the platform of August 14 and that a reconciliation with the socialists could only be insincere, though it might be practically a necessity for a class that had so much to lose.   It was precisely that sort of half-hearted reconciliation which occurred in the famous handshake of Bublikov and Tsereteli.[5] Thus, the combination of elements somehow soldered together by Tsereteli was artificial and purely superficial.   The artificiality displayed itself when, in the final analysis, the last link proved to be Kerensky's personality. Kerensky was necessary to both sides as the lesser evil—and this was what kept him in power. But such support was only and could only be temporary. It lasted only because—and during the period that—the crucial questions which the revolution should have resolved remained unresolved and were merely deferred for future consideration. These deferrals might have been useful if the authority of the Provisional Government had lasted until the meeting of the Constituent Assembly. But what could be done when the anarcho-communist faction, supported by the logical inconsistency of the socialists and by the lack of consciousness of the masses, did not wish to wait for the Constituent Assembly and even began to fear it, and to inculcate this fear in all social elements that were profiting from the existing situation? To seize the moment without waiting for an uncertain future—this meant for them above all to consolidate their own revolutionary gains at the most favorable time for them. But this also meant an end to the compromise on which Kerensky depended.

On the other hand, moderate public figures and the "bourgeoisie" in the broad and narrow sense depended on Kerensky—in part, they did so despite rising dissatisfaction with and even repulsion from him—only because they saw in him the last guarantee of a peaceful and rational solution to the fundamental political problems of that same uncertain future. Yet over time it became clearer and clearer that the resolution of certain problems could not wait, for to wait was tantamount to predetermining the solution to the problems. The problem of the battle-readiness of the army, land reform, the condition of industry and productive forces, the arrangements dealing with peripheral areas of the old empire and the nationalities, and, finally, the basic question of the future political system—all these questions had had their answers predetermined by fruitless waiting during long months, and predetermined not in the fashion that genuine statesmen had projected. In particular, the problem of the army's battle-readiness could be put off no longer; it was necessary to begin serious work toward the revitalization of the army in August if the government expected that in spring, at the time of a possible new offensive, it might see the results of its labors. Such was the opinion of the best military minds, such as General Alexeev. That was why General Kornilov told Verkhovsky, who two days before the uprising had presented a plan to revitalize the army, that Verkhovsky's plan "was too slow; the Germans are attacking and therefore it is essential to try his [Kornilov's] method, however risky it might seem."[6]

One could no longer defer solution of the most fundamental issue of that time, the issue of the war, for on the solution of this question depended the solution of the other capital question—that of a strong government. And after answers to both these crucial questions were predetermined by the position Kerensky took in the Kornilov affair—and the answers were not in the interests of the state—further waiting became simply useless.

That is why Kerensky, who long since had become useless to the extreme leftists, became at that moment useless to the so-called "bourgeoisie." For both groups he ceased to be the lesser evil: for both now regarded as harmful the continued existence of the fictional system of the "coalition." The irrevocable decisions that had been made under the cover of the "coalition" contradicted the "bourgeoisie's" political views or class interests, while the leftists found the decisions insufficiently reflected their own theories. Thus, the alliance was broken at both ends. The only people who could defend it any longer were doctrinaires of pure form, empty of all content—or the personal friends and partisans of Kerensky, those few who still preserved faith in his personal charm. It was possible superficially to maintain such a government only until the first strong blow. The government had the strength neither to foresee the moment of nor to survive that blow, although it knew quite well from whence the blow would arrive. It was helpless against that blow because, in the final analysis, on that flank where there was real strength, no one wanted to defend the government, and because in the center, where the government was still weakly supported, there was no real strength, only ideology. We have observed in the preceding chapters how, under the shocks of reality, even this ideology gradually lost faith in itself and turned into mere words, into "a conditional lie." The "bourgeois republic," defended by the moderate socialists alone (and defended by them *à contre coeur*), and no longer supported by the masses or by the "bourgeoisie"—such a platform could no longer survive. Its entire content had been emptied out, and now only the empty shell remained. Under different forms here was established that system of official hypocrisy from which the old monarchy had perished. And the fate of the new system would have to be the same as that of the old: they both prepared the ground for revolution, and on the day of the revolution neither one found for itself a single defender.

The inherent contradiction of the new situation in which Kerensky found himself after the suppression of the Kornilov uprising immediately revealed itself as soon as the first problem created by the disintegration of the cabinet was faced—namely, how to reorganize the government.

The majority of members of the Soviet Executive Committee learned only on the morning of August 27 about Kerensky's evening conversation with V. N. Lvov and about the nocturnal session of the government in which the ministers had given full powers to Kerensky.[7]

Kerensky had already thought of surrounding himself by a collegium of four "directors," two of whom from the beginning of the revolution had belonged to the inner nucleus that had directed all the government's affairs (Nekrasov and Tereshchenko). It was proposed to give the other two places to B. V. Savinkov and N. M. Kishkin. The last possessed Kerensky's personal trust: in the directory Kishkin was supposed to represent Moscow and the "bourgeoisie."[8]

This plan was discussed at the nocturnal meeting of the ministers and seemed more or less to have been accepted. Kerensky immediately summoned Kishkin from Moscow. But the Soviet's sanction was still required. In the afternoon the bureau of the Executive Committee met in extraordinary session and heard a report on the Kornilov affair and on Kerensky's proposal concerning the reorganization of the government. The bureau, on its own initiative, suggested another idea: to create under the directory a standing committee of representatives of "revolutionary democracy." Both proposals were submitted for preliminary discussion to the central committees of the parties who were participating in the Soviet. A plenary session of the Executive Committee along with the Soviet of Peasant Deputies, the representatives of political parties, trade unions, and cooperative societies, was called for that evening.

Of course, the Bolshevik newspaper and Soviet faction opposed both proposals. Their policy had always been, under all conditions, to give "all power to the Soviet." The Socialist-Revolutionaries, having received two places on the directory (Kerensky and Savinkov), rejected Savinkov and demanded Chernov[9] as replacement; in addition, they wanted to add a sixth person to the directory. The Mensheviks also agreed to the directory under the condition that Tsereteli be added to it. Only the Popular Socialists and the Trudoviks were against the directory from the very beginning and, for reasons of expediency, they supported the preservation of the existing government the origins of whose authority would not be a matter of dispute and whose capacity to govern would therefore be stronger. At the plenary session the objections of the Trudoviks and Popular Socialists found support. The majority inclined to keep executive power in the hands of the old government.

The question of whether to strengthen the government through a constantly functioning agency like the standing committee of representatives did not stimulate controversy. Everyone agreed to the creation of such a committee, although some preferred to see in it only representatives of democratic organizations, and others broadened the committee to include most of the elements of the Moscow State Conference except for the members of the four State Dumas.

At 11 P. M. after all these meetings there was a closed session of the Executive Committee and its invited guests. Orators from the various factions presented all the views of the political parties, from the Trudoviks' proposal of unconditional support for the government to the Bolsheviks' proposal to replace the government by Soviets. The parties of the center agreed to reject a directory and passed a resolution to leave the government as is, except that members of the Party of Popular Liberty would be replaced by "democratic elements." It was decided to convene in the immediate future a democratic parliament of representatives from all organizations who had united in Moscow around the platform of August 14. Around 2 A.M. on August 28 the presidium broke off its meeting to report its decision to Kerenksy. At 3:45 A.M. the presidium returned from the Winter Palace and the meeting resumed. The presidium informed the members that Kerensky insisted on a directory and on transfer to it of full power, and that he had accepted a six-member directory. The prolonged debate that followed was interrupted by the summons of Tsereteli and Chernov to the Winter Palace where "their presence was essential."

It was at this moment when the stage of "misunderstanding" in the Kornilov affair ended and the stage of "panic" began. First, General Alexeev and Tereshchenko were summoned, then Savinkov, after Savinkov Nekrasov, and after Nekrasov came Tsereteli and Chernov. This order of emergency nocturnal summons was evidence of the prime minister's anxiety. Kerensky's exclamation, "very sad," when he discovered at 4 A.M. that it was too late to stop Nekrasov's release to the newspapers accusing Kornilov of "treachery," was the final payment of tribute to the more moderate elements with whom Kerensky desired a reconciliation. After 4 A.M. obviously it was a foregone conclusion that Kornilov would accept Kerensky's challenge, and it therefore became "essential" for Tsereteli and Chernov to come to the Winter Palace.

The issue of how to reorganize the government of the directory thereupon took second place on the agenda: now the main problem was how to organize resistance to Kornilov.

This became clear at the morning session of the Executive Committee which convened at 8:30 A.M. The participants, who had gathered after a sleepless night, were struck by M. I. Skobelev's[10] reading of Kornilov's manifesto to the people, in which Kornilov accused Kerensky of provoking his [Kornilov's] actions and accused the entire government of being in the Bolsheviks' power, of facilitating Russia's defeat, and of harboring in its midst defeatists and traitors.[11] Kornilov justified his own decision by declaring that he did not wish Russia to perish. Having read the proclamation, Skobelev added that Kornilov had ordered military units to move toward Petrograd, that the situation was very serious, and that in response to the threatened Kornilov dictatorship it was necessary to create the kind of government that could bring all its powers to bear against the usurper. After this the assembly no longer had the leisure to discuss the reconstruction of the government. Tsereteli summarized the course of the latest negotiations with Kerensky and asserted that it was essential that the government have complete and broadbased support without petty arguments. The Bolsheviks, Menshevik-

Internationalists, and Left SRs alone continued to object, promising the government "only purely technical and military support." The overwhelming majority accepted the resolution formulated by Tsereteli in the most sweeping terms: "Having entrusted Comrade Kerensky with the task of forming a government, the central task of which must be to conduct a decisive battle against the conspiracy and General Kornilov, the Central Executive Committee of the Soviet of Workers' and Soldiers' Deputies promises the government its most energetic support in that struggle."

We have seen how that "energetic support" was manifested, including "unauthorized arrests" and the "decisive actions" of Petrograd and other local "committees to save the revolution." The "democratic organizations" assembled soldiers, arrested generals, officers and deputies, seized the telegraph and radiotelegraph, stopped railroad traffic—in a word, they showed much tactical skill, paid no attention to formal legal barriers and gave an effective demonstration of their power in relation to everyone who wore the label of "counter-revolutionary." In order to organize *its own* forces against Kornilov, the Executive Committee published a proclamation which was full of demagoguery. Kornilov wanted to resurrect the old order and to deprive the people of land and liberty; "Kornilov is ready to open the front to the Germans, ready to betray the motherland," and so on.

These undertakings of the Soviet distracted it from the question of reorganizing the government, but not for long. Once they returned to the question, the "democratic organizations" brought to bear even greater influence on its solution than formerly.

As we already know, the day of August 28 passed with the government in a state of panic, and toward evening this mood reached its apogee. Kerensky was forced for the first time to hear from his socialist comrades a very pessimistic evaluation of their actions, and he was brought to propose his own resignation from government and the transfer of authority to stronger figures. On that day "stronger figures" meant more moderate figures, the only people who could build a bridge to the future victor, as Kornilov was now imagined to be. Several voices spoke in favor of Kerensky's dismissal and of his replacement by General Alexeev, and many of those who were silent obviously sympathized with this plan. On August 29 Kerensky's position was strengthened again, but now the political pendulum swung in the opposite direction—to the left.

That night Kerensky had to choose between Nekrasov and the leaders of the Soviet. In a moment of fear Nekrasov had lost Kerensky's trust, and it was on the basis of this trust that Nekrasov had played his role in the "triumvirate." At the time of the meeting in the Winter Palace Nekrasov already understood that the card on which he had wagered his entire career as a statesman was a loser. In his own words, he "twice bowed to Kerensky's requests that he remain in the cabinet": on July 7 and when he had accepted the portfolio of the Minister of Finance on July 24. This time Kerensky not only did not ask Nekrasov to stay on, but dismissed him. At one time Kerensky had valued Nekrasov as a useful intermediary with a political camp with which Kerensky had to reckon but where he had no firm support. When Nekrasov parted company with his [liberal] political friends, he ceased to be useful to Kerensky as an intermediary. Forced to explain to the press the reason for his exit from the government, Nekrasov said bluntly that he not only "cannot count on the support of any public group," but he had against him "a significant part of Russian society." Moreover, the "blows directed against him personally" struck the government in view of the "legend," which had grown from a "grain of truth," that he was an indispensable member of the governmental triumvirate.

The days of Kornilov's possible victory came to an end with the dismissal of a minister of the opposite camp—the man who at the Moscow Conference and in Kornilov's orders had been branded publicly as a "traitor"—Chernov. Chernov was the last minister to submit a resignation to Kerensky and he did so most unwillingly; he then immediately concocted a new plan to become Kerensky's replacement in the future cabinet. He opened against his party comrade, whom he had tried unsuccessfully to exclude from the SR Central Committee, a cruel and systematic campaign in the party newspaper *Delo Naroda*. [The People's Cause].

Besides Kokoshkin and Iurenev[12] who had left the ministry for good, there was yet another minister who was forced by the course of the Kornilov affair to try to resign from the cabinet. This was another member of the "triumvirate," Tereshchenko. He was smart enough to understand that his card was also a loser. Nothing had come of the attempts to make the interests of Russia fall into accord with the Zimmerwaldist tendencies in foreign policy, except for a weakening of our influence among the Allies. Twice during his tenure in office Tereshchenko had tried to demonstrate his independence *vis-à-vis* the Allies and the "revolutionary democracy." But both attempts were rather unsuccessful. The protest against the overthrow of the Germanophile Greek King Constantine certainly satisfied the principle of the "self-determination of peoples," but was not at all motivated by our national interests. The announcement that the Stockholm Conference was the "private affair" of political parties, not of the government, caused a real scandal both at home and abroad; it deprived the government of a certain standing in the Russian "democracy," and yet prevented the government from taking a definite stand on the issue itself. In Russia Tereshchenko's first move passed unnoticed. The second, on the contrary, was given too much scrutiny and led to corrections and denials. In any case, after the one and the other act the minister could not but experience an aftertaste of bitterness. Obviously, no fancy turn on the dance floor could correct the fundamental mistake of agreeing with the Zimmerwaldists, and so Tereshchenko would have to live with the consequences. In the Kornilov affair Tereshchenko must have felt quite acutely his awkward external ties to the Zimmerwaldists, for here his natural love for the motherland conflicted too sharply with the demands of formal discipline imposed on a cabinet officer. Having failed to convince Kerensky to think that Kornilov's actions were the product of a "misunderstanding," Tereshchenko, against his own will, was forced to look on the affair as "mutiny"; yet he soon had a painful encounter with the first victim of Kerensky's tactics, with the suicide Krymov, a pure and idealistic officer whose services to the Russian Revolution Tereshchenko felt duty-bound to acknowledge after Krymov's death. Tereshchenko submitted his resignation after Nekrasov did. But no candidate was found to take his place, or to take the place of the Supreme-Procurator of the Holy Synod, Kartashev.[13] Both men had to remain in the cabinet temporarily.

Whether for political or personal reasons, the cabinet was disintegrating. In order to strengthen it, Kerensky thought only to invite N. M. Kishkin who had participated, as we have seen, in the meeting of August 28. On August 30 there occurred the final "private conference" of ministers, including the Kadet ministers who were leaving the cabinet. The Kadet Central Committee did not refuse to allow Kerensky to select a new party representative for the government, and it approved Kishkin's participation in the cabinet. However, through its representatives in the "private conference" the Central Committee of the Party of Popular Liberty announced its conditions. The Central Committee wished to bring into the administration authoritative representatives of the military high command. General Alexeev was first on the list. After Alexeev's appointment as chief of staff, the Kadet demand was changed into a request for military appointments to the offices of War and Navy ministers; this harmonized with Kerensky's desire to fire Savinkov and to appoint Verkhovsky and Verderevsky—both being in contact with the Soviet. Moreover, the Party of Popular Liberty proposed that representatives of the commercial-industrial class be brought into the cabinet, a proposal that had been made earlier, in the July negotiations. Kerensky accepted this proposal as well, and he asked Kishkin to undertake talks with the commercial-industrial class. Industrial Moscow nominated Smirnov for the post of State Comptroller. Kerensky himself selected the deputy Buryshkin, but later this candidacy collapsed, since it was not supported by Moscow's merchantry; Buryshkin was replaced by another representative of the commercial-industrial class, S. N. Tretiakov.[14]

The Kadets' third demand, a result of the sad experience of the "triumvirate," was that there be no more government within the government and that all members of the cabinet have an identical right of participation in government affairs. This demand harmonized with the socialist parties' objections against the formation of a "directory." But a "directory" remained a favorite notion of Kerensky, who had grown accustomed to acting autocratically and to surrounding himself with those comrades who could reconcile themselves to this autocratic fashion of rule. The Kadets' fourth demand was that the Kornilov affair be resolved without sacrificing the battle-readiness of the army and without further exacerbating civil strife by dividing the nation into two camps, the "counter-revolutionaries" and "revolutionary democracy." This demand, as we know, fully accorded with the mood of those days when General Alexeev was appointed chief of staff and when the army orders inspired by Alexeev were published. But with General Verkhovsky's appointment as War Minister and with the Soviet's swift emergence in a dominant role this demand could not be met by Kerensky.

In fact, it soon became evident that, in inviting General Alexeev and Kishkin into the government and in giving Kishkin the commission to discuss more rightist, even purely "bourgeois" ministerial candidacies, Kerensky had failed to take into account his master. On the same day, August 30, in the Executive Committee of the Soviet there appeared a most intolerant attitude to keeping the Kadets in the government, and the man who expressed that attitude was none other than a member of the cabinet, the Minister of Labor M. I. Skobelev. Having underscored the services of the Soviet and of the Commission for Popular Struggle Against Counter-Revolution, which had just presented its report, Skobelev turned to the question of government reorganization, and he informed the Soviet of the appointments that had already been made. The names Verkhovsky and Verderevsky were greeted with loud applause. However, the hall was silent at the announcement that the new Supreme Commander-in-Chief was Kerensky and his chief of staff would be General Alexeev. The silence was the more noticeable because the maladept orator paused for effect before announcing these names in the expectation there would be applause. Now having been put on guard, the audience listened in distrust to the following words of the the orator. Skobelev said that the coalition must be preserved, for it "is not the fruit of intrigues within the cabinet;" but, he added, "of course, in the cabinet there can be no place for anyone connected in any fashion with Kornilov." "Can't you be more precise?" asked voices from the audience. Skobelev, accommodating himself to the wishes of the assembly, then spoke more "precisely." "That party which stated in its party newspaper that Kornilov is a real force with which one has to contend, cannot count on its representatives being admitted into the cabinet." The cries from the audience, "Thank God! Down with the Kadets!" made explicit the orator's reference. However, later, in the speech of another minister, Avksentiev, these statements were made even more "precise."[15] When the Minister of Internal Affairs accused Kornilov of leaving the army "defenseless against the enemy's advance," cries resounded from the audience of "death to traitors." Acceding to the mood of the assembly, the orator, to loud applause, demanded the death penalty for the general who had managed to reestablish the death penalty in the army. The minister then repeated false reports about Kaledin,[16] and he informed the audience concerning the new government that "no one may enter the cabinet who has not publicly distanced himself from the partisans of the rebellion or who places all the blame for the rebellion on the Provisional Government. Nor may anyone enter the government who has proposed to begin negotiations with the rebellious general." At these words there were shouts from the audience of "Arrest Miliukov!"

The next speaker was Tsereteli. Far from objecting to the statements of the two ministers, he merely emphasized more sharply the significance of the coalition, "an idea that had justified itself." But he also not only demanded "the elimination of certain parts of that coalition"—asserting, in harmony with the auditorium's mood, that this did not amount to "narrowing the base of the revolution"—but he insisted on "the destruction of those centers around which there gather dark forces." Here he meant that there should be a purge of the officer corps at Stavka and the dismissal of the Fourth Duma, for "the interest of the nation and of the revolution demand that the government secure us against a repetition of such events."

On the next day, August 31, speeches by the Bolsheviks and Internationalists Kamenev, Steklov, and Lapinsky demonstrated the mood against which the government would have to contend.[17] These speakers not only condemned the idea of the coalition, they also represented as insufficiently decisive the demand for a complete change in the composition of the government. "Kornilov's rebellion is not a crime by a single person, but a crime of the organized bourgeoisie," said Kamenev.

"Only a coalition of the proletariat, peasantry, and soldiers will save the revolution, and only such a coalition is practical at present." Steklov added: "The coalition with the bourgeoisie is undermining the political power of the democracy's representatives, who are forced to pursue a policy of conciliation and to permit constant sabotage from the right wing."

To this extreme, but quite logical position, the moderate "democracy," as usual, opposed its own internally-contradictory plan: to preserve the coalition, but without the participation of members of the Party of Popular Liberty.

Before the Executive Committee of the Soviet reached a final decision on this question, two of Kerensky's comrades from the Socialist-Revolutionary Party, Gots and Zenzinov,[18] reported to Kerensky in the Winter Palace the opinion—"at the moment not yet an ultimatum"—of his political allies. It was impermissible to include Kadets in the cabinet. "But," Gots added, "this does not exclude the possibility of certain representatives of that party entering the government," those representatives who had distanced themselves from the followers of Miliukov, as, for example, the Moscow Kadets had done in the Moscow City Duma when they had accepted the formula of the Socialist-Revolutionaries . . . . "From this perspective Kishkin's entrance into the government would not cause any particular difficulties." That was what Gots told journalists at midnight on August 31/ September 1. Thus, Kerensky continued to conduct negotiations with the Kadets and with the industrialists. On the evening of September 1 N. M. Kishkin, S. A. Smirnov, and P. A. Buryshkin left Moscow for Petrograd. Kishkin published a letter in the newspapers in which he stated that he "is entering the Provisional Government with the approval of the Party of Popular Liberty," in order to counteract "the struggle of classes and parties" and in order to promote unity. However, on the morning of September 2, when the threesome arrived in Petrograd, the situation had changed completely.

The change was the result of the position taken by the Petrograd Soviet on the issue of the government. For a long time the Soviet had manifested an inclination toward Bolshevism, and on this question a Bolshevik majority came into being. On August 31, after the session of the Executive Committee described above, the Petrograd Soviet opened its own session. It began with Bogdanov's speech[19] about the "unauthorized" actions of the Committee of Popular Struggle Against Counter-Revolution from which we quoted above in Volume 2. This speech ended with the statement that the committee already demanded payment from the government for services rendered: namely, the liberation from prison of the Bolsheviks arrested in connection with the affair of July 3-5. The rest of the meeting was in accord with this beginning. Tsereteli's speech, which unsuccessfully attempted to defend the principle of coalition government, was so frequently interrupted by protests that the presiding official, Chkheidze,[20] finally had to remind the members that the Soviet possessed sufficient forces "to eject those who violate rules of order." The attempt to defend the Moscow Kadets, who had agreed to the SR resolution on the Kornilov affair, was greeted by an especially loud commotion, thus provoking Tsereteli to a stern rejoinder: "Do not overestimate your strength. If Kornilov's plot did not succeed, this is solely because it was not actively supported by the entire bourgeoisie: otherwise, the democratic forces alone could not have overcome it." "It would be a very great misfortune if the government should fall into the hands of a single class."

But arguments were of no help. The mood of the auditorium had already taken shape, and, to Tsereteli's chagrin, the audience gave a loud ovation to Iu. Steklov, who repeated his afternoon's speech. All the subsequent speeches—by Kamenev, Martov, Volodarsky and Rozanov—were against the coalition.[21] S. R. Boldyrev added other demands: a purge of Stavka; dismissal of the State Council and State Duma; the trial of the government, which was answerable to the Soviets, before a revolutionary parliament of all democratic organizations—this trial to be scheduled before the summoning of the Constituent Assembly. In vain Tsereteli tried again to demonstrate that the transfer of power to the proletariat was not in accord with the actual constellation of forces in the nation and that the Bolsheviks' promises could not be fulfilled. He concluded his speech, however, with a pessimistic admission: "It is obvious that the banner of the revolution, which for six months we have held in our hands, is now being transferred to other hands. One would like to believe that in these new hands it will survive for even half that time. But I fear this moment, for the enemies of the revolution impatiently await the transfer of power to the Soviet of Workers' and Soldiers' Deputies in order to deal the revolution a decisive defeat." Tsereteli undoubtedly articulated a mood that was widely felt at that time; he only failed to note that this mood was the result of the tactics adopted by moderate socialists.

This session of the Petrograd Soviet ended, of course, with the defeat of the [old] Soviet majority. By a vote of 279 to 115, with 51 abstentions, the Soviet adopted a Bolshevik-sponsored resolution with the following provisions. There must be an end to all vacillations in the organization of the government. Not only representatives of the Kadets, but representatives of propertied society in general must be excluded from the government. The only solution was to create a government from the representatives of the revolutionary proletariat and peasantry. The new government should take up the following agenda: proclamation of a democratic republic; the immediate abolition of private property on seigneurial land; the announcement that secret treaties shall henceforth have no binding force; and an immediate proposal to all peoples of the belligerent states to conclude a democratic peace. In addition, it was necessary to halt all repression of workers and of workers' organizations; the death penalty at the front should be abolished immediately; complete freedom of agitation should be restored in the army and bourgeois newspapers should be confiscated. The resolution also demanded the election of commissars, realization of the right of the nationalities living in Russia to self-determination—in the first instance, satisfaction of the demands of Finland and the Ukraine—and the dissolution of the State Council and the State Duma.

Thus, the old majority in the Soviets was defeated. Tsereteli had calculated correctly the psychology of the assembly. In view of its defeat, the entire presidium of the Petrograd Soviet surrendered its plenary powers. And in the presidium was the whole flower of Soviet leadership: Chkheidze, Anisimov, Gots, Dan, Skobelev, Tsereteli, and Chernov.[22]

Among the ranks of the "revolutionary democracy" the defeat of the old Soviet majority in the Petrograd Soviet brought extreme confusion and disorientation. At 2 P.M. the next day, September 1, the Executive Committee was scheduled to continue debate over the speeches of Skobelev and Avksentiev. It was necessary to approach the meeting with some kind of prepared plan of action. But there was no such plan of action. The meeting was put off from 2 P.M. to 7 P.M., and then from 7 to 11 P.M. Finally, the impatience of the Executive Committee members, who had waited an entire day for the meeting, forced an opening of the session under the chairmanship of Filippovsky. But only at 2 A.M. did the ministers arrive—alas, not the *former* ministers—and so began the long-awaited debate.

What had transpired during that day?

The leaders of the "revolutionary democracy" spent the entire day traveling back and forth between the central committees of their parties and the Winter Palace. The Bolsheviks' victory in the Petrograd Soviet forced the moderate majority of the socialist parties to make a choice: either to concede to the Bolsheviks on the issue of the government, or to await a new Bolshevik uprising in Petrograd. In case the parties decided on the latter course, there was already circulating a list of ministers that included Chernov as prime minister, Riazanov as Minister of Foreign

Affairs, Lunacharsky as Minister of Internal Affairs, and Avilov as Minister of Finance.[23] On the other hand, it is true, the defensist group of socialists issued an appeal to the citizenry in which they implored citizens "not to interfere with the government's efforts to consolidate and *broaden* the social foundation of its political power." This appeal was published on September 1 in three socialist newspapers, the Socialist-Revolutionary *Volia Naroda* [Will of the People], Plekhanov's *Edinstvo* [Unity], and the Populist *Narodnoe Slovo* [People's Word]. But none of these groups, as everyone knew, had any influence within the working masses, whose mood during this time was very buoyant. In reckoning with this mood and with the danger of a Bolshevik uprising, the leaders of the moderate majority resolved to force members of the Kadets to stay out of the government—to make this demand an *ultimatum*. The SR Central Committee backed up this demand by threatening to pull its own members out of the government if the Kadets should remain in it: if this were to occur, Kerensky would lose the right to think of himself as a representative of the SRs.

This ultimatum put Kerensky in an impossible position. In objecting to Kadet participation in the government, but not objecting to a coalition, the Soviet leaders, in essence, made a coalition impossible. Kerensky explained to them that General Alexeev had been invited to serve on the condition of a broad coalition, and that Generals Ruzsky and Dragomirov would resign if that condition were violated, while the more rightist elements, such as representatives of the commercial-industrial class, would not enter the government without Kadet participation. Finally, Kerensky himself already had entered into negotiations with candidates of the commercial-industrialist group and had bound himself by promises to Kishkin and Alexeev. If the ultimatum were not withdrawn, then Kerensky himself would have to resign his office.

These statements were discussed anew in the central committees, but on this occasion they did not have the desired effects. Even Kerensky's resignation was not as frightening as the Bolsheviks' wrath. In fact, there was powerful resentment against Kerensky even within his own party. At 11 P.M. the ministers began their meeting in the Winter Palace, and the issue had still to be resolved. At midnight representatives of the Executive Committee—Tsereteli, Gots, Dan, Rakitnikov and others—arrived at the Winter Palace with bad news.[24] They had managed to inform themselves as to the mood of the Executive Committee then in session at Smolny. There was nothing that could be done. "We have run into a deadend, and there is no way out." Neither the ultimatum nor the threat of pulling socialist ministers out of the government could be withdrawn. Kerensky heard these repeated assertions in silence. The delegates left for Smolny. The ministers continued to debate the issue in the Winter Palace. The majority[25] agreed that no other decision was possible other than a continuation of the coalition on its present basis. When, toward 2 A.M., this majority opinion became clear, M. I. Skobelev and N. D. Avksentiev, who considered themselves bound by the decision of the revolutionary agencies of the democracy, announced that they could no longer remain in the government and they asked to be excluded from the cabinet. Zarudny added his wish to resign. The mood in which Skobelev and Avksentiev acted became clear from speeches given by them shortly after their arrival at Smolny.

Only two days earlier Skobelev and Avksentiev had delivered fiery speeches to the Executive Committee of the Soviet; now nothing of this fiery tone remained. Both orators were close to total despair and had lost their bearings. Skobelev stated that he was leaving the government not because he disagreed with its political line, but because the Soviet of Workers' Deputies did not agree with this line. He himself had only one goal: "to make sure that you start to act according to the dictates of cold reason. If my resignation can calm you down in the least, and if your minds can operate more clearly, then I shall consider my duty to have been done." As we see, the former Minister of Labor had stopped mincing words with the "revolutionary democracy." What do you want? he asked his auditors. If you agree that "the Russian Revolution is a bourgeois revolution, then why do you want to throw out of the government all bourgeois elements? Not all the bourgeois supported Kornilov. If you argue the opposite, if you say that everyone except us is counter-revolutionary, then I say that this is the death-agony of the revolution. If that is what you think, then you might as well say publicly that we and the nation are doomed to destruction." "If so, then let us stop writing resolutions and say: 'We are ready for foreign passports.'" Are you ready to proclaim a government of the Soviet at a moment "when the officer corps is prepared to turn anywhere in order to avoid such a circumstance?" To proclaim a Soviet government "will be the best way to cause a counter-revolution. At the moment Kornilov's army fraternizes with us. But when the soldiers find out that a government of the Soviet of Workers' and Soldiers' Deputies occupies the Winter Palace, they will no longer approach us in order to fraternize. Do not forget that Petrograd is not Russia, and before you decide on such a course, keep in mind the mood of all Russia." If it should happen that the Executive Committee did not heed his advice, Skobelev stated: "I am prepared to go together with you, but not into the government: rather into the opposition. There we will sit on the extreme left, and we shall be in the minority. Then the responsibility will rest with you.

We shall sit here and criticize you more conscientiously and constructively than you have criticized us. But know full well that this path will lead to Russia's destruction."

Nor did Avksentiev stand on ceremony with the "democracy." His accusation made an enormous impact on the committee: "The Provisional Government has reliable information that the Germans are planning an invasion of Finland, yet at the same time the Military Commission of the Central Executive Committee has recalled from Finland to Petrograd several minelayers, troops, and submarines." Avksentiev implored the "democracy" to support, not to undermine the government. "If here in Petrograd the government does not receive support, then Russia is doomed. Comrades, this is a tragedy. Do you understand that we are on the brink of destruction, or are already over the brink? . . . . Please, support the government, for Russia's sake. Do you not see that the nation is already perishing?"

Apparently, the "comrades" were beginning to understand and to see. The meeting was adjourned temporarily, and party groups met in caucuses. When the debate recommenced at 4:30 A.M., the committee rejected the Bolsheviks' resolution, adopted the day before in the Petrograd Soviet. Kamenev's assertion that "the new government is a government for Kerensky, not for us" had no effect this time. Tsereteli characterized this attack as false; Kerensky himself had turned to the Executive Committee over the issue of how to reorganize the government, and the committee had "commissioned" him to form the government; in addition, Tseretili added, "the best solution has been found—a government without propertied elements." However, in the draft of the projected resolution this point was softened: "The government must be free of any compromises with counter-revolutionary propertied elements." Very skillfully the resolution changed the center of gravity from the contested issue to another matter on which everyone was agreed: to the matter of creating a new government through a special Democratic Conference that would be convoked no later than September 12 (that is, in ten days) in Petrograd. The resolution adopted by the Executive Committee stated: "(1) There should immediately be convoked a congress of the entire organized democracy and of the democratic agencies of local self-government, which will decide the question of the organization of a government capable of ruling the nation until the Constituent Asembly meets. (2) Until this congress shall meet, the Central Executive Committee proposes that the government *retain its current membership* and . . . the committee calls on the democracy to render energetic assistance to the government in its efforts to organize the nation's defense and to struggle against counter-revolution, particularly by democratizing the army and decisively renewing the high command of the army. (3) . . . The committee finds it essential that the government, in taking measures to preserve order, shall act in close contact with the Committee of Popular Struggle Against Counter-Revolution under the direction of the All-Russia Central Committee." In all respects this was a clever resolution. It left everything as it had been and conceded nothing of the "democracy's" demands. The chief difficulty was deferred to the future, a future distant enough so that decisions could be made in the short term, but not so distant as to frighten the "democracy."

That this delay not only failed to diminish, but actually increased the difficulty of creating a "strong revolutionary government" was something which the leaders of the Soviet may not have considered at all, and which, in any case, they were afraid to discuss. To survive the day somehow, to muddle through until tomorrow, remembering that "sufficient to the day are the evils thereof"—that was a tactic to which Tsereteli had become accustomed long ago. He possessed enough skill to avoid dealing with genuine problems whose solution, in any case, was impossible within the confines of "revolutionary-democratic" tactics. Thus, the problems were put off and allowed to accumulate, and the difficulty of solving them increased. Yet while awaiting the day of reckoning, the democracy was able to live from day to day—to live as peacefully as its inexperience and lack of farsightedness permitted.

Such, in essense, was Kerensky's current tactic, which was directed to a single end: somehow to lead Russia until the convocation of the Constituent Assembly, no matter what effect this should have on Russia. Kerensky's intention was entirely compatible with Tsereteli's compromises. The question of reorganizing the government was decided the same night, as soon as the Executive Committee meeting made clear its response to the speeches of Avksentiev and Skobelev. Just after 2 A.M. on September 2 journalists, who had been awaiting a decision in the Winter Palace, were given good news from the ministers: "The crisis has been resolved successfully . . . . It has been decided temporarily to concentrate power in the hands of five men on issues of government administration and state defense: Kerensky, Nikitin, Tereshchenko, Verkhovsky, Verderevsky."[26]

Thus, the government also conceded nothing, and did not prejudice its future activity. Kerensky got his "directory," but "temporarily," and he did not have to renounce the principle of the coalition, or even the introduction into the government of "propertied elements." The five members of the directory were simply those members of the existing cabinet whose participation in a future government was certain. The remaining ministers were to be considered, until the final decision about the future list of ministers had been made, simply as acting directors of their agencies who did not share with the "five" the plenitude of governmental power. Since this state of affairs was also "temporary," the Kadets could not regard their demand for the equality of ministers to have been rejected. The temporary decision on the ministers also meant that that the government would not immediately have to fill those administrative posts that became vacant. The places of departed ministers were taken *for the time being* by their respective assistants. Finally, the matter that especially interested the "democracy"—the right of the projected "Democratic Conference" independently to create a new government—was deliberately obscured from the very start. The "democracy" could think that it had that right, but the government continued to think that it had simply put off the completion of appointments to the cabinet "until such time as it shall become possible once again to formulate a list of members of the Provisional Government along the lines of the former coalition." It was for this reason that Kerensky could make a promise even to Kishkin, who was Kerensky's sole selection from the three candidates who had arrived from Moscow on the morning of September 2. They could not become ministers, but they did not cease to be candidates.

Having thus preserved what was chiefly necessary to him, Kerensky decided to make concessions to the democracy on those demands which were of fundamental importance to it. It was easiest of all to satisfy the demand of the "revolutionary democracy" to declare Russia a democratic republic. This declaration had no legal significance at all. Otherwise, as one of the jurists close to the government noted, some other cabinet might declare Russia a monarchy. This declaration of the republic preempted the voice of the highest court and the sovereign: the voice of the people at the Constituent Assembly. This objection had been raised habitually by members of the government from the time the idea of proclaiming a republic had first been discussed in the cabinet—that is, when Prince Lvov had resigned.[27]

But on this occasion Kerensky had a new argument. During the Moscow Conference the venerable emigré, Prince P. A. Kropotkin,[28] had demanded the immediate proclamation of a republic, and the conference had responded with deafening applause. What could really be said against this in an assembly where even Kornilov was a republican? The issue of the form of government gradually lost its significance—to the degree that the acts of the Provisional Government lost their significance generally. And now there was but one serious argument against the immediate proclamation of a republic: the lack of seriousness of this act and the lack of authority of the government which carried it out.

We noted above that the first blow to the democracy's heretofore inviolable and sacred idea of the Constituent Assembly had come from the democrats themselves, who had used the issue of when to convoke the Constituent Assembly as a weapon in partisan struggle and who had made a schedule for convocation that was obviously impractical. A similar blow was dealt to another of the democracy's sacred notions—to the idea of a republic, which was proclaimed in an act signed on September 1 by Kerensky and Zarudny. This idea gained nothing from the formal connection between its implementation and the "suppression of General Kornilov's rebellion." "Considering it necessary to bring to an end the external amorphousness of the governmental structure, and recalling the unanimous and enthusiastic recognition of the republican idea at the Moscow State Conference, the Provisional Government"—at a time when formally it did not exist and all power had been transferred to Kerensky—declared "that the order of government which shall rule the Russian nation is the republican order of government, and it has proclaimed the Russian republic." Here the governmental proclamation noted the "transfer of the plenitude of governmental authority to five persons among the members of the Provisional Government," although, as we have noted, this transfer was accomplished not by the government, but by Kerensky, and it occurred only on September 2 after the resignation of Zarudny, who signed this proclamation on September 1.

The governmental proclamation went on to speak of a new program and of the future plans of the "directory." "The Provisional Government considers its first task to be the reestablishment of political order and of the fighting capacity of the army." It "shall strive to broaden its membership by attracting into its ranks all those elements who place the eternal and general interests of the motherland above the transient and private interests of individual parties or classes." The Provisional Government "did not doubt that this task shall have been accomplished by it within the coming days." As we see, there was not a word about a "Democratic Conference." The moralistic sentence about "eternal and general" interests concealed a quite definite content, which turned out to be a repetition of Kishkin's words on "parties and classes" from his letter to the newspapers. The "democracy" would have to swallow this entire dish, seasoned only by the condiment of "a democratic republic."

A more serious concession to the revolutionary agencies was the new tactic on the issue of raising the "fighting capacity of the army," mentioned earlier. Here the issue was not a matter of mere words: we have seen with what ease the government of five rejected support for the

program of Kornilov and Alexeev, that aged "expert," and how selfless-
ly, in the person of General Verkhovsky, it attempted to reconcile
"fighting capacity" with the "democratization" demanded by the Executive Committee's resolution. A purge of Stavka and wholesale change
in the officer corps—this condition also presented no difficulties. A. F.
Kerensky occupied himself with this matter as soon as it became possible for him to appear at Stavka without danger.

Kerensky's third concession was the release from prison of those Bolsheviks arrested in the uprising of July 3-5. The government, of
course, had just demanded the condemnation of Kornilov's "rebellion"
on the same grounds that it had condemned the "rebellion" of the Bolsheviks. But now, when Kornilov's "rebellion" had been suppressed and
the Bolsheviks could threaten with impunity a new uprising in Petrograd, now was not the time to hold too strictly to this principle of *equal*
punishment.

The leaders of the "revolutionary democracy" had insisted for some
time on a reexamination of the Bolshevik case. Under pressure from
these requests, A. S. Zarudny had obtained a copy of the investigative report from the public prosecutor, N. S. Karinsky,[29] held this report from
more than three weeks, and thus effectively stopped the course of the
investigation. Although Karinsky did not agree to release the arrested
leaders, Trotsky and Lunacharsky, Zarudny neverthless released the latter. On the next day *Izvestiia* [News] stated that Karinsky should be dismissed from office. Indeed, within two days the Minister of Justice invited the prosecutor to the minister's office. Zarudny began by saying
that he fully approved of Karinsky's actions in the Bolsheviks' case, and
approved the publication by Karinsky of the results of the investigation. But Zarudny ended by inviting Karinsky to accept the high position of the senior chairman of the judicial chamber. When Karinsky
said that "at the moment, in view of the Soviet's demand, he did not
wish to step aside and did not desire a promotion," Zarudny, after long
attempts at persuasion, finally told Karinsky directly: "As a Trudovik,
I am bound by party discipline. As soon as the Soviet demands of me
your dismissal, I must act to secure it. For the Provisional Government the Soviet's demand has the force of law. If I do not submit, I
shall be obliged to resign myself." After reflection N. S. Karinsky sent
Zarudny a letter. "Having considered the difficult position of the Minister of Justice, I agree to the promotion."

All this had transpired before the Kornilov uprising and, in part, before the Moscow Conference. On August 30 Karchevsky was appointed
Karinsky's successor, and it became apparent at once that the government had changed its attitude toward the Bolsheviks' case: it was

decided to release from prison all arrestees against whom no criminal charges had been brought. A specially appointed commission to investigate the legality of the incarceration of the Bolsheviks revealed that, as of September 1, of 87 Bolsheviks imprisoned in connection with the uprising of July 3-5, and twelve other Bolsheviks imprisoned for other reasons, there was not one who had been imprisoned without legal foundation. However, after the Executive Committee's renewed demand on September 2 to release the arrested Bolsheviks, the government decided to ignore the report of its investigative commission. Karchevsky was asked to cut short the period of incarceration, and that he did. On September 4 Trotsky was released on pledge of good behavior. A number of other Bolsheviks—soldiers and sailors from the *"Aurora"*—were freed with him. On September 5 several more soldiers and sailors were let go. On September 6 in the Petrograd City Duma the Bolsheviks and SRs raised the question of the release of the Bolsheviks and simultaneously disturbing rumors began to circulate around the city about a demonstration of Bolshevik workers scheduled for that day. On September 9 the Petrograd Soviet passed a resolution demanding that comrades Lenin and Zinoviev (who had avoided arrest) be given "the possibility of open activity in the ranks of the proletariat; that all revolutionaries charged with political crimes should be released immediately on recognizance; and that there should be an immediate and authoritative public inquiry into the entire process of criminal investigation." Throughout this period the release of Bolsheviks from prison on recognizance continued.

Of the other demands of the "revolutionary democracy" it was easy to fulfill the one calling for dissolution of the State Council and State Duma. To that effect a manifesto was prepared in the first days of September. But again Kerensky could not bring himself to raise a hand against the institution that had created his political reputation. The publication of the decree was delayed. Nevertheless, the sovereign powers of the Fourth State Duma came to an end in October.

The Executive Committee's resolution demanded that the government cooperate with the Committee of Popular Struggle Against Counter-Revolution. Meanwhile, the "directory," immediately after its formation, hurried (on September 4) to declare closed all branches of "committees for the salvation of the revolution" across Russia. The central "Committee of Popular Struggle" decided simply not to recognize this directive, and on the following day it adopted a resolution in which, "noting with a sense of deep satisfaction the energy and steadfastness shown by the local agencies of the revolutionary democracy in the struggle against counter-revolution," it expressed its conviction that "the corresponding local agencies, in view of the continuing disturbing state of affairs, *will work with the same energy and persistence* in a close alliance with the Committee of Popular Struggle Against Counter-Revolution." In other words, an organ of the Executive Committee openly called for insubordination to the government, a government to which the Executive Committee had just repeatedly promised support. This was made even clearer by the inter-district conference under the aegis of the Petrograd Soviet, in a resolution adopted on September 6. "Having discussed Kerensky's directive on the dissolution of the revolutionary organizations for struggle against counter-revolution, the inter-district conference states, that in the difficult days of armed uprising by the *bourgeoisie* against the revolution when the Provisional Government was impotent and disoriented, the entire burden of struggle . . . fell on the shoulders of these organizations, created on the initiative of authoritative democratic organizations . . . . *Not recognizing the government's right to dissolve* revolutionary organizations that have been created by authoritative institutions, the conference resolves: *not to disband* the revolutionary organizations of struggle against counter-revolution, which have been created by the inter-district conference. The Central Executive Committee shall be informed of this decision."

The political standing that had been obtained by the Bolsheviks after the Kornilov uprising, quite apart from all these demands submitted to the government and quite apart from the government's concessions, was underscored by Tsereteli's attempt to check the vote that overturned the presidium of the Soviet at the midnight session of the Petrograd Soviet on September 1. At an unusually crowded session of the Soviet on September 9, the outgoing presidium of Chkheidze and Tsereteli put the question as to whether the vote of September 1 had been the accidental result of the absence of certain members, as a representative of the soldiers had asserted, or whether the passage of the Bolshevik resolution signified a complete change of tactics which the Soviet must now follow. The Bolsheviks tried to shift the political question to a tactical one by proposing to reelect the presidium on the basis of proportional representation and thus to include Bolsheviks and internationalists in its membership list. But Tsereteli objected firmly. "You Bolsheviks explain the vote as a change in the mood of the entire proletariat. We must know if this is so or not so, for we cannot support nor can we carry out Bolshevik tactics." The draft resolution, proposed by the Mensheviks and SRs, stated that the resolution of September 1 had been passed by a portion of the Soviet membership that had met fortuitiously that night, and therefore did not correspond to the general political line of the Soviet taken as a whole, and that the Petrograd Soviet had complete confidence in the former presidium as enumerated by Tsereteli. After an incident provoked by the absence of Kerensky's name from the list of presidium members (this weakened the position of the [presidium's] opponents but put Kerensky into an ambiguous situation), a roll-call vote of confidence was taken, spelling defeat for Tsereteli, Chkheidze, Gots, and the former presidium. There were 414 votes for the Mensheviks' resolution, and 619 against it, with 67 abstentions. Tsereteli had received the answer to the question he had put. The old line of the Soviet was condemned. Now the Bolsheviks' turn had come.

As we see, the political circumstances under which the government was forced to reorganize itself and to transform the "council of five" into a full cabinet were quite unfavorable to it. Keeping an external appearance of independence from the "revolutionary democracy," to whom it had been compelled in fact to make one concession after another, and supporting the principle of the government's lack of accountability to the "Democratic Conference" which was supposed to meet in ten days, the government of the five promised to augment its membership "in the next few days." In fact, having deferred for now the question of whether to add Kadets and commercial-industrialists to the cabinet, Kerensky quickly opened negotiations designed to add socialists to the cabinet. For Zarudny's slot he selected P. N. Maliantovich, to whose candidacy the Soviet was well disposed. Oldenburg's place was taken by S. S. Salazkin,[30] who had pleasantly surprised the "democracy" at the Moscow Conference by endorsing the formula of August 14 on behalf of the Zemstvo. Above all, the Soviets were unhappy with the appointment of General Alexeev and with the candidacy of the Kadet N. M. Kishkin for the important post of Minister of Internal Affairs. But General Alexeev himself understood that he did not belong as chief of staff, given the radical purge of Stavka and of the high officer corps: he publicly protested against the new course as leading to the destruction of the army. The Ministry of Internal Affairs was to be given to a socialist who would not draw the Soviet's protest—to A. M. Nikitin, the Minister of Posts and Telegraphs.

The decrees appointing the new, and from the perspective of the "revolutionary democracy," uncontroversial ministers were almost ready. It was proposed to publish them on September 10 without waiting for Kerensky's return from Stavka. Thus, at least formally, the government had completed its reorganization before the Democratic Conference. But it was precisely this that the Executive Committee found irritating. On the evening of September 9 the Executive Committee sent a delegation headed by Chkheidze to M. I. Tereshchenko, Kerensky's deputy. The delegation stated that a reconstitution of the government before the

Democratic Conference and on coalition principles was unacceptable; the council of five could function only temporarily. The publication of the new appointments had to be delayed. At this juncture the last member of the Party of Popular Liberty in the government, A. V. Kartashev, finally lost patience. On the morning of September 10 he sent Tereshchenko a petition, "in view of the obvious domination of the socialists over the Provisional Government and the infeasibility of a genuine coalitional cabinet . . . to relieve him of his post as Procurator of the Holy Synod and member of the Provisional Government."

Thus, before the opening of the Democratic Conference the government was composed exclusively of socialists, with the lone exception of M. I. Tereshchenko (who, however, also raised the question of retirement). Of course, this did not determine in advance the ultimate character of the government. But, in expectation of being attacked from all directions, the government was adopting a defensive posture.[31]

CHAPTER II

THE DEMOCRATIC CONFERENCE

On the Democratic Conference was now concentrated the general attention if not of the nation (for it the idea of the conference was extraneous and artificial), then of the party press and of political circles. As we have seen, the "Democractic" Conference was from its very beginnings a clever political maneuver designed to defer the resolution of an insoluble conflict. Since the conflict had arisen from the midst of this self-same "democracy," no one could expect anything new in the sense of solving the difficulties encountered. Here for the first time an issue relevant to all citizens, the structure of the government, was declared the affair of a group of political parties, which themselves admitted that they only imperfectly and incompletely represented that insignificant part of the democracy which was "organized" and "conscious." For the first time an institution, composed of representatives of these groups of the population was prepared to act not only as an expression of the "democracy's" opinion, but also as an expression of its sovereign *will*.

Thus, the Democratic Conference was to be superior to the government, which would become responsible to the conference. But this was exactly the same thing that the Bolsheviks had been trying to achieve when they wanted to transfer "all power to the Soviets." Tsereteli's enterprise was essentially a complete capitulation to the plans of Lenin and Trotsky. Of course, when the presses of the Bolsheviks and of the "bourgeoisie" pointed to this political consequence of calling the conference, the Mensheviks and SRs heatedly disputed the assertion. They tried to prove that by making this concession to Bolshevism they would free themselves from Bolshevik pressure on the masses.

When, however, it came time for each political faction to clarify just what the arrangers of the Democratic Conference had wanted to achieve, if indeed they thought of it as something beyond a tactical move to delay solving the nation's problems—then opinions were divided even among political allies, and there was complete confusion. The Right-SR *Volia Naroda* quite maliciously described the confusion in socialist thinking: "The SR party has not managed to reach a single decision. It is divided into at least two sections. The Menshevik faction of the Social Democrats has divided into four sub-factions." Then there were resolutions

by the Bolsheviks, Popular Socialists and emendations of all sorts issued by individuals.   Some favored a coalition, others opposed it.
Some recognized a coalition of all the living forces of the nation; others
wanted a coalition of everyone except the Kadets; and still others wanted
a coalition excluding the Central Committee of the Party of Popular
Liberty, the Kadets from *Rech* [Speech].   Some wanted a coalition to
unite on a definite platform, without defining concretely the parties and
classes involved in such a coalition. Others added to this the condition
that the coalition government be responsible to the Soviets.   Still
others substituted for responsibility to the Soviets responsibility to an
executive body that would be selected from the membership of the Democratic Conference. There was no agreement even concerning the composition of this executive body: some said that the bourgeoisie should also be represented in it, others protested against such an "ill-assorted mix-
ture." There were those who defended the thesis that the government
should not be responsible to anyone. These disagreements even manifested themselves among opponents of a coalition. Some said that
broadly democratic elements, not purely socialist ones, ought to take
power; others said that the socialists should be in power; a third group
defended Soviet power; a fourth group—exclusively proletarian rule, and
so on. The newspaper ended with the question: "What kind of opposition would greet such a government, what sort of protest would such a
government provoke all over Russia?"

One thing was beyond doubt. The intention of the "revolutionary democracy" to summon a conference that would select a government on
the basis of the desires of those groups represented within it, caused immediate protests to be lodged by all those public circles operating outside the party discipline of the socialist factions. The Party of Popular
Liberty issued such a protest on September 6 and forbade its members
to participate in the election of delegates to the conference. The Kadets
justified their protest on the ground that the views of broad elements of
the populace already had been expressed at the Moscow Conference; that
the newly-scheduled conference, compared with the Moscow Conference, would be one-sided, for it was a conference solely of those who accepted Chkheidze's platform; that such a conference, being useless even
as a forum to *illuminate* political questions, certainly could not be considered competent to *decide* them; and that, despite all the above objections, the groups dominating the Soviet already had decided to make the
conference a permanent agency and had directed it to organize a government.

Even earlier, on September 4, the Soviet of the All-Russia Cooperative Congresses, along with the All-Russia League of Consumer

Societies, the Moscow National Bank, the Central Association of Flax Producers, and the League of Siberian Dairy Artels, sent the following telegram to Kerensky, Chkheidze, and the Soviet of Peasants' Deputies: "The All-Russia Conference must be an undertaking of all nationalities and must be convoked by authority of the state; all strata of the population must be represented in it. This conference must be convened in Moscow." The participation of the cooperatives was to be determined at a Congress of Cooperatives, convening in Moscow on September 11. For its own part the Soviet of Cooperative Congresses announced in advance its "unconditional advocacy of a coalition government." "We are certain that this opinion is shared by the overwhelming majority of those in the Russian cooperative movement. The majority of the population does not share the [Petrograd] Soviet's enthusiasm and certainty that the only way to cope with universal chaos is through organized agencies of the Soviets; this enthusiasm and certainty will lead to civil war and the destruction of Russia."

Indeed, at the Cooperative Congress, after a series of passionate and deeply felt speeches in favor of a coalition, the following instruction was adopted for "cooperative representatives Prokopovich, Skobelev, E. D. Kuskova, and others in the Democratic Conference."[1] "Whereas the Democratic Conference is a *private* assembly of the organized democracy, whereas it *cannot by its very nature be an expression of the will of the entire nation* and a source of governmental authority . . . , the cooperative instructs its delegates to form a temporary bloc of cooperative organizations in union with those currents in the socialist parties that stand for the statesmanly perspective, and with those non-socialist groups and parties of Russian society which have striven and strive to defend the achievements of the revolution and social reforms. Resting on such a basis, the bloc should organize a national coalition government, which should include various social groups—both socialist and bourgeois—capable of subordinating their personal interests and the interests of their class to the national interest, and who are not besmirched by participation in rebellious uprisings against the revolutionary government *from whatever perspective*. This government must be free from any dependence on individual groups and organizations, and it *should be responsible only to the entire nation and to the Constituent Assembly*." Concerning the government's program the cooperatives' leaders expressed two desires, by which they carefully distinguished themselves from the Soviets of the "revolutionary democracy." In internal politics they were satisfied by the "general principles" of the program of August 14; they stressed, as the main goal, "putting in order the deeply troubled life

of the nation and *defending all the past achievements of the revolution*"
[and not its "creative work" and future "deepening"]. In foreign policy,
while agreeing with the desire to achieve "peace on the principles announced by the Russian 'revolutionary democracy,'" the cooperatives'
leaders emphasized that such a peace could only be achieved though "an
active defense of the nation against enemy attacks, a defense conducted
in union with the world's progressive democracies, now allied to us."
One can tell how strongly felt was this political mood in Moscow from
similar resolutions adopted by the Moscow Council of Barristers and
the Moscow Council of Teachers, who *refused* to be represented at the
"Democratic Conference."

The Cossacks also expressed their doubts in a set of questions forwarded to the government on September 5, questions that the Cossacks
wanted answered before deciding to participate in the Democratic Conference: "Is this conference meeting on the government's initiative? Will
members of the Provisional Government be taking part? Does the government attribute national significance to this conference? If the conference is convening with the participation of the Provisional Government, then will the Soviet of the Union of Cossack Soldiers be given
its legally proper number of representatives?" The government's response
was evasive: of course, it recognized the "national significance" *of all assemblies* of influential groups in the populace.

In view of the variations in opinions and of the strong opposition issuing from democratic, but not from narrowly-partisan, circles, the question of how to distribute seats at the Democratic Conference became
very important. In the invitation of September 2, the Executive Committees of the Soviets decided upon the following numbers: there would
be 100 representatives from the Soviet of Workers' and Soldiers' Deputies; 100 from the Peasants' Soviet; and 50 from the regional committees of each of these two Soviets. Thus, there would be 300 representatives from the "revolutionary democracy" of the Soviets. In addition,
150 seats were assigned to the cooperatives, whose mood we have described above. One hundred seats were allotted to the trade unions, who
recommended themselves in Moscow as most loyal allies of the Soviet
democracy; 84 seats to the military organizations; 50 to the Zemstvos;
59 to ethnic groups; 20 to the railroad union; 10 to the peasant and telegraph unions; 15 to the teachers' union; 3 to Zemstvo employees; 2
each to journalists, engineers, lawyers, doctors, feldshers, and employees of the commercial-industrial committee; and one each to pharma-
cists and architects.

A number of complaints were lodged about this distribution of representation. Representatives of Moscow municipal and Zemstvo self-

government demanded "no less than half the votes in the conference" for Zemstvos and cities, and many Zemstvos and cities made their own demands for greater representation. These demands had to be satisfied: after all, these were "democratic" municipal dumas and Zemstvos. The cities got 300 seats, the Zemstvos 200. On the other hand, the Bolsheviks in the Executive Committee stated that the apportionment did not guarantee spots to a number of organizations on which the Bolsheviks were counting to make their weight felt in the conference: they demanded that the representation of local Soviets be increased by 50 seats; that each army organization receive 5 seats instead of only 3; that the trade unions have 25 more seats; and that the factory committees be given 22 places. The Executive Committee rejected this proposal, although the representation of the Soviets was increased from 300 to 460 seats. In any event, the impression created by the statements of the cooperative movement and of local self-government certainly changed the disposition of the Executive Committee; the central agency would now be more amenable to more moderate programs and to the selection of a more moderate government.

However, even the more moderate position of the conference organizers continued to be internally contradictory as the plenary session of the Soviets Executive Committee on September 12 demonstrated. Tsereteli formulated the following "concrete proposals" which the "revolutionary democracy" would bring to the conference. "As a basis of future activity we should propose a democratic platform, like the one announced at the Moscow Conference. The Democratic Conference should elect from its midst an agency that will function until the convocation of the Constituent Assembly. *The government should be responsible to this agency* and should preserve its unbreakable bond with the entire democracy. The membership of this agency should include all those elements who *accept our conditions* for organizing a government. *Otherwise, it will be necessary to create an exclusively democratic government.*" The same contradiction manifested itself in voting. The principle of coalition was endorsed by a vote of 119 to 101. But the session also endorsed an amendment offered by a minority of the Mensheviks. The coalition would be a "coalition without Kadets," although Tsereteli quite properly stated that this amendment violated the very principle of coalition. He failed to notice, however, that the principle of a coalition *had already been violated* in his own formula, which set as conditions for entering the coalition acceptance of the "democratic platform" and responsiblity of the government to a permanent agency of the Democratic Conference, an agency that was clearly intended to replace the Executive Committee of the Soviets.

For the extreme left this compromise position, which undermined the coalition principle for the sake of the Bolshevik principle of "all power to the revolutionary democracy," was still unacceptable. The Bolsheviks again demonstrated their intransigence by selecting as delegates from the Petrograd Soviet the fugitives Lenin and Zinoviev.[2] (True, the government responded to this challenge by reissuing warrants for their arrest.) The Bolsheviks' "concrete demands" were articulated by the Baltic Fleet, which on September 8 began to fly red battle flags, and which on September 9 explained the logic of this demonstration through the following resolution: "The fleet is demonstrating its readiness to fight with all its resources *for a transfer of power to the revolutionary democracy*, the proletariat, and the laboring peasantry, and it insists that the Democratic Conference implement this plan of action. Down with agreement with the bourgeoisie! We demand an immediate truce on all fronts in order to begin negotiations for a peace without annexations and indemnities on the basis of the self-determination of peoples. We demand an *immediate transfer of all land* into the control of the land committees before the Constituent Assembly shall meet. We demand *workers' control* over production. The flags will be lowered at 8 A.M. on the day when the Democratic Conference meets."

The Democratic Conference opened two days late, on September 14 at 5:30 P.M. in the main hall of the Alexandrinsky Theater. The total number of representatives with credentials reached the enormous sum of 1,775. Of these approximately 1,200 were present at the opening. After all the changes in the conference's membership, the distribution of votes between the two contending opinions—favoring or opposed to the coalition—remained unclear. The uncertainty lent a measure of drama to the debates.[3]

The government was represented at the session by all members of the directory except for Tereshchenko. Kerensky, who came somewhat late, entered the former tsar's loge during the introductory speech by the chairman, Chkheidze.

Chkheidze's speech sketched out the conference's intermediate position between two extremes. One extreme was the ambition of the "imperialists" to take Constantinople and Hagia Sophia. The other extreme was the ambition to "extinguish the fire of the capitalist war by transforming the revolution into a socialist and world revolution." Half a year of revolution had shown that both extremes had created the soil for counter-revolution. "Instead of a leap into the realm of liberty there has been a leap into the realm of anarchy." Governmental authority, caught between the two warring camps, "has been almost paralyzed." "The nation yearns for a government"—naturally, a government that was "revolutionary" and "responsible"—but the task of this government would be to implement the platform of the Moscow Conference.

The inevitable chairman of all "democratic" conferences and agencies, the honest Chkheidze, would not have been suited to a more responsible and complicated role. His revolutionary reputation far exceeded his personal resources. This "revolutionary against his will" long ago had become frightened of the revolution, and, unlike many others, he had covered up this fear by ambiguous use of revolutionary cliches to the extent that this was required by his position. To admit before such an assembly that, instead of leaping into the socialist realm, the revolution had leapt into the realm of anarchy, that the government's authority had been paralyzed and that the nation yearned for a real government—this was certainly to move much closer to an accommodation with "propertied elements" than the membership of the given assembly would permit.

After Chkheidze's speech and the election of the presidium, it was Kerensky's turn to speak. In avoiding personal encounters with the "revolutionary democracy," Kerensky rarely had visited its committees. He visited only when clouds rose above his friendly majority, when storm clouds gathered above his own name. A single visit usually sufficed to disperse the bad weather. On this occasion he thought to achieve the same result. In distinction from the Moscow Conference, he was here in the midst of the "democracy," among his "own." Before the "democracy" he wanted to make a display of dropping his armor and the attributes of his power, to win trust for himself at a single stroke. He would adopt a confessional tone and speak candidly, as a man and as a comrade.

Passing through unabating applause on his way from the loge to the stage in the company of the traditional two aides, Kerensky began boldly in that tone. "Before the assembly of the democracy, by whose will and in whose company *I made* the revolution, I cannot say nor do I feel that there is anyone here who can hurl at me personally the reproaches and slanders that I have been hearing recently." Such personal references in a public auditorium are dangerous, for they assume that the audience will respond positively. Kerensky discovered the danger, for on this occasion his calculation proved wrong. "There are such people, there are," the Bolsheviks screamed at him from their benches, thus destroying the triumphal rhythm of the speech.

Indeed, here were gathered not only Kerensky's friends, but also his enemies and detractors on whom candor would have no effect. And from that moment Kerensky's speech met with a strong psychological resistance from that signficiant portion of the audience who did not share his perspective on events and who wished at all times to demonstrate their opposition. This unnerved the speaker. Being excited by the ironic exclamations and interruptions from the audience, he was continually diverted into improvisation—a most dangerous path for him. One touchy matter that he could not avoid discussing was the question of his own involvement in the Kornilovshchina.

The Executive Committee already had introduced a resolution most unpleasant for Kerensky, a resolution calling for a careful investigation of the government's role in the Kornilov affair. Kerensky should have accepted the challenge, but he supposed that he could win over the "democracy" by confidential disclosures about the dangers which had threatened it and from which he, Kerensky, had saved it. He confessed that "I learned of the incipient coup long before the events themselves. And from the very day I discovered it, I took all necessary steps." Instead of expressions of gratitude from the audience, Kerensky heard the malicious words: "The first general of the Russian Revolution has let the cat out of the bag." Kerensky continued: the Kornilovshchina "was unmasked *by me* in a timely fashion and most thoroughly." The Bolsheviks corrected him: "It was unmasked by the Soviets and the democracy." "Yes," replied Kerensky, "by the democracy, because everything that I have done and everything I do, *I do in the name* of the democracy." And once again Kerensky returned to *his own* services to the revolution. "I predicted the coming of the 'white general.'" "Already in June," here the speaker cut off in mid-sentence the admission that was ready to pour out of him, but he could not help himself and quickly returned to it. "I knew what they wanted to accomplish, because, *before they turned to Kornilov, they came to me and proposed the same plan*"

At this sensational revelation, the left screamed: "Who came to you? What did they propose?" Having placed himself so close to the alleged criminals, the head of the government could not stop here without reinforcing the impression that he "had let the cat out of the bag." Kerensky sensed the problem, but there was not really much he could say, for one cannot make a criminal conspiracy out of private conversations. Ignoring the question, he continued: "I said: Make no mistake, do not suppose that there are no forces of the democracy standing on my side . . . . If you try to arrange anything of the kind [a coup d'etat], everything will stop in its tracks; the troops will not move, your dispatches will not be sent." But who was this "you" to whom Kerensky had predicted in June the failure of the Kornilov conspiracy? Feeling the impossibility of stopping halfway once he had embarked on the road of revelations—revelations that would have been more in place in an investigative commission, Kerensky disclosed the facts. But which facts? "I affirm that even before V. N. Lvov appeared before me, another former public figure approached a certain prominent individual in Moscow and demanded, for especially weighty reasons, a meeting with me.[4] At the end of this encounter [with the prominent individual], the public figure said: 'Let Kerensky bear in mind that in the future no changes in the Provisional Government will be permitted without the consent of Stavka.'" We have seen that Tsereteli made precisely the same statement to the government on behalf of the democratic agencies. The government had not agreed to Tsereteli's conditions and saw in them no conspiracy, but this other case was considered a conspiracy. Then there followed another confidential disclosure that was easier to verify. "Before the Moscow Conference itself I faced a dilemma: either to fulfill their demand, or they *would blow up* the Moscow Conference. I rejected this demand. Kornilov's report received no hearing in the Provisional Government, and no one blew up the Moscow Conference." No one had threatened "to blow up" the Moscow Conference, and, as we know, all Kerensky's fears on this score were exaggerated. The "demands" sent to Kerensky before the Moscow Conference were not all "rejected" in their entirety. True, Kornilov's report was not read at the meeting of the Provisional Government on August 10, but it was read and discussed at a private meeting of the "triumvirate." Kokoshkin's threat of resignation lead to a discussion of part of the report even in the Provisional Government (on August 11), during which members of the government reached agreement concerning Kornilov's "demands."

Kerensky's confession did not succeed, and the speaker made a motion as if to depart from the stage. But he remembered that before him lay the main part of his speech—the part in which he had wanted to prepare the assembly for a serious understanding of its task. Kerensky stopped, and delivered that section of his speech. This time it was not his fault that this portion of the speech failed to win the requisite sympathy or even understanding. He spoke of the anarchy growing everywhere, of the need "to apply all the forces and intelligence of the nation." He cited as a dangerous symptom the new revolutionary action of Finland—the unauthorized opening of the Diet that had been dispersed by the government—and the cooperation in this matter of the Russian revolutionary soldiers at a moment when "a German squadron, well-informed about the situation, is nearing the Gulf of Finland." Alas, from the Bolsheviks' benches there were loud cries approving Finland's behavior. And in vain the speaker tried to win the conference's sympathies by threats ("if the nation is not convinced of our collective political wisdom," then the revolution will suffer defeat), and, on the contrary, by flattery (he expressed, "under pain of being considered a dreamer and visionary," complete "faith in the rationality of the nation"). "We sense," Kerensky assured his audience, "that in the moment of danger everyone will come together and reason together." In response his opponents shouted to him: "And what about the death penalty?" And they called him the Russian Marat. They knew how best to wound the speaker who in Moscow had threatened to "kill his own soul."

Having lost his composure, Kerensky, in a shaking voice, now uttered words that are impermissible in the mouths of heads of state: "I say to you, you who shout from the audience, that you should wait until I, as Supreme Commander-in-Chief, have signed even one death sentence. Then I shall allow you to condemn me." What was the point of passing laws when the supreme commander refused in advance to apply them, solely to avoid ruining his reputation among the Bolsheviks? But even this concession won no mercy for Kerensky. A young soldier approached the stage barrier and, pointing to the supreme commander, loudly shouted: "You are a disgrace to the motherland." This drop finally caused the cup to overflow. Kerensky's pride was wounded: he finally remembered that he was the head of the army and the government. The speech that had begun in a tone of comradely candor he now ended in the more customary tone of a threat. "When I come here, I forget about convention, about the post that I occupy, and I speak to you as one human being to others. Not everyone here understands a human being, so I shall now speak to you as a government official. Whoever shall dare to infringe on the freedom of the republic, whoever shall dare to stab the Russian army in the back, that person shall learn the power of the Provisional Government, which commands the trust of the entire nation."

Alas, Kerensky already had left an impression on the audience. It was the same impression that he had made in Moscow, but it was now sharpened by the circumstance and by the failure of the orator's tactics. And this failure was significant. It signified that, as a result of the constant contradiction between word and deed, the government had lost the use of both the contrary means of influencing the masses: loyalty and fear. To be more precise, having lost its old means of influence—motivating by fear—the government failed to acquire a new means—motivating through loyalty. The masses no longer had faith in the government, and no one was afraid of it.

The same impression had been made in Moscow. But there it had been obscured by the superficial effectiveness of the delivery, by the threatening, if also theatrical gestures of the man who had been invested with all the attributes of supreme power. Here, in a democratic auditorium, the speaker, who wanted to disarm his auditors by divesting himself of the attributes of power, failed to achieve even a superficial success. He was defeated in the struggle against the psychology of the audience. His enemies took advantage of his confidential tone publicly to dethrone and humiliate him. Thus, the government, which at this time should have been stronger than ever before, showed itself to be weaker than ever before. Even among its partisans, the government aroused not respect, but pity. The weakness of the government also manifested itself in the decision of the cabinet, which was attending a conference that it had not convoked, to say nothing concerning the main task of the conference: the reorganization of the government. The cabinet left the task of defending its cause to its political allies in the conference.

The duel between speakers of the various political parties began after War Minister Verkhovsky's ambiguous and useless speech. Chernov, Kamenev, even the Menshevik Bogdanov all spoke against the coalition. The first attempt to defend the coalition was Tsereteli's address, which was adapted to the membership and mood of the assembly. If, in the Executive Committee, he had frightened the democracy by indicating that a coalition with propertied elements was necessary because of the *weakness* of the democracy standing alone, he now flattered the democracy and indicated the need for a coalition because of the democracy's *strength*. "Bourgeois" elements of the coalition had always done the bidding of the democracy while in the government. That was why representatives of the bourgeoisie "ran from the government" during every crisis. Now, after the "tragicomic rebellion of Kornilov," who was supported only by "adventurist elements" and whom "propertied elements of Russia had not supported," the democracy was stronger than ever before. That was why the democracy had less reason than before to fear collaboration with elements of the bourgeoisie who would involuntarily side with the democracy, "picking the lesser of two evils." And now the bourgeoisie would have to accept in full, without emendations, the old program of the democracy, which was formulated in the government's declarations on May 6, July 8, and August 14. Here Tsereteli was studiously silent about the fact that the "old" program, which in its original formulation on May 6 had served as the basis for the activity of the government's "bourgeois elements," was transformed in its two subsequent formulations into a completely new program, one that was in many respects unacceptable to the "bourgeoisie." One of these subsequent versions of the program (that of July 8) was, like the declaration of a republic, composed and published during an interregnum, between two coalitions. The other version (that of August 14) was not endorsed by the government.

Chernov made the same point as Tsereteli, but much more frankly, when he said that "a coalition must form around a program, not the program around the coalition." But Chernov was at least logical in his exposition, and he understood quite well that a coalition based on these (Tsereteli's) conditions was the negation of a coalition.

The second day of the Democratic Conference was of especial interest. The former socialist-ministers grasped that it was impossible to defend a coalition by advancing, as Tsereteli had done, from propositions which the "revolutionary democracy" was accustomed to take for granted, but which actually contained the cause of its errors. The former socialist-ministers tried unsuccessfully, based on their ministerial experience, to show that some of these assumptions were questionable and to convince the "revolutionary democracy" that its thinking rested on mistakes and illusions rather than on sure axioms. A. V. Peshekhonov[5] asked the assembly: "You say that there is a *struggle* for power. But I, having seen how people have taken power and how they have thrown it away, must testify that power is now something that no one wants anything to do with." You claim that the "bourgeoisie" in the government defended the interests of its *own class*. But "I must remind you that when very serious issues having to do with the interests of the lower classes were raised, the Kadets did not oppose passage of these laws. Don't forget that the bread monopoly, which strikes a very cruel blow against the interests of the commercial class, was promulgated under Kadet ministers; A. I. Shingarev[6] pushed through an onerous financial assessment." You claim that the Kadets "sabotaged" revolutionary legislation? In fact, the Kadets "opposed the passage of certain laws not so much for ideological, as for technical reasons: these draft laws were so weak that even we, the socialist-ministers, did not always find it possible to defend them." Quite right, agreed M. I. Skobelev: "When we came forth with concrete proposals and clearly formulated all the steps that had to be taken immediately and that were essential to the workers, we always succeeded in overcoming the class opposition of the propertied elements." On the other hand, an exclusively socialist government could not do everything. "The broad masses will not receive tangible benefits in the next few months from even the most radical measures. Moreover, trust in the democracy can quickly be squandered, and broad strata of workers and peasants will condemn even a socialist government and shower hatred upon it, just as on any other government that proves unable on the day after taking power to provide bread and peace."

A. V. Peshekhonov also pointed to the danger of programs "of group and class pretensions" that "quite easily win popularity among the broad masses." "The program (of August 14), for whose sake we made the revolution, conceals within itself a grave danger. Its implementation would be dangerous even in peacetime, but it is the more dangerous in time of war, when its enforcement will present incredible difficulties for the nation." Peshekhonov stressed that at the present "what is necessary from all sides is not the satisfaction of demands, however justifiable they may be, but restraint and sacrifice." And he conscientiously stated that the sacrifices made *by the "bourgeoisie"* "have not been matched by the democracy, which is very wary of calling for them." "I must say," he added, "that we socialists, being in the government and knowing clearly that *there is no other way to safety than to put a limit* to demands and pretensions, *have not yet found within ourselves* the strength to enforce such a limit." A. S. Zarudny said the same thing. "The government which will be summoned to power should understand that *this is not the time for us to talk about the details of a program.* Is it really feasible in one month to solve the agrarian question and institute control over capital? . . . The only question that the government must resolve in the next week is the question of how to guarantee the minimal security of our nation and when to call the Constituent Assembly."

From all these perspectives the three ministers found that to get along without the Kadets—or, what amounted to the same thing, to get along without the "industrial bourgeoisie"—in the future government was impossible. As to the accusations of Kadet complicity in the Kornilov conspiracy, all three ministers—Skobelev and Zarudny and Peshekhonov—testified in one voice to the complete absurdity of such suspicions in relation to the Kadet ministers. Zarudny saw the only shortcoming of the former government to be Kerensky's inclination "toward issuing sovereign decrees and toward dictatorship." And Zarudny was extremely critical of those ministers who, at Kerensky's first hint, "took pieces of paper and signed their requests to resign." "I refused to do so," Zarudny added to general applause.

Tsereteli agreed with Zarudny, but he placed the responsibility for Kerensky's despotic behavior on the democracy. "Let the democracy blame itself alone, if its representative has grown dizzy with power." But Tsereteli immediately provided an excuse. What was to be done? Already in July it had become necessary to make concessions to Kerensky, "given the weakness of the revolutionary agencies." "Having weighed the situation, we concluded that we had two alternatives: either the government of the Soviets of Workers' and Soldiers' Deputies faced civil war, or we would have to accept that imperfect form of govern-ment resulting from the personification of authority and from the coali-tion . . . . We chose the latter. If the revolutionary democracy were more organized, then no one would have considered this alternative."

Having thus justified Kerensky's regime and the coalition only as the lesser evil, Tsereteli returned the debate to its traditional channel, within which it continued to run. The speeches of Skobelev, Peshekhonov and Zarudny, which were free from the conventional illusions, had little effect, their authors being voices crying in the wilderness. To their voices were added—besides the statements of the cooperative move-ment's leadership whose opinions we already know—only the warning voices of Chkhenkeli and Minor, whose speeches resounded with im-measurable pain over the suffering and humiliation of the motherland.[7] Chkhenkeli spoke apropos of the statements by delegates of the various national minorities. He said that he "sensed here what was perhaps one of the very saddest acts of the Russian tragedy." What was at stake was not only the destiny of the non-Russian peoples, but also the destiny of the ethnic Russians — a crucial question for every country. "Where is it, this [Russian] nation?" asked Chkhenkeli. "I would like to hear al-so from its representatives." "We Georgians have a national feeling which is very difficult to distinguish from Russian patriotic feeling: and it would be nice if the Russians would say that their patriotic feel-ing differs very little from the national feeling of the Georgians." But, alas, there was nothing of the sort. "Midst the rumors about every pos-sible political, social, economic, and other kind of change, one thing is lacking: there is no national anxiety for the fate of Russia; a proper concern for national health is no longer evident." The orator continued: "When the Kadets asked us by what means we wished to save the coun-try, we always answered: 'By revolution.' But six months have passed, and my confidence has begun to be shaken in whether revolution will save Russia . . . . The sacred words of the Petrograd Soviet's declara-tion to all peoples of the world continue to be significant today. But one does not see actions to back up these words. With every day we grow weaker at the front, behind the lines chaos deepens, and our influ-ence in the concert of nations becomes more and more negligible . . . . I began to ask myself the question: can we really perform the very great tasks we have set ourselves? . . . If there is a desire for national self-preservation, if there is anxiety [over our country's fate], if there is enthusiasm—then we can overcome all the dangers. If not, then all our desires will come to nothing . . . , and we shall then have to ask the question whether Georgia will be the Tabriz of the Great Russian Revolution."

The same note of doubt, close to despair, resounded in the speech of the old revolutionary and internal exile, Minor. "Where is your sense of history, where are your own views?" he asked his comrade-socialists. "Is everything really forgotten and, do you suppose that one can really leap from the confines of the existing order straight to new forms of living? . . . Can an exclusively socialist government satisfy the demands that the coalition government failed to satisfy? Can a socialist government fix broken locomotives in order to transport grain from Siberia to Moscow?" This was "an objective circumstance which we socialists are powerless to alter in wartime." Enough of "brilliant speeches that are substitutes for brilliant ideas." "The more lies we tell, the worse it will be for the revolution." And Minor implored the conference to vote overwhelmingly in favor of a coalition. Otherwise, the majority—it made no difference what majority—would have *to force* the minority to submit. "If you do not achieve some unity, then, you know, we shall be facing the times of the Great French Revolution. Keep this in mind: there is no point in self-deception. We shall slaughter." "Slaughter whom?" asked voices from the audience. "We shall slaughter each other," concluded Minor, amidst a funereal silence throughout the auditorium. No one dared to applaud a man who, in this most unreceptive gathering of people trying to deceive themselves with words, dared to take upon himself the mantle of the Cassandra of the Russian Revolution.

"Achieve some unity?" But *Volia Naroda* now counted six possible solutions to the basic question of how to reconstruct the government: (1) all power to the Bolsheviks; (2) all power to the Soviets; (3) all power to an exclusively socialist government, which would be responsible to a Pre-Parliament; (4) all power to a coalition government excluding the Kadets, a government that would be based on the program of August 14 and would be responsible to the Pre-Parliament; (5) the same formula as above in number four, only including the Kadets; and (6) all power to a coalition ministry, which would include the Kadets and be responsible only to the Constituent Assembly.

Naturally, the conference's sympathy was not equally distributed among these options. No one really spoke directly in favor of the first option. Even Tsereteli could still provoke the Bolsheviks with impunity; he dared them to "seize power," and then argued that they did not want to seize power at all—indeed, that they could not do so; they only wanted to criticize others. In favor of the second option was a cohesive Bolshevik group, obviously not the majority of the Bolshevik faction, which group found additional support from the Left SRs. The third option received support from part of the Mensheviks, and it would probably be victorious, though by a narrow margin. The fourth formula, artificial and contradictory, for without the Kadets a coalition could not be realized—and everyone understood this—this fourth formula found a large number of adherents who looked on it as a compromise. Tsereteli and Bogdanov and Chernov could all support it. The fifth option was the one that Tsereteli and Chernov were prepared *personally* to support, but only the right wing in the conference collectively endorsed it, because the presence of the Kadets in the government was irreconcilable with support for the program of August 14 and with responsibility of the government to the Pre-Parliament. The only logical formula that might have been used to oppose the two Bolshevik formulae was the sixth option. But only the right wings of the SRs and Mensheviks and the more conservative socialist parties (the Popular Socialists) supported it. It was only among these rightist groups, the groups of Argunov and Breshkovskaia, Plekhanov and Potresov, that Kerensky found unconditional support.[8] Avksentiev already wavered between Breshkovskaia and Chernov, while Tsereteli sharply distinguished himself from Potresov and moved toward Bogdanov.

However, when Trotsky asserted that "No one has taken upon himself the enviable role of defending the five in the directory and its representative Kerensky," the conference immediately sensed that this statement came from a common enemy. The lack of enthusiasm toward the head of the government suddenly was replaced by an almost unanimous and noisy demonstration in Kerensky's honor. Zarudny might speak about Kerensky's "despotism," and Tsereteli might joke that Kerensky "was dizzy with power." Kerensky was *one of their own*. But when Trotsky said that Kerensky, by his refusal to sign death sentences, "transforms the decision on the death penalty into an act of capriciousness, which is really a criminal act," Trotsky spoke as an *alien*. Naturally, one had to remain silent when from the audience someone shouted, "Quite right." Kerensky's reputation, as a politician and as a man, was obviously in decline. But here, amidst "the revolutionary democracy," they stood behind Kerensky as the last point of support capable of restraining the body politic from plunging into the abyss, which was how the majority of those at the conference imagined a Bolshevik victory.

With the exception of this motive, one that was instinctive rather than conscious, nothing united the members of the conference. The Democratic Conference had no opinion on the concrete question that it had been charged to discuss. This became clear in the votes taken at the concluding session of the conference on September 19.

It was decided to vote first on the general question: either for or against a coalition. The second vote was to be on the nature of the coalition. The opponents of the coalition insisted by a majority of 650 to 574 that the vote should be a roll call, in the hope that a roll call would terrorize the adherents of the coalition. The pressure on the conference was increased by a speech concerning the motives behind the voting, a speech delivered by a representative of the Baltic Fleet, which was at the moment in open conflict with the government. The fleet's representative threatened "to defend the Soviets of Workers' and Soldiers' Deputies" by force against a coalition. The vote for or against the coalition yielded the following results:

	In Favor	Opposed	Abstentions
Cooperatives	140	23	1
Soviets of Peasant Deputies	102	70	12
Cities	114	101	8
Food procurement, land committies, economic organizations	31	16	1
Military organizations	64	54	7
Other organizations	84	30	1
Soviets of Workers' and Soldiers' Deputies	83	192	4
Unions	32	139	2
Nationalities organizations	13	44	2
Zemstvos	9	29	2
Totals *	672	698	40

It was no accident that in this vote the cooperatives, peasants, and those organizations connected with real economic work supported a coalition. Here land hunger was a factor. It was also no accident that the proletarian organizations (the Soviets of the workers and the unions) voted *against* a coalition. The voice of reality came from the military organizations at the front. It was also characterisitic that, despite the predominance of radical opinions in the new municipal self-governing institutions, the voice of the cities inclined to support the rational alternative. On the other hand, the vote of the democratized Zemstvos, which had less than their proper numerical representation, must be considered an accident. The nationalities' organizations, of course, were represented exclusively by extremist socialist elements; but this was

* Miliukov's breakdown of the vote gives the mistaken impression that the conference voted against the principle of coalition rule. In fact, the principle of coalition rule was endorsed by a vote of 766 in favor, 688 opposed, with 38 abstentions. [Editor.]

typical of the fashion in which the nationality question was posed, as Chkhenkeli had noted. It is curious that the address by the speaker from the Kiev Congress of Nationalities produced the impression of a comic episode. The Democratic Conference had no sensitivity to the tragic aspect of the matter, a tragedy quite clearly understood by Chkhenkeli.

The not so significant counterweight provided by the adherents of the principle of the state and of political rationality provoked the opponents of a coalition to their final attack. The conference would now vote on the next question: how to understand the coalition? This issue was fought over two "amendments:" (1) "Elements both of the Kadets and of other parties which took part in the Kornilov rebellion shall remain outside the coalition;" and (2) more decisively, "The Kadet Party shall remain outside the coalition." L. Trotsky immediately revealed the Bolsheviks' future ploy: they would vote in favor of both amendments, and then, having perverted forcibly the sense of the resolution by virtue of these amendments, they would vote against the resolution as a whole. Without any resistance the conference allowed itself to fall into this trap. The first amendment was accepted by the same groups as accepted the resolution itself. By a vote of 797 in favor, which number included the Bolsheviks, (139 were opposed and 196 abstained), the majority stated that it understood the coalition to be free of persons directly involved in the Kornilov rebellion. In essence, this resolution eliminated the need for the second amendment. However, the conference also voted on the second amendment, despite Tsereteli's protest, and it was also adopted by a vote of 595 in favor (this number included the opponents of the coalition) to 493 opposed (these were proponents of a coalition), with 72 abstentions. The formula that resulted—that of a coalition without Kadets—had almost no supporters. Gots asserted that "since the second amendment adopted by the assembly in fact destroys the very possibility of a coalition, the section of SRs supporting the coalition will vote against the formula as a whole and washes its hands of responsibility for the current situation." Berkengeim, speaking on behalf of the cooperatives, associated himself with Gots' position: the cooperatives would also vote against the resolution and would consider that in doing so, they also voted against a government of the Soviets. Kamenev, speaking for the Bolsheviks, and M. Spiridonova,[9] speaking for the Left SRs, asserted more logically that they would reject the resolution because they were *in favor* of all power going to the Soviets. Only Martov, speaking for the Menshevik-Internationalists, unexpectedly announced that he was prepared to accept a coalition without Kadets, for this was "a big step forward toward the liberation of the democracy from Kadet influence." On behalf of the Menshevik supporters of the coalition Dan spoke quite candidly. The Russian democracy had split to such a degree on the fundamental question of the moment that it was not in a condition to act as a united force. Now the fragmented sections of the democracy would resolve the question, each at its own risk, to the very great detriment of the nation as a whole. Responsibility for this outcome Dan placed on those members of the conference who struggled the whole time against the coalition; yet it would seem that this wing had merely remained true to itself and that it had known what it wanted.

Against the formula of "a coalition without the Kadets" there were 813 votes (from supporters of a coaliton and from its opponents), while 183 doctrinaires of the Tsereteli stripe and advocates of a coalition whatever its form voted in favor of the resolution. There were 80 abstentions in this confusing situation. On the root question of its entire program the conference remained without an opinion and without a formula.

Amidst the embarrassed confusion of some and the triumph of others, at about 1 A.M., a break was announced. After forty minutes the conference reconvened itself and Tsereteli proposed a way out of the dead end. "The presidium, having discussed the situation that has arisen, *has determined unanimously that amidst the organized democracy there is no unity of will which might lead to action*." For that reason, "taking this vote as an indicator of the conference's mood, the presidium appeals to the democracy and to all organizations in general to meet each other halfway and to make concessions so that a formula may be found in which the united will of the democracy can be articulated." To that end, it was proposed that all groups and factions meet with the presidium in a special session, to which they would send one representative from each group and three from each party, and, if they should so wish, the entire membership of their party's central committee. The exhausted assembly unanimously decided to relieve itself of the burden of decision in this puzzling matter. To satisfy its conscience the conference also unanimously "resolved that it will not disperse until there are established forms of organization and methods of work for the government that *meet the specifications* of the democracy."

The poor conference! It had only just stated in its votes that, proceeding from its universally-accepted yet mistaken assumptions, it *could not find* an acceptable formula, no matter how hard it tried. But it was necessary to find a way to save face. And Tsereteli's conventional hypocrisy was there to lend assistance . . . .

CHAPTER III

"DEMOCRACY" AND "BOURGEOISIE" COMPROMISE

The Provisional Government followed without especial anxiety the "war of words" in the Democratic Conference. On September 10, as we have seen, the government decided not to form a cabinet before the conference's resolution was made clear. But already on September 13, that is, on the eve of the actual opening of the conference, A. F. Kerensky invited the Moscovites N. M. Kishkin, P. N. Maliantovich, and also the representatives of the commerical-industrialists, A. I. Konovalov, P. A. Buryshkin, S. N. Tretiakov, S. Smirnov and S. M. Chetverikov to come to Petrograd for a continuation of negotiations.[1]   Having worked out in advance the preconditions for their entry into the government, the Moscovite figures arrived on September 14 and presented their six demands—demands that were the same as before: (1) decisive struggle against anarchy; (2) a guarantee of free elections to the Constituent Assembly; (3) equality of rights among all ministers entering the government; (4) organic work to restore the battle-readiness of the army, without any deviations into demagogy; (5) independence of the Provisional Government from all irresponsible political parties and class organizations; (6) inclusion in the cabinet of members of the Party of Popular Liberty. Kerensky did not object, but neither did he make any concrete proposals. He waited for the conference's decision. Kerensky's friends gave him the hope that there might appear in the conference a majority favorable to the government. On the morning of September 15, however, Kerensky took a step forward: he indicated to the Moscovite candidates the portfolios that they might receive. These were the ministries of State Charities and Commerce, the position of State Comptroller, and the chairmanship of the Economic Council. The Muscovites did not object, but they repeated that for them the main thing was the program that they had presented, plus the condition that the socialist-ministers would not outnumber them. On the evening of September 15 there was a meeting of all the candidates for ministerial posts at which it was established that there were no disagreements among them over the program submitted by the Muscovites. On that same evening, the candidates departed for Moscow for final negotiations with their political allies. The question of the cabinet's reconstruction continued to be an open one.

In the next few days, however, a step was taken which showed that Kerensky was moving toward his objective without waiting on the conference's decision. S. N. Prokopovich was transferred from the Ministry of Commerce, which wanted a representative from the commerical-industrial class, and was appointed Minister of Supply in place of A. V. Peshekhonov, who finally was leaving that position. This directive was published in the Legal Digest on September 17. At the evening session of September 19 the ministers discovered first that the conference majority had accepted the principle of a coalition, and then that in the second vote the conference had rejected a coalition. However, since what had been rejected was not a coalition in general, but a coalition without Kadets, it was possible to consider the first vote as remaining in force. On the other hand, one might draw the conclusion that the conference had no opinion at all about the reorganization of the government. In either case, Kerensky thought he had the right to hold to his former line of conduct. On the next day, September 20, he sent his assistant Galpern to inform I. G. Tsereteli at Smolny that the council of five, basing itself on the first vote of the conference, had already drawn up a cabinet including representatives of the propertied elements, and that it proposed to publish a complete membership list of the government on the next day. At 3 P.M. of the same day Kerensky informed S. N. Tretiakov in Moscow that Tretiakov, Konovalov, Kishkin and Smirnov already had been appointed to ministerial posts, and that on the next day, September 21, these appointments would be announced.

At Smolny from 12:30 on the conference's presidium sat in session with representatives of the central committees and of the groups taking part in the conference. As soon as the issue of reorganizing the government was raised, endless speeches again poured forth. Each political party continued to defend its own opinion. The Mensheviks did not favor a coalition ministry. The Bolsheviks did not express the desire to support unconditionally even an exclusively socialist government based on the program of August 14. In the middle of these arguments Tsereteli received Kerensky's communique, as cited above. Tsereteli begged to inform Kerensky that such a solution to the existing difficulties was unacceptable and could not lead to the desired results, because a government with the composition proposed by Kerensky could not receive the support of the "revolutionary democracy." Having received that answer, Kerensky expressed the desire personally to appear at 5 P.M. at the presidium meeting. The presidium would have to hurry in order to prepare at least some kind of opinion before the head of the government arrived.

Tsereteli then proposed momentarily to set aside as moot the issue of the government and to deal with an issue on which everyone agreed: the question of the Pre-Parliament, which was supposed to create a government responsible to itself. It immediately became clear, however, that the Bolsheviks wanted to create this "Pre-Parliament," or as they called it, "Convention," from the workers', soldiers', and peasants' deputies, and for this reason they proposed to delay its formation by two weeks, until the new Congress of Soviets met. The cooperatives and representatives of self-government found such a delay to be intolerable, for a government would have to be formed quickly. At 4 P.M. there was a break in the session; the advocates of an exclusively [socialist] government held a caucus, after which it was proposed to reach a decision. During the break the adherents of an exclusively [socialist] government met with the partisans of a coalition, Chkhenkeli, Gots, and others, whom the former began to sway to their position. As soon as word of this reached the lobby, the cooperatives issued a sharp protest; they believed that the first vote of the Democratic Conference, the one on the principle of a coalition, could not be abrogated by absurd additions to the formula that obscured its purpose.

However, when the session recommenced following the adjournment, a vote was held on the issue of a coalition ministry; *fifty members* voted for a coalition, while *sixty voted for an exclusively socialist ministry*. Kamenev magnanimously agreed not to overthrow such a government . . . before the Congress of Soviets. The advocates of a coalition stated that, while they bowed to the results of the vote, they could not enter such a government, because they thought it disastrous for Russia. Tsereteli claimed that the presidium had not fulfilled the task with which it was charged, for voices again were divided and one could not "force through" an exclusively socialist ministry against the opposition of half the assembly. "How can one speak at this moment about governing the nation with the forces of the democracy alone," he asked despairingly, "if in our modest group we cannot create a coalition?" Tsereteli saw the only hope of a solution in removing the issue of the coalition from discussion, and letting "our elected agency decide the question about which persons shall serve on a definite platform." In other words, the agency to which the Democratic Conference had entrusted the decision, proposed to entrust it to someone else, to a third body.

Shortly after 5 P.M. Kerensky arrived and delivered a long speech to the conference presidium. After finishing the speech, he quickly left. Kerensky's speech made an impression—not so much by the dark picture he drew of the country's situation, a picture which, coming from him, was no longer new—as by his definite hints that, in case the conference decided to establish a uniformly socialist government, he would take no part in its formation. Kerensky also expressed the desire that the "Pre-Parliament" not be elected by the conference, but appointed by the government.

The debate resumed after Kerensky's departure. The adherents of a coalition demanded a reconsideration and cancellation of the decision just made. The coalition's opponents protested. In the heated arguments that followed it became evident that neither Tsereteli nor the other socialist-ministers would take part in an exclusively socialist goverment. Again the presidium found itself in a dead end. Tsereteli's advice would have to be followed—that is, having admitted that it could not come to a decision, the presidium would have to entrust the making of a decision to another agency, with the agreement of the conference as a whole. The presidium assembly could only state that it had reached agreement on three issues: (1) on the need for the government to be responsible to a representative agency, which would be organized by the democracy; (2) on the requirement that the government operate on the basis of the program of August 14, augmented by a provision for "the active conduct of foreign policy with the goal of immediately concluding a universal democratic peace;" (3) on the decision to elect a special body to be entrusted with organizing the government, this agency not being bound by any instruction to include this or that kind of ministers. This body would be staffed, according to Tsereteli's suggestion, by all political parties represented in the conference, and also by the cooperatives in proportion to their numbers. If it should turn out that a government must be organized on a coalition basis, then this agency would include in addition representatives of the propertied elements, although, of course, the democracy would retain its numerical advantage. This last point passed by a vote of 56 to 48, but only because there were 10 abstentions. Limiting amendments suggested by the proponents of an exclusively socialist ministry were rejected on this occasion. Finally, the presidium meeting came to an end. Throughout the day, simultaneously with the presidium session, the party factions met, delivered speeches, but reached no decisions because they were waiting for the results of the presidium meeting. Only now, in the evening, were the factions informed of the resolutions adopted by the presidium. New speeches followed. After prolonged discussions among the Mensheviks, Tsereteli's proposals passed, and everyone from Potresov to Martov promised to abide by them. Things did not go so smoothly among the SRs, who quarreled until midnight: Chernov's group accepted Tsereteli's proposals only with several caveats.

Finally, at 11:30 P.M., some five hours late, the Democratic Conference opened its meeting in the Alexandrinsky Theater. Tsereteli's speech was adorned with official optimism. "We have found a common language;" "we have raised a common banner;" "the specter of a split that yesterday cast such a pall over the conference has disappeared today;" "the danger that the unity of revolutionary democracy would be destroyed" had been averted. Tsereteli presented the presidium's decisions as the fulfillment of the conference's decision to "find something in common that will unite the entire organized democracy." The program of August 14, the responsibility of the government to "agencies of the popular will," together with the "corresponding reorganization of the government on new principles, and, finally, the creation of an agency that would reflect the popular *mood* (here Tsereteli deliberately refrained from saying "will") "during the two months before the convocation of the Constituent Assembly"—such were the links of the chain, which were logically connected and which artfully hid from the democracy the failure that awaited it when its fine-sounding proposals would encounter the real mood of the government and of the dedicated partisans of a coalition. For the right wing of the conference and for Tsereteli himself, who had been warned by Kerensky, this danger was already apparent. They hoped to avert it—not in substance and not by means of compromise, but by word games and by deliberate vagueness calculated to pass over a large and inattentive auditorium. Thus, "the permanent government agency" to which the cabinet would be answerable was, according to the draft resolution, to be "selected from the midst" of the conference, whereas for the negotiations with the government there would be created a special collegium of five, which would also quickly "take the necessary *practical* steps to assist the formation of the government on the basis of the above-mentioned principles." The third point of the resolution said: "the government must render account to this agency and must be responsible to it." But, at the request of the cooperatives and in harmony with Kerensky's wishes, Tsereteli inserted a phrase after the first two words of the point that contradicted the rest of it: "the government must *sanction* this agency."

The chairman of the conference proposed to accept Tsereteli's draft resolution without debate, but this proposal was rebuffed. It is true that the resolution was accepted unanimously, but party speakers received the right to speak concerning the motives behind the vote. The majority of parties did not take advantage of the possibility of speaking for the sake of arguing. The United Mensheviks, the Menshevik-Internationalists, the Socialist-Revolutionaries, Popular Socialists and Trudoviks, the moderate cooperatives and the extremist representatives of the workers' cooperatives, and, finally, the Cossacks grudgingly, with various reservations, agreed to vote for Tsereteli's resolution. Only Trotsky remained inexorable. On behalf of the Bolsheviks he agreed to accept the conditions defining the government, the platform and the government's responsibility, but he did not agree to accept the method of selecting the Pre-Parliament; nor would he accept the participation of propertied elements in the Pre-Parliament or in the government. He had announced earlier that, in case this section of the resolution were accepted, the Bolsheviks would vote against the entire resolution. Part of the assembly, hoping to keep the Bolsheviks in solidarity, exclaimed naively from their benches: "Trotsky, this is no time to made trades."

The voting began. The platform of governmental responsibility, "a representative institution before the Constituent Assembly shall be convoked that reflects the nation's will"—in a word, the entire content of the first point was accepted by an enormous majority of 1150 votes against 171, with 24 abstentions. The opposition more than doubled on the vote over the second point, which contained the proposal concerning the "propertied elements," and on "selecting" the representative agency "from the midst" of the conference; this was the point to which Trotsky had objected. The second point was accepted by a vote of 774 to 385, with 84 abstentions. This was the best showing of the opposition, and the Bolsheviks saw that they did not have the strength to influence the outcome of the voting. Then they passed over to the tactics of resistance. When an amendment was introduced to the second point to the effect that the democracy should have numerical preponderance in the representative agency, the amendment passed by a vote of 941 to 8. But there were 274 abstentions. On the third point Tsereteli's proviso about a government "sanction" of the representative agency provoked such an upheaval that before the vote Tsereteli himself withdrew the proviso. Then the provisions for "rendering of account" and "responsibility" were approved by the center of the conference and also by the Bolsheviks, while the rightists objected. The vote was almost the same as on the first point: 1064 in favor and 1 opposed, with 123 abstaining. The last point of the resolution obliged the presidium "to present tomorrow a plan for elections to the permanent institution from the membership of the conference," and also to elect five representatives from its own ranks for immediate "assistance" in the formation of the government on the above-mentioned conditions with "the sanction of and under the condition of reporting concerning its work to the above-mentioned government institution." This point was adopted by a vote of 922 to 5, with 233 abstentions.

The mood of the assembly finally had been expressed. The assembly included a strong center, which defended a useless compromise that was unacceptable to the government, and two wings, which stood for clear and logical tactics: the stronger wing favored the Bolsheviks' tactics, the weaker wing favored the Provisional Government's tactics. One could measure these sections of the assembly numerically: the center had around 774 votes; the right wing (the cooperatives, self-government, the countryside) had between 123 and 171 votes; the left wing (the Bolsheviks and Left SRs) had from 233 to 274 votes. The last group, having noted its inability to influence the conference, hurried to part company with the conference.

At the end of the conference the left provoked a scandal. Before the vote on the resolution as a whole, Lunacharsky announced that the Bolsheviks would vote against it, because the sense of the resolution had been significantly altered by so-called "stylistic" amendments. Thus, he ironically observed, due to "the cooperation of the cooperatives" the government had "sanctioned" the representative agency; instead of "creating the government" the projected agency would only assist in the creation of the government, in addition to which the degree of assistance was ill-defined. The objections were justified: in the incriminating words there were not merely "stylistic," but also substantive differences. The conference had been driven to this expedient in order to paper over disagreement. But now, after the matter had been brought loudly to everyone's attention, Avksentiev and Tsereteli hurried to the rescue, fully prepared to sacrifice the points in the resolution itself that revealed a principled disagreement with the Bolsheviks. The proviso concerning the "sanction" had already been removed, stated the chairman. In place of the words "to assist" Tsereteli proposed to say—and this was basically just as vague: "to take steps to create a government." But he was incautious enough to add: "From now on, when speaking with the comrade-Bolsheviks, I shall bring a notary and two clerks." There was an unimaginable commotion in the hall. The Bolsheviks demanded that Tsereteli be called to order, and they threatened to walk out. Tsereteli's partisans applauded him. After a break in the session, at 3:30 A.M., Tsereteli announced that his criticisms applied only to the two Bolsheviks who were speaking, to Lunacharsky and Kamenev. The matter was declared closed.

In the absence of part of the Bolsheviks, the entire resolution was put to a vote. The result was that 829 votes (the center and right wing) supported the resolution, 186 (leftists) opposed it, and 69 abstained.

On the next day, September 21, the parties entered into negotiations over the number of places to be allotted in the "Russian Democratic

Soviet." At 6:30 P.M., after a delay of three and a half hours, in a half-empty hall Voitinsky read a report to the Democratic Conference about this. Then there were new negotiations between the parties and groups. The peasants' deputies demanded two-thirds of the seats, the workers demanded half. The center and the left wanted to conduct elections by parties, the right wing wanted elections by interest groups. At midnight Voitinsky[2] made a final proposal, which was accepted without debate. The total number of members of the Soviet was to be 308. Each party or group would be able to send about 15 percent of its representation to the Democratic Soviet. Thus, with the changes, there would be: from the cities and Zemstvos 45 members each; from the Soviets of Workers' and Soldiers' Deputies and of Peasants' Deputies 38 members each; from the cooperatives 19 members; from the workers' cooperatives 5 members; from the active-duty army 26 members; from the navy 3 members; from military-district organizations 2 members; from the Cossacks 6 members; from the commercial-industrial, service, and railroad organizations 5 members each; from the land committees 7 members; from the economic organizations 6 members; from the peasant leagues, the teachers' union and the postal and telegraph workers 2 each; from the lawyers 1 member; and from other organizations 7 members.

At the meeting of the Democratic Conference on September 22 there was an announcement and confirmation of a list of those elected by the groups and parties to the "Democratic Soviet." Then Voitinsky delivered a concluding word, which sounded rather pessimistic. "We carry from the assembly a sense of anxiety, for the profound internal disagreement that paralyzed the revolutionary democracy has not been overcome by our labors . . . . We have not found within ourselves enough strength to resolve the problems facing us, . . . We have not found new paths . . . . Nevertheless, we have found several common positions, which unite us . . . . We carry away from here the profound realization that the democracy must find a common language, a common path, and common tactics." "If this does not occur, then the collapse of all our hopes and the failure of the revolution are unavoidable." As if in illustration of this funeral speech, the last session of the Democratic Conference ended in a new conflict with the Bolsheviks over the Mensheviks' attempt to find a "common language," at least in the matter of an "active foreign policy" and accelerating "the democratic peace." Dan read the draft of an "appeal to the democracy of all nations"—one of the refrains of the Zimmerwaldist melody. But the Bolsheviks claimed that the Mensheviks had caught them unawares: essentially, the Mensheviks were trying to take away the Bolshevik monopoly over Zimmerwaldism.

After a prolonged commotion and a considerable interval Riazanov read an indictment of the conference's majority. "The responsible leadership of the conference" has "worked behind the scenes for conciliationism," and although the fruits of this labor had been snatched away from them, the official leadership had led a portion of the conference's members to capitulate to irresponsible and propertied elements. The membership of the Pre-Parliament had been "hand-picked, just like the membership of the conference," because "the objective of the organizers of the Pre-Parliament was not the creation of a democratic government, but, as before, the search for conciliation with the bourgeoisie." In view of this, the Bolsheviks, "insisting all the more, after the experience of the Democratic Conference, on the necessity of transferring all power to the Soviets of Workers', Soldiers', and Peasants' Deputies, are sending their representatives to the Pre-Parliament" only in order "to unmask within this new stronghold of conciliationism every attempt to fashion a new coalition with the bourgeoisie."

Compared to the vacillations of the Menshevik center, this was at least a definite position. The people who took it were not embarrassed by their opponents, and they did not soften their position by making concessions. They knew where they were headed, and they were moving in a single direction, decided once and for all, toward an objective which drew nearer with each unsuccessful experiment of "conciliationism." The Petrograd Soviet of Workers' and Soldiers' Deputies had already become a firm base in this struggle. To the Soviet the Bolsheviks came with a sharp critique of the "rubber-stamp allies of Kornilov" in the Democratic Conference (the so-called "commercial democracy" of the cooperatives), and there [in the Soviet] they voted to adopt the desired resolutions against "conciliationism," and from there they brought their resolutions to the tribune at the Alexandrinsky Theater. The Petrograd Soviet and the Petrograd workers were the audience for whom they put on their spectacles in the "Democratic Conference."

The Provisional Government formally followed its own course in the reconstruction of the cabinet. We have seen that as early as September 20 Kerensky considered as complete the negotiations with Moscow's "propertied elements," and that on September 21 he intended to publish a list of members of the new government. But in fact he had to await the results of the conference, since Tsereteli did not consider acceptable the formation of a government in a fashion so demonstratively independent of the conference, and since the Muscovites had decided not to return to Petrograd until at least the principal barriers to their entering the government had been removed. Those obstacles included the program of August 14 and responsibility of the government to a new representative agency to be elected by the conference. For Kerensky himself only the second condition was unacceptable.

Tsereteli and Chkheidze called at the Winter Palace. In their view the resolution accepted that night did not contradict in any sense Kerensky's intentions and left him complete freedom to continue negotiations with the Muscovites. They encouraged Kerensky to believe that "responsibility" to the "Pre-Parliament" could be interpreted not in the political sense of "parliamentary" responsibility, but in the more general sense of "moral responsibility and of a partisan rendering of accounts. The ground having thus been cleared of obstacles, further negotiations were now possible. In response to Kerensky's new invitation the Muscovites agreed to depart for Petrograd on September 22.

At 5 P.M. in the Malachite Hall of the Winter Palace the full cabinet met, together with representatives of the Democratic Conference (Chkheidze, Tsereteli, Gots, and Avksentiev), the mayors of Petrograd and Moscow (Shreider and Rudnev), the representative of the Zemstvo group (Dushechkin) and the representative of the cooperatives (Berkengeim), the four Muscovites who were ministerial candidates, and two members of the central committee of the Party of Popular Liberty (Nabokov and Adzhemov).[3] In his introductory remarks A. F. Kerensky formulated the goals of the meeting in the same way as the representatives of the "propertied elements" understood them. The tasks of the government, which was face-to-face with growing international and domestic difficulties, were quite elementary: to raise the fighting capacity of the army, to avert economic collapse, and to fight against anarchy. In its activity the government was guided only by those programs worked out in its own agencies, taking into account the interests of all elements of the populace. The publication of new broad declarations was a vain endeavor: what was needed was not declarations, but the adoption of certain measures. The resolutions of the Democratic Conference were of enormous importance as an indicator of the mood of broad social strata. But these resolutions were not binding on the government, just as the resolutions of the previous preliminary assembly of Muscovite public figures had not been binding. The source of the government's authority was the revolution of February 27 and the traditional transfer of powers from the government created by the revolution. The government, like the revolution that had created it, embraced all nationalities of the empire, and was sovereign, beholden to no one. The appointment of a new government was its right alone. In view of the difficulty of the situation, the government, acting on its own initiative, had decided to strengthen itself by means of an ad hoc agency [the Pre-Parliament] with which it [the government] would try to act in solidarity. But, of course, the government could not be responsible to such an assembly, which it [the government] was now organizing from representatives of various parties, classes, groups in the populace, and which would have only an advisory character. The Provisional Government maintained that the nation's safety was possible only with the formation of a solid and coherent bloc of bourgeois and democratic elements—a position with which the conference's majority agreed. A government with such a membership should be organized now, on the spot, and tomorrow its membership would be announced.

V. D. Nabokov could only agree with everything the prime minister had said. But in agreeing, Nabokov indicated that there was an enormous difference between Kerensky's point of view and the views of the Democratic Conference. He noted three basic points of difference. (1) The *source of governmental authority,* according to the government, was the traditional transfer of power from the revolution of February 27, while the Democratic Conference considered itself to be the source of governmental authority. (2) *The program of August 14,* according to Kerensky, was merely a program of particular groups in the populace; according to the conference, it was supposed to be binding on the government. (3) *The Pre-Parliament,* according to the prime minister, should be only an advisory agency, while the Democratic Conference demanded the responsibility of the ministers to this agency. V. D. Nabokov asked the representatives of the conference to explain how the "revolutionary democracy" looked on these issues.

Tsereteli's response was distinguished by his usual serpentine guile. The question of the source of governmental authority, he answered, remained now as it had been previously. Then and now the government had been created by an agreement of propertied and democratic agencies (this, of course, was legally inaccurate). Only now what was needed was not the agreement of these classes alone, but an agreement of the entire nation that might be achieved by the implementation of a "manifestly democratic program." That program was the program of August 14, augmented by Verkhovsky's plan for raising the fighting capacity of the army and by the demand for "immediate talks with the Allies concerning the conclusion of a peace on the basis of the integrity and independence of Russia and in the spirit of the ideas of the Russian Revolution." There was also nothing to argue about concerning the Pre-Parliament: "We have already created it;" it remained for the government "to sanction" it and to add propertied elements. The Pre-Parliament "should be granted the function of controlling the government, the right of interpolations, and of expressing confidence and lack of confidence in the government." The main obstacle to agreement was a possible lack of trust. The propertied elements did not credit the democracy's love for the motherland, while the democracy did not credit the propertyowners' love of the revolution. One would have to eliminate this obstacle, and then it would not be difficult to create a coalition.

S. N. Tretiakov correctly pointed out that Tsereteli had not given a clear and definite answer to Nabokov's questions. What was necessary was to throw a bridge across the chasm separating the views of Tsereteli and Kerensky, especially on the Pre-Parliament: then one could talk about an agreement. The subsequent speakers tried to "throw the bridge." Adzhemov, Avksentiev, Berkengeim, Prokopovich, Nikitin, and Konovalov tried to persuade the assembly to reject superfluous formalism, to pronounce the disagreement to be semantic, and to locate points of contact in a spirit of mutual trust. It was not necessary that the government be strictly responsible to the Pre-Parliament, but if the Pre-Parliament should vote no confidence in the government, then the government, in fact, would resign. "Would it be necessary for the government to announce that it would be guided by the program of August 14, or would it be enough if the government included individual points in its declarations?" Kerensky asked. Of course, Rudnev agreed, the Democratic Conference "has no right to create the government," because it [the conference] was an agency expressing the political opinion of the democracy, and certainly not expressing the popular will. After an hour-long break, Tsereteli made a concession to Kerensky: it was of no import that the government's declaration should refer directly to the program of August 14; it was sufficient that the government implement the measures enumerated there—measures, it should be added, that would require not months, but years to implement. In response to Adzhemov's argument that the Pre-Parliament was "an anti-democratic surrogate for a real Parliament," Tsereteli asserted that the Pre-Parliament was necessary to prepare "the masses' psychology" for parliamentary rule. Tsereteli provoked a sarcastic objection from Nabokov, who said that an institution violating the elementary principles of democratic representation would scarcely lead to parliamentary rule; indeed, from this perspective the Pre-Parliament was worse than the Bulygin Duma.[4] V. D. Nabokov also restored the purity of the social-contract position that had been obscured by the "conciliationism" of many previous speakers. If the government's responsibility to the Pre-Parliament were to be recognized, this would mean that a new revolution had occurred. The government would be transformed from sovereign, as it had been until now, into a mere agency of executive authority that had conceded its sovereign rights to an institution which in no way could express the people's will, but only the opinions of various groups in the populace.

After the first break, from 2 to 3 A.M., the Muscovites and the spokesmen of the central committee of the Party of Popular Liberty formulated their final demands in the following, quite concrete declaration. "The activity of the coalition government should be determined by the same routine tasks that were placed before it at the Moscow Conference—namely, the raising of the army's fighting capacity, the fight against anarchy, the reestablishment of law and order in local areas, and the fight against economic collapse. The Provisional Government's program should be worked out on the basis elaborated by public organizations at the Moscow Conference, in accordance with the requirements of the moment and the feasibility of these programs, and also taking into account the proximity in time of the Constituent Assembly. In view of the desirability of the closest possible relationship between the government and broad strata of the populace for the purpose of mutual exchange of information and the rendering of assistance to the government by these strata of the populace, we recognize as expedient the formation of a temporary special state conference to meet until the convocation of the Constituent Assembly, which conference could be an expression of public opinion. The conference should be organized by the government, which will determine its membership and competence and write its regulating charter, while preserving its own [the government's] complete independence."

To this Tsereteli responded that the representatives of the "revolutionary democracy" could give a final answer concerning the bases of an agreement only tomorrow, after consulting with democratic agencies. For his own part, he expressed a readiness to agree that the Pre-Parliament should be established by the government, which would not be responsible to the Pre-Parliament in a formal, parliamentary sense. Thus, a final agreement seemed possible, given the readiness of the representatives of the Democratic Conference to depart from their principled positions. For their part, the representatives of the propertied elements, given the restraints on them, showed the greatest possible willingness to find a compromise. If the conciliatory mood of the leaders of the "revolutionary democracy" was explained by an awareness of the complete hopelessness of the situation into which their internal disagreements had led the "democracy," then the chief motivation of the "propertied elements" was the need immediately to assist the motherland in circumstances whose onerousness was again made clear in the statements of the conference's participants.

The representative of the new democratic Zemstvo, the pedagogue Ia. I. Dushechkin, spoke about the complete collapse of the government's authority in local areas, about the high rate of absenteeism at

elections, about the indifference of the populace to reforms and their preference for the old volost elders over the new democratic committees,
about the inability of the new institutions to guarantee not only the
property, but also the very life of a citizen. The mood of the more conscious strata was reflected in the railroad strike that had threatened to occur for some time and which broke out on that very night, September
23. The conflict with "Tsentroflot," which had been dissolved by the
government, had not really been laid to rest, and was being renewed.
The Gomel Soviet of Workers' Deputies, under pressure from a crowd
of thousands, had been compelled to pass a resolution for the immediate
conclusion of peace. M. I. Tereshchenko stated that, with the destruction of the army's command system and with the deepening of economic collapse and anarchy in the nation, our prestige among our Allies had
fallen drastically, and that we had nothing that we could offer in the conference with the Allies that was scheduled for the middle of October. It
was obvious why the appeal to the democracies of the world just introduced by the Mensheviks "spoke the language of a beggar-woman." In
such circumstances the entire order that had been achieved by the revolution was in danger. According to Kerensky, in Kostroma, Tobolsk and
other provinces there were signs that the mood was beginning to shift
in favor of monarchy. S. S. Salazkin, speaking of the possible failure
of the coalition, threatened the meeting with the notorious "general on a
white horse." Others more correctly pointed to a more immediate and
more serious danger: to a seizure of power by the Bolsheviks, a danger
that was particularly clear to the leaders of the "revolutionary democracy." Given the rising pressure from this front, they had nowhere to
move. And it was not surprising that Chkheidze, to the complete surprise of the meeting, asked: "Would the bourgeoisie *alone* accept power, if the democracy would promise its support?" V. D. Nabokov took
this question as a trap, or at least, as irony, and so he answered in kind:
we are not empowered to negotiate about a purely bourgeois or a purely
socialist ministry, but only about how best to arrange a coalition. But
at that moment Chkheidze was asking a serious question, and it sounded
more of despair than of irony or mockery . . . .
     For their part the representatives of "propertied" elements placed no
hopes whatsoever on a coalition, and they regarded the various combinations with extreme skepticism. They did not believe that a coalition
could endure; they did not believe even in the signs of support [for a coa-
lition] from the improvised representative agency, which, as the official
organ of the "revolutionary democracy," *Izvestiia* [News], had already
stated, had been created to carry out a new "open and organized class and
partisan struggle through the practical discussion of political issues."

Most of all, the representatives of the "propertied elements," like the "democracy," did not believe in Kerensky or in Kerensky's associates. Of course, Kerensky was now saying the same thing—or almost the same thing—as the Kadet ministers; of course, he sought support from his old friend, A. I. Konovalov, who associated himself with the Kadets after leaving the ministry; of course, even that other representative of the former triumvirate, M. I. Tereshchenko, now manifested his complete disillusionment with the democratic organizations, impatiently threw himself into struggle against them, and publicly displayed the patriotic anxiety that had grown within him. Nevertheless, on the one hand, the *will* of these people, and above all, Kerensky's will, had been crushed by events; and, on the other hand, one was forced to ask whether it wasn't already too late. Was it not too late to declare war on the Bolsheviks, after the Soviets' tactics had prepared the ground for a Bolshevik victory? During those very days *Rabochy Put* [Workers' Path] reminded everyone who intended to "isolate" the Bolsheviks and to "liquidate" the Soviets: "You have forgotten that now the Bolsheviks are the Soviets of Workers' and Soldiers' Deputies. It is *with them* that you wish to deal by means of an 'iron fist.'"

Alas, none of the socialists declared "war" at all against the Bolsheviks. Tsereteli, who was asked at the conference if it were true that he intended to "cut off the Bolsheviks from the democracy" (This was Kishkin's question: "We have cut off our Bolsheviks from the right; have you cut off your Bolsheviks from the left?"), answered on September 23 the same way that he responded at the Jubilee Session of the State Duma on April 27: "The democracy will struggle against them by political means only, and will consider other means to be impermissible." And it was in vain that Plekhanov[5] warned Tsereteli in his *Edinstvo* [Unity]: "Having preserved the unity of the democratic front which has directed its energies toward seizing power [instead of publicly dividing the front into the advocates of the principle of the state and the adherents of the Bolsheviks and of anarchy], Tsereteli himself has pronounced the letter 'A.' Lenin's followers want Tsereteli to pronounce the letter 'B.' It is unlikely that he will do so. But the Leninists will get along without his help. Once 'A' is pronounced, 'B' will be pronounced as well: the very logic of events will guarantee it. But what do you have to be happy about, good sirs? You who do not stand in favor of Lenin's view? We are talking about a very great misfortune, which might well affect the Russian worker, and also Russia . . . ." No, they had no understanding of this. They believed so much in Marx that the notion of a Bolshevik seizure of power did not enter their field of vision. It was so "clearly senseless and intolerable." Even Gorky's and Sukhanov's *Novaia Zhizn* [New Life][6] thought at that time (we are quoting the issue of September 23) that "the formation of a government of the proletariat and the poorest peasantry is . . . not a solution to the problem, but simply an admission of defeat," for "the proletariat, isolated not only from other classes in the nation but also from the active, vital forces of the democracy, does not have the technical skill to run the state apparatus and force it to function in an extremely complicated set of circumstances, nor is the proletariat politically capable of withstanding the pressure of inimical forces that will sweep away not only the dictatorship of the proletariat, but also the entire revolution."

Did these essentially correct observations mean that Lenin would hold back from this clearly hopeless and dangerous experiment? Very many people who understood theoretically the absolute necessity for a coalition with "propertied elements" held fast to the conviction that the democracy was safe from Bolshevik experiments because these experiments were obviously doomed to fail. This conviction prevented them from understanding the gravity of the situation and the necessity to prop up the "bourgeoisie" with all their remaining resources. In any case, the "propertied elements" not only did not share that conviction, but, on the contrary, were convinced of the opposite. On September 24 *Rech* [Speech] wrote: "If after everything that has happened, after the accumulation of hatred, of threats, of the demagogy that the last week has brought, if after this the coalition were to take shape, then, it is terribly unfortunate but one must conclude that our situation is already, perhaps, beyond saving. In any case, one can say with certainty that the broader the coalition, the clearer it will be that no future combinations based on orderly succession of government will be possible: this is the final experiment, after which, in case of failure, we are threatened by the cannibalistic triumph of the Leninists over the ruins of great Russia."

Such was the mood in which the "propertied elements" entered the coalition on this occasion. This was also why they did not attribute much significance to the particulars of the agreement. In any case, they wanted to conduct the "final experiment" with all the seriousness the situation demanded. Taking responsibility upon themselves at this critical juncture, they wanted to enjoy the requisite freedom of action: they wished neither to bind themselves to discharge impossible duties, nor to subordinate themselves to the formal control of an institution that was insupportable even from a strictly democratic perspective. After the representatives of the democracy had refused in principle to demand the formal responsibility of the government to the Pre-Parliament, the center of gravity shifted to another controversial question—to the government's program.

The conference in the Malachite Hall on September 22 had already indicated that even here the leaders of the democracy would not insist on a literal fulfillment of the "democratic" demands; they agreed to a reexamination of the program of August 14 and to the incorporation into the government's declaration of only those elements of the program that were most immediate and practical. From this perspective it was decided to reexamine the program of August 14 at a new meeting on September 23. At this meeting only the two sides locked in argument—the "revolutionary democracy" and the "propertied elements"—participated. The government absented itself so as not to interfere with the two sides coming to an understanding. Of the former ministers only Kartashev[7] was present; his resignation had not been accepted formally, and he was here not in the role of a member of the old government, but in the role of a Kadet party candidate for the new cabinet.

After substracting from the program of August 14 all those points which had been covered by the government's measures and had therefore lost their importance, or which were too complicated to be carried out in the two months remaining before the Constituent Assembly, or, finally, which predetermined the latter's will—there were a few substantive points in the program that were completely unacceptable. Moreover, they were unacceptable not so much because of their contradiction of "propertied interests," as because of their theoretical nature and their anti-statist character. From the economic section of the program the point concerning state syndicalization was ruled out. In the financial program all the heavy taxes on the "bourgeoisie" were accepted: the tax on inheritance, and on the increase of valuables, and on items of luxury, and even on property (without the stipulations that it should be a high, one-time tax). But the view was expressed that every tax had a limit and a tax should not be levied if it would destroy the source of the tax payment. On the land question the transfer of all land to local land committees was declared unacceptable in principle. In military questions the program of August 14 still needed to take account of Kornilov's program. Now Verkhovsky's program was triumphant, and unfortunately one was compelled not to argue against the view that it would restore the fighting capacity of the army. Thus, the most important of the questions of the day was sacrificed to the "democracy's" mood.

On the other hand, in the matter of local administration the "propertied elements" pushed through their view that the commissars should not be elected from local areas, but appointed by the central government, and that the authority of every conceivable kind of public organization and their executive committees should be eliminated following the election to the democratic agencies of self-government. In the nationality question the right of all nationalities to complete self-determination, to be realized by means of a compact in the Constituent Assembly, was labelled unacceptable; the propertied elements also thought it impractical to take immediate measures to assure the autonomy of the nationalities. The "revolutionary democracy" contented itself with the following text: "We recognize the need to publish a declaration of the Provisional Government recognizing the rights of all nationalities to self-determination on bases which will be established by the Constituent Assembly, and the need to form under the aegis of the central government a council on nationality affairs, with the participation of representatives of all the nationalities of Russia, for the purpose of preparing materials on the nationality question for the Constituent Assembly."

Turning to the question of the Pre-Parliament, both sides agreed to give about one-fourth of the places in it (120-150) to the propertied elements. Given the advisory character of this body, the need to argue about the numerical representation of the "bourgeoisie" did not arise, although events subsequently showed that the results of the elections to the Pre-Parliament certainly had an impact on the course of events. On the issue of responsibility the propertied elements remained firm, and they did not agree to recognize even a "de facto" governmental responsibility to the Pre-Parliament. Nor did they consent to the immediate recognition of the Pre-Parliament—whose membership now consisted of democratic elements *alone*, elements that had already been elected by the Democratic Conference—as a legally functioning state institution. Before they would give their consent, they demanded the addition to the Pre-Parliament of propertied elements—and, of course, as soon as possible. The competence of the Pre-Parliament was also defined according to the wish of the propertied elements: it could address the government with "questions" (in the sense of article 40 in the Duma Charter), but not with "inquiries" (the government's response to these in a certain period would be mandatory and a vote might lead to consequences similar to an expression of no confidence); it could elaborate legislative proposals, but for the government these proposals would have the significance of background material only; and it could discuss issues introduced by the government or raised by the Pre-Parliament itself, but only in an advisory fashion, without the power to make decisions binding on the government. The propertied elements rejected the proposal to dissolve the Duma as unnecessary in practice and as politically inexpedient and demagogic. The leaders of the "revolutionary democracy" reserved to themselves the right to raise this issue through the socialist-ministers in the future Provisonal Government. Finally, the demand of the "democracy" to have its own representative at the conference of the Allies in

Paris on October 16 (to propose a "democratic peace") was accepted in an altered form: the democracy would indicate its candidate, but the representative would be appointed by the government and would have to represent at the conference only the point of view of the entire governmental delegation.

Throughout that entire day, September 23, the representatives elected by the Democratic Conference sat in the Alexandrovsky Hall of the City Duma, under a large sign hanging at the entrance doors: "Entrance to the Pre-Parliament." But they could go no further in constituting themselves, and they broke up into party factions while awaiting the result of the negotiations at the Winter Palace. Only at 8 P.M. did the meeting recommence. After some rather pointed exchanges the assemblage accepted Tsereteli's proposal to hear his report in a closed session. As was his wont, in his report Tsereteli softened his language and smoothed out the sharp edges to such an extent that the Left SR Karelin could justifiably reproach him with being less forthcoming in his descriptions of proceedings at the Winter Palace than were the newspapers. In the debates over Tsereteli's report, debates that took place in public session, Tsereteli received an enthusiastic appraisal only from "Grandmother" Breshko-Breshkovskaia, who, together with another patriarch of the revolution, N.V. Chaikovsky,[8] occupied the extreme right wing of the assemblage. From the opposing wing Trotsky made the accusation that in opening negotiations with the Kadets the delegates of the Democratic Conference had violated their instructions; he added that Kerensky, whose irresponsible power the conference "had said must be curbed once and for all," had "played the role of super-arbiter [between Kadets and the conference]" in the affair. The Menshevik-Internationalists and the SR Internationalists also spoke against a coaliton. Both Dan, who had introduced a resolution with a provision on the government's responsibility [to the conference], and Tsereteli himself in his concluding remarks had revealed their "uncertainty as to whether their platform concerning the coalition fully harmonized with the moods of the single united family of the majority of the organized democracy." But Tsereteli took upon himself the responsibility for "conciliation" with the bourgeoisie, because the democracy alone was "not strong enough to resolve the problems facing the revolution," and "the lesson the Bolsheviks would teach" if they should seize power "could cost the nation dearly." Tsereteli and his political group "cannot carry out the kind of extravagant experiments contemplated by Trotsky and Martov." "We cannot repeat after Martov that the revolutionary democracy is loading its weapon, for he who loads a weapon must be prepared to fire it; we do not wish to do this, for we know that the bullet will strike the heart of the revolution."

The vote on Dan's resolution was delayed until 6 A.M. on September 24, because the Bolsheviks and Left SRs were making their final efforts to "break the coalition." Trotsky and Kamenev stated that to this end they were proposing a series of amendments. When Kamenev's amendments (the abolition of the death penalty and the dissolution of the State Duma) failed after disorderly and bitter debate, the Left SRs introduced an even more insidious proposal: they insisted that the agreement [on a coalition] include a point on the transfer of land to the jurisdiction of the land committees. Chernov and his friends announced that they would vote as the chairman of the Soviet of Peasants' Deputies, Avksentiev, voted. In vain were all Minor's reproaches of "filthy demagoguery," and Breshko-Breshkovskaia's conscience-stricken handwringing. At first Avksentiev tried unsuccessfully to leave the hall; then he mounted the rostrum to announce that his group would vote *for the amendment*, but that his group proposed to add another to go with it: "If the fate of the coalition shall depend upon this amendment, the SRs withdraw it." There was a new and unbelievable commotion in the hall and disapproving shouts addressed to Avksentiev and Gots. Chernov and his friends were walking the whole time between the SR benches and accused the majority of being prepared to betray their banner. In spite of all this, Chernov's amendment was rejected by a vote of 100 against to 75 in favor, with 6 abstentions. The assemblage adopted the following resolution by Dan: "The Democratic Conference, having heard the report of Comrade Tsereteli, recognizes the formation of a Pre-Parliament, to which the government is obliged *to render accounts*, as a large step toward the creation of governmental stability and the implementation of the program of August 14, a political program whose purpose is the quickest possible achievement of a general democratic peace and the convocation of the Constituent Assembly at the appointed time. The democratic Soviet finds it *necessary to assert the formal responsibility* of the government to the Pre-Parliament and, *recognizing as acceptable the agreement outlined by the delegation*, the Soviet states that governmental authority can belong only to that government which enjoys the trust of the Pre-Parliament." This ambiguous resolution, which unsuccessfully attempted by means of stylistic maneuvers to save the face of the "revolutionary democracy," was the victory for which the parties involved had to waste a week on endless arguments, nocturnal meetings, scandalous votes, and for which three times they had put off the resolution of the fundamental question, a question that the democracy was powerless to resolve according to the admission of its own leaders.

On the following day, September 24, in the Malachite Hall of the Winter Palace the representatives of the "propertied elements" asked the leaders of the "revolutionary democracy" how to reconcile the conference's agreement via the resolution to certain provisions and the conference's demand for formal [governmental] responsibility [to the Pre-Parliament], which contradicted those provisions. Having resolved so many insoluble difficulties, the sophists of the "democracy" did not shrink from this last difficulty. Tsereteli said that the sense of the resolution was that the democratic Soviet recognized the necessity of *struggle* to establish "formal responsibility" *as one of its own goals,* but it did not require the propertied elements to accept this demand immediately. The Soviet simply reserved to itself the right to pursue the goal of establishing governmental responsibility in the Pre-Parliament. For their part, the representatives of non-socialist groups had become accustomed to interpretations which later proved to be unjustified; the non-socialists only wished that Tsereteli's interpretation be conveyed both to the Provisional Government and to the democratic Soviet. For their part, the representatives of the "democracy" won a new stylistic concession in the question that Chernov had wanted to place before Avksentiev's peasants. The following version was adopted: "The immediate regulation of agrarian relations should be turned over to the local land committees; they shall receive, under conditions specified by law [and not in a mandatory fashion, as the program of August 14 demanded] and without violating the existing forms of landownership, jurisdiction over lands devoted to agricultural pursuits in order more completely to utilize these lands so as to save the national economy from final collapse."

Thus having laid aside their final difficulties, the two sides now informed the government in a joint meeting of the results of their negotiations. With this the governmental crisis that had begun a month earlier formally came to an end. But on the next day, September 25, the Petrograd Soviet, which the Bolsheviks dominated, rejected the proposal of the Mensheviks and SRs, and adopted the following resolution, which defined the attitude of the Petrograd democracy to the new governmental authority: "The Petrograd Soviet of Workers' and Soldiers' Deputies stated: after the experience of the Kornilovshchina, which showed that all propertied Russia occupies a counter-revolutionary position, any attempt at a coalition government amounts to nothing other than a complete capitulation by the democracy to the Kornilovshchina. A reflection of this capitulation is the membership of the ministry now being formed, in which the decisive place is allotted to the commercial-industrialists, the intransigent enemies of the workers', soldiers' and peasants' democracy. The so-called democratic ministers, who are responsible to no one and to nothing, are incapable of changing or softening the anti-popular character of the new government, which will *go down in the history of the revolution as the government of civil war.* The Petrograd Soviet stated: to the government of bourgeois dictatorship and counter-revolutionary violence we, the workers and the Petrograd garrison, shall offer no support whatsoever. We declare our firm conviction that the news concerning the new government will meet with one response from the entire revolutionary democracy: the government should resign. And based on this unanimous voice of the genuine democracy, the *All-Russia Congress of Soviets* of Workers', Soldiers', and Peasants' Deputies *will create a truly revolutionary government.*" Here we see the program of a new revolution already outlined.

On September 26 the government published directives concerning the appointment of A. I. Konovalov as Minister of Commerce and as deputy prime minister in place of M. I. Tereshchenko; of A. V. Liverovsky as Minister of Transport; of S. M. Smirnov as State Comptroller; of N. M. Kishkin as Minister of State Charities; of M. B. Bernatssky as Minister of Finance; and S. N. Tretiakov as a member of the Provisional Government and chairman of the Economic Council. Only the Ministry of Agriculture was unoccupied. Later S. N. Maslov was appointed to that position.

On September 27 there appeared the proclamation "of a Provisional Government with augmented membership," as the new cabinet officially called itself. The proclamation collected in one place all the individual compromise decisions worked out in the agreement between representatives of the Democratic Conference and the representatives of the "propertied elements" and the Party of Popular Liberty. In the areas of the national economy, agrarian relationships, finances, local self-government, and the nationalities question, the proclamation introduced all the above-mentioned cuts and changes in the program of August 14 without ever mentioning that program. The declaration indicated in its conclusion that, of course, "not all these tasks can be completed in the short time that remains before the Constituent Assembly." "But the very beginning of their implementation . . . will give the government a solid basis . . . for the organization of an active defense, the revitalization of the national economy . . . and the fight against manifestations of counter-revolution and anarchy" and "will facilitate the future work of the Constituent Assembly."

In the field of foreign policy and "raising the fighting capacity of the army" the program accepted the views of the "revolutionary democracy": the program promised "to continue" and tirelessly "to develop" a dual foreign policy "in the spirit of democratic principles proclaimed by the Russian Revolution, which has made these principles into a universal property." In specific, at the forthcoming Paris Conference the program pledged "to strive for an agreement with the Allies on the basis of the principles proclaimed by the Russian Revolution." It also pledged that the army reform "would proceed in a democratic fashion, which alone can provide favorable results." Thus, the new government subscribed to the most dangerous of the illusions of the "revolutionary democracy," and assumed responsibility for the implementation of its program. In the same manner the declaration specifically connected the "profound disturbance now occurring in the nation" with "General Kornilov's uprising," and it saw the main danger to "the freedom of the Russian people" lurking in the calculation "of counter-revolutionary elements" that "exhaustion now grips the entire nation." In the struggle against counter-revolution and anarchy the government promised "to act in the closest cooperation with the organizations of the people," although these organizations were not mentioned by name. Turning in conclusion to the promise "to work out and publish in the next few days a statute on a Provisional Soviet of the Republic" (the title was suggested by Tsereteli), the declaration stated that, "preserving as inviolable the unity and continuity of governmental authority according to its oath of allegiance, the Provisional Government will honor its responsibility to bear in mind in all its actions the [Soviet's] great social significance." Thus, the "democracy" reclaimed in the declaration a part of the position it had lost in the negotiations, while the new government did not obtain in the declaration the solid basis of support for the kind of action that alone could have justified a last attempt to halt the nation's progress toward a Bolshevik victory and toward civil war.

One cannot say that the new ministers were oblivious of their responsibility on this final occasion to try a new approach and new methods different from those tried previously, or at least to try *some sort of method*. The new deputy prime minister, to whom Kerensky at first entrusted all his own powers during Kerensky's absence from the country, sensed the acute need for some kind of definite plan and system. S. N. Tretiakov, who was entering the government for the first time, was prepared to invest in the search for a plan the fresh energy and faith which were solely lacking in A. I. Konovalov who was already worn out and had returned to the cabinet against his will. N. M. Kishkin was one of those active characters who by nature cannot remain passive. A. V. Kartashev, a religious thinker, very quickly familiarized himself with an area of politics that was alien to him and brought to it seriousness and earnestness, combined with great powers of observation and a capacity to understand people and situations. This tightly-knit circle of people sought and found support in the central committee of the Party of Popular Liberty, which delegated several members to act as liaisons with this circle of ministers. These members were Nabokov, Adzhemov, and also P. N. Miliukov and M. M. Vinaver,[9] both of whom had returned after an absence.[10]

There was no shortage of good intentions. But all the good intentions of the cabinet members inevitably ran up against the same obstacle: the psychology of A. F. Kerensky. The prime minister brought to this new cabinet his habit of making autocratic and uncontrolled decisions. In Konovalov and Kishkin, Kerensky had in the cabinet personal friends whom he trusted. Yet both these ministers used their positions not to reestablish a triumvirate, with its atmosphere of secret decisions and dark intrigue, but rather to implement the general views and decisions of the above-mentioned circle. In certain cases M. I. Tereshchenko also affiliated himself with this circle. Tereshchenko brought to the struggle against the pretensions of the democratic agencies all the bitterness of hopes deceived and of disappointments long endured. A. F. Kerensky also felt himself now alien from the "revolutionary democracy" that had turned away from him. But he did not find within himself the courage to meet halfway those people, whom, in the language of the revolution, he should have considered his enemies—and after the Kornilov affair many of these also saw him as their irreconcilable enemy. Having lost his footing, Kerensky more and more manifested all the symptoms of that pathological state of mind that might be called in the language of medicine "psychic neurasthenia."

A close circle of friends had been long aware that, after a morning period of extreme enervation, Kerensky began the second half of the day in a frenetic state under the influence of the medicines that he was taking. Kishkin's influence on Kerensky had perhaps as one of its sources the skillful mode of address used by an experienced and professional psychiatrist with a patient. However this may have been, both this and other influences on Kerensky now remained external and did not really reach to the sources [of Kerensky's psyche]. In his eternal indecisiveness, in his constant vacillations between pressures from the right and the left and his searches for an equilibrium, Kerensky gradually arrived at a condition in which it was genuine torture for him to make a concrete decision. He instinctively avoided these torturous moments, as only he could. Meanwhile a hypertrophied instinct and taste for power, a peculiar pride inflated by the exceptional circumstances, permitted him neither to resign his office nor to escape. Amidst the increased difficulties in holding onto power, Kerensky's hunger for power took the form of a desire somehow to retain his offices until the opening of the Constituent Assembly. To this end all other ends were sacrificed. To this end conflicts were avoided, and so as to avoid conflicts and frictions, concrete decisions were avoided in general. Even to his closest friends Kerensky became inaccessible. He could not be matched in the art of avoiding the necessity to make up his mind to do something. So the precious days and the weeks dragged on, and directives deserving immediate action were delayed, the most efficacious measures were not adopted, the most crucial questions remained without discussion. Between the head of the government and its members there was literally no communication, and all the noble intentions of the ministers were not acted upon, having been stopped on the threshold by the absence of the will to act.

The new government might have been able to escape from this condition of paralysis if the moderate socialist majority that had insisted on the government's formation had not limited itself to placing responsibility on others' shoulders, but had given to this last government of "the bourgeois revolution" active and consistent support. But the obvious inconsistency, the clear retreat from positions just occupied, the pitiful grasping for verbal camouflage during a forced retreat—all of which the leaders of the "democracy" had just been forced to display, exhausted their last reserves of strength. And whatever they thought about the new coalition among themselves, they could not support it loudly and openly. Their inconsistency and timidity were made apparent in those sections of the program, the military and international, that even Plekhanov labelled in his *Edinstvo* a return to Zimmerwald-Kienthal. On September 28 Plekhanov wrote: "I ask any citizen who has not yet become completely callous toward the fate of his country and who has not lost the capacity for logical thought whether it is possible to improve the fighting capacity of the army by the same means which diminished this fighting capacity to such a horrifying extent." The disinclination of the moderate "democracy" to support the government was made apparent in the composition of the socialist part of the cabinet. Kerensky had selected these people long ago from the ranks of those who could not be his rivals. Independent political leaders who could stand on their own merits had been pushed aside gradually or had left the government of their own volition. Now both better and less well-known names were leaving. After Tsereteli and Chernov, Avksentiev and Skobelev left as well. Skobelev left as Minister of Labor his assistant Gvozdev, a simple worker, a man with common sense and civil courage, but, of course, a man unprepared for the role of Russia's savior in the critical moment of its existence. As far as the representatives of Social

Democracy [the Mensheviks] in the new cabinet were concerned, *Izves-tiia Moskovskogo Sovieta* [News of the Moscow Soviet] wrote: "The Social Democratic Party is represented by Nikitin, Prokopovich, Gvoz-dev, and Maliantovich. The personal political influence of these men, of course, varies from one to another. But surely it has not occurred to any-one that these men can be seen as authoritative representatives of Social Democracy." And, as if to illustrate this point, the central committee of the Social-Democrats at this very juncture, under Bolshevik pressure, asked Nikitin to leave party ranks.

The psychology of this tendency to make concessions will become clear if we recall the results of the district duma election just completed in Moscow in late September. Here are the comparative figures for the municipal elections of 26 June and the September voting.

	June	September
SRs	374,885 (58%)	54,374 (14%)
Mensheviks	76,407 (12%)	15,887 (4%)
Bolsheviks	75,409 (11%)	198,320 (51%)
Kadets	108,781 (17%)	101,106 (26%)

The increasing absenteeism of disillusioned residents; and, against the background of this indifference, the terrible collapse of the SRs, who had been victorious in June because of the accident of their list of candidates being third (the number 3 resembles the Russian letter "3"—the first letter of *zemlia* [land]); the almost complete disappearance of the Mensheviks, whose vacillating tactics made them incomprehensi-ble to everyone; the decisive departure of the active elements of the pro-letariat from adherence to the socialist intelligentsia and the allegiance of these proletarian elements to the demagogues; and finally, the stable position of the conscious section of the non-socialist democracy (the "bourgeoisie")—such was the instructive picture of the political mood of the old capital. This picture was corroborated by the situation in Pet-rograd. "Whoever is acquainted with the situation prevailing in the large organization of Petrograd Mensheviks, which not long ago numbered around 10,000 members," wrote *Novaia Zhizn* [New Life] on Septem-ber 29, "knows that this organization has in fact ceased to exist. Dis-trict meetings involve a paltry 20-25 people, members' dues are not be-ing paid, the circulation of *Rabochaia Gazeta* [Workers' Gazette] is fall-ing catastrophically. The last all-city Menshevik conference could not meet because of the lack of a quorum." And this is what the Bolshevik *Rabochy Put* [Workers' Path] wrote about the SRs: "Comrades, it is time to understand that the SR party no longer exists. There are only the 'diffuse' masses, part of which have gotten mixed up in the '*Savin-kovshchina*,' a second part of which have remained in the ranks of the revolutionaries, and a third part of which uselessly mark time by providing cover for the 'Savinkovtsy.'"[11]

The moderate leaders of socialism had fallen under suspicion of surrendering democratic positions to the "Kornilovites." At the last session of the Democratic Conference Tsereteli was even called a "Kornilovite." *Novaia Zhizn* called the socialist leaders' tactics "the pitiful fruit of cowardice and opportunism . . . of the true knight . . . and commissar of the Provisional Government in the democratic organizations"—that is, Tsereteli. Quite naturally the socialist masses turned away from this result of their works, or, in any case, they adopted a defensive posture toward it. The central committee of the Social Democrats resolved: "While recognizing the bases of the agreement concluded between the democracy and the propertied elements as not altogether satisfactory, and finding it necessary to strive to change these bases, both in the sense of establishing the formal responsibility of the government to the Pre-Parliament and in the sense of ensuring a more consistently democratic implementation of the individual points of the program, the central committee . . . considers that the agreement . . . is the only way out of the current situation." At the same time, the central committee, appraising the current role of the Social Democrats in the ranks of the united democracy, and permitting members of the party "in each individual case," to remain in the cabinet, "reserves to itself the right to call on members of the party to resign from the government when the central committee determines that their presence in the government is incompatible with the proletariat's interests." In the same dour fashion but with further caveats the SR central committee approved the agreement just concluded by its representatives. "Assuming that the revolutionary government must be built on the basis of the program of August 14 and on the responsibility of the government to the democratic Soviet, and that the make-up of the ministries should include *individual representatives* both of the revolutionary democracy and of the propertied elements, the central committee recognizes that the aforementioned bases of agreement, although they represent a certain deviation from the desired principles of forming a government, nevertheless, given the political and economic circumstances and the international situation facing the nation, must be accepted by the SR party." As we see, in the declarations of the central committees of both the dominant parties there was no enthusiasm for the new combination.

What a difference there was between these declarations and the bellicosity of the Bolsheviks who through the Petrograd Soviet called the new government the "government of civil war," and who publicly demanded that this government "resign"! Here were positions in the front lines where the real battle was being waged. Compared with them, the positions taken by the moderate majority, which was becoming the minority, were located far from the scene of battle. On the day after the agreement was reached, Gorky's *Novaia Zhizn* already was calling his troops from this reserve position to the first line of trenches: he called for rapprochement with "the healthy elements in Bolshevism" and insisted on "the reestablishment of unity if not of the entire, then at least of the greatest possible portion of the democratic front," in order to create the "dictatorship of the democracy," which was "the only way to save the revolution." And we can already sense in advance in which direction would turn the gazes of the hesitating socialist center in the future "Soviet of the Republic," if on one fine day, a day not chosen by them, they would be forced to make a decisive choice.[12]

Compared with these influential groups whose attitude toward the new coalition was more than skeptical, the political attitude of the less well-organized groups that might have rendered support to the coalition was not very significant. Among these groups one must include, as the Democratic Conference had indicated, the countryside and the cooperative movement. The Soviet of Peasants' Deputies no longer represented the true mood of the peasantry. But it had to take the peasants' true mood into account—and this had its effect in the contents of the Soviet's platform which was elaborated by its Executive Committee in early October. The committee called all peasant deputies "to support energetically the Provisional Government recognized by the revolutionary democracy, a government which alone could lead the nation to the Constituent Assembly." This goal—the preparation of the Constituent Assembly—and the defense of the nation the committee thought to be the only items on the agenda, and "whoever distracts the people" from this preparation "does not consider the Constituent Assembly to be a great, decisive event in the affairs of the people," and thus "shows himself to be moving, either consciously or unconsciously, against the popular interests." Therefore, the committee considered even the Congress of Soviets of Workers' and Soldiers' Deputies, scheduled to meet on October 10 in Petrograd, as "*ill-timed and dangerous*," as *capable* "of delaying the convocation of the Constituent Assembly and *of squandering all the revolution's achievements in civil war*." Thus, the committee instructed all its members in the army and the army reserves "not to send delegates to the proposed congress." In sharp contradiction to the "revolutionary democracy" and even to the governmental declaration, the platform of the peasant delegates recognized that, although "peace is a cherished dream of the peasantry, the peasantry will receive peace only when our army becomes able to fight and to defend the Russian land from the impending partition." Therefore, the Executive Committee "considers as traitors those who leave the front and leave the Russian army defenseless before the enemy." The committee called on soldiers "to stand firm before the enemy and not to permit peasant hopes for a better life to perish in an enemy attack."

The Russian cooperative movement also embarked on the same path; at its September congress it had issued a declaration with special instructions for the Democratic Conference. On October 4 an emergency congress of the cooperatives opened in Moscow, and, referring to the September instructions that had been carried out, Berkengeim had the right to say that "without the cooperatives the composition of the Democratic Conference would have been different," and that it had been precisely the cooperative movement that "provided the crucial margin of votes in favor of the coalition government." This led the cooperatives to the logical conclusion that in the elections to the Constituent Assembly the cooperative movement could not refrain from a political role, a role generally alien to it—that it was obliged to enter the elections as a separate political group. "The general impression among us at the Democratic Conference," said Berkengeim, "was this: the rapid and spontaneous organization of workers and the peasant masses is occurring around the nation. This organization feeds on demagoguery, and various political factions are attaching themselves to the tail of this anarchical beast . . . . But I am convinced that not all of Russia will become an insane asylum, that, for the time being, it is mainly the inhabitants of the big cities that have lost their senses."

Berkengeim's observation was, of course, correct. It was corroborated by the results of the elections to municipal self-governing institutions. On September 2 there were elections in 643 cities out of 779, and, according to the Ministry of Internal Affairs, here are the results:

	Provincial capitals	Other cities
Elected as deputies [glasnye]	3,689	13,246
Of these in percentages:		
Bolsheviks	7	2
Mensheviks	6	4
SRs	16	9
Socialist Bloc	36	21
National Minorities	8	7
Party of Popular Liberty	13	5
Nonpartisan	14	50

As we see, the small group of people who had demanded "all power" for themselves on behalf of all Russia received only 7 percent of the deputies in the big cities and only 2 percent of the deputies in the remaining cities. Half of all the delegates in the small cities, where the way of life was transitional between urban and agricultural, were nonpartisan: that is, the political parties in general had not penetrated into this milieu. To the extent that they had penetrated, the small town inhabitants gave most of their votes to non-socialist elements rather than to socialists, which, in total, had control over only a third (36%) of the deputies in small towns. In relation to the distribution of the votes of the municipal section in the Democratic Conference, this meant, according to the calculation of B. Veselovsky,[13] that 13,800 out of 16,935 deputies were in favor of coaliton government (Veselovsky counted 9,100 bourgeois deputies—the nonpartisan, Kadets, and national minorities—plus 60 percent of the socialist deputies, that is, 4,700 as favoring the coaliton). Clearly, not all of Russia had been "turned into Bedlam." But, unfortunately, the groups nearer to the center and to the rudder of state, groups constituting an insignficant minority in the nation, were close to an actual seizure of power in the capital.

The cooperatives were right that, given the divisions and hesitations of the socialist parties, given the obvious inability of the villages to make sense of the socialists' arguments, given the increased role of demagoguery among the dark peasant masses who were unaccustomed to political life, elections to the Constituent Assembly might yield a quite accidental, and perhaps a lamentable result. The role of "the ten million cooperative agents" who were close to the masses and who had merited the masses' trust, was therefore quite irreplaceable. Telegrams to the cooperatives' congress from local areas showed that, in essence, life itself had settled the argument about the participation of the cooperative movement in the elections. Of 66 published telegrams 54 were in favor of independent participation by the cooperatives in the elections, and only 12 opposed participation. The opponents were obviously moved by the same reasons that had animated opponents of participation in the congress (including the workers' group)—namely, they feared that the cooperatives would spoil the success of socialism. The resolution of the congress, adopted after heated debate by a vote of 81 to 17 with 7 abstentions, stated "that those elected to the Constituent Assembly should be *people of action*, dedicated to the Russian Republic, capable of subordinating group, class, and partisan interests to the immediate need to defend the fatherland at the front and in the rear and to consolidate the revolution's achievements." Standing on this platform, "cooperative organizations should strive to unite all democratic factions which support the energetic and vigorous defense of the nation and of liberty, who support the restoration of law and order in the nation through the forces of a state-oriented democracy, and who believe it impermissible to elect to the Constituent Assembly the representatives of defeatism and anarchy."

"For this purpose," of course, it ought to have been possible to unite all "democratic factions supporting the principle of the state," including the Party of Popular Liberty, whose platform the resolution quoted verbatim. But even here the fatal weakness of Russian progressive society made itself evident. By "democratic" they meant only the socialist parties. The cooperatives' resolution directly called, where possible, "for cooperation in forming *blocs with the socialist parties* and factions who favor the principle of the state;" where this was not possible, they called for "entering into an agreement with *individual* [also socialist] parties and factions;" and where neither the one nor the other course succeeded, they [the cooperatives] should offer their own list of candidates. This alienation of all non-socialist democracy, given the extreme weakness "of socialist parties favoring the principle of the state," stood in direct contradiction to the basic task—the unification of people "capable of subordinating class interests to the immediate needs of the defense of the fatherland." The position of the majority of the socialist parties, even the moderate ones, was, above all, a class-oriented one. This turned out to be the underwater rock against which the Russian Revolution was fated to shatter itself. In order somehow to get out of this contradiction between class-oriented and state-oriented politics, the cooperatives resorted to the favorite means of the Russian citizen. They juxtaposed the "activists of political parties" who were bound together by "party dogma," with "people of action who are well acquainted with the most varied aspects and peculiarities of the nation's economic and material life." These latter should enter the Constituent Assembly "not with closed minds," but "only to engage in careful, long work on each painful question . . . to make their free judgment on the basis of the general ideas and principles that answer the interests of the working populace." This unsuccessful attempt of the cooperatives to depart from the political parties is best explained as follows: the existing *socialist* parties did not suit the cooperatives, while the parties that did defend the cooperatives' program did not call themselves socialists. And so even "people of action" who contemptuously brushed aside mere phrases, became themselves the prisoners of phrases that had hypnotized the Russian "democracy" and had deprived it of secure footing on that dangerous incline down which it was sliding toward the destruction of the revolution.

True, there was one socialist party other than Plekhanov's which, it seemed, was capable of assuming the state-oriented position demanded by the cooperatives. We have in mind the modestly-sized group of the intelligentsia called the "Popular Socialists," who were the old Populists of *Russkoe Bogatstvo* [Russian Wealth], combined with a group—inchoate and unclear in its political outlook—which during the First Duma had been christened the "Trudoviks" [Laborites], a name that served to substitute for a program. Russian Populism by tradition was less bound together by socialist dogma, than was orthodox Social Democracy. Populism had always shown a greater capacity and desire to investigate more closely the "peculiarities of the nation's economic and material life." It was this current of thought [Populism] that attempted unsuccessfully to create an independent theory of Russian agrarian socialism. True, this current of thought was more closely bound up with the cultural and ideological traditions of the Russian intelligentsia, and that for this reason it had been a special target for the attacks of the "scientific" Marxists. However that may be, around the banner of Mikhailovsky and Annensky[14] there gathered a group of people who were talented, knowledgeable, who loved the motherland, and who were of unquestioned integrity. In Russian political life they occupied the unique position of inhabitants of a "cultural monastery in the wilderness," of voluntary anchorites whose sacred task it was to preserve the eternal flame on the old altar. But now Russian life had called them out of seclusion. They might have turned out to be more useful than many others in this process of transforming the fanatics of abstract socialism into sober political figures—a process with which Russian life was so regrettably late. Their political attitude can be divined from the speech of A. V. Peshekhonov, one of the "leaders" of the group, at the Democratic Conference.

The second Congress "of the Trudovik-Popular Socialist Party" (that is how the group labelled itself after the fusion with the Trudoviks) gathered in Moscow on September 26 to determine its preelectoral platform for the Constituent Assembly. The congress was not well attended. Representatives from the provinces were often meeting for the first time here with the central leadership. Only about 70 members of the party came to the congress. Peshekhonov was elected chairman; the spokesman from the central committee was V. A. Miakotin.[15] Much of what Miakotin had to say could have been said by a Kadet. He noted the destruction of many hopes since the first congress. There was no government. There was not even a set of several governments. There was anarchy. Members of the first congress had feared "counter-revolution," which did not then exist. Now counter-revolution did exist, "having been nurtured by the errors of the revolution." The party had not opposed these errors with sufficient vigor. The party had not protested against the violation of all civic freedoms by democratic institutions or against the effort of these institutions to stand alongside the government. In the Soviets the party was a "yes-man of other parties, the Mensheviks and SRs." Meanwhile, the party did have its own slogan. "Now this slogan is not popular, for it demands sacrifices from the masses; but we have never sought *only* popularity." This slogan, so essential at that moment, was "a common national bond" [obshchenarodnost], the serving of the common popular interests—the old slogan of the party. On the nationality question "we are federalists, but also partisans of the Russian state." As far as attitudes toward other parties were concerned, "we were the first to disassociate ourselves from the Bolsheviks, for they have but one method—violence, for they are not, in essence, socialists." Of the three groups into which the SRs were divided, the Party of Popular Socialists was closer to *Volia Naroda* and to Avksentiev—that is, to the right wing and to the center; Chernov and his followers were the same as the Bolsheviks. But all three groups were "organizationally connected," and therefore the party could not enter the election lists with any of them. But "how to behave with respect to the Kadet party"? The Kadets were not socialists, and on a series of issues were opponents. But the Kadets were not "rightists" at all, their program was not at all the "program of the landowners." "We and they have common ideas:" "the tasks of political construction of the nation, of inculcating legal consciousness into the people."

This report was by no means banal, and it provoked angry objections from a typical representative of the Trudoviks, a member of the First Duma, Bramson.[16] He argued that the party should not reject an agreement with socialist parties: otherwise, "we will isolate ourselves." One should not approach the Bolsheviks with simplistic assumptions: they were fused with the masses, they lived in the masses, and the party of the laboring classes would be forced to "compete" with them [the Bolsheviks]. On the other hand, "one most assuredly must put distance" between oneself and the Kadets. The Kadets, of course, were "old capital accumulated by the people," "the cultural party," "not Kornilovites." But . . . "they have never had civic courage." Stahl objected more candidly that the Kadets wanted to remain at positions taken on March 1. But the revolution was a social phenomenon, and not merely a political one. And therefore one could not "go to the people with the gospel of self-limitation alone: the people, who feel themselves to be the victors, will not understand such a gospel." It was necessary to force the people "to hate monarchy," and to do that one would have to take out of the briefcase a bill of indictment against august personages. In view of these objections from his new allies, A. V. Peshekhonov attempted to take a conciliatory position, and, thus, he sacrificed the Kadets. He said that the party was striving to channel the spontaneous struggle of classes into state-oriented forms. The only parties which had sharply defined their political positions—the Kadets and the Bolsheviks—on the contrary, were dividing class struggle from state-oriented struggle. The Bolsheviks recognized only the elemental struggle of classes, while the Kadets took the "opposite course: they wanted to recognize only purely state-oriented forms." A coalition with the Kadets (as with state-oriented members of the intelligentsia) he "understands and approves." But behind the Kadets stood the commercial-industrial class; and so he "does not understand" "a coalition with the bourgeoisie." One must make clear the substantive goal of the party, and not be embarrassed by the lack of correspondence between its resources and its goals. The resources will come to us "if we will explain ourselves more clearly, more fully, and more vigorously."

As a result of the debate, the congress adopted a resolution whose entire content came from Miakotin's report, but whose practical conclusions were taken from Miakotin's opponents. The goals of the current efforts were the motherland's defense from the external enemy and the assertion of the democratic principle of the state, which depended upon the inalienable rights of citizens and on the freely expressed will of the people; the struggle against everything that interefered with these ends—against infringements of the inviolability of persons and of liberty, against anarchy, against the fragmentation of governmental authority and the usurpation of authority by class-oriented and other organizations which could not by their nature express the will of the entire populace; an organization of government that would give the government not a class character, but a common national character; opposition to vigilante justice [samosudy] and the attempt to resolve social and political issues by means of law, promulgated and enforced by the government, rather than by means of violence; the preservation of the political unity of Russia from the maximalism of certain peripheral areas and of ethnic national parties, and the energetic struggle against these same maximalist demands, which threaten to lead the state to dissolution; the subjugation of class and group interests to common national interests....

Here was a fine summary of everything for which the Party of Popular Liberty had striven during the seven months of the revolution and about which, as is evident from this book, it had spoken many times in its resolutions at party congresses and in the statements of its ministers *in contradiction* to the efforts of socialist parties and the "democratic" organizations to "deepen" the revolution and to create "revolutionary laws and justice" [revoliutsionnoe pravotvorchestvo]. How did the

"Trudovik-Popular Socialist Party" propose to attain these ends? Just as V. A. Miakotin's opponents had recommended! The party was also socialist, and therefore "during elections agreement with non-socialist parties is out of the question."

Here we see the line which the "revolutionary democracy," including the "Trudovik-Popular Socialists," was either incapable of or unwilling to cross. On the contrary, in spite of everything done by the socialist parties of the Soviet majority—and that contradicted so sharply the program just summarized above—the congress found it possible to cooperate both with the SRs, "to the extent that they have distanced themselves from the maximalist wing," and with the Mensheviks. The congress preferred to shut its eyes to the fact that the SRs were not only "organizationally" but, in the final analysis, ideologically tied with the "maximalist wing." It was sufficient that maximalism not make itself obvious in party slogans or in the personalities of electoral candidates. The congress even agreed to go along with "extra-partisan organizations, if they did not contradict the program of the Popular Socialists." The only desideratum was that these organizations not bear the labels of one of the "bourgeois" parties.

Such was the limit of statesmanly good sense and tactical restraint of the most rational of the socialist parties. In order to save the revolution from the consequences of "maximalism," this limit was utterly inadequate. And the inability to move beyond it constituted one of the main reasons for the failure of the entire revolutionary movement. This circumstance best explained why, in all the practical steps it took, the "revolutionary democracy" was compelled to yield the initiative to that same non-socialist party, the formal agreement with which the democracy so carefully guarded against. Having preserved the purity of their party facade, the leaders of the Soviets gave to the "state-oriented intelligentsia" the right to govern the course of actual national political life. For *that reason* the Soviet leaders needed a coalition with "bourgeois" elements in power.

CHAPTER IV

STRENGTH AND WEAKNESS OF THE
THIRD COALITION

Thanks to the end of the governmental crisis that had dragged on for an entire month and to the renovation of the coalition cabinet, the Provisional Government in late September and early October enjoyed one of its *lucida intervalla*: a period of clarity in political thinking. These periods, as we have seen, always strengthened the government. And whenever the government grew stronger, it had to settle accounts—accounts that had been confused and long overlooked as a result of the crises—with the "maximalist" seizures of territory by nationalities of the peripheral regions and by the Russian political parties. No sooner had the government begun to consider its political course than the long-standing peripheral conflicts in Finland and the Ukraine announced their claims to the government's attention.

We left Finland at the moment when the Provisional Government had dissolved the Finnish Diet for its attempt at autonomous legislation on the fundamental question of the mutual relations of Russia and Finland. The Social Democratic majority of the dissolved Diet did not wish to submit to the dissolution, did not announce the dissolution in a meeting of the Diet, and attempted unsuccessfully on August 16 to reassemble on its own initiative. This attempt was frustrated by the energetic efforts of the Provisional Government, at whose order Governor-General Stakhovich[1] sent Hussars to occupy the Diet's meeting place. Although the deputies gathered even after this in the hall of the four Estates, the government could view this meeting as a meeting of private citizens, the former deputies, in a private place, and not attribute to the meeting any juridical significance. A month later, three days before the elections, the Finnish Social Democrats decided to repeat their experiment, and they sent to all political factions of the Diet a notice about a meeting on September 15. At the directive of the Provisional Government N. V. Nekrasov, who was the newly appointed replacement for M. A. Stakhovich, quickly left Petrograd for Helsingfors, and he found in Helsingfors a different picture than existed a month earlier. On this occasion the Helsingfors Soviet of Workers' and Soldiers' Deputies refused to support the troops sent to forbid the unauthorized meeting of the Diet. The Provisional Government received a telegram, later read by Kerensky in the Democratic Conference, that "local revolutionary forces will not permit anyone, especially the Provisional Government, to interfere with the unauthorized meeting of the Diet." Quickly dispatched delegates of the Central Executive Committee of the Soviet of Workers' and Soldiers' Deputies were not allowed into the courtroom for negotiations with the sailors.

Given these circumstances, N. V. Nekrasov was forced to limit himself to symbolic actions and to announce that he "had ordered a seal to be placed on the door of the Diet so that everyone would know that the meeting scheduled on September 15 was illegal." The representatives of all the other parties announced in advance that they would not take part in an unauthorized meeting: they had no interest in doing so, since in the impending elections they were counting on a victory of the bourgeois parties over the socialists. At 12:45 P.M. on September 15 the chairman [tal'man] of the dissolved Diet, Manner,[2] appeared at the Diet session in the company of 80 deputies, constituting 40 percent of the Diet membership; he ordered the seal taken off the door, opened the door and declared the meeting open. Within 20 minutes the assembly examined in three readings the legal project of July 5/18 on the sovereign rights of Finland and voted to adopt it. Before the vote the deputy Airola articulated the convictions of the other participants. The Diet had been dissolved illegally. The present meeting should be considered as having convened legally, for the Diet's charter did not require a quorum. If the bourgeois deputies were absent, that was their misfortune: they did not want to do anything to attain Finnish independence by taking advantage of circumstances that would not be repeated. As far as the election to the new Diet was concerned, the Diet could either declare the election to be illegal, or could agree to it if the election yielded favorable results. Since two Diets could not exist, the current Diet could proclaim that its session had come to an end, and could determine when the new deputies should assemble, for the Russian government's directive that the Diet be convened on November 1 was not binding. Then, acting on the basis of the law just enacted, the assembly unanimously voted to adopt laws on the eight-hour day, on communal elections, on the rights of Russian citizens, on Jewish equality, and other laws that had been passed by the Diet previously. After this meeting, which lasted 35 minutes, the chairman closed the meeting.

The government reacted to this by drawing up an act, asking the Judicial Department of the Senate to conduct an investigation of the violators of public order.

On the next day, September 16, Social Democratic deputies gathered at a second session, but this one was closed quickly by Manner. Nekrasov explained this closing (in a conversation with journalists) as follows: "The assembled deputies learned that the joint conference of democratic organizations looked negatively on their [the Social Democrats'] demonstration." One must then assume that the symbolic victory over Russia changed the deputies' mood after their telegram to Kerensky. However this may have been, it was obvious that the Social-Democratic deputies could have done no more than they had already done. They had given a demonstration of their position in the elections, which were to begin on September 18, and they had tested the new governor-general from whom the Russian leftist and the Finnish press expected "a policy of concessions, instead of the policy of strict adherence to law" carried out by Stakhovich.

However, the elections demonstrated that the nation did not approve the tactics of the socialist majority from the dissolved Diet. The electors came to the polls in unusally large numbers and awarded victory to the bourgeois parties. In comparison with the old Diet, the membership of the new Diet changed in the following fashion:

	Old Diet	New Diet
Social Democrats	103	91
Bloc of Finnish bourgeois parties	57	61
Agrarians	18	26
Swedish Constitutionalists	21	21
Peasant Workers	1	0
Representative of Lapland[3]	0	1
	200	200

Thus, neither the unauthorized declaration of Finland's independence, nor the promises of radical social reforms were effective. This did not mean, of course, that the Finns had rejected independence. But they wanted to move toward it by a surer path. The Diet was in the hands of groups that were accustomed to act not by revolutionary, but by constitutional methods. By the Provisional Government's charter on September 30, the convocation of the legal Diet was scheduled for October 19/November 1. Before that date it would be necessary to work out the long-desired new "form of government." Of course, this "form of government" was imagined now, in this revolutionary period, by the young generation of Finnish politicians quite differently than it was depicted by old Mäkelin[4] and his associates. On September 22, that is, as soon as the electoral victory of the bourgeois parties became apparent, the

Finnish newspapers published projected legislation on the establishment of a republican form of government and on the mutual relations of Russia and Finland. These projected laws, drawn up by Finnish jurists, had been awaiting consideration by the Juridical Collegium of the Senate, but had not yet been examined. With the consent of the Provisional Government, it was proposed to introduce in the Diet the draft on the new form of government, while the draft on the mutual relations of Finland and Russia would be introduced simultaneously in the Finnish Diet and the Russian Constituent Assembly.

In accordance with both drafts, Finland would declare itself a republic, united with Russia but having its own constitution and a government that was independent from the legislative and executive branches of government in Russia. Legislative authority would belong to the Diet and to the president of the republic, who would be elected by a direct and general election for a term of six years and who would receive the right to convene and to dissolve the Diet, schedule elections, and appoint the members of a Council of Ministers. The president was to be commander-in-chief of the Finnish armed forces in peacetime, and, with the consent of the Council of Ministers, he could announce mobilization. The issue of war and peace was a general question of state that would be decided according to the fundamental law of Russia for both countries. The Russian government would conclude treaties with foreign powers, if it did not delegate this right to the Finnish government. Until the formation of a Finnish army had been completed, Russian forces would remain in fortifications in Finland; these forces would take advantage of identical rights of quartering, transport, and requisition with the cooperation of the Finnish authorities. After the formation of the Finnish army, it alone would be quartered in Finland and would have as its purpose the defense of Finland; *in this manner* it would cooperate in the defense of the Russian state. Each citizen would have a military obligation, and the Finnish government would be obliged to keep a quantity of men under arms such that, in peacetime, expenditures would be no less than 10 Finnish marks per person. The Russian government would have the right to inspect these forces and to demand their placement onto a war footing. In wartime Russia could introduce into Finland a certain number of troops, and Russians would take command of the Finnish armed forces. To build new fortifications the Finns would have to seek the consent of the Russian government. Russia could station its own institutions, officials, and agents in Finland to deal with matters pertaining to the Orthodox Church, the telegraphs, monetary accounts, commerce, and shipping. There were provisions for mutual extradition of criminals.

The relations of the two governments would be conducted through a high representative of Russia in Finland (or of Finland in Russia) or through a state secretary. The application of the law on mutual relations could occur only by identical resolutions of the legislative agencies of the two countries, in the manner established for fundamental laws. In case of a difference in the interpretation of a law, the controverted issue would be turned over to an arbitration commission composed of three representatives from each country, and, in case they disagreed, to the decision of the international arbitration court in The Hague, if this court were willing to assume jurisdiction.

The attitudes of the Finnish parties and press to these proposed laws were various. Naturally, the socialists regarded them quite negatively. But even the Swedish Constitutionalist *Hufvudstadsbladet* [Capital News] thought that such a resolution of matters could not satisfy the majority of the Finnish people. On the contrary, the Old Finnish *Helsingin Sanomat* [Helsinki News] asserted that all parties could unite on these proposals and that the projected law on the form of government "will satisfy the most extreme demands."

On September 26 and 28 the proposal on the mutual relations of Finland and Russia was discussed by the Juridical Commission of the Provisional Government. The speaker B. E. Nolde immediately directed attention to the main peculiarity of the proposed law: that it radically altered the rights of Russia concerning Finland's domestic legislative process, and thus significantly diminished Russia's sovereignty. Of course, the principle of Finland's independence with respect to its local affairs was not challenged by Nolde. On October 1 a commission of jurists (B. E. Nolde, N. I. Lazarevsky, D. D. Grimm, M. S. Adzhemov, A. Ia. Galpern)[5] left Petrograd for Helsinfors, and in two joint sessions with the Commission on Fundamental Laws of the Finnish Senate discussed the proposal. On returning to Petrograd (October 5), B. E. Nolde informed journalists that both sides had made clear a desire to come together, and that an agreement had been outlined. Russian members had agreed that the right of self-determination in the sphere of purely internal affairs should be recognized as belonging to Finland in full measure. Finnish members had agreed that without Russia's consent there would be no change in the mutual relations of Finland and Russia, or in the form of government [in Finland]. The office of the president, to whom all the rights of Russian monarch were transferred, was hard to reconcile with Russia's sovereignty. But the necessity of a person who would sanction Finnish government directives and would stand as its head was recognized in full. The Russian members only preferred that this person be called a "vice-president." Two substantive

questions, however, led to irreconcilable disagreement and remained unresolved: one was the question of the right to quarter Russian soldiers
in Finland during peacetime, and the other was the transfer of controverted questions to the Hague tribunal for decision. Both for strategic
and for international reasons, Russia could not renounce the right to
quarter its soldiers in Finland at any time—including peacetime. And
referral of issues to the Hague tribunal could only occur if Finland were
completely independent, in which case all of the troublesome issues
arising from Finland's tie to Russia would disappear. Such questions,
of course, did not enter the jurisdiction of a normal court of arbitration,
and Finland was not numbered among the 40 sovereign states who had
signed the Hague Convention and who could conclude amongst themselves treaties providing for arbitration. Of course, Finnish jurists who
would not agree to concessions on these questions [were so stubborn]
precisely because they valued an indirect proof of Finland's complete independence.

Two weeks later, on October 19, a new Diet opened its sessions.
The Young Finn Lundson was elected chairman, and the vice-chairmen
were the Old Finn Ingman and a member of the Agrarian Party, Alkio.[6]
Having foreseen that the issue of the mutual relations of the two
countries would be raised in the Diet, the Provisional Government sent
to the governor-general a directive that all decisions on this issue must
be made in a fashion which would guarantee their juridical force—that
is, not unilaterally, but on the basis of a voluntary agreement that
would bind both sides, the Diet and the Provisional Government which
was reponsible to the Constituent Assembly. In essence, the Russian
government agreed to transfer matters of domestic legislation and administration to purely Finnish agencies, and it insisted, in the name of the
continuity of Russian and Finnish law, on the preservation of the status
quo in relation to matters affecting both Finland and Russia, until such
matters were settled by the proper legal procedures. On October 23
both the legal projects discussed above were transmitted in final form
from Helsingfors by Nekrasov and the State Secretary for Finnish Affairs Enckell,[7] and were approved at a session of the Provisional Government. Finland, while preserving its tie with Russia, received its own
legislature and government. The governmental structure of Finland was
defined as a republic in which supreme executive authority would belong to a "ruler" [pravitel]. The power to make war and peace and to enter into treaties would remain Russia's. Thus, before the Bolshevik uprising and final victory the long-standing quarrel between Finland and
Russia promised to be resolved to the mutual satisfaction of the two

countries and with full allowance for their respective interests. Fate decided otherwise.

In the Ukraine, as in Finland, the striving for autonomy and, in the final analysis, for independence continued to develop and win adherents. But in the Ukraine the process was more turbulent, because of the temperament of the populace and because of the lack of "continuity" in law, for it was completely impossible to rely on a legal tradition springing from the practice of Ukrainian institutions and from the fundamental charters of public law. A new public law, which had only now begun to be created under the pressure of usurpations by Ukrainian politicians, was full of omissions and gaps which each side interpreted in its own fashion. The institution of the "General Secretariat" itself had been created on July 4 not in a legislative act, but in a "declaration" which served to inform the public of a governmental "decision." Of course, this was not done accidentally. The "Instruction to the General Secretariat," which was based on the "declaration" of July 4, had no legal foundation and the Senate for this reason even refused (on October 2) to publish the "Instruction as law, without simultaneously promulgating an organic law on the Secretariat itself, as a new public statute." Moreover, the "Instruction" itself, especially its final section which defined the administrative authority of the General Secretariat, remained incomplete.

According to article 5 of the "Instruction," the set of issues in local administration on which the Provisional Government could bring to bear its plenary powers via the general secretaries (mentioned in article 3) was supposed to be defined in a "special appendix." This appendix was not published, and, as a result, the administrative competence of the commissariat was juridically undefined. This not only did not hinder, rather it even assisted Ukrainian politicians covertly to broaden the competence of the secretaries throughout the entire sphere of administration. Here we are not even raising the issue that the General Secretariat, which in the "Instruction" was labelled "an agency of the Provisional Government," actually functioned as a parliamentary ministry of the Ukraine, a ministry whose existence and membership depended on the "confidence" of another institution that was ill-defined juridically and was self-appointed to boot—the "General Rada," a sort of Ukrainian Pre-Parliament.

From the narrow and limited parameters of the "declaration" of July 4 the Ukrainians rushed toward complete liberty under the concerted pressure of the "separatists" who had begun to find room to operate.

In his book on the Ukraine Vinnichenko wrote that, "Aside from the naive, no one paid serious attention to the Instruction. Everyone knew that this was not peace, but a temporary cease-fire, that a battle would occur and must occur. Both camps, took advantage of the cease-fire to gather their forces, measure their strengths, and to organize themselves . . . . And neither side hid this from the other."[8] While Vinnichenko's observation was not necessarily true for the Provisional Government whose intentions the Ukrainian leaders continued to regard with extreme suspicion, it was certainly true for the other camp to which Vinnichenko himself belonged. Vinnichenko admitted that the advocates of Ukrainian autonomy extracted the advantage from the very "Instruction" that they so disliked. He said: "For us the Instruction had many positive elements. It was, in the first place, the primary support of our 'legal,' 'juridical' right to statehood; and this 'legality' had a tremendous psychological importance for the broad circles of poorly-informed, forgotten citizens who were accustomed to every 'legality' . . . . The Instruction played an enormous role in agitation and propaganda." The negative aspects of the "Instruction"—and especially its limitation of the Ukraine's territory—gave impetus, according to Vinnichenko, to "national activism" that now developed under the slogan of "a single, indivisible Ukraine." And the General Rada "measured the effects of its activity by one criterion: how soon it could free its hands." The Rada "decisively set out to broaden both its jurisdiction and the ties uniting all separated provinces with the entire Ukraine."

We have spoken already of the foreign connection of the "Union for the Liberation of the Ukraine." The foreign influence continued to make itself felt in this period. The Ukrainian paper, *L'Ukraine* [The Ukraine], which was published in Lausanne, publicly expressed the political slogans of the day. The freedom of the Ukraine was connected here with liberation from the Leninists and with an energetic defense of the Slavs against Germanism from which defense "Moskovia" refrained under the influence of "Lenin's hypnosis." The paper asserted that Lenin had influence only among Great Russians, whereas among other peoples of Russia—the Poles, Ukrainians, Latvians, Armenians, and Jews—one encountered patriotic enthusiasm. "If Moskovia does not reconsider its policy," threatened *L'Ukraine*, "and does not take into its own hands the defense of the Slavs against the German Empire, then there can be no more question about the right of the Great Russians to represent the Slavic peoples and to play among them the dominant role. Naturally, this role devolves upon the strongest nucleus in the group of nation states which ought to form a federation. If the Great Russians continue to behave incorrigibly, then the Ukrainians will be permitted *to demand more than autonomy*, and to strive to raise up again the scepter of the

Grand Dukes of Kiev which has slipped from the hands of the Muscovite and Petrograd tsars."

A characteristic step to strengthen this ideology, which undoubtedly
had been spread by agitation from across the borders, was the convocation in Kiev of representatives of the peoples and regions of Russia
who coveted a federated system. While, on the one hand, the Congress
of Nationalities in Kiev was influenced by of the propaganda of the "au-
tonomists and federalists" who had been active since the First State Duma, it was, on the other hand, a definite continuation of wartime experiments designed abroad with the participation and financial support of
Germany. In particular, the immediate predecessor to the Congress of
Nationalities in Kiev was the Congress of Nationalities in Lausanne in summer 1916, at which the directing hand of the Germans was quite apparent.

At the Kiev Congress of Nationalities from September 10-15 there
were roughly 100 delegates (of whom 86 were actual voting members),
representing many nationalities: Estonians, Latvians, Moldavians, Georgians, Crimean Tatars, Transcaucasian Turks, Buriats, and Kirgiz; there
were representatives from several Islamic military committees; and there
were also representatives of the Union of the Twelve Cossack Hosts.
The Armenians, Yakuts, Bashkirs, Kalmyks, and the mountain peoples
of the Caucasus and Dagestan sent greetings and subscribed themselves
in advance to the decisions of the congress. It goes without saying that
what was actually represented was certain political factions among these
nationalities, and even they often were represented haphazardly. Characteristically the government, or, more precisely, Kerensky (this was during the "directory") took a positive view of the congress and sent to the
congress its delegate, M.A. Slavinsky, who at that point was still a
moderate Ukrainian and collaborator of *Vestnik Evropy* [Courier of Eur-
ope]. Slavinsky informed the congress that the government was aware
of "strong and vigorous outgrowths" of autonomy in the Caucasus, Siberia, Estonia, Latvia, and even among the Cossacks, but that it did not
consider itself justified in proclaiming in advance of the Constituent Assembly a federated structure; meanwhile, it would "not hinder work in
local areas for the creation of such a structure." The government already
had created a special conference to elaborate plans for regional self-government under the chairmanship of Slavinsky himself; Slavinsky indicated that this special conference "considers its task to include entering
into contact with all the nationalities and regions of Russia in order to
take stock of all their autonomous-federalist sentiments" and to introduce a responsible draft of legislation to the Constituent Asssembly.

Professor Hrushevskyi,[9] who was elected an honorary representative, used his opening remarks to tie the idea of federated autonomy to Kiev, the "home" of this idea; he also indicated that among the Ukrainians the idea of a federation had never died.   Petliura,[10] the chairman of the Ukrainian Military Committee ("the War Minister"), advocated creation of a Ukrainian national army both "to defend [Ukrainian] land," and to make the voice of the Ukrainians heard at the Constituent Assembly. In conclusion, in complete agreement with the editorial in the newspaper *L'Ukraine*, Petliura stated that Russia was on the brink of an abyss, and could only be saved by an appeal to the vital sources of strength of the individual nationalities.   In the resolutions adopted by the congress the delegates recognized the need to reconstruct Russia on a federated basis; Russia would be divided into autonomous-federated states, and there would be a common federal agency whose tasks would include not only external defense but also domestic unification.   To bring about this restructuring, the congress suggested two approaches: the internal work of the national groups and decisions of local constituent assemblies, on the one hand, and unifying work, in collaboration with the agencies of the Provisional Government and with the participation of representatives of the nationalities, on the other hand.

Beyond this the congress did not venture. Even the Georgian Baratashvili, who claimed that Georgia could not be satisfied by a republican-federated structure of Russia and would soon announce its autonomy, was forced to take his words back. Here is a typical episode of the same sort.   *Kievskaia Mysl* [Kievan Thought] reprinted from *Vestnik Soiuza Osvobozhdeniia Ukrainy* [Courier of the Union of Liberation of the Ukraine] a telegram of greetings to an Austrian general concerning his "brilliant victories on the native land of the Ukrainian Grand Duke Liubart and of the warrior for the independence of the Ukraine, the Grand Duke Svidrigailo." This telegram also expressed the desire for "a *future victorious advance of the glorious Austrian-Hungarian army into the very heart of the Ukraine, Kiev*, to the glory of his Imperial Majesty, Franz-Joseph." The telegram was signed by Vladimir Doroshenko on behalf of the "presidium of the union of a liberated Ukraine." Our Ukrainians hastened to point out that this Doroshenko had nothing in common with D. Doroshenko, the government commissar.[11]   Thus, *officially* no separatist statements were permitted. But in the private, candid statements of the Ukrainians it was often admitted that for them a federation was only a step on the road toward complete independence.

However this may have been, Ukrainian reality was far away even from a federation, and the Ukrainians took advantage of the Democratic

Conference officially and publicly to present their immediate demands. At the end of the session of September 17, in an empty hall and amidst ironic exclamations from those present, the delegate of the Ukrainian Rada, Porsh, read his mandate.[12] He complained that the government had done nothing on nationality questions. He stated that the nationalities no longer desired to wait to be freed and were prepared "to enter the path of active struggle," that they demanded from the government now, without waiting for the Constituent Assembly, recognition of the right of all nations "to unfettered self-determination" and to convoke local constituent assemblies. Concerning the Ukraine, he demanded reconsideration of the "Instruction of the General Secretariat," so as to broaden the territory falling in the Ukraine, and to broaden the administrative jurisdiction of the secretaries.[13]

If in the Ukraine people generally were not waiting for the decision of the Russian government before going over to "active struggle," then after the unfriendly encounter at the Democratic Conference these tendencies were intensified. Already on September 1 the government had confirmed, on the Rada's request, those general commissars recognized by the "Instruction": Finance (Vinnichenko), Nationalities (A. Shulgin), General Comptroller (Zarubin), Education (Steshenko), General Clerk (Lototsky), Agriculture (Savchenko-Belsky), and the Commissar for Ukrainian Affairs under the Provisional Government (Stebnitsky).[14] But the question of transferring to the General Secretariat's jurisdiction agencies having a common national character remained open. Commissars of Supply, Transport, Justice, Post and Telegraphs, and War were not confirmed. This last was especially irritating to the Ukrainians. The "Ukrainian Military Committee" had been recognized by the government—and by its representative in Kiev, the commander of the region's military district, K.M. Oberuchev—as a private institution. Moreover, this committee had long been engaged in covertly equipping the first Ukrainian military units. Oberuchev opposed this; he argued that it was "clear legitimation of a collection of deserters and of soldiers absent without leave." The Military Committee was detaining in Kiev echelons that had been scheduled to augment units on the Southwestern Front, and Oberuchev officially stated that, as a result of the confusion created by the committee, he could not send reinforcements to the front during the June and July engagements. A.F. Kerensky had prohibited the Ukrainization of the military, but this did not prevent the general committee from circumventing Oberuchev and from obtaining directly from Kerensky a series of special decisions and executive orders that led to the same result. A systematic campaign was begun against Oberuchev, as an opponent of Ukrainization. Things went so far that on

October 20 the commander of the 2nd battalion of the 1st Ukrainian Reserve Regiment refused to submit to an order of the commander of the military district to move to a different place; this junior officer referred to the resolution of the battalion committee which stated that this transfer (to Chernigov) was evidence of Oberuchev's hostile attitude toward the Ukrainian infantry. Then Oberuchev, who did not wish to sanction such dual power, tendered his resignation. True, Kerensky responded by expressing confidence in Oberuchev and asking him to remain at his post. But this did not change the situation. After a second request to be permitted to resign Oberuchev was replaced on October 17 by the fighting General Kvetsinsky.

Following in the footsteps of the army, there was also an attempt to "Ukrainize" the navy. Here Kerensky's inconsistent behavior also helped the Ukrainians. On September 12 in Sevastopol Kerensky's order concerning the "Ukrainization" of the *Svetlana* was published. Then, under the influence of rumors about the commander-in-chief's favorable disposition toward Ukrainization, the Ukrainian Military Committee decided to Ukrainize the entire Black Sea Fleet. And the entire fleet unfurled Ukrainian flags and transmitted the signal: "Long live the free Ukraine!" The Black Sea Ukrainian Rada resolved (on September 15) to consider the entire Black Sea Fleet to be Ukrainian and to staff it in the future only with citizens of the Ukraine.

That was how matters stood before the Democratic Conference and before the formation of the third coalition cabinet, under the "directory." When the government grew stronger with the new coalition, a new note was immediately heard [from the government] concerning Ukrainian pretensions. And the Ukrainians noticed it at once. In Kiev preparations were under way to publish the "Third Universal." Now it was decided (on September 27) that the right to publish "Universals" ought to rest with a general congress of the Rada, and in the meantime the Ukrainians would limit themselves to an appeal and to the publication of a declaration by the Secretariat. In both these documents, which were published on September 30, the Secretariat went much farther than had been permitted heretofore by the government. In the appeal the Secretariat proclaimed itself "the highest organ of government of the region," "having been elected and established by the will and the word of the revolutionary parliament of the Ukrainian people and the Ukrainian Central Rada, in complete agreement with the government of the revolutionary Russian people." "We, the Secretariat of the Ukraine," the appeal went on, "*guided by this unwritten law* of all the democracies of the Ukraine, are preparing our region for autonomy and for the federation of the Russian Republic." In the "declaration," which summarized the program of the Ukrainian government, the Ukraine delcared itself "a body politic equal in rights to the united, federated Russian Republic."

But from the remainder of the declaration it became clear that the Ukraine was demanding more than simply being "an equal member of a federation," like a state of North America. The "declaration" promised to obtain for the Ukraine separate representation in a world confederation—that is, to endow the Ukraine with the rights of a sovereign state unconnected to any [federated] union. The document projected the creation of a Ukrainian constituent assembly—that is, another symbol of sovereignty would be created. Under the pretext of "the struggle against those elements committing excesses and acts of piracy," the declaration sanctioned the Ukrainian "free Cossackdom," which had appeared already "by virtue of life itself," as a means of self-defense for agencies of local self-government. In social relations the Secretariat promised to "recreate the social structure of the peoples of Russia" in a "proletarian-peasant federated republic." The Ukraine would receive its own budget and new financial resources through "an increase of taxation on the possessing classes of the populace." A "National Ukrainian Bank" would take the place of branches of the State Bank. Naturally, the territory of the Ukraine would be extended to include all five provinces stipulated by the Provisional Government, and full administrative authority would fall to the Secretariat.

In particular, in military affairs the Ukraine would have all power over its army, including power to appoint and dismiss military officers in the territory of the Ukraine in Ukrainian military units. The Central ("Small") Rada, by a vote of 24 in favor to one lone Kadet dissenter, approved the declaration and demanded of the Secretariat the swift and unwavering implementation of the declaration's *minimum transitional demands* which had been placed before the Ukraine by the course of the revolution, while simultaneously "the Secretariat should strive to *broaden and deepen* its work until it had fulfilled *all* the tasks of the revolution." One could not have said more clearly that the entire Rada already considered the ideal of Ukrainian "separatism" to be the "maximum" which must be achieved by taking advantage of the revolution and by relying on its own [Ukrainian] army and on free Cossackdom. In the appeals of the "Union of the Ukrainian State," which had been formed on the model of the Polish union, this goal was not even concealed. On October 29 a plenary session of the Central Rada was scheduled for the resolution of all the basic questions: peace, the [Ukrainian] Constituent Assembly, and unification with those parts of the Ukraine which were not autonomous.

The scope of the Secretariat's activity, combined with the unauthorized directives in military matters and with the new attempt to raise the Ukrainian flag on the ships of the Black Sea Fleet, finally drew the attention of the reconstituted government of the third coalition to the Ukraine. According to the report of A.I. Konovalov (on October 16), the government decided to take the necessary measures. Minister of Justice P.N. Maliantovich suggested that the Procurator of the Kiev Judiciary immediately carry out an exacting investigation into the actions of the Rada and the Secretariat, which were agencies of governmental authority whose members were appointed by the Provisional Government. The Navy Minister Verderevsky then sent the Central Rada a telegram, in which he stated that "raising any flag, other than [an authorized] military flag, on the ships of the Black Sea Fleet, which is the Fleet of the Russian Republic and is supported by the state treasury, is a wanton act of separatism." On September 17 the government sent a telegram inviting Vinnichenko, Steshenko and Zarubin to come to Petrograd to clarify the position of the Rada concerning the Constituent Assembly. Their arrival was expected on September 19. At the same time the government proposed not to send to the Secretariat its usual credit for 300,000 rubles until the matter of the [Ukrainian] Constituent Assembly was clarified.

Several days earlier the Kievan committee of the Party of Popular Liberty had condemned the "separatist" ambitions of the Rada and had recalled its minister, Zarubin, from the commissariat. Even earlier, for the same reason, the Kadets had left the Rada, and the 10th party congress had approved this step by the regional committee. The press also took a disapproving line toward the immoderate ambitions of the Rada and the Secretariat.

All this had an effect on the Ukrainians, and their leaders sounded a retreat.[15] Vinnichenko published a letter in the local newspapers in which he claimed that "the sovereignty of a Ukrainian Constituent Assembly does not necessarily mean that the Ukrainian democracy favors separation from Russia and independence." In Rada committee meetings on October 18 and 19 Vinnichenko presented this letter, stressed the declaration's commitment to "the unity of a Russian federated republic," and announced that a draft project on the convocation of a Ukrainian Constituent Assembly would be submitted for the Provisional Government's approval. The issue of sovereignty was a subject of impassioned debate and divided the assemblage. Finally, the "Small" Rada adopted a compromise formula that was supported by all the Ukrainian factions, although this formula did not by any means satisfy the representatives of Russian democracy in the committee. "Reemphasizing the need for unity of the federated Russian republic," the Small Rada stated that the will of the peoples of the Ukraine for self-determination could be expressed only through a Constituent Assembly of the Ukraine and that, once expressed in this fashion, "the will of the peoples of the Ukraine will be coordinated with the will of all peoples who live in Russia, which will be expressed through the All-Russia Constituent Assembly."

And with this the concessions came to an end. Vinnichenko, acting in accord with the Rada's resolution, refused to travel to Petrograd on the summons of the government. The unauthorized steps toward Ukrainization of the civil and military administration continued more energetically than before. On October 21 the Third All-Ukraine Congress opened in Kiev; its members began with a demonstration in front of the Khmelnitsky monument. The Rada protested against Kvetsinsky's appointment and forbade military units to obey his orders. The mood of the Ukrainian nationalists was completely in tune with the Bolsheviks. At the congress, which elected a Ukrainian front committee for the Western Front, the delegates resolved to demand that the government immediately enter peace negotiations and that it conclude a cease-fire on all fronts. Moreover, since "the hour of doom does not wait," the Central Rada, without waiting for a response from the government, should take into its own hands the matter of ending the war [by confronting] "the bourgeoisie which is prolonging the fighting." The Provisional Government's commissar declared that this resolution contained a direct incitation to commit treason. He proposed not to recognize the front committee and not to give it funds to operate. Nor did the government recognize the Ukrainian front committee on the Southwestern Front. In short, just before the Bolshevik uprising (they were preparing for an uprising in Kiev too) the Ukraine, despite external concessions, was in open conflict with the Provisional Government. Only the conflict with the Black Sea Fleet was resolved successfully; from the fleet Commissar Shreider telegraphed that the whole matter amounted to a "misunderstanding," for the raising of Ukrainian flags had been ordered only on one day, in celebration of the Ukrainization of the cruiser *Svetlana*.

The checklist of difficulties facing the third and last coalition would not be complete if we did not mention here the complications which were the results of constantly growing aspirations in social questions and the progressive collapse of governmental administration. Immediately before the formation of the third coalition *Russkie Vedomosti* [Russian News] wrote in its issue of September 20: "An enormous wave of disorders has swept across all Russia. Kiev, Bakhmut, Orel, Tambov, Kozlov, Tashkent, West and East, center and periphery, either simultaneously or by turns have become the arena of pogroms and various sorts of disorders. In some places the disorders arise because of problems in food supply; in other places the impetus for them comes from a crowd of soldiers breaking into a wine cellar; in still other places no one can answer the question of why the disorders occur. A city was living an apparently peaceful life, but suddenly a crowd came forth onto the street and began to destroy the small shops, to demand violence against certain individuals, to turn over to vigilante courts the representatives of the administration, even though the administration was elected. The spontaneity and senselessness of the pogroms are striking, yet these peculiarities of the disorders significantly hinder the fight against the disorders. Should one attempt persuasion, an appeal to reason and to conscience? But it is precisely reason that is lacking here, and conscience sleeps fast. Should one resort to repressive measures, to the assistance of armed force? But it is precisely the armed forces, embodied in the soldiers of the local garrisons, who play a big role in these pogroms . . . . Only two weeks ago the Minister of War spoke quite reassuringly about the situation in the Moscow military district [praising his "democratic" methods of administration there—PNM], yet at the end of these two weeks it became necessary to equip a special military expedition from Moscow in order to put down disorders among soldiers in Orel, Tambov, and Kozlov. The *crowd* in the worst sense of the word more and more often goes out onto the street and *begins to feel itself master of the situation*, and it recognizes no authority superior to itself. Sometimes this crowd tosses about one or another of the Bolshevik slogans, but, in essence, one cannot call it even Bolshevik or anarchistic. It is simply a crowd, and like all crowds it is dark, profoundly ignorant, capable of recognizing nothing other than vulgarly personal interests."

Within several days the newly-formed government had set itself to work, and the first issue on its agenda was this very problem of anarchy across the country. In the government's meeting on September 27 Minister of Internal Affairs Nikitin reported that, according to information from local respondents, anarchy continued to grow both in the cities and in rural areas. He also took note of the spontaneous character of the movement, which was especially dangerous in the countryside. According to this information, agrarian disorder in the majority of cases were taking the form of senseless riots that manifested themselves in the destruction of noble-owned country houses, of herds of cattle and so on. Indeed, at this same time the official SR paper of the Chernov stripe, *Delo Naroda*, published a report from a party activist, Sletova, about agrarian disorders in Kozlov district, which presented a clear illustration of Nikitin's information. In that district by September 18 more than 30 estates had been set afire, and in the most impressive estates not a stone was left upon a stone. "They burn and threaten not only the noble landowners, but also the peasants, especially the small individual farmstead owners and those whose lands were consolidated from the communes. One village goes to destroy another either because of property divisions or because of the refusal to participate in the destruction." "The peasants are begging that help be sent to them to defend them. In a few cases soldiers are sent who merely join the rioters . . . . Now Cossacks have been sent to Kozlov. Their appearance has been greeted with joy even from the most extreme elements." But against the Cossacks, Sletova continued, "someone is agitating among the soldiers. It is pitiful and sad to see how people celebrated the approach of the Cossacks, while now against the Cossacks there is terrible anger, although they merely dispersed without touching anyone." What were party workers doing against this agitation? "A handful of local party workers, *not the demagogues*," Sletova said, "are exhausting themselves, but there are laughably few of them . . . . Influential representatives of the party and the Executive Committee need to come to these local areas . . . . but . . . I tried to talk with this person and that, and I begged them for permission for me to give a report at a session of the government without waiting in line. They said: 'Wait,' and they dismissed me. 'We have an important matter to discuss: two new places may be added to the presidium; we'll have to settle this first.'" And as it was in Kozlov, so it was in Petrograd and everywhere else: partisan arguments over precedence in the government interfered with the use of authority, and means were transformed into ends.

An excellent example of how the "democratic organizations" themselves exploited the increased weakness of the government is the story of the railroad strike and the demands of Tsentroflot. Both conflicts coincided with the governmental crisis. They came to an end after the establishment of a cabinet, but they were ended by forced compromises to which the government had to resort, to the detriment of the state treasury and its own authority.

Since May a general railroad strike had been threatened. The railroad workers resorted more than once to the threat of this trike, while demanding an increase in the number of their food warehouses. Additional warehouses, as recommended by the so-called Plekhanov Commission, were planned in accordance with considerations of the state's economic resources. The railroad workers were not satisfied with these additions, the more so because the price of food continued to rise. The All-Russia Railroad Congress, which ended on August 25, entered into new negotiations with the Minister of Transport, and, in addition, raised anew the threat of a strike. P.P. Iurenev succeeded with great difficulty in delaying the strike when the Kornilov movement began.[16] Under Iurenev's replacement, A.V. Liverovsky, the railroad workers succeeded in playing a major political role in confronting the Kornilov movement. For good reason Kornilov had thought it necessary to win their favor; not long before the uprising he sent them a personal telegram in which he recognized their services and their right to an increase in material rewards. By not permitting Kornilov's trains to reach Petrograd on schedule, the railroad workers spoiled Kornilov's entire plan and contributed substantially to his defeat. This naturally raised the political self-esteem of their central organization. From now on the famous "Vikzhel" (the All-Russia Executive Committee of the Railroad Workers' Union) moved prominently into the ranks of those major "democratic organizations" with which the government was forced to contend as influential factors in domestic politics. And immediately after the liquidation of the Kornilov uprising Vikzhel decided to force the government to feel and recognize its [Vikzhel's] strength.

On the night of September 7 the full staff of the railroad union's Executive Committee journeyed to Petrograd to present to the government the union's demands, which were backed up by the threat of a strike. The committee found in Petrograd a new commission, charged with reexamining the norm for compensation of railroad work, under the chairmanship of the Assistant Minister of Labor, Gvozdev.[17] Not being satisfied with what it regarded as the overly broad and vague mandate of this commission, Vikzhel, "which considers the railroad union to be a democratic organization," entered into direct contact with the Executive Committee of the Soviet of Workers' and Soldiers' Deputies, and there it received official recognition.

Along with representatives of the Bureau of the Executive Committee of the Soviet and of the All-Russia Soviet of Trade Unions, Vikzhel became part of a conference which in three days was supposed to resolve the question of "the terrible poverty and starvation threatening the railroad workers." The bureau guaranteed to Vikzhel full support for the commission's recommendations before the Provisional Government. After making certain reductions in the wage rate, the conference forwarded its recommendations to the Gvozdev Commission where a final decision would be made within a week. Vikzhel expected that the government would simply confirm the results of the Gvozdev Commission's work. But the government, having discussed the matter on September 19 (that is, at the moment of its collapse), decided *preliminarily* to balance the new expenditure falling on the treasury from the addition to the number of warehouses by adding a new source of income from a tariff on passengers and freight; the government also contemplated decreasing expenditures by paying the railroad workers in kind. These decisions were to be reviewed in a new commission of ministers to be chaired by Liverovsky. Vikzhel stated that, "this referral of a question that already has been decided to a new commission provoked a natural outburst of dissatisfaction among rank-and-file railroad workers." Judging by the disagreements "among the rank-and-file" that manifested themselves later, this statement was not quite true. But the Union Executive Committee decided in any case to make use of telegrams from branch local affiliates to assert that "starving railroad workers cannot wait any longer," and to take a decisive step. Let us listen to Vikzhel's own words.

"Being inspired by the masses and clearly recognizing that uncoordinated strikes on individual lines will lead to complete disorder in transport and will bring complete chaos into the economic life of the nation, will reduce by half the shipment of supplies to the cities and to the front, will generate hunger riots, and will lead to the complete ruin of the nation and the revolution, the Central Executive Committee of the Railroad Workers' Union, obeying its bounden duty, was forced to take into its own hands the leadership of a railroad strike, in order to introduce into it rational planning so that the populace and the popular army will not suffer from this dispute." Subsequently, in announcing the end of the strike, Vikzhel, it is true, admitted to less-elevated motives. "Our goal was to win the fullest possible satisfaction of our demands with the least possible sacrifices by the army and the nation." It even admitted that this goal had not won the general sympathy of the "democracy." On September 26 Vikzhel stated: "To prolong a strike at this moment which is so difficult for the nation is very dangerous to the revolution and to the All-Russia Railroad Workers' Union. *Railroad workers risk being isolated without the support of the remainder of the democracy.*" And so Vikzhel knew quite well what it was risking and what were the dangers to the nation: but it made concessions only because of the future risk to itself, not because of the risk to the nation. In any case, its calculations were true and exact: the government, "at this moment which is so difficult for the nation," could not resist. The government made concessions precisely at the moment when future resistance was becoming "very dangerous"—for Vikzhel itself.

Here for the first time a "democratic organization," which had abandoned the customs of the Russian intelligentsia and had learned to act practically in practical matters, came forward without a slip—in the American fashion. For history's sake one must preserve the names of the initiators of the new period of Russian political tactics, the more so because in every other respect these names are unknown to Russian society. They were: the chairman of the strike committee of Vikzhel. A. Char; the assistant chairman, Fedotov; secretary, Afanasiev; and its members, Bakanchikov, Ilichev, Dobytin, Kravets, Shekhanov, and Magitsky.

The government did not give in at once. The strike was scheduled to begin at midnight on September 24 for express trains, at midnight on September 27 for local trains, and at midnight on September 29 for all trains except hospital and military trains, food and military freights. On September 21 Kerensky announced that the government "intends to set new norms for wages in the next few days," although he considered it his duty to warn that these norms could be met only if there were an immediate increase in railroad tariffs, since the treasury could not possibly defray these expenses from its current resources. But the prime minister also stated that "the government cannot permit any interruptions in the proper work of the railroads, since this would entail innumerable problems for the army and the populace of large cities, and would be a grave crime against the motherland and the army." Therefore, Kerensky "expressed his hope that the Provisional Government will not have to take severe measures, which by law apply in cases of nonfulfillment of the orders of railroad authorities in wartime," for he was "certain that in these days of terrible trials the railroad workers will not betray the motherland." Minister of Posts and Telegraphs Nikitin adopted an even more decisive tone in his telegram of September 22: "An appeal to terminate railroad traffic," he reminded everyone, "is a crime punishable by law, and is tantamount to betraying the motherland. All citizens are called on to defend the motherland against the new blow, *which is like the Kornilov conspiracy*. I order all telegrams of a clearly criminal content to be confiscated, and I should be informed of them."

Alas, in spite of all these warnings, a strike was nevertheless called for the 24th. Over Magitsky's signature Kerensky received an angry and sharp response: "The railroad workers have never been and will never become traitors to the motherland and the revolution; you, comrade Kerensky, know this better than anyone else [This was a hint at the railroad workers' services during the Kornilov movement]." But "the senseless game being played by the Minister of Transport had made the railroad workers very angry . . . . The initiative is not coming from us, but from the broad masses. Comrade Kerensky, we have exhausted all our options. It is now the turn of the Provisional Government to speak . . . . Responsibility for the threatening events rests not with us, but on those who six months ago toyed with the patience of the starving railroad workers." Nikitin and the Postal Workers' and Telegraphers' Union now entered into open conflict, for the union's Excecutive Committee, in contradiction to the minister's telegram, asserted that Vikzhel's motives were "serious and completely justified" and it ordered that "telegrams from the branches of the railroad workers' union be sent on without hindrance." Nikitin answered this order with his own order to confiscate the telegram of the Executive Committee of the Postal Workers' and Telegraphers' Union, and "to regard the Executive Committee of the Postal Workers' and Telegraphers' Union as having joined a subversive movement." He threatened "to cut off all relations with the union." In response the Executive Committee of the Postal Workers' and Telegraphers' Union and an assembly of workers in the Ministry of Posts "explained" that they considered a strike "ill-timed," but that nevertheless, they "cannot permit members of the Postal Workers' and Telegraphers' Union to serve as a tool to be used against a fellow trade union organization." "Categorically protesting against the comparison of an economic strike with the Kornilovshchina," the union members took "the only possible position—one of strict neutrality" and they condemned "as provocative rumors assertions about a possible postal-telegraphers' strike" and labelled such assertions "attempts to interfere with the affairs of the railroad workers' organizations and to frustrate proper planning for a strike" by Vikzhel. For its part, Vikzhel pointedly reminded Nikitin—and in this reminder was the political essence of the test of strength begun on behalf of the "starving railroad workers"—that Nikitin's telegram "is an appeal for the destruction of the democratic organizations, for the army of railroad workers is a part of the common democracy, and the Central Committee of the Railroad Workers' Union enjoys in this strike *the support of the Moscow Soviets* of Workers' and Soldiers' Deputies." "However," Vikzhel added disdainfully, "your attitude toward the Soviets which put your name forward and put you into the government, is well known . . . . and therefore we view your telegram as a work of provocation and we are responding to you solely in order to place this issue before the eyes of the democracy and of the entire populace."

The government quickly began to make concessions. In its meetings on September 24 and 25 the government worked out and immediately conveyed to the Executive Committee of the Railroad Workers' Union in Moscow a governmental decree, which set the norm for railroad workers' wages twice as high as the norm suggested by the Plekhanov Commission, although these new norms were somewhat lower than those recommended by the Gvozdev Commission. Moreover, the railroad workers received exclusive privileges of access to food supplies. Their food supply committees were made independent of the provincial food supply committees; if for three weeks they did not receive food shipments, the railroad workers' committees had the right to make their own purchases and to ship them as priority items; finally, in case of necessity, the railroad workers could receive food supplies from the army quartermasters' warehouses. The new monetary burden assumed by the treasury was 760 million rubles a year, and for the remainder of 1917 the government encumbered 235 million rubles for these purposes.

Nevertheless, Vikzhel was dissatisfied. According to the public statement of A. Ia. Char, Vikzhel had addressed to the government not only economic, but also purely legal demands which concerned the rights of Vikzhel itself; about these rights the decree had not said a single word. Vikzhel demanded that the Railroad Workers' Union be recognized as the legal bargaining agent during the final working out of an agreement with the government; it demanded from the ministry an immediate order to establish an eight-hour working day everywhere; and, finally, it demanded "at least an agreement in principle" on "the democratization of the central administration." The economic concessions made by the government were also declared to be insufficient. But here Vikzhel agreed to await the decision of the new Railroad Workers' Congress that had been summoned on an emergency basis. Having departed Petrograd on the eve of this congress, Vikzhel's delegation received the appropriate instructions.

There followed new negotiations, and on this occasion a special part was played by Minister of War Verkhovsky, to whom the railroad workers' delegation was sent directly. Government headquarters at the Winter Palace received visits from representatives of the Soviet of Workers' and Soldiers' Deputies, Chkheidze, Gots and Krupinsky, from the representative of the trade unions, the Bolshevik Rozanov, and the delegation from Vikzhel. These parties proposed that the government immediately publish additions to the earlier decree, the preliminary text of which additions they had already drafted at a meeting in Smolny. Minister Liverovsky categorically stated that the government could not provide more money, but he said that the failure to mention Vikzhel's rights in the decree was the result of hastiness and he promised to form a special commission to set the exact length of the working day. This commission would include Vikzhel and the ministry, with both groups having equal rights in deliberations. With these caveats the government accepted the additions to the decree and published them. Vikzhel received formal recognition. The government obligated itself to seek Vikzhel's participation on "all points where an agreement must be arrived at between different governmental agencies or where instructions must be worked out." After this

Vikzhel could announce to its union membership: "We have succeeded in attaining more or less significant results . . . . In their struggle the railroad workers have shown the maximum of political wisdom and the greatest display of strength . . . . To work out the forms of future struggle we have decided to summon an emergency congress on October 15." Now "fearing only that the nascent Railroad Workers' Union may be destroyed utterly in this gigantic struggle, and that it may wind up in complete isolation, the Central Executive Committee of the Railroad Workers' Union has recognized the need to end the All-Russia strike." This was done by telegrams sent to all lines in the railroad network: after midnight on September 27 the movement of traffic on the railroads was restored to full capacity. The new "democratic organization" received its political baptism and declared its equality with others by adopting the acronym "Vikzhel."

The incident involving the other "democratic organization," the Central Committee of the All-Russia Military Fleet under the Central Executive Committee of the Soviets of Workers' and Soldiers' Deputies, or, in the shortened version of this long title, "Tsentroflot," provided an even more depressing spectacle. A conflict arose here over a completely trivial matter, but the "democratic organization" manifested such an exaggerated sense of its own dignity and such an inability to preserve the dignity of the national, "revolutionary" and "republican" government, that a trivial matter became a terrible symptom and an even more terrible harbinger of future ordeals. Tsentroflot raised the question of increasing its office space in the Admiralty building. The Navy Minister Verderevsky, having looked over the office situation, found this desire to be well-founded, and he issued the appropriate instructions. But Tsentroflot did not like the minister's decision, and it preferred to act without authorization. On September 14 Verderevsky received from the chairman of Tsentroflot, the Bolshevik Abramov, the following short statement: "Mr. Navy Minister, by resolution of Tsentroflot it has been decided that we shall occupy the quarters set aside for Chief-of-Staff Egoriev for our work and plenary sessions. You are being notified of the above for your information." Admiral Verderevsky wrote on the document this message: "From the form and manner of this notice to me I surmise that Tsentroflot presupposes it to be necessary and feasible in the resolution of questions that have heretofore fallen within a minister's purview to replace the minister. Not considering such conduct to be useful or legal, I do not see that it will be possible for me to continue to work effectively under these circumstances. I shall make this known to the prime minister." However, Kerensky did not accept the resignation of the Navy Minister, and the directory decided not to yield to Tsentroflot. Then Abramov sent the minister a new telegram: "Tsentroflot, in view of the obstacles encountered . . . is refraining from occupying Egoriev's apartment, but, given the position in which Tsentroflot has been placed, it will consider itself as lacking the possibility to continue its work and it will not carry out its duties until the departure of its members to places of service." By offering to resign the minister appealed to the government, and by its "failure to carry out its duties Tsentroflot appealed" to the Soviet of Workers' and Soldiers' Deputies.

There followed an attempt to resolve the affair through long negotiations. The Navy Ministry offered Tsentroflot a huge office with 12 rooms and the largest hall in the Admiralty, the library, for its plenary sessions. If even this did not suit Tsentroflot, the minister offered money to rent whatever office space in the city that Tsentroflot might find appropriate. But the "democratic organization" wanted to have Egoriev's apartment no matter what, and on September 17 it dispatched to the minister the following note: "Considering abnormal a situation in which the Navy Ministry will not compromise, Tsentroflot decided to occupy the vacated apartment of the chief-of-staff. It is bringing this item to your attention and to the attention of the prime minister." And so, Tsentroflot initiated acts of war. The Navy Minister for his part took defensive measures and placed a seal on the apartment. Then on September 18 there followed an ultimatum: Tsentroflot demanded of the Provisional Government that Egoriev be dismissed from his posts and that the assistant telegrapher of the Naval Staff, Romanov, also be fired. The government would leave "the contested apartment" "by rights" to Tsentroflot and would appoint to the post of First Assistant to the Navy Minister Captain Veiner, the chief-of-staff at Kronstadt.

All these demands were supposed to be met within 24 hours; otherwise Tsentroflot threatened to consider "the rights of the supreme naval democratic organization to have been violated and all relations with the Navy Ministry to have been sundered." This was already too much—even for "the directory." And Kerensky's government decided: to dissolve Tsentroflot and to schedule new elections, "to consider as treason any attempt to incite an uprising among the command, given the threatening situation in the Baltic Sea." "In case of a renewal of difficulties on these same grounds, the current membership of Tsentroflot would be treated as instigators." In carrying out the order to dissolve Tsentroflot, the government demanded that it [Tsentroflot] vacate all its current offices by 3 o'clock on September 19. The Admiralty was surrounded by a detachment of cadets, Tsentroflot's offices and the Hughes apparatus were placed under sentry. The Navy Minister sent a telegram to the naval committees in Helsingfors and in Sevastopol informing them that the navy might become the target of "provocations," and that simultaneously with the Tsentroflot ultimatum, the government "received another series of indications about an impending German attack on the Baltic Sea in connection with the unceasing disturbances in the naval command." "In view of the absolute necessity of avoiding an interruption of Tsentroflot's real work," the minister asked that elections of a new Tsentroflot staff be expedited.

As the commander of the Baltic Sea Fleet, Admiral Razvozov, [18] informed the government over the Hughes apparatus, a meeting of representatives from various shipboard commands in the Baltic Sea, which gathered at 1 P.M. in Helsinfors, had "an expectant, if anxious character, in view of the trust and respect which bind the fleet and the Navy Minister." But, nevertheless, the central committee of the fleet found the "dissolution of Tsentroflot in such a dangerous period to be inconceivable," and insisted that the order to that effect be cancelled. The meeting of the shipboard commands asked Admiral Razvozov "what measures to take against the dissolution." When Razvozov informed Verderevsky about this, the latter responded that the government's decision about the dissolution of Tsentroflot had been unanimous, and that no government could permit "individual organizations to make irrational demands," for in that case every demand of any group of people would have to be satisfied by the government and the government would transfer *de facto* power into the hands of the masses who lack any organization whatsoever. Verderevsky "appealed to the intelligence and compassion of the shipboard commanders," and he begged them "not to descend anew onto the path of destruction in view of the enemy, which is standing at the gates."

Three o'clock arrived and Tsentroflot had not even given a thought to vacating its offices. It held a meeting under its chairman, Abramov, and "made decisions of the greatest import that would be published only after they had been put into effect." Admiral Verderevsky, probably under the influence of conversations with Helsingfors, then proposed new conditions. He would not insist on the offices of Tsentroflot being vacated or the reelection of the Tsentroflot staff, if the latter "in written form, categorically and unambiguously, would withdraw its ultimata of September 18."

This compromise was acceptable to the Executive Committee of the Soviet Workers' and Soldiers' Deputies, which approved it, in the presence of the Tsentroflot presidium, in the evening session of September 19/20. On the afternoon of September 20 members of the Executive Committee, Gots and Avksentiev, looked over the offices which the Navy Minister had proposed to give to Tsentroflot and found them to be quite suitable. After this, there was no reason to hold out any longer. On the same day Tsentroflot members resolved to inform all units of the fleet about the cause of the conflict and about the successful resolution of it. Basing itself on a document that was signed by members of the Executive Committee and that stated that Tsentroflot was withdrawing all its demands, the government cancelled the order for the dissolution of Tsentroflot.

But this decision did not satisfy the self-esteem of the "democratic organization." On the night of September 23 Tsentroflot, taking advantage of Kerensky's negotiations with representatives of the Soviet about the composition of a new cabinet, made a new decision: they would not enter into any negotiations or take part in any agreements with the directory; their demands and decisions remained in force; and they would await a resolution of the conflict "not from the current directory, but from the Central Executive Committee of the Soviet of Workers' and Soldiers' Deputies and from the new government that was now being formed, which would be responsible to representatives of the organized democracy." The Navy Ministry turned to the Executive Committee of the Soviet for proof that this document was a "misunderstanding" and that Tsentroflot was withdrawing not only the *forms* of the ultimatum in its demands, but the demands themselves in substance. But Tsentroflot had already gone into battle with the Executive Committee of the Soviet itself, whose "Naval Section" Tsentroflot resolved "to abolish, and whose personnel should not be recognized as expressing the will and the needs of the fleet," in view of their "counter-revolutionism" and "two-faced behavior." The Bolshevistic tactics now manifested themselves in all Tsentroflot's maneuvers, in complete harmony with the mood of the Baltic Fleet.

The calculation that trouble might be incited during the formation of the new cabinet proved incorrect on this occasion. The government was formed, and this government was not responsible to the organized democracy. Nevertheless, Tsentroflot succeeded in insisting on the satisfaction of its original demands. At a new meeting of the Executive Committee of the Soviet of Workers' and Soldiers' Deputies, Tsentroflot's ultimatum was investigated, and the committee decided to form a commission, consisting of the members of the Executive Committee, of Tsentroflot and the Navy Ministry, to . . . look over the disputed apartment. The Navy Minister stated that he would respect the decision of this commission. And the commission decided to award the apartment of the chief-of-staff to Tsentroflot! The chief-of-staff himself, Egoriev, whose dismissal Tsentroflot had demanded, had to abandon his post. This was a complete capitulation by the government to the arbitrary caprice of a "democratic" organization.

CHAPTER V

LAST CHANCE OF THE LAST COALITION

It was clear under the circumstances, given the more than unenthusiastic attitude of the moderate socialist parties toward the new government, given the aggressive attitude of the extremists, given the anarchy that had finally erupted after seven months of non-government in the cities and in the countryside, given the callous disregard for the state's needs and ends by the "democratic organizations" which had grown like mushrooms and which, like a thick ring, had cut off the government from any prospect of influencing the masses, the third coalition could not count on success. Of course, the creation of each coalition government following progressively longer political crises was accompanied by a temporary increase in the government's authority. But each time this occurred, the increase in authority was less significant. The political barometer of four revolutionary governments, of which three were coalition governments, could be plotted on a curve with a whole series of decreasing high points and with sharply plunging low points, and with the amplitude of the swings between high point and low point increasing. The "history of the illness" of the Provisional Government could be graphically represented by this curve.

In the situation that took shape in early October there was a new feature. For the first time since the revolution two groups that were becoming more and more antipathetic toward each other were to meet in one and the same representative assembly: "the revolutionary democracy" of the so-called "democratic organizations;" and the so-called "propertied elements," which included the entire non-socialist and non-party democracy. Both antagonistic elements were loosely connected with the lower classes. But the advantage of demagoguery, the advantage of the loud slogans of "class struggle" was on the side of the "revolutionary democracy," and within its ranks this advantage had already shifted to the extreme left wing.

What kind of encounter would there be between the two competitors for the right to represent the popular will? To what extent would it be possible in a personal encounter to lay to rest the monstrous legends that circulated, and to establish some kind of pacific relationship?

Would they succeed finally in confining those real disagreements that did remain within the channels of a purely parliamentary struggle? Would it be understood that above this parliamentary struggle there were common national tasks on whose execution depended the future existence of a democratic and republican Russia? To what extent would this understanding remain above partisan and class considerations? Would the assembly demonstrate, along with an understanding of common national issues, a discipline sufficient to strengthen the government in the common national struggle for their successful resolution? In particular, would the assembly rise to an understanding of the two most important problems on whose solution depended not only the existence of a democratic and republican Russia, but the future existence of Russia in general: the problem of the war and the international problem? To all of these questions the answer was already obvious in the material evidence accumulated in the last seven months, and this answer was negative. But, nevertheless, it was necessary to await the outcome of the last attempt. Those political figures who were accustomed to responsible work were shaking their heads but were not giving up. In order to make use of this last chance, they went to work with the same seriousness they would have manifested had they believed that they might succeed in the end.

The "Statute on the Provisional Soviet of the Russian Republic," which was based on principles established by the leaders of the Soviet and by the "propertied elements," was published on October 3 along with a governmental statute providing for the convocation on October 7 of the Soviet of the Republic and its termination "a week before the opening of the Constituent Assembly" (that is, on November 20). Thus, the Soviet was to be in session for six weeks. In the first days of October Kerensky raised in the government the question that was being discussed by the "democracy" as to whether the seat of government should be moved to Moscow and the Soviet of the Republic convoked there. In view of the German victories in the Gulf of Riga, the issue of the evacuation of Petrograd was raised anew, and the government had already decided to move to Moscow those sections of the ministries which were tightly connected with central administration and which were essential to the government's functioning. N. M. Kishkin had already started to carry out the tasks entrusted to him: to prepare office space in the old capital for the government, the ministries and the Soviet. But when news of Kerensky's intentions appeared in the newspapers, the "revolutionary democracy," and in particular its left wing, sounded the alarm. They had no doubt that Kerensky would make use of the move to Moscow to distance himself from the Soviets.

Moreover, they did not doubt that it was this calculation that prejudiced the government's decision in the disputed question of where to convoke the Constituent Assembly, so that the government's decision coincided with the desires of the moderate elements and went against a concrete decision of the Soviet. One of the Soviet's leaders told a member of the government that the transfer of the government to Moscow was a "knife in the revolution's back." He received the response, quite characteristic for that moment, that to remain in Petrograd was "a German bayonet thrust in the chest." The Bolsheviks had discussed already in their central committee the possibility of establishing communes in Petrograd in case the government should leave. A member of the Executive Committee, Bogdanov (a Left Menshevik), had predicted that "if Kerensky's government seats itself in Moscow, a new government will form in Petrograd."

All these rumors stopped the government. It decided to turn over the question of whether to evacuate the capital to the Soviet of the Republic, which was supposed to open its sessions in Petrograd. The hall of the Mariinsky Palace was adapted quickly for the Soviet of the Republic, because the hall was large enough to accommodate the 550 members of that body. It was merely necessary to replace the cushioned armchairs, in which the officials of the old State Council had sat so contentedly, with democratic chairs that were more suitable to the membership of the new assembly. Of course all reminders of the old system of government were removed from the hall: the coat of arms that was hanging above the chairman's rostrum was hidden by a curtain, and white linen covered the famous painting of Repin that depicted the statesmen of the old State Council in jubilee session under the chairmanship of Nicholas II.

The membership of the Soviet of the Republic was distributed as follows:

Representation of Democratic Organizations
(socialist democracy)

Parties

Socialist-Revolutionaries	63	Popular Socialists	3
Menshevik-Defensists	62	*Edinstvo* Group	1
Bolsheviks	53	(Plekhanov)	
SD Internationalists	3	Ukrainian SDs	1

Organizations

Executive Committee of		Teachers' Union	2
the Peasants' Soviet	38	Peasants' Union	2

continued . . .

Zemstvo Group	37	Bureau of the	
Representatives of		Conference of	
the Front	25	Lawyers	1
Cooperatives	18	Military District	
Workers' Cooperatives	5	Committees	2
Economic Organizations	6	Provincial Executive	
Land Committees	5	Committees	4
Cossack Self-Government	5	Zemstvo Workers	1
Cossacks	3	Women's	
Railroad Workers' Union	4	Organizations	1
Postal Workers' and		Wounded Veterans	1
Telegraphers' Union	2	Democratic Clergy	1
Fleet	3	Miscellaneous	
		Democratic Groups	15

TOTAL   367

Representation of "Propertied Elements"
(non-socialist parties and the "bourgeoisie")

Party of Popular Liberty	56	Old Believers	2
Representatives of		Ecclesiastic Academy	1
Commerce and Industry	34	All-Russia Council of	
Council of the Moscow		Clergy and Laymen	1
Conference of Public		All-Russia Council of	
Figures	15	Teachers of Church	
Council of Landowners	7	Schools	1
Cossacks	22	Central Military-	
Academic Union	3	Industrial Committee	1
Radical Democratic Party	2	Central Bureau of All-	
All-Russia Society of Editors	2	Russia Council of	
League for Women's Equality	2	Engineers	1
Main Committee of the		Various National	
Women's Union	1	Minorities	5

TOTAL   156

(Socialist) Representation of National Minorities

Jews	4	Estonians	1
Muslims	4	Armenians	2
Ukrainians	2	Georgians	2

continued . . .

Belorussians	2	Soviet of Mountain	
Poles	2	Peoples	1
Lithuanians	2	Volga Basin	
Latvians	1	National Groups	1
?	1	Buriats	1
Soviet of National			
Socialist Party	1		

TOTAL   27

Representatives of All Groups Listed Above 550

After the Bolsheviks (53) walked out, there remained 497 members of the Soviet of the Republic, of which 314 belonged on the list of the "democratic organizations" and exactly half as many (156) belonged on the list of the "propertied elements." If, however, we recall the political position of the cooperatives and of the peasants, and of part of the Zemstvo groups and the economic organizations at the Democratic Conference, then we see that the majority held by the "revolutionary democracy" on all the most important issues of the day was far from certain. If one transfers the cooperatives and the peasant deputies, along with the Plekhanovites and the Popular Socialists, to the side of the non-socialist elements of the Soviet of the Republic (67 votes), one gets, instead of a two-thirds majority for the socialists, 247 delegates to 223. The votes of the Zemstvo group, of the economic organizations and the land committees (48) even gave to the "propertied elements" a majority, and that was true even if all the representatives of the nationalities sided with the socialists (226 socialist votes to 271 for the "propertied elements" and their allies). Of course, this breakdown of votes could occur only on common national issues. But it was precisely on such issues that the partisan struggle was concentrated at the moment. The position taken by the above-mentioned groups, from which one might expect moderation and freedom from subordination to the party discipline of the socialist parties, would now determine whether the Soviet of the Republic would render that support to the government which was a logical consequence of the very idea of a coalition regime, or whether, on the contrary, the Soviet of the Republic would deal this idea, and along with it the revolutionary government in general, the final *coup de grâce*.

When the members of the Soviet of the Republic gathered at their first meeting, an hour before its opening at 4 P.M. on October 7, many sceptics felt somewhat relieved. In this hall were gathered all the in-any-way prominent figures who had been thrust forward by the revolution. Many of them who had been rank novices at the beginning of the revolution now had lived through a series of difficult ordeals, which, to a certain

extent, had given them statesmanly experience. One involuntarily compared this group, appointed by the central committees of the parties and
organizations and almost entirely lacking the usual ballast of the large
meetings, with that for-the-moment mysterious assembly, the face of
the future "master of the Russian Land," which would meet in a month
and a half at the Tauride Palace as a result of the first experiment with
universal suffrage in the atmosphere of Russian ignorance and political
unpreparedness. The members of the Soviet of the Republic said to
each other looking from side to side: "It would be good if the Constituent Assembly were no worse than this!"

The members of the Soviet seated themselves on chairs of various
fashions in this order. On the extreme right were the commercial-industrialists; then, in the places of the "old guard" of the State Council,
sat the Party of Popular Liberty, which soon grew to 75 members.
Then, immediately adjacent, in the second third of the hall, were the
Popular Socialists, the Zemstvo group, the Mensheviks and Right
SRs. Next to V. D. Nabokov sat E. K. Breshkovskaia; behind her Vera
Figner.[1]   The extreme left wing of the hall remained almost empty
since the Bolshevik faction was absent. The meeting opened without
them. The Bolsheviks gathered at Smolny Monastery to decide the
formal pretext for their planned walkout. Indeed, the hall was half
empty, since many deputies had not yet arrived, and the general mood
was far from the usual festiveness of first meetings. Here were people
who were accustomed to dealing with each other; they met here accidentally and for a short period, as if they were meeting on the road.
Soon they would again disperse—and would encounter each other again
in the Tauride Palace. They sat down here just for a minute's breather.
In Russia it was so gloomy, and there remained little hope that even the
collective intelligence of revolutionary Russia, gathered here, could
succeed at last in finding the proper road. In a word, this was not the
place and not the time for phrases and empty speeches: the mood was
rather subdued and businesslike, and even the noisy assessors of Smolny here, in the midst of the quiet setting of the Supreme Court, face-to-
face with the "propertied elements," grew somewhat timid and quieted
down. A different ambience, different customs—and even different cos-
tumes . . . .

The introductory speeches by Kerensky and by the elected chairman of
the Soviet of the Republic, N. D. Avksentiev, were most appropriate to
the gravity of the moment and the seriousness of the situation. Past
failures as speakers had taught both men to be careful. On this occasion Kerensky spoke without impromptu digressions and almost without departure from the basic positions that had been approved by the

government. Avksentiev read his welcoming speech directly from a text. The themes of both speeches were almost identical: the common national tasks of the moment. Both the speakers considered these tasks to be the restoration of the fighting capacity of the army and the energetic struggle against the enemy, the introduction of order and the organization of the economic life of the nation, and the persistent struggle against anarchy. While subscribing in passing to the "idea" of "swiftly concluding a democratic peace," both Kerensky and Avksentiev concentrated their speeches on an apotheosis of the army and the navy. They both called for further struggle, which would give our Allies the possibility of "boldly counting on our collaboration and assistance," while the enemy would be forced "to count us among those people with whom there is no other way to talk except as one equal to another," and with whom it would be possible to conclude only "an honorable peace" along with "the great Allied nations," but whose will to the victory of right and justice "no matter what the ordeal, cannot be broken by force." Kerensky continued from time to time to make advances to the "revolutionary democracy," promising it, for example, that the government in the future, as in the past, "will not resort to measures which will be abhorrent to the idea of freedom, equality, and fraternity." Avksentiev's speech was in all respects sincere and honest, and it made no concessions to current revolutionary phraseology.

The tone and content of the speeches, however, were not appreciated by the entire auditorium. Much of the applause came from the right and the center. The entire hall applauded only the greetings that were extended to the army. The extreme left, the Bolsheviks and the Internationalists, sat in sullen silence and did not rise from their places even when the entire assembly arranged an ovation for the diplomatic representatives of the Allies.

Immediately after the speech of Avksentiev, Trotsky asked for the floor to make the Bolsheviks' first and last statement, which justified their formal break "with this government of popular treachery and with this Soviet [of the Republic]." According to the Bolsheviks' custom, the entire declaration was devoted to demagogic revelations. The Soviet of the Republic was a new piece of "stage setting," behind which "murderous work against the people" would be done. The Democratic Conference was supposed—this was its "official goal"—"to replace the irresponsible personal regime with a responsible government capable of ending the war and guaranteeing the convocation of the Constituent Assembly at the scheduled time. Meantime, behind the back of the Democratic Conference, by means of behind-the-scenes intrigues, Kerensky, the Kadets, and the leaders of the SRs and Mensheviks, had achieved the opposite results: the formation of a government in which and around

which Kornilovites—both avowed and secret—are playing a fatal role."
The "bourgeois classes" who were directing the policy of the Provisional Government had set themselves the goal of smashing the Constituent
Assembly. "The propertied classes are provoking a peasant uprising
and civil war." They "openly hold course toward the bony hand of fam-
ine [the expression of Riabushinsky[2] at the First Congress of Public
Figures in Moscow], which must strangle the revolution and the Constituent Assembly. No less criminal is foreign policy . . . . The idea of
surrendering the revolutionary capital to the German troops does not
arouse the bourgeois classes to action, but, on the contrary, it is accepted as a natural link of the general policy, which will make easier to
achieve their counter-revolutionary plans." "Instead of a public proposal of immediate peace over the heads of all the imperialist governments
and diplomatic chancelleries," in order "to make the waging of war a *de
facto* impossibility, the Provisional Government, on the order of the Kadet counter-revolutionaries and the Allied imperialists . . . has doomed
to a senseless death many hundreds of thousands of sailors and soldiers
and has prepared the surrender of Petrograd and the destruction of the revolution." "The leading parties of the Soviet are serving as voluntary
protectors of this policy." But "we, the Bolshevik faction of the Social
Democrats, have nothing in common with them and do not wish either
directly or indirectly to serve as protectors of them for a single day."
"In abandoning the Soviet [of the Republic], we are appealing to the
vigilance of workers, peasants, and soldiers of all Russia; . . . only the
people can save themselves, and we are appealing to the people: long
live an immediate, honorable democratic peace, all power to the Soviets, all land to the people, long live the Constituent Assembly."
Trotsky's speech was interrupted more than once by cries of dissatisfaction, and Avksentiev was forced more than once to ask the assembly
to hear the speaker out. But the interruptions and the cries from the audience were heard, unfortunately, only from the right and the center.
The left was a silent observer of this controversy, since it had not
resolved, even at this critical moment in its own destiny, openly to condemn the kind of tactics of which Trotsky's speech was a clear example.
   In walking out of the Mariinsky Palace, the Bolsheviks showed that
they did not recognize parliamentary forms of struggle, and that they
would continue the battle against the government and against the "leading parties" of the Soviet outside this hall, on the streets. They had
spoken and they had acted like people who sensed strength behind them,
who knew that tomorrow would belong to them. To this challenge those
who still had the power to change the course of events responded with an
ambiguous silence. And so the first day of the Soviet's session already

cast a ray of light on its expected fate. As one newspaper observed the next day, "When you compare the beginning and the end of the first day, you involuntarily conclude that the new Soviet of the Republic and the government that wishes to depend on its support will only be able to lead the nation out of the present situation of ever-increasing anarchy when the ministers show the same decisiveness and will to act as Comrade Trotsky, and when the Soviet of the Republic is the only Soviet expressing the will and political reason of the nation."

But, alas, the newspaper added, neither precondition existed. The government not only displayed none of that "persistence" in the struggle against anarchy that Kerensky had demanded of society in his speech, but continued to put up with the manifestations of anarchy; and this was true, by the way, even in Kerensky's own speech. Words continued to be divorced from deeds, and "a government in words alone is no government at all."

Several days later (on October 14) at the congress of the Party of Popular Liberty, Minister of State Charities N. M. Kishkin, with complete candor, gave exactly the same characterization of the government's mood and lucidly pointed to the basic reason why "daring" did not translate into "deeds." Kishkin said: "The basic problem is that the revolutionary government has no revolutionary daring. The second problem is the omnipotence of words, which cover everything in a thick layer. And the third problem is that on the banner which now waves above the nation is written 'Immunity from Punishment.'" How should one struggle against this triple evil? Did the government have the will and the organization for this? Kishkin answered: "The observations made by us after a short presence on the cabinet give me reason to say that the government's weakness is to a considerable extent the product of self-hypnosis." Kishkin would personally appeal to the government to liberate itself from this hypnosis; he would call for "daring." But the speaker added, "Here is the sad thing: within the government itself one can still come to an understanding—and this was so difficult, almost impossible, during the former coalition governments. *But there is no assurance that the things one agrees on will be put into action.* And so the new task is to take care that action follows agreement."

Kishkin's psychological characterization harmonized completely with our previous description. Even given the large degree of unanimity of the ministers, it was extremely difficult to push the head of the government onto the path of daring. During the first days of the new cabinet Kerensky left Petrograd for Stavka and placed the responsibility for running the government on his assistant; Kerensky stayed at Stavka until early October. Having just opened the Soviet of the Republic, he dreamed up a new trip—to Stavka and from thence to the Volga and elsewhere around Russia. Only the very energetic urgings of A. I. Konovalov had forced A. F. Kerensky to put off his decision to make a long trip and to confine his travels to Stavka, to which he departed on October 14. But even while he was in Petrograd, he showed the same fatal passivity, which perhaps resulted from his recognition of the hopelessness of the situation but which, in any case, ultimately reinforced that hopelessness.

The Soviet of the Republic had to turn its attention to discussion of the basic problems, military and international, and the fruits of this discussion would show its worth.

When the Soviet took up the problem of the fighting capacity of the army, the situation was more serious than ever before. For the first time since the beginning of the war one sensed that there was a real possibility that the enemy might draw near to the capital by taking the shortest route—the coast of the Gulf of Finland. In late September the enemy landed successfully on the islands of Ezel and Dago. In the first days of October they penetrated into the Gulf of Riga and tried to cut off the egress of our flotilla to the Gulf of Finland, having first obstructed from the north the strait between Moon Island and the coast of Estonia. The navy was compelled to depart, having lost the destroyer *"Grom"* and the old ship-of-the-line *"Slava."* Then the Germans opened a siege on the Verder Peninsula against Moon Island in Estonia itself: they fortified themselves thus on both sides of the Moon Sound, and threatened to move toward Gaspal and Revel. From this point on large German zeppelins could move to the outskirts of Petrograd.

Despite all the conferences of the Supreme Commander and the War Minister with the new chief of staff (Dukhonin)[3] at Stavka and in the capital about ways of raising the fighting capacity of the army, the military situation did not improve. It was easy to dismiss the army high command, but it proved impossible to inculcate "revolutionary discipline" into the army by the methods of Verkhovsky and Kerensky. Reports from military commissars and the staff to the War Ministry continued to paint a picture of complete anarchy and destruction. Here and there soldiers refused to go to the front; they preferred to devote themselves to commercial operations in the cities, and they forcibly seized passenger trains and grain illegally purchased from the peasantry. Units at the front demanded an end to the war no matter what the cost, even by means of a disgraceful—or as the soldiers' delegation put it to the Executive Committee of the Soviet of Workers' and Soldiers' Deputies—an "obscene" peace. They demanded their own transfer from the front to the rear, and their replacement by reserve units. The disorganization of transport, which had begun to manifest itself in the shortage of food supplies and of equipment for the army, intensified the nervous irritation among the troops. The reserve units pouring into the front

brought with them the dissolute spirit of the capital and the ready slogans of class struggle.

While certain units at the front, having preserved their discipline, refused
to accept such reserves and asked that no more be sent, other units, on
the contrary, succumbed to the influence of the reservists, and, by and
by, began to adopt Bolshevik resolutions. From October 1 to 9 the
War Minister counted among the reserve units of the army, which were
stationed all over the country, 16 pogroms, 8 drunken pogroms, 24 unauthorized demonstrations, 16 cases of the application of armed force to
suppress anarchistic outbursts. This breakdown of discipline had an effect on the most recent military operations. Commissar Vishnevsky,
who fell into captivity on Moon Island but who later managed to
escape, recounted in Tsentroflot that complete disorganization and confusion reigned on the islands of Moon and Ezel during the enemy's attack.
Many soldiers refused to go into battle, and said that they preferred to be
shot by their own comrades. The level of the enemy's information
about all the details of our defense was striking. On one of the downed
German airplanes was found a map with the exact disposition of all our
officers quarters and batteries. A large part of the garrison fled in panic.
There were cases where regiments went to surrender themselves while
singing songs. Part of the command of the Verensky artillery batteries
(on the southern tip of Ezel), according to Verderevsky's statement in
the Soviet of the Republic, "disgraced themselves forever." In the Executive Committee of the Soviet of Workers' and Soldiers' Deputies Verderevsky gave a more detailed account of this incident: at the approach
of the enemy, the gun crew and the commanders of several shore batteries abandoned their posts and ran; in order to stop this flight, the gun
crews of other batteries turned their artillery against the fleeing
men—and at the decisive moment the entrance into the Gulf of Riga
was completely undefended.

How all this was reflected in the consciousness of the army, which
had been diverted from its task by internal and enemy agitation, can be
seen from a telegram sent to Tsentroflot by the Soviet of Soldiers' Deputies of XII Army. Face-to-face with the enemy, this army understood
that "there is no immediate way out of the war, that Wilhelm's troops
are attacking us, and that, without losing a minute, we must defend ourselves." But, "going to our deaths," we "have a right to demand"—and
they did demand—the implementation "of the people's most cherished
demands in the revolutionary program *within the nation*,"—that is: the
transfer of land to the land committees; the immediate attainment of a
democratic peace; and only after this the "immediate suppression of the
pogromist movement in the nation;" the supply of the army with bread
and fodder, warm clothes and boots; and to accomplish this, the struggle

against the "criminals" who were slowing down the work of transport and supply; and, finally, the immediate dispatch into the army of the other "criminals," "the idle, satisfied, carousing soldiers of the reserve units," but only on the condition that the reserves be "trained reinforcements." "We have no need of base cowards, of the pitiful rabble which the home front bestows on us." But the home front gave what it had in hand. A sick army, a sick home front; this is a vicious circle, as General Alexeev said in response in the Soviet of the Republic.

We shall now see that the soldiers' demands, forwarded through Tsentroflot, were law for the authorities. The program of XII Army was the program of the public speeches of Verkhovsky and Verderevsky. Whatever the ministers might have been thinking and however they might have understood matters—and they could not but think as military specialists, and they could not fail to see the root of the problem—was all the same. They would say in public what was demanded of them. But did the Soviet of the Republic really not hear the voices of independent people and of the parties whose hands were not tied by the orders of the "democratic organizations"? Was that member of the Soviet of the Republic really correct when he responded to a remark about the opponents of a "democratic" army structure with this exclamation from his seat: "There are no such people here!"

Of course, there were such people there. The Party of Popular Liberty, having discussed this question on October 9, decided that nothing had changed since it had endorsed a plan for the revitalization of the army, a plan that had been labelled as "Kornilovite," but which was shared by the entire former high command, headed by General Alexeev. The Party of Popular Liberty reasserted its belief that even now the reestablishment of the fighting capacity of the army was possible only under the condition that disciplinary authority be returned to the military commanders and that the activity of the "democratic" army organizations be limited to economic and educational functions. At the same time in Moscow there was a meeting of the Second Congress of Public Figures, which represented, in addition to the Kadets, the more rightist elements of Russian society and of the Soviet of the Republic. This congress heard speeches by two former supreme commanders of the army, A. A. Brusilov and N. V. Ruzsky,[4] who both bitterly lamented the destructive consequences of the introduction of politics into the army. Moreover, General Zaionchkovsky, the former commander of the army on the Romanian Front, categorically denied that Verkhovsky's program had been endorsed by any of the military authorities, whether Russian or foreign. The naval officer S. V. Lukomsky refuted Verkhovsky's assertion that discipline, based on the new principles, could yield a victory in the field.

After this the congress moved on October 14 to adopt a very detailed resolution on military issues that had been introduced by the military group. The resolution demanded that the army stand "outside parties and partisan influences," so that appointments to military posts would depend on "military and service abilities," and not on the results of "political oversight and inquiries presently being conducted by military commissars and organizations;" that lists of officers "who have been dismissed from duty under the influence of irresponsible and unauthorized organizations" be reexamined; that the power to give out awards and to administer discipline be restored to commanders of all ranks, providing, of course, there be a guarantee against commanders exceeding their authority; "that the jurisdiction of army committees be limited exclusively to cultural-educational, economic and supply questions, with their decisions being subject to the approval of the commander and with the commander having the right to dismiss the members of a given committee in case it should exceed its rights;" finally, that "propagating subversive and anti-national ideas, as well as doctrines that deny the need for the existence of the army and of military discipline," not be permitted in the army and be subject to prosecution.

In the Soviet of the Republic all these concrete solutions would inevitably run against the tendency to soften the sharp corners, and to find grounds for conciliatory formulas capable of bringing closer together differing opinions, even those that by their very nature were irreconcilable. This tendency was natural among people who had just won a brilliant victory over the "revolutionary democracy." After all, it was only by means of agreement that they had forced the leaders of the "democracy" to set aside resolutions that had been formally adopted; that they had realized, despite the "democracy," a coalition with the "bourgeoisie" and with the "Kadets;" and that they had completed their victory by publishing a compromise declaration that replaced the "democratic" platform of August 14 with the creation, in the Soviet of the Republic, of an *advisory* agency whose membership was *appointed* by the government. Within the Party of Popular Liberty this conciliatory tendency was represented by V. D. Nabokov and M. S. Adzhemov, and later by M. M. Vinaver[5] who had returned after a respite from party activism. We should recall that it was precisely the military and international sections in the declaration of the new coalition that made the largest and most dangerous concessions to the "revolutionary democracy," and that it was with these two most important sections that the work of the Soviet of the Republic began. The Party of Popular Liberty asked the recently returned A. I. Shingarev, who had a special acquaintance with defense issues from the Fourth Duma commission which he had chaired, and also M. S. Adzhemov, who was a participant in the talks that led to the third coalition and was the author of a project for the creation of a Soviet of the Republic that served as the basis of the plan that was eventually confirmed by the government, to speak in the Soviet of the Republic on the military question.

On October 10 the Soviet of the Republic opened its debate on the issue of restoring the fighting capacity of the army. Superficially the atmosphere in the hall of the Mariinsky Palace was dull and businesslike. The members gathered slowly, and the session began after such a long delay that the chairman, Avksentiev, was forced to direct to the members a request unusual for Russian representative bodies—that they arrive on time "for at the current difficult juncture every minute is important." Everyone seemed to sense that political life was already bypassing this auditorium, and that the most important decisions were being made outside its walls. One could also sense this in the statements of the War and Navy Ministers, who too obviously concerned themselves in their speeches not with what needed to be done under the circumstances, but with the probable reactions to their speeches by members of the "democratic organizations," to which the ministers felt responsible.

The War Minister, Verkhovsky, began by denying the existence of the very problem that needed to be investigated. "People who say that the Russian army does not exist do not understand what they are saying. The Germans have committed 130 divisions on our front—that is how they evaluate the Russian army . . . . One is forced to listen to nonsensical speeches about how, with the beginning of the cold season, the army supposedly will leave the trenches and not fulfill its duty. This is pure nonsense," said Verkhovsky to applause from the left. In general, he was the first minister to win applause not from the "right and a section of the center," but from the "left and a section of the center." And there was good reason for that. "The government's military program, which I presented at the Democratic Conference three weeks ago," the minister claimed, "is being implemented in the most energetic fashion. All those in the high command who took part in one way or another in the Kornilov movement have been dismissed from their posts. Their places have been taken by others who understand the current circumstances." Alas, several sentences later the War Minister was forced to add: "Even under the old regime there were people who followed the prevailing winds, and now, under the new regime, there have appeared generals—and even generals of the highest ranks—who definitely have understood what direction the wind is blowing and how they must behave in consequence." An opposition speaker later observed that "this also can be applied to certain people who are occupying the benches of the Provisional Government."

In any case, one could certainly apply this comment to Verkhovsky's speech. The War Minister could not entirely ignore such negative developments as "the anarchistic movement at the front and in the reserves, and the baneful influence of reinforcements, which come to the front full of ill-trained and undisciplined reserves, in complete disarray." But Verkhovsky very cleverly inserted this admission between a reminder about the "tragic Kornilov affair," "as a result" of which there had occurred one or another "incalculable harm," and the frank statement: "One of the reasons for this [disorder in the army] is a misunderstanding by the troops about the goals of the war. The task of the current government and of the Soviet of the Republic is to make clear and concrete to every man that we are not fighting for the sake of territorial acquisitions, ours or anyone else's." Verkhovsky also very skillfully passed off even the "creation of Ukrainian, Estonian, Georgian, Tatar and other units" as a measure that "will raise the fighting capacity of the army," . . . for this was a "gradual transition to a territorial system of supplying the troops." The equipping of the army was poor, but that was because "at the beginning of the revolution people had thought that one could destroy and rebuild everything in the army at once" . . . . and "they had replaced the quartermaster service with a series of organizations" whose "reduction" the minister could discuss and demand . . . quite without danger. These were not "democratic" organizations, but Zemstvo and municipal organizations which had fallen into the soldiers' disfavor as agencies that assisted in keeping troops in the reserves rather than sending them to the front lines.

Finally, there was "the most important question," the question of discipline. Was it possible to restore order "through the use of force by one group against another" or "by involving a punitive force from the outside," "by pacification and subjugation?" the minister asked. And he answered, continuing his juggling of realism and political intrigue: after all, "There is only one force standing outside that can pacify and subjugate: that is the force of German bayonets." And then, instead of rejecting with disgust this solitary "external force," the minister was not above trying to use it to frighten his audience. "If we do not find within ourselves the strength and capacity to restore order within the nation, then German bayonets will restore order for us." Later the purpose of this threat became clear. Heretofore order was in the process of being restored by military organizations, but in order *to apply armed force* with the goal of forcing the submission of people *within the nation*, it would be necessary "for the Soviet of the Republic *to say that it wanted this to be done.*"

This unexpected appeal was directed to the right majority. The left was certain that this was a trap and a provocation in its own style, and therefore from the left they screamed: "Correct!" Yet, by this vague phrase the minister, without losing the confidence of the left, in fact suggested to the right his candidacy for the post of military dictator and successor to Kornilov. So that there would be no misunderstanding, he even returned to this theme at the end of his speech. "I ask the Soviet of the Republic directly and specifically whether it finds pleasing the continuation in the nation of pogroms, drunken excesses, demonstrations and so on? Or would it prefer, in cases when an anarchical crowd comes out onto the streets, to use force against the crowd? . . . Kornilov also tried to use his authority to restore order. Kornilov's attempt failed and could not help but fail. But to allow the continuation of anarchy, such as we currently face, is a crime against the state, and against the entire nation. Therefore, let the representatives of the entire Russian people say that they think it necessary to restore order for the sake of the motherland."

Evidently, this young man did not wish to end his meteoric career as War Minister, and he was looking for support to rise higher. But he was in too much of a hurry, and therefore he gave himself away. He had all the following: a slender figure that had not become portly; a voice that broke into a falsetto at the most emotional points; turns of speech that were too bold, risky, not weighed, that jumped out quite unexpectedly for the orator himself; and, finally, the ideal position for making confidential proposals. All this smacked of something incomplete and immature. Obviously, Verkhovsky did not lack for courage and ambition; nor was he lacking clarity of vision. But a lack of discrimination in his choice of means and a lack of principle in the overly glib argumentation were so obvious that he could not but "fail" himself. Perhaps before the homogeneous audience of the Executive Committee his cleverness might have been taken for seriousness and strength of conviction. Here, in this heterogeneous and demanding auditorium, where he was forced to argue simultaneously on two fronts, the examination confronting him proved too difficult.

The Navy Minister, Verderevsky, spoke more simply and directly. He also, in the words of old Horace, "saw and approved the better path, but took the worse one." He concealed this contradiction by choosing more rewarding themes, by avoiding the more difficult ones, and, in the most crucial places, by covering himself with the mantle of the democratic agencies. In all the fleets the situation was not bad. If in the Baltic Fleet, at a moment when it was being forced to carry out the difficult task of defense, the situation was far from ideal, if the productivity of factories had declined sharply, if the attitude of workers toward their responsibilities was negative, then, in the first place, "the workers and their organizations are not solely to blame;" the factories did not have enough coal and metal. Second, the appearance of German forces near our shores would make clear to the working masses and their organizations that efforts to raise the fighting capacity of the fleet [by increasing the supply] of war materiel depended on them, and that each hour of dilatoriness in this work was dangerous. As far as the central issue was concerned, the personnel of the fleet, Verderevsky related how smoothly things went from the very beginning of the revolution in Revel, where "there was not a single excess." In Helsingfors things had turned out differently; but here the fault lay "with the habit of those traditional figures, who spent their entire military career under the old regime, of hiding the truth from the masses." "Commissars from Helsingfors testify that there are no counter-revolutionary tendencies there." At the bottom of the chasm between sailors and officers was only "bloodshed for no reason." The minister was "profoundly convinced" that those guilty of shedding this blood and deserving punishment "will fall under the onus of accusations from their own peers." Moreover, he placed hopes on the "conclusions that will be drawn from the recent naval operation" which testified to "the absence of discipline." The penetration of these conclusions into the consciousness "of the mass of sailors" would be the "only way to reestablish normal relations in the fleet." For those who understood matters, Verderevsky's statement meant that there was no way to restore discipline and the situation was hopeless. But . . . the Navy Minister "spoke yesterday with representatives of the sailors," and when he mentioned that even in the American army attention was paid to neatness of dress and promptness in saluting and that discipline there "is accepted by everyone consciously and voluntarily," then "this word 'voluntarily' caused a great disturbance" amongst his collocutors.

"They told me that, of course, true discipline should be voluntary: this is really the only way." This was, of course, not the conclusion to which the minister wished to lead them. But he readily bowed to the circumstances and presented this conclusion about "voluntary discipline" as the voice of the people from the rostrum of the Soviet of the Republic. Small caveats—for example, that "individual violations of discipline and order, of course, cannot pass without punishment, even under a system of voluntary discipline," or that "a subordinate has no right to judge his superior" "in view of the unusual circumstances in which the fleet finds itself," and that therefore "officers will be unconditionally subordinate only to the personal authority of their superior"—these and other passing observations were essentially just details and trivia: they

were introduced into draft legislation, as were Verkhovsky's proposed
limitation of disciplinary trials among the troops to a forty-eight-hour
period and his establishment of the peculiar "punishment regiments."
Mostly the minister calculated that "by means of [his] personal exertions on the spot, in Helsingfors," he would "elicit a response in broad
circles, and sailors will learn to adopt a rational, honorable, intelligent
attitude toward their duty."

After all these verbal contrivances and attempts to console, after all
the conventional statements of official optimism and hypocrisy made
by the leaders of the army and navy who were so well loved by the "revolutionary democracy," the direct and honest speech of the former supreme commander, General Alexeev, had an especially powerful impact.
Alexeev neither concealed nor understated the problem; he called a spade
a spade, yet he did not succumb to pessimism and despair. And even
now it was not too late, if they wanted honestly to examine the situation and to show genuine decisiveness: that was the sense of his
speech. The whole problem was that we had convinced ourselves that
we could not continue the war and that we needed peace whatever the
cost. But General Alexeev asked the audience to think seriously about
whether peace was possible. The old leader prophetically asserted that
"a dispassionate assessment of the situation will show that the immediate conclusion of a peace will mean disaster for Russia, its physical disintegration, the inevitable fragmentation of its territory, and the destruction of the work of all the generations of the preceding three centuries.
But even a peace purchased at such a great price will not improve our
economic situation, will not revitalize our disorganized economy, and,
this is the main thing, will not give us bread or coal, and cannot long
ease the burdens of our personal existence. After such a peace we will
be the complete slaves and tributaries of stronger peoples, and, ultimately, a swift and immediate peace will destroy Russia as a state, will remove Russia from the concert of great powers, and will condemn the remainder of our people both in a spiritual and in an economic sense."

But did this mean that the situation was hopeless? After all, Germany was also exhausted, although it sustained itself "by virtue of its
national spirit, national discipline and its system." "Russia can, if it
wishes, survive the days of its weakness; it will receive help from its
Allies; it is only necessary to resurrect the national spirit." But in order
to do that, it was necessary above all to stop flattering the people. It
was necessary, on the contrary, "boldly and publicly to look reality in
the eye." Yes, the army was ill, seriously ill. "The masses, who have
tasted the sweetness of disobedience and of the non-fulfillment of operative orders, of complete idleness, who have wallowed in the desire for

an immediate peace as if this peace would arrive of its own accord, masses who, practically to a man, desire only to save their own lives—[have created] a dangerous situation." It did not make sense "to console ourselves on the grounds that we have at the front a reliable means to defend the motherland." The calculation that a "lack of discipline will be overcome by enthusiasm and by a rush forward"—the calculation on which the attack of June 18 was based—was mistaken. "There was no enthusiasm and no rush forward." Of course, Alexeev admitted, the *entire army* would not leave the trenches and return home; but one could not fail to recognize that among the masses the concept of honor, duty, and of the most elementary human justice was somnolent. That is why, in the most recent battles, the army "did not show that perserverence of which it was always capable, even in the difficult years 1915 and 1916." People say: "Make the homefront healthy, and the army will be resurrected." "But will it be possible to restore order on the homefront without stable armed forces, with some troops dependent on local agencies, and without the resolve in case of necessity to use this force? . . . Consequently, the army cannot wait to be saved by a revitalized homefront; the army itself must work energetically and decisively to save itself." General Alexeev indicated that the purpose of such work should be the implementation of the program discussed more than once since June but never put into action. Alexeev wanted to hear echoes of that program even in the statements of the new War Minister. But one could not tell from Verkhovsky's promises about future legislation what the content of these future laws would be, especially given the prevailing atmosphere.

Substantively speaking, these three addresses on defense exhausted the subject. After that there was only "politics." The entire basis of the Internationalist Martov's speech amounted to a distorted interpretation of Alexeev's words that you cannot cure the homefront with an unhealthy army. From this Martov drew the convenient conclusion that Alexeev wanted the fighting capacity of the army to be restored in order "to suppress popular movements." In its "class interests" the bourgeoisie opposed even the introduction of a "democratic structure" into the army, although "every political actor should have understood in the February days that there could be no political revolution that did not shatter the army's organization in general and [that] its old organization" would have to be replaced by a new "organization, permeated by a contrary principle." Thus, the bourgeoisie and tsarism were to blame for the disorganization of the army, for the disorganization of the army had begun under tsarism. Moreover,—and here was the heart of the argument—"Russian society could not have carried out a revolution, if from the very beginning the soldier masses had not risen against the officer corps, which at that time favored tsarism." The formula of the revolutionary transition suggested by Martov proposed to recognize the necessity for a real purge of the officer corps, for granting to army organizations the contested right to dismiss and to certify the character of officers, for granting to the central agency of the "revolutionary democracy" control over the action of commissars, for the aboliton of capital punishment and for the liberation of all prisoners who had violated discipline "for ideological reasons," for the immediate proposal to all belligerents of a general peace and the immediate conclusion of a cease-fire on all fronts.

After Martov's speech Kerensky had the opportunity to occupy a favorable position between the two extremes. And he took advantage of this opportunity. He defended common sense against Martov and the "honor of the Russian army". . . against Alexeev. He said that the army would not defend the class interests of the bourgeoisie, nor the partisan desires of internationalism. The government had always struggled against the tyranny of the minority over the majority, whether the case in question was the uprising of August 27 or of July 3-5, and whether this minority was called Kornilovite or Bolshevik. The failure of the attack of June 18 was not caused by a mistaken calculation of the army's enthusiasm, for there was enthusiasm present; rather blame lay with "unconscious fanatics along with a small group of conscious traitors to the fatherland," who "destroyed the fruits of the colossal, concerted labor of the entire Russian democracy." Martov's statement that the success of the revolution could be explained by the soldiers' uprising against the officer corps—a statement that was true with respect to the extremist tendencies of the revolution—gave Kerensky the opportunity to move his carefully balanced speech somewhat to the right and to render justice to the Russian officer corps. "The brilliant and rapid completion of the struggle against the old regime and the bloodless defeat of the dynasty within a few days was the result of the fact that, in general, with a few exceptions, the old regime did not find suppport among the officer corps . . . . The army as a whole, both its officer corps and its enlisted men, went once and for all over to the side of the people and of service to the democratic state." But, of course, this praise did not apply to the 10,000 retired officers about whom Alexeev had spoken as a "precious resource, which is scorned only because [these retired officers] are regarded as proponents of the old regime," although "they are in heart and mind dedicated sons of their country." Kerensky said that everyone who opposed "public" organization in the army "not out of misunderstanding, but out of an incapacity to understand and because of ill will, must be decisively swept aside." Here Kerensky stressed that he agreed with Verkhovsky, with whom Martov had agreed. "Not one iota has been conceded to the program of the so-called Kornilovshchina,"—with the exception of what was done in the first period under the influence of general fear, "at the moment of the great pogroms in Galicia, on the demand not only of the officer corps, but also of the local army organizations" (the creation of military-revolutionary courts and the reinstitution of the death penalty). That even in Verkhovsky's program there were further concessions to the "Kornilovshchina," which concessions had won Alexeev's approval—about that Kerensky, of course, said not a word.

Kerensky's speech was successful among all parties, with the exception of the Menshevik Internationalists. After the Bolsheviks walked out of the preceding session, this small group of 25 members felt itself to be in the Bolsheviks' position. The Menshevik Internationalists decided publicly to justify themselves for not having walked out with the Bolsheviks, but for having stayed in the Soviet of the Republic. Before the close of the session this Menshevik splinter group read its declaration which in all respects corresponded with the Bolshevik statement. Here was the same "sabotage" of the Kornilovites, and the "capitulation of the entire organized democracy," and the "half-breed, legally-advisory Pre-Parliament," to which "a significant part of the working class, having become disturbed by too much marching in place, turned its back." But above all it was announced that the Menshevik Internationalists "are remaining in the Soviet, because they see in it an arena of class struggle," and they would use the tribune to unmask "the counter-revolutionary character of the coalition" and to await the time when "the temporary lull of the revolution . . . will inevitably give way to a new upheaval."

What was the result of the first session which was devoted to questions of defense? Was there, aside from Kerensky's diplomacy and stylistic posing, common ground on which all parties could meet? The future work of the commission would reveal concealed disagreements. But it was already clear from the general debates that between the various sections of the assembly there were profound differences—the same ones as before, and that new military defeats and the enemy's threats at the front could not pierce the armour plating of revolutionary doctrinairism. The second session on October 12 uncovered still more sharply the divergence of these groups than even the general debate. The chairman of the Left SRs, Shteinberg-Karelin[6] stated frankly: "The basic tragedy of the revolution is that, having commenced under common slogans, its defenders soon split into various factions. If the revolution was necessary to the propertied elements in order to clear the road for their military successes, for the democracy it was the first step toward ending the war. And since these goals were diametrically opposed, there was no way of bringing about unity." "Given such circumstances it is clear that conversations about defense are fruitless, for we have different points of view."

What was worse, the Menshevik-Defensist, Goldman-Liber,[7] also had a "different point of view." He dedicated his whole speech to strident attacks against the "Kadets," who "for years permitted what is now being denigrated," who wished "to fulfill duties imposed by the old regime," and demanded war "to a victorious conclusion," instead of "telling the army that the Russian army will not *wage a defensive war in order to assist our Allies' attack.*" The formulas of the Menshevik-Defensists read by Liber enumerated the "deep roots" of the diminution in the army's capacity to fight: the prolongation of the war and economic disorganization, the soldiers' lack of trust in the officer corps, the excesses of soldiers "who are being led by politically immature elements and anarchistic organizations." There followed a list of positive demands: to foster in the army a clear understanding of the war's aims in harmony with a foreign policy "that strives by all means toward the rapid attainment of a universal democratic peace;" to guarantee the successful supply of the army through an energetic economic policy "that subordinates the interests of private groups to common national principles;" to raise the level of organization and of discipline in the army "through the concerted actions of the officer corps, the commissars, and the soldiers' organizations;" to abolish the death penalty, "which has not justified itself from the perspective of restoring military discipline;" and to fight mercilessly against counter-revolution, against vigilante justice, against violence and pogroms. Only the last words of the resolution—"without an energetic and strengthened defense the rapid conclusion of a peace is impossible"—were supposed to indicate that the speaker and his party understood much more than they dared to say to the faces of their critics from the left. Only N. G. Chaikovsky, speaking on behalf of the Trudovik-Popular Socialist group, had enough courage to take Shteinberg-Karelin's set of options (war or immediate socialist reforms) and to choose the first option, war. "I have said since the very beginning of the war," Chaikovsky stated, "that the implementation of social-economic reforms in their full measure during wartime is a crime, and we are committing this crime." After a rude interruption from the left, the seventy-year-old Chaikovsky, one of the patriarchs of Russian socialism, had the right to respond proudly: "Let those who do not believe me demonstrate by their actions that they are correct."

The only voices from the ranks of the other socialist groups who ventured publicly and consistently to associate themselves with this voice of experience and common sense were the voices of two women socialists—one of whom, E. D. Kuskova, spoke in the name of the cooperatives, and the other, L. B. Axelrod-Ortodox, spoke on behalf of the group *Edinstvo*. Both speeches had the kind of impact that is always generated by a true and bold word in a milieu accustomed to conventional hypocrisy. The impression was all the stronger because it was the result of the debut of women in Russian representative institutions. Of course, the women delegates did not speak as experts on the military questions. But both spoke about the elementary preconditions without which there can be no order and no defense. Kuskova demanded of the government not words, but deeds: "Those who have not been instructed by everything that we have said cannot be instructed by words." She "did not ask, she implored" the Pre-Parliament to leave aside declarations, to take into account "the lack of consciousness and the lack of organization of the masses," who "are utterly weary of what we are doing, we their intellectual leaders," to put away "the pupil's notebooks of public activity" and "to find those points of unity, which would surely guarantee the defense of the nation and [the survival] of the state which is now plunged into chaos." She concluded with an appeal that the Pre-Parliament "fashion an exclusively defensive alliance for the motherland's defense."

This was a very astute way of posing the question of the nation's fundamental task, and Kuskova's appeal was also shrewd: "If we have these points of contact, let us show them in the next days and hours." The very least that needed to be done was to unite if not the entire Pre-Parliament, which was obviously impossible, then at least the majority of the Pre-Parliament, on a common formula of transition. The Party of Popular Liberty took the initiative in the field by drafting its own formula and conveying the draft to the cooperatives. Since the cooperatives were the natural center in this assembly, the Party of Popular Liberty conceded the initiative of introducing the common formula to them. The formula turned out to be acceptable to the cooperatives. But when they entered into negotiations with more leftist groups, they discovered that it was necessary to make changes and additions, to strike out something here and to go farther there. The negotiations dragged on. There was no common draft of a formula, and while waiting for the groups to reach an agreement it was impossible to halt debate. Thus, another session, that of October 13, was devoted to speeches and to discussion of the question of Petrograd's evacuation. Apropos the evacuation Kerensky protested against the accusations that were so often repeated in these days of Bolshevik demagoguery—that the government wanted to surrender Petrograd to the Germans, and that it wanted to "escape to Moscow." Kerensky simply removed this question from the agenda; he said that "since the time when the government first discussed this issue internally, the situation has changed significantly for the better, and at present the government does not think it necessary to insist on a discussion of the evacuation of Petrograd as an immediate measure."

During the interval between sessions of the Soviet of the Republic the All-Russia Congress of the Party of Popular Liberty met in Moscow, on October 14 and 15. Its debates were closely concerned with the issue of the political role of the Pre-Parliament. As was indicated earlier, opinions in the party were divergent. V. D. Nabokov, M. S. Adzhemov and M. M. Vinaver thought essential the further use of the tactic of conciliation, which had led to the creation, with the active participation of Nabokov and Adzhemov, of the third coalition and of the Soviet of the Republic. By means of negotiations and concessions to the more leftist groups they were hoping to create in the Soviet of the Republic a "healthy majority supporting the principle of the state." They viewed conciliation in the Pre-Parliament as the first step toward elections to the Constituent Assembly. On the contrary, P. N. Miliukov and A. I. Shingarev, who associated himself with Miliukov in this matter, argued that there were no healthy elements with which to build a stable majority in the Soviet of the Republic, for even the moderate socialist parties would not risk publicly entering an agreement with the "propertied elements" and would not renounce the ideology and phraseology that would make them victims of the extremist leftist elements.[8] If they were not looking for support from the "propertied elements," that was because they had been separated from their social and political base at an auction where the extreme left kept raising the price. Under these circumstances they were impotent allies, and as a result were useless, and there was no reason to sacrifice for this dubious and unreliable alliance the clarity of the Kadet program, which was being accepted gradually by broader circles of the public. The Pre-Parliament should be seen not as an arena for agreement, which probably would not occur, but as a means for further agitation before the elections to the Constituent Assembly. The elections required not agreement, but struggle. The elections were our last chance, for "if the composition of the Constituent Assembly were the same as the Soviet, then this would be disaster for Russia. Now there is a process of disillusionment with the slogans of the extreme leftist parties, and we must hasten this process." This would be possible only if we posed quite concretely all the basic issues of state.

On this occasion a majority of the central committee and the party faction in the Soviet were in favor of conciliation. But the overwhelming majority of the congress favored the tactics of P. N. Miliukov and was prepared to go even further than he. M. S. Adzhemov's passionate and sharp attack was met by just as sharp a rebuff from P. I. Novgorodtsev.[9] P. N. Miliukov asked the congress not to exacerbate the disagreements and to adopt a compromise formula in the expectation that the next few days would justify in fact one or another of the contending views. In the formula that was adopted, the "effort to form in the Soviet a guiding center of political thought, uniting healthy political elements, giving the Provisional Government the opportunity to rely on them, and leading the government on the path of undeviating completion of the immediate political tasks," was accepted as the "immediate goal of the party in the Soviet [of the Republic]." But, in addition, it was stated categorically that this goal should not lead to the sacrifice of another goal—the preservation of continuity with the party's preceding activity during the revolution—activity whose purpose was to "inculcate into the consciousness of the masses a firm and concrete view of the way to save the motherland." Long ago the party had drafted for this purpose a minimal national program "which was not contested anywhere, except in Russia," but which had achieved recognition here by a whole series "of heterogeneous and ever more numerous public groups."

The next sessions of the Soviet of the Republic justified all P. N. Miliukov's fears. The two days before the session of October 16 were spent in the search for a common formula. To the efforts of the cooperatives to create a right majority with the Constitutional Democrats, the Social Democrats counterposed their own attempt to create a new majority with the SRs. But this effort also came to nothing. The session of October 16 also had to be devoted to a continuation of debate. After the over-long interval between sessions, it was decided, while awaiting the results [of the negotiations], to give the floor to M. I. Tereshchenko who spoke about foreign policy. Finally, the session of October 18 opened, and there was still no common formula. The matter would have to be resolved by the uncertain means of voting. Before the vote, on behalf of the united group of the cooperatives, of the Popular Socialists, of *Edinstvo,* of the Peasant Union, of the Party of Poular Liberty, of the Radical Democrats, of the Cossacks, of the commercial-industrial and several other national groups, N. V. Chaikovsky presented in public a proposal for a common formula. Everything that was in any way controversial and concrete had been stricken from this formula. The attitude of the Soviet toward the revitalization of the army, that is, the choice between Alexeev and Verkhovsky, was left open "until the government and commissions of the Pre-Parliament present measures worked out in detail." However, the formula did say that the goals "of broad socialist reforms and of the guarantee of land to the peasantry must be subordinated to a more immediate goal—the repulsing of the enemy and the defense of the integrity and independence of the motherland." It stated that "the nation's forces cannot be considered exhausted" and that it was necessary only "to introduce into the nation and the army a democratic order" in order to eliminate the disorganization of economic life. In the field of military regulations the formula demanded only the definition of precise rights and responsibilities for the committees and commissars, in order "by this means to bring to an end the further usurpation of state authority by unauthorized groups and individuals." The formula also asked for an energetic struggle against arbitrary rule [samoupravstvo], and for the subordination of the interests of all classes to the common national tasks. Of the army and the navy the resolution asked that, "while cooperating with the government, they take measures to restore their own faltering strength." All citizens were enjoined to "tireless work, self-restraint, and self-sacrifice."

This compromise formula, which declined to respond to the fundamental question facing the Soviet of the Republic, satisfied neither the right nor the left. P. B. Struve, speaking on behalf of the Congress of Public Figures, expressed reservations, and the Cossack Anisimov was also unhappy "with the general phrases."[10] A. V. Peshekhonov explained in detail why the Trudovik-Popular Socialist Party had agreed not to introduce into the formula leftist principles. In the end, all these groups agreed to the compromise. And on the first vote the formula was adopted by the insignificant majority of 5 votes—141 to 136, with 6 abstentions. But when this vote was being checked by means of a division of the house, the majority disappeared. The formula was rejected by a vote of 139 to 139, with one abstention. None of the other formulas managed to win this many votes. The SR formula got only 95 votes, with 126 opposed and 50 abstentions (from the extreme left). The Mensheviks formula received only 39 votes, the Left SRs' formula only 38, the Menshevik Internationalists, and Left SRs' combined formula only 42 votes. Thus, on the first and most important question left to the decision of the Soviet, the Soviet of the Republic was without a formula and without a common opinion.

As the chronicler of *Russkie Vedomosti* noted, "In the hall there was general commotion and confusion."

CHAPTER VI

"NATIONAL POLICY" OR "OBSCENE PEACE"?

Then the Soviet of the Republic directed its attention to a second cardinal question of state policy, which was closely connected to the first: to the question of the basic tenets of our foreign relations. In this sphere, as in the sphere of military questions, the government was hopelessly mired in contradictions between the ideology of "revolutionary democracy" which it professed and the real interests of Russia, without the protection of which the government would find it impossible to implement even this very same "democratic" ideology.

There was a difference between the military and foreign policy issues. Whereas mistakes in the military program were immediately reflected in the diminution of our fighting capacity and in the bitterness of defeat, which forced the government, however reluctantly and unsystematically, to think about immediately returning to the old path, here, in the field of diplomacy, the loss of our international influence did not become apparent so quickly and directly, partly thanks to the conventions of diplomatic language, and partly due to the necessity of reckoning with even the weakest ally. People continued to speak of Russia as a "great power." But the abnormality of the existing situation, as well as its true causes, were very well understood by the official head of our foreign office. We have already taken note of M. I. Tereshchenko's increased irritation with the agencies of the "revolutionary democracy" when he failed to come to an understanding with them after having appeared to make concessions. He had entered the last coalition with a firm resolve to break with this policy of concessions. Tereshchenko had not spoken to the Democratic Conference, but on the very day of its opening, September 14, the newspapers had carried an interview with him that showed he was conscious of the internal contradiction which we have noted and whose victim he was to become. "Speaking of the future," he "expressed the hope that from now on the general Russian policy will not be a *policy of paradoxes*, a policy that has cost us dearly during the last months." "In fact," explained the Minister of Foreign Affairs, "we have spoken in favor of peace, but our actions have created conditions that prolonged the war. We have striven to reduce casualties, but, as a result, we have increased bloodshed. We have worked for a democratic peace, but instead we have brought nearer the triumph of German imperialism. Such misunderstandings are not permissible. In order to end the war in a manner consistent with the principles enunciated by the Provisional Government, it is necessary that all the vital forces within Russia unite and that they give the government the opportunity *to carry out a genuine national policy.*"

The former Assistant Minister of Foreign Affairs, B. E. Nolde, was right when he pointed out in the newspaper *Rech* (on September 16) that this brutal criticism of the "policy of paradoxes" was a criticism of the policy that had been pursued by M. I. Tereshchenko himself. Nolde also indicated that one should not take lightly the German peace proposals (Tereshchenko's interview dealt with the German response to the peace proposal of Pope Benedict XV),[1] for given the weakening of Russia and given circumstances in which Russia might prove physically unable to continue the war, these proposals could be tendered separately, at Russia's expense, to its Allies. In fact, Tereshchenko had reason to assert that Germany's new response was just as hypocritical and that it yielded just as little as the earlier proposals. But he could add that when preliminary negotiations were being conducted between Germany and the Papacy about the publication of the papal note, Germany had considered giving a more concrete answer and allowing more latitude for concessions. If these intentions were later modified and if the German response had turned out as vague as before, one should not forget that in the interim the Germans had taken Riga, thus raising the spirits of German patriots and opening new perspectives to Germany.

Among the concessions to the "revolutionary democracy" which threatened in the future to keep our foreign policy in the realm of "impermissible misunderstandings" and "costly paradoxes" that deprived the government of the "chance to carry out a genuine national policy," there was one particularly harmful concession. Already in the declaration of July 8, which was published in the interval between the walk out of the Kadet ministers and the creation of the second coalition with their participation, the "revolutionary democracy" was promised the peculiar right directly to conduct foreign negotiations, parallel with the official diplomats. To this was added a commitment that at the forthcoming Allied conference—which was scheduled for August, but had been postponed precisely for this reason—representatives of the "democracy" would take direct part in overseeing negotiations, along with specialists from the Ministry of Foreign Affairs. During the negotiations over the formation of the third coalition the "democracy" issued a reminder of this commitment and demanded its fulfillment. We noted that at that time there was especially great pressure from the left in the Soviet, which pressure took the form of a demand for immediate negotiations with the Allies about the conclusion of a "democratic peace" and a simultaneous cease-fire on all fronts. Representatives of the Party of Popular Liberty, of course, could not sign the politically illiterate declaration of July 8. Yet because they were conducting negotiations in a spirit of conciliation, they could not categorically reject this concession once it had been tendered. They chose a middle path: they agreed that a "person enjoying the special trust of the democratic organizations" should be included in the official membership of the Russian delegation. But they insisted that this person be *appointed* by the government, that he be considered the government's representative, and that he speak together with and in solidarity with representatives of the diplomatic corps. This condition was written in black and white in the governmental declaration of September 27. A. F. Kerensky repeated the condition in his speech at the opening of the Soviet of the Republic.

However, the "revolutionary democracy" had no desire to accept this condition, for representation of such a nature had no value to the "democracy." And at the same time that M. I. Tereshchenko was conferring at Stavka and in Petrograd with General Alexeev and with the newly appointed ambassador to Paris, V. A. Maklakov,[2] whom Tereshchenko planned to accompany to the Paris conference that finally had been scheduled for the second half of October, the Central Executive Committee of the Soviet of Workers' and Soldiers' Deputies charged its bureau with working out a special "Instruction" that was supposed to guide at the conference the conduct of the delegate of the "revolutionary democracy," M. I. Skobelev. This "Instruction" was published on October 7. Its content was such that sending a representative of the "democracy" along with the government's representatives to the Allied conference was out of the question.

As if purposely to highlight the peculiarities of this "Instruction," the manifesto of the organizing committee of the Stockholm Conference had been published two days earlier. A delegation of specialists from neutral nations sent this manifesto to parties affiliated with the International in all countries. The material for the manifesto was based on the detailed questionnaires submitted to socialist delegations of various nationalities that had visited Stockholm in May and June.

The convocation of the Stockholm conference, as is well known, was delayed more than once as a result of the internal disagreements between different socialist groups, disagreements which intensified after the weakness of the Russian Revolution became apparent.

Finally, the organizational committee decided to make use of the collected material in order to formulate concrete conditions for what was called in Germany a "conciliatory peace."

In accordance with the general tendency of the Stockholm committee, its conditions for peace were formulated in such a manner that, without manifesting obvious bias, they would nevertheless be acceptable to Germany. Of course, all the fundamental theses of the international movement for peace were included in full: mandatory arbitration, universal disarmament, peace "without the victor coercing the vanquished," "without annexations and indemnities," and with "free national self-determination." But the center of gravity of the manifesto lay not in these pacifistic notions, but in the special conditions. These last conditions reflected very transparently the opinion of socialist delegations of nations inimical to us. Belgium must be reestablished "economically" (there was nothing said about political and military independence) and divided, in accordance with the recently published demand of Germany in its supplementary response to us, into Flanders and Wallonia, which would receive "cultural autonomy." Russian Poland was to receive independence, but the Polish regions of Austria and Germany were to receive only "the greatest possible autonomy," in complete contradiction to the principle of the "self-determination of nationalities." With the same kind of care the manifesto approached the Italian regions of Austria, which would not be conceded to Italy. They "would be granted cultural autonomy," while the Czech people would be "unified" with no mention not only of independence, but even of autonomy. In addition, the generous hand of the manifesto fostered the "independence of Finland and Ireland" and gave "territorial autonomy to the nationalities of Russia within the framework of a federated republic," thus emphasizing the connection of Russian national minority organizations and of the "Congress of Nationalities" in Kiev with the international ties and influences that had been cross-breeding in Stockholm. The Balkan issues were dealt with in a superficially just fashion. An "independent Serbia, united with Montenegro" was to be established "politically and economically," and it was to receive from Bulgaria and from Greece Macedonia to the west of the Vardar, "which will remain a communication line of Serbia—and across it a link of Austrian commerce—with the sea," and also "the right of free access to the Salonika region and to the port." The demand for the independence and territorial reestablishment of Armenia was unquestionably just and impartial. Finally, the Jewish question was recognized as an international issue and was resolved by suggesting "personal autonomy" for the Jews in Russia, Austria, Romania, and

Poland (obviously, what they had in mind was non-territorial national autonomy) and "assisting the Jewish colonization of Palestine."

The "Instruction" to M. I. Skobelev went far beyond the limits of these more or less popular theses of international socialist pacifism. Rereading its text parallel with the text of the Stockholm manifesto, one cannot rid oneself of the impression that there were two hands responsible for the "Instruction": one was the inexperienced hand of a pacifist-utopian, who introduced into the text specifically Russian pacifist illusions; the other was a very experienced hand, acquainted with details of the controversial issues that would have been unknown to the uninitiated. This hand accumulated decisions favorable to Germany much more systematically and openly than was done in the document by the Dutch-Scandinavian committee trying to maintain neutrality.

To the first category of the pacifist demands one can assign the demands for the abolition of secret treaties, for the statement by parliaments of the conditions of peace, for the conclusion of the peace at a conference "through plenipotentiaries elected by the agencies of popular representation," for participation in a "League of Peace" "by all states with equal rights, given the democratization of foreign policy." All these proposals naturally flowed from the hidden assumption that peace and future international relations would be established not by "predatory imperialist governments," but by the "revolutionary democracies" of all countries, which would overthrow [imperialist] governments after the Russian example. In any case, this Bolshevistic-Zimmerwaldian idea, which found no place in the confines of the Stockholm manifesto, fitted cozily into the framework of the "Instruction" to Skobelev.

The other category of changes introduced into the "Instruction"—the result of rewriting by the knowledgeable Germanophile—ran like a red thread through all the *concrete* conditions of the peace. The German armed forces, of course, "will leave the occupied regions of Russia." But . . . "Russia will grant full self-determination to Poland, Lithuania, and Latvia:" in other words, in the place of the occupied provinces there would be "buffer states," in accordance with the old dream of the German nationalists.[3] The "Instruction" was simply silent about the German and Austrian sections of Poland. The issue of Alsace-Lorraine was resolved as in the Stockholm manifesto, but not in "a specified period after the conclusion of the peace," as the manifesto provided in accordance with the wishes of French socialists. Instead, the resolution of the problem would occur "after the withdrawal of the armed forces of both coalitions," when "the local self-government will organize a referendum of the populace under conditions of complete freedom of voting." In other words, the administration created during the period of

German dominance would involve in the voting the recently-arrived German element, while the French exiles, who would not yet have managed to return to their native land, would be prevented from deciding their own fate. Belgium would also receive its former borders, but the "Instruction" said nothing about its independence (even its "economic" independence). Its losses would be compensated "from an international fund," since even the German government had agreed to return to Belgium part of the "contributions" exacted from it.

The "Instruction" also provided advantages for Germany's allies: Serbia would receive only "access to the Adriatic Sea," to which the Austrians had consented even in 1909, but Bosnia and Herzegovina would receive only "autonomy." The "Instruction" limited itself to granting autonomy to "the Italian regions of Austria," but also provided for a "subsequent plebiscite." The concession to Italy of even a part of [the Italian regions of Austria], as forseen by the Stockholm manifesto, was not contemplated. Just as Russia was to give Poland, Lithuania, and Latvia "complete self-determination," so would Romania grant it to Dobrudja: this meant that Dobrudja would become part of Bulgaria, which would also receive all of Macedonia—not only the eastern section up to the River Vardar, as the Stockholm manifesto had proposed without even mentioning Dobrudja. The "Instruction" made a special reference to the return to Germany of its colonies, which the manifesto made contingent on the return of all occupied territories in general. The "Instruction" also spoke about the "reestablishment" of Greece and Persia, which was to be understood only in the sense of restoring German influence in the former and eliminating Russian and English influence in the latter. Probably the reference to the "neutralization" of the long-ago neutralized Panama and Suez canals was also to be understood as implying the establishment of certain special German rights and the elimination of English and American rights. The usual German demands for "freedom of the seas," a renunciation of an economic blockade after the war, and free trade were also elaborated. With respect to free trade the "Instruction" said that each nation would receive "autonomy," but without the right "to form separate customs unions" (obviously, new customs unions) and without the right of granting "most favored nation status," which should apply "to all nations without distinction."

The publication of the "Instruction" produced a scandalous impression even in the "democratic" circles. Having realized some of the implications of what they had done, the agencies of the "democracy" began to say that not everything in the "Instruction" was binding, and that, in general, the "Instruction" might be reexamined. But the shortcomings of the "Instruction" were, as we have seen, not alien, accidental features in it, but, so to speak, its very substance. And for the government to make an accommodation with the "revolutionary democracy" on the basis of this "Instruction," which so clearly protected the enemy and betrayed our friends and Allies, was out of the question. M. I. Tereshchenko gave the "democracy" to understand that he could not adhere to the "Instruction" and that he would not go to the conference together with M. I. Skobelev.

That was the situation when the Soviet of the Republic turned to a discussion of foreign policy. It was possible for the government to find a compromise position on the issue of peace. In fact, it had already declared itself in favor of a compromise in principle: it was prepared to seek some kind of minimum program under which the "democratic" formula for peace might be reconciled with Russia's national interest. But the sort of minimum that Verkhovsky had found on the military question was not in evidence on the peace question, and the "democracy" would not have accepted it even if it had been. Yet for any self-respecting government it was impossible to adopt the perspective of the "Instruction." Thus, in the field of foreign policy the government remained without a compromise and without the possibility of proposing one with any hope of success. M. I. Tereshchenko did not even have the kind of support that Kerensky, Verkhovsky, and Verderevsky had had in the debate on the army's fighting capacity.

Perhaps it would have been sensible under the circumstances to speak publicly about a "genuine national policy." M. I. Tereshchenko did not lack an understanding of what such a policy consisted. But, fearing a quarrel with the "democracy," he could speak only under his breath. And so his speech to the Soviet of the Republic was half-hearted, lame, incapable of satisfying anyone, obviously insincere, and utterly unworthy of the director of Russian foreign policy.

The connection between foreign policy and defense gave the minister his first theme; in developing it he could have returned to his own observations about the "paradoxes" that had "cost Russia so dearly" and were now "impermissible." Even the leftist press was developing the notion that the chances of a "democratic peace" were swiftly diminishing in proportion to the success of the democratic utopias. But such a treatment of the theme before the audience of the Soviet of the Republic would not be without danger . . . . So the minister confined himself to two observations. First, one could not say everything in public about defense and foreign policy. Second, both defense and foreign policy should be based on "one and the same feeling of love for the motherland and on a desire to guard its interests." However, this second observation immediately frightened Tereshchenko. Could one really speak here about love for the motherland and about its interests as something that was objectively necessary and universally accepted? And catching himself in this carelessness, M. I. Tereshchenko immediately added the proviso: "I would like to speak here quite candidly and concretely, without bringing up the questions of national honor and dignity, but only the matter of political expediency." And based solely on considerations of "expediency," he concluded that "Russia must not remain isolated, and that, *leaving aside the questions of duty and honor*, the constellation of forces which exists at present *is advantageous for her.*"

Probably the Minister of Foreign Affairs found himself before the only auditorium in the world, where at that juncture he could not speak about the "obligations of honor and of the dignity" of the motherland, where he would have to excuse himself for uttering such words, and where these words could be disregarded as being controversial! What a difference, what a chasm separated this moment [in Russia], from that in the House of Commons, when, before England's decision to come to the assistance of France and Russia, Sir Edward Grey said: "You are free from obligations, no alliances bind you, but remember the honor and dignity of England!" Even the Soviet audience felt awkward and loudly applauded a reference in the forbidden zone of "dignity and honor," which reference slipped from the minister when he tried to introduce under the flag of "expediency" another contraband idea: "In Russia no one will permit a peace that is *humiliating* for Russia and which would violate its national interests." The internationalism of the left wing permitted the minister to finish this thought with an argument that was used more often in the parliaments of the Allies—and which was acceptable both to Martov and to Miliukov: such a [humiliating] peace would "for decades, if not centuries" delay the triumph of the "democratic principle" in the rest of the world.

In any case, having propagated heretical ideas about the advantage of unity with the Allies and about the harm to Russia of a peace at any price, Tereshchenko had to break the traditional association of these notions with past Russian policy and to connect them to the repetoire of ideas about a "democratic" foreign policy. Tereshchenko tried to do this by means of a risky historical reference. However, he cast aside this reference in mid-road, as he approached the most difficult moment. It turned out that the "humiliating" peace threatened Russia not as a result of the "democratic" policy of "paradoxes," but as a result of actions taken before it [the policy of paradoxes] was adopted; indeed, the real reason for this threat was that Tereshchenko's predecessors and his former comrades in the first coalition cabinet had not wanted to adopt it [the policy of paradoxes]. We know, however, that certain French and English socialists had understood government policy precisely in this fashion. "Future historians," said Tereshchenko, turning upside down the entire history of the revolution, "will note with surprise that Russia stood closest to a shameful separate peace" during the first months of the revolution, when the patriot Guchkov[4] began to ruin the Russian army, and the "great power politician" Miliukov led Russian foreign policy. M. I. Tereshchenko dated to this period "the spontaneous movement, the spontaneous wave, which, running counter to the true interests and tasks of the motherland, pushed Russia toward unforeseen consequences." It was at that point that "the cease-fire arranged on our front threatened to end the war under the influence of a spontaneous force, the simple exhaustion of military action at the front." By adopting the principles of a democratic policy, Tereshchenko and Kerensky had saved Russia from the danger of "unforeseen consequences." Yet this policy was now bringing about the "unforeseen consequences" of Zimmerwaldism and was sanctioning through Kerensky's signature that very "harm," which supposedly had been inflicted on the army by Guchkov!

Tereshchenko managed to steer around this underwater rock by means of an obscure and general reference to "those goals" which the government "firmly set for itself" in May and to which it now "holds and will continue to hold." But at this point he ran up against another, more serious obstacle. Had the enthusiasm which the Provisional Government had tried to engender in the Russian army by means of great "exertions and effort" and with the aid of the ideas of a democratic foreign policy and "revolutionary discipline" turned out to be short-lived? Had those signs of "fear of the Russian Revolution," which the minister had seen in Austria and Germany after the "success that encouraged our army" in late June and early July, also swiftly given way to an impression which was noted in Europe by members of the delegation of the Soviet of Workers' and Soldiers' Deputies and which Tereshchenko himself described in these words: an impression of "confusion and disillusionment?" Did this mean that the "Russian Revolution, which already in March was calling so loudly for a fraternal peace, had not given its people strength, but had weakened them?"

This underwater rock the minister could not avoid—and, perhaps, did not wish to avoid, for his historical reference was chosen not for the "future historian," but for the special mentality of his listeners, to whose consciences he was trying to appeal and whom he was trying to persuade by using their own arguments. After all, your own comrades, who were sent abroad by the Soviet and who returned from there, told you: "It is essential that Russia win some kind of a victory somewhere." If you want to demonstrate that your "statements renouncing territorial acquisitions come not from weakness and not from the impossibility of capturing a certain territory, but rather from the will of the Russian democracy and its ideals," if you wish, in a word, "for the voice of the Russian democracy to be strong," then raise the fighting capacity of the army! He, the minister, of course, was not placing blame on anyone for the failure of democratic policy; this was "not my domain."

Tereshchenko also tried carefully and delicately to interpret "the ideals of Russian democracy" accepted in May as "concrete goals of our foreign policy." The renunciation of annexations and indemnities was fine; but it was necessary that there also be "a refusal to accept the enemy's imposition of these penalties *on us,* and the confiscation of *our* land." This meant, in the language of Russian national interests, the "inviolability of Russia's territory." Moreover, why did the "democracy" tend to forget about the second half of its slogan—the self-determination of nationalities—"especially in statements which had to do with the central powers?" "The government finds it impossible to renounce either part of this slogan, the negative or the positive." "The right of nations to self-determination is just as essential as the renunciation of territorial acquisitions." And if one should recognize this right, then how could one approve of Germany's ambition to keep its Polish lands and to seize Lithuania and Courland, the plan for the settling of which by German colonists was already prepared? One had to agree with this, and M. I. Tereshchenko then transformed a "democratic slogan" into a patriotic statement: "Here Russia must stand absolutely firm: to be deprived of that which all Russian people desire and which is a real national interest—an access to the warm-water Mediterranean Sea—this Russia cannot tolerate." It should struggle against the plan of creating buffer states on its western borders. This struggle was certainly not hopeless, for Germany was also exhausted and also longed for peace. Even after the German announcement, following its response to the papal note, that it would no longer extend its hand, Germany nevertheless extended its hand. Moreover, the fight against "disannexation" on the western border was also important—and the army should understand this: otherwise, Russia was threatened with economic conquest by Germany, and "the future fate of the Russian people will be terrible." Finally, even military failures in the struggle would not be so terrible, as long as we were not isolated, and as long as our Allies, as they categorically claimed, made an effort to analyze "all the pluses and minuses" of the coalition "as a whole."

On this ground M. I. Tereshchenko again confronted the demand of the "democracy"—to speak with the Allies only on the subject of concluding a democratic peace,—and to speak immediately, as soon as the belligerents showed a readiness to renounce territorial acquisitions and without waiting for a definitive statement by them on the actual purposes of the war (that is, a statement which Germany stubbornly refused to make). This was one of the points of the "Instruction" to Skobelev, which was clumsily put there by the person who had been thinking from the German perspective. We have seen that neither the Allies nor the Russian minister could accept this "Instruction" as a basis for discussion, much less for guidance. One way or another, one had to say this, for one could not pass over *this* "Instruction" in silence. M.I. Tereshchenko did say so, but he did it as carefully as he possibly could.

The purpose of the conference "had been defined by Lloyd-George," and the Russian minister "could do little but associate himself with Lloyd-George's statement." At the conference, as in the debates of the Soviet of the Republic, the delegates would turn from military-strategic issues to the goals of foreign policy: the one concern was interconnected with the other. Moreover, there was no doubt that the conference would articulate those points of view, which, *as Lloyd-George had said,* would "bring an end to this terrible bloodshed." This would be done for "the first time since the beginning of the war." But, "in order that there be no misunderstandings on anyone's part," the minister proposed that at the conference Russia "represent itself as one unit." "The views, which will be presented there, must be united and coherent." And he hastened to soften the blow and to calm his audience: "After all, our delegation is a broad coalition, which will be workable if people speak truthfully and sincerely, if they have a common cause—the interests of the motherland—and if they agree on a definition of tasks."

But did the audience agree to understand "the interests of the motherland" in such a fashion? In the way of this harmonious understanding stood the "Instruction" to Skobelev, and the minister, in spite of all his tact, could not say that he was in agreement with it. Tereshchenko noted that even the program of the Dutch-Scandinavian group, "which the representatives of Allied democracy had viewed with mistrust out of the fear that this group places the interests of the central powers above other considerations,"—even this program did not go so far in the direction of German interests as did the "Instruction" to Skobelev. "Take the second point, which is not in the Scandinavian manifesto: the complete self-determination of Poland, Lithuania and Latvia," that is, the independence of these regions. "Without the warm-water harbors of the Baltic Sea Russia will return to the pre-Petrine period . . . . Delegates to the conference must not speak in favor of this point. Russia will condemn them," stated the minister to vigorous applause from the right and center. Furthermore, the neutralization of the Straits, in the event that complete disarmament shall not have occurred, was also "a shameful violation of the interests of Russia, a return to a situation much worse than that obtaining before the war." (Again there was vigorous applause from the right and center.) From these two examples M. I. Tereshchenko drew the conclusion that "the attempt to shape a new peace demands, perhaps, a greater acquaintance with the facts and an even greater love for the interests being defended."

This conclusion naturally divided the auditorium. From the right people shouted, "True!"; from the left, "Strongly put." But the speaker still had to say that one should not completely ignore the responsibilities falling on our adversaries and should not demand sacrifices from our Allies, such as the concession of Dobrudja to Romania—as the "Instruction" had done. The good will—or neutrality—of the left had already been exhausted. And the minister literally in two words, as if in passing, mentioned what he considered the positive task of the Russian delegates at the conference: the demand "that Russia's territory be inviolable and that the conditions which had made possible the economic development of Russia to the north and south be guaranteed in a responsible fashion." At the end of this last sentence Russian interests in the Black Sea, including even the problem of the Straits, were carefully smuggled in . . . . In his concluding words the minister hastened to assure the "democracy" that the Provisional Government "does not renounce those slogans, which it has endorsed—and *which it considers genuinely to uphold the interests of Russia.*" It would not repudiate "a single section of them" and would consider their implementation "*in the light of our military failures and of the difficult circumstances within the country.*" But, "in order that the word of the representatives be firm," he reminded citizens that "each of them, and not the government alone, is responsible for the historical fate of Russia;" everyone must be a "servant of the great ideal and a worthy child of a great nation."

The minister finished to applause *only* from the right and center. The leftists were quite dissatisfied. Their reactions in the press suggested that Tereshchenko had gotten by with generalities, that he had not expressed concretely his attitude toward the demands of the "democracy," and had not explained "why the army should sustain inhuman casualties." (This from Dan, Gots, Skobelev.) In negotiations with Kerensky they went even further, and stated that, in general, Tereshchenko was not able to represent at the conference the views of the "revolutionary democracy." This was true: Tereshchenko had interpreted the slogans of the democracy in his own fashion, translating them, where possible, into the language of statecraft, and where this was not possible, he drew from these slogans no practical conclusions. In turn, Tereshchenko also said that, in case of disagreement with the "democracy," he would prefer to step down and not to go to the conference at all. The final decision now depended on how the majority of the Soviet of the Republic and its commission on foreign policy viewed the conflict between the "revolutionary democracy" and the minister.

The first speaker in the debate was Tereshchenko's predecessor in the ministry, P.N. Miliukov. In order to stay in the good graces of the "democracy," Tereshchenko found it more advantageous to have Miliukov as an adversary than as an ally. But to support the minister by *this* method was not Miliukov's wish. On the contrary, he revealed what Tereshchenko had left unsaid in order to demonstrate that, in essence, the minister had not changed anything of substance in his [Tereshchenko's] former views on Russia's war aims; Miliukov also wished to juxtapose Tereshchenko's views with the latest statements of Asquith in Leeds. Miliukov merely deflected the minister's attack [on the first coalition] by putting to Tereshchenko this question: "When was Russia closer to a separate peace—at the point when deputations came from the army to the Provisional Government and proposed to defend it from the Soviets and the Bolsheviks, or now, when the same army delegates come to the Petrograd Soviet of Workers' and Soldiers' Deputies and propose that the Bolsheviks arrest the government and transfer all power to the revolutionary democracy, in order to make what they themselves call an 'obscene' peace?" He also brought it to the minister's attention that he [Miliukov] had always struggled against "great power" politics, if what was meant by that term was "imperialistic" politics.

The main content of Miliukov's speech was a criticism of the "peculiar, truly Russian view of the goals of foreign relations, which view pretends to be international." True, "formally speaking, this view was imported into Russia from abroad and it pretends to a tie with the International. But originally it was exported abroad from Russia, and is a specific product of the hot-house atmosphere of our emigre circles." This view had been nurtured in the sphere of abstract thought, and specifically of Russian, doctrinaire thought characteristic of the intelligentsia. The nobleman Lenin only repeated the nobleman Kireevsky[5] when he said that from Russia the new word would come forth which would regenerate the decayed West and put in place of the old banner of "scientific" socialism a new banner of the direct, extra-parliamentary action of the starving masses, who by physical force would compel mankind to break down the door to the socialist heaven. Only from the perspective of this new world-historical illusion could one make sense of the unconscionable treason, which at the height of a war summoned soldiers to leave the trenches and, in place of the war against the "imperalist" governments, to fight another war—a domestic civil war of the international proletariat against the capitalists and landowners of all nations. To the question from the left: "Who says that?", Miliukov cited from the rostrum the basic propositions of Martov's Kienthal speech—and he thus elicited from Martov the statement that Martov did not call for soldiers to leave the trenches during wartime. P.N. Miliukov then pointed out the connection that continued to exist between the pure Zimmerwaldian doctrine of the extremists and the views of the moderate socialists, between the views of these last and the government's foreign policy. He added that in its truncated form, without the calls to use force and to an immediate worldwide socialist revolution, the Zimmerwald doctrine lost whatever sense that it had had in its original, "pure" form. The last hope of the Zimmerwaldists was for the insignificant Zimmerwald minority to win over by logic the European majority of socialist-patriots, and through them morally to compel bourgeois governments to accept the point of view of the International. Obviously, this *was not the shortest path* to the "democratic" peace demanded by the Russian "revolutionary democracy." The delegates would have to be convinced *a posteriori* abroad that "a real possibility for the international conference that they dream about, does not exist." However, they continued to preserve the mask of "official hypocrisy," as the "Instruction" to Skobelev demonstrated.

In order to explain why the publication of the "Instruction" made the sending abroad of a person pledged to defend it a blatant contradiction to Russia's honor and dignity, P.N. Miliukov subjected that strange document to a careful analysis. He divided its contents into three concentric circles of thought. (1) There were *general pacifistic notions* (concerning arbitration, disarmament, control by parliament over foreign policy, the self-determination of peoples in the broadly accepted sense): he agreed with these ideas as a pacifist and an opponent of the current war. (2) There were *specifically* Dutch-Scandinavian or *Stockholmian notions* (the responsibility of *all* governments for the war; no one could win the war; the self-determination of peoples in the one-sided German interpretation; and the renunciation of economic struggle, in which was the same tendentious idea): with these notions he did not agree, just as the Allied socialists had not agreed. (3) There were the *specifically Soviet notions*, which were amusing where they constituted a "caricature" of pacifistic ideas, but which provoked "a feeling of indignation and of burning shame" where they were mere faithful reproductions of German desires. These notions included the creation, "in the worst case," of buffer states on our western periphery, and "if the effort to disorganize our army continues at the same rate as in the past," then what was contemplated was "complete surrender of this strip of land" as "compensation for the concessions to our Allies on Germany's western frontier."

Miliukov then pointed out all the sacrifices which the "Instruction" to Skobelev imposed on our Allies in the interests of Germany. The left section of the auditorium, which after the first mention of "German interests" in the "Instruction" made a loud commotion, interrupted the speaker and demanded that he be called to order. This section, after Miliukov cited the objective facts, sat silent at his conclusion: "The German Mark is obviously firmly attached to the Instruction." The speaker concluded with an appeal: not to take pride in a false democratic superiority over the Allies, but to bow before the progressive democracies of the world, "who long ago traversed a significant part of the path on which we have just set out with shaky and uncertain steps;" to bow and take a lesson from [the Allies'] ability to combine real military power with the pursuit of actually obtainable democratic goals, instead of proletarian utopias.

The continuation of the debate on foreign policy was put off until October 20. In the interim the leaders of the revolutionary democracy tried very energetically to determine the extent of the conflict that had arisen unexpectedly between the Minister of Foreign Affairs and the "democratic agencies," and to take steps to resolve the conflict one way or another. It would have been most inconvenient for the "democracy" if the conflict had revolved around the "Instruction" to Skobelev, the indefensibility of which was beyond question after it was criticized in the Soviet of the Republic. On *this* point the leaders of the democracy would have to concede. In order to save face, the Executive Committee of Peasants' Deputies moved to assist the Executive Committee of the Soviet of Workers' and Soldiers' Deputies. On the day of the reopening of the debate, the Bureau of the Executive Committee [of Peasants' Deputies] drafted *another* "Instruction" to Skobelev, from which were eliminated all the specific peculiarities of the "Instruction" of Workers' and Soldiers' Deputies that had made it absolutely unacceptable and which had cast a shadow on the agency that had written it. In the peasant "Instruction" to Skobelev the first point restored, as Tereshchenko had demanded, both parts of the Russian democratic formula for peace ("without annexations" and "self-determination"). The second point detailed the general-pacifistic notions that P.N. Miliukov had recognized as acceptable and formulated them with proper care. The third point mentioned the responsibility of the Allies not to conduct separate negotiations for peace, and not to conclude a separate peace. The fourth point combined the renunciation of economic blockades, which renunciation was desirable to Germany, with the complete freedom of trade for all nations.

The second section of the "Instruction," which was devoted to the concrete conditions of peace, also retracted not only the concessions to the Germans which had been made in the other "Instruction," but also those that had been made in the Stockholm manifesto. The first point of this section demanded the evacuation of foreign troops from occupied territories; the second affirmed the fundamental principle of the inviolability of Russian territory, and it also subjected the right of self-determination of Russian national minorities to "the decision of the Constituent Assembly." The third point, which affirmed the *independence* of Poland by a reference to a Russian governmental act of 13 March 1917, extended to the Polish regions of Germany and Austria the "right to self-determination with an international guarantee." The fourth point obliged Germany to compensate at least that portion of Belgium's losses which was incurred as a result of violations of the laws of war, as specified in the Hague Convention. The fifth point left Serbia and Montenegro in the same position [as did the other "Instruction"]. The sixth point demanded the "reestablishment" of Romania without separating Dobrudja from it. The seventh point permitted a plebiscite in Alsace-Lorraine on the condition that "persons who are in the German state service, and those who are not natives of Alsace, and also their families" could not take part in voting. The eighth point guaranteed "full autonomy to Armenia" "via an international guarantee" and left the right to arrange Armenian autonomy to "an Armenian national assembly, under the same guarantee." Finally, the ninth point spoke of a "real guarantee of free voting" after the final resolution "of all national-territorial issues resulting from the current war or connected intimately with it, such as the Yugoslavian, Transylvanian, Czech, and Italian questions in Austria." This was a complete retreat along the entire line and a direct admission that the criticism of the first "Instruction" to Skobelev had been justified. Thus, the main pretext for conflict [between the "revolutionary democracy" and the Minister of Foreign Affairs]—the content of the "Instruction" that was inimical to Russia's interests—was eliminated.

But this did not mean that the conflict itself had been resolved. On the contrary, it was transferred to more defensible points: to the ministry's attitude toward the democratic delegation generally; to its attitude toward the Stockholm congress; and particularly to the chief point of disagreement—the negotiations with the Allies for an immediate peace. The issue of whether to fight or to make peace, to prepare for a continuation of the defense or for a cease-fire on all fronts, continued to loom in all its enormity just as before, and the sharpness of the debate about it only intensified after the public exchange of opinions in the Soviet of the Republic. The adherents of the contending perspectives all agreed that the resolution of the question of foreign policy should be connected with the resolution of the military question. But on the military question the "democracy" had made its choice: this was Verkhovsky's solution, which had been approved by Kerensky. On the issue of foreign policy Tereshchenko's opinion could not have been accepted by the "democracy." And so the conflict between the two sides of the question turned into a conflict between the two persons who were defending incompatible decisions: Verkhovsky and Tereshchenko.

During this time Verkhovsky showed that he was quite conscious of the role he was playing, and that he wanted to take advantage of the situation, which for him was quite favorable. In his dealings with the agencies of the democracy, which dealings were becoming ever more frequent and systematic, he argued the view that, because of the indissoluble link between the war and foreign policy, it would be necessary to make the same choice that he had made: not to augment the means of fighting, but to make an immediate peace. Gorky's *Novaia Zhizn* took Verkhovsky under its protection during these days and pointed out that, in the persons of Verkhovsky and Tereshchenko, "There is a confrontation of two world views:" one was acceptable to the democracy, the other was unacceptable. "For General Verkhovsky it is clear," wrote the newspaper, which stood on the outskirts of the Bolshevik camp, "that for a successful defense and for the aversion of further devastation to the army, the soldier masses must be clearly aware of the aims being pursued by Russia. Any obscuring of these aims, any delay in peace negotiations inevitably will be interpreted by the army as treachery and deception. Only a consistent and resolute policy of peace can dissipate such suspicions . . . . The War Minister arrived at this view not under the influence of theoretical considerations, but as a result of the bitter lessons of reality itself . . . . As a fighting man, he could not hide this truth, to which everyone coming back from the front testifies—namely, that without the acceleration of peace negotiations it will be not only impossible to raise discipline in the army, but *even to hold the army in its current positions.*" *Novaia Zhizn's* conclusion expressed the view of the left wing of revolutionary democracy: "In spite of attempts at intimidation, the democracy must support General Verkhovsky against Tereshchenko."

In this atmosphere the debate over foreign policy was reopened in the Soviet of the Republic on October 20. M.I. Tereshchenko, who had

departed for Stavka before P.N. Miliukov's speech, returned to the Mariinsky Palace only for the second half of the session of October 20.
Consequently, he could not participate in the negotiations of these days.
Tereshchenko's absence had an effect on the character of the leftist
speeches by the Menshevik Gurvich-Dan, the Internationalist Lapinsky,
and finally, by Chernov, who spoke at this session. The jaded attitude
toward the debate, an attitude that manifested itself in the late opening
of the session in a half-empty auditorium, continued throughout this
session and the following one, on October 23.

Dan and Lapinsky argued virtually the same old theses of the "revolutionary democracy," although, of course, with much greater precision
than would Tsereteli, who by now had entirely faded into the background. The demoralization of the army was not the fault of the "revolutionary democracy," but the result of the war, which was incomprehensi-
ble to the people and which was also "imperialistic." "Our participation
in this war was a crime of tsarism, which had been seeking to save itself from impending revolution." This stereotypical presentation included, of course, a response to the question of responsibility for the
war—naturally, a response favorable to the Germans, and not favorable
to our Allies. "The broad masses and the army understood the revolution as a revolution *against the war,* a revolution for the *swift attainment of peace.*" To understand it as a "revolution for the better prosecution of the war" was "a profound mistake of many in Russia and in the
West." This mistake, "in particular, the policy of Miliukov," which
was based on it and which had continued the foreign policy of tsarism,
"more than anything else facilitated the development of anarchy within
the country and the demoralization of the army." If the army still existed, "if the legitimate desire for peace has not demoralized it beyond re-
pair, then the credit for this belongs entirely to the revolutionary democracy, which has worked alone to organize our army." In May the coalition government through Tereshchenko promised to aid the democracy
"by directing its active foreign policy toward a swift attainment of a universal peace" on the basis of the democratic formula. But the government "expended too little effort to bring about the realization of this policy." In Tereshchenko's speech there were "no democratic nor revolutionary elements, which alone might be able to lend support to a strong and
resolute foreign policy." Under Tereshchenko Russia was conducting itself like a "poor relation" of its Allies, and it was counting on the Allies' "pluses" to outweigh Russia's "minuses," when the revolution in
and of itself was a "colossal plus." "The dignity of Russia has not been
sufficiently defended in past debates:" "We do have the capacity to advance the cause of a democratic peace, and all and everyone *must*

contend with this fundamental demand of the Russian democracy—*to enter immediately* into peace negotiations."

Lapinsky even found that the government of the coalition did not know how to speak a resolute language to the Allies and did not conduct itself according to democratic slogans. "The moment has come when revolutionary Russia *must frankly tell the Allies that it cannot continue to fight any longer*, and that it is senseless to drag out the war without any definite purpose. It is necessary to demand that the Allies immediately enter peace negotiations on the bases proclaimed by the Russian Revolution." Dan expressed himself more carefully: "Our delegate and the entire delegation should place on the agenda the question of all Allied powers declaring their readiness for an immediate cease-fire, as soon as all nations agree to renounce territorial acquisitions." This was the chief demand of the "Instruction," a demand about which the minister had remained silent. Chernov was even more restrained, for he apparently understood that what was demanded of Russian diplomacy was only a platonic demonstration. "Now the question of precise conditions for peace is not on the agenda." At the conference "only principles can be worked out, and first attempts made to apply them to concrete questions. The publication of principles will already be a huge step toward ending the war. They are mistaken who assert that they possess a magical way to end the war: the proclamation of an immediate cease-fire on all fronts. A cease-fire is a natural consequence of making public the results of the future Allied conference." In this connection, "while conditions are not yet ripe for peace on all fronts," more importance should be attached to the issue of "hastening their maturation" through a "preliminary peace conference" [predkongress mira], at Stockholm. Dan's demand—that the Russian government should not confine itself to treating the Stockholm conference as a "private affair," as Tereshchenko insisted, but should consider the conference to be its own business, "indivisible" from the democratic foreign policy proclaimed by the government—also made sense in this context.

P.B. Struve's speech again underlined the profound difference between this view and that shared by the right wing of the Soviet of the Republic. True, Russia's desire for peace had not yet yielded any results. But this was so not because Tereshchenko's policy was mistaken, for this policy nevertheless provided for at least "a minimum of that which healthy national sensibility and the true interests of Russia required." Rather this failure occurred because, from the very beginning of the revolution, peace propaganda had been based on utopian assumptions. The German Social Democrats, on whose activity the entire calculation [of the propaganda's effect] rested, were "first and foremost, Germans and good bourgeois." As Germans they would not rebel in wartime, and as good bourgeois they were utterly incapable of making a revolution. The most submissive Russian Kadets were much more revolutionary than the most fierce German Social Democrat. That is why "the democratic formula" merely kindled the appetite of German imperialism for the Baltic region and led to a prolongation of the war. It was senseless to explain to the soldiers the reasons for which the war was being waged, "when the enemy is approaching the outskirts of the capital and there are discussions about the evacuation of Petrograd." Furthermore, the propagandists of an immediate peace "are leading the people into a delusion when they promise that, with the swift ending of the war, the people's lives will become easier. On the contrary, such a catastrophic termination of the war, which could not occur in conditions of a rationally regulated international and economic order, will mean a sudden catastrophic worsening of the living standards of the working class in general and of broad strata of the cities in particular. The revolutionary liquidation of the war will certainly cause the masses much greater suffering than that caused by [continued] war."

The aphorisms of one of the founders of Russian Marxism were very painful to his former political associates. In one of the profound paradoxes he hurled at them, Struve said: "You are bad socialists, because you did not benefit from a good bourgeois uprising." "Bonaparte," Martov shouted from his seat. Others reminded Struve about Kornilov. The last reminder provoked from the speaker an angry reply: "Kornilov escaped from German captivity after receiving serious wounds, and his name we here hold to be honorable." This elicited vigorous protests from the left, but the right answered them by rising to to their feet and arranging in honor of the arrested "traitor," as Chernov had called Kornilov here, an impromptu ovation.

It was clear that, given such a divergence of opinions, given almost two world views, the general formula for the transition period was still more hopeless than it had seemed during the military debates. There were attempts to compose such a formula both from the left and from the right, by the Social Democrats and by the Party of Popular Liberty. But the negotiations over the formula by the different groups came to nothing. And once again it became necessary to delay the end of the debates until the next session, that of October 23.

Before this session, however, the political circumstances again changed significantly. On his return from Stavka Tereshchenko renewed negotiations with the representatives of the "democracy" concerning the concessions the "democracy" had made on the matter of the "Instruction." However, Verkhovsky did not wish to give up the role of the

true representative of the democratic world view. Having conducted negotiations with the leftist groups, he evidently decided that his hour had
come. Within the Provisional Government Verkhovsky's relations with
the left wing of the "democracy," including the Bolsheviks, aroused
doubts at that juncture about whether he should remain a member of the
government, especially considering the Bolshevik movement that then
threatened the government. Verkhovsky decided to confront these rumors directly and raised the possibility of his resignation, but over a
question of *principle*—over the *entire* policy of the government, or,
more precisely, over the basic question of its entire policy: the connection between the war and foreign policy. On the evening of October 20
there was a meeting of the Committee on Defense of the Soviet of the
Republic. Detailed reports were read by the heads of the departments
dealing with various aspects of army supply. In the middle of these reports, late in the evening, Minister Verkhovsky arrived at the meeting,
and, having taken the floor without making any attempt to deal with
the issues being discussed, announced that this was all trivia and details,
and that it was essential to discuss the main issue of whether we could
continue the war in general. This strange interference in the debate provoked puzzlement and confusion. The members of the committee from
the Party of Popular Liberty proposed that the chairman, Znamensky, restore order to the debate that had been disrupted by the minister. Verkhovsky's interference was so obviously inappropriate that the chairman
could only accede to this demand, and this he did with rather sharp remarks.

On the next evening, October 21, Verkhovsky repeated his attempt,
but this time he planned it carefully. In connection with the debate in
the Soviet of the Republic a special joint session of two committees—that of defense and foreign affairs—was scheduled, where the two
ministers, Verkhovsky and Tereshchenko, were supposed to speak one
after another. If the former should contend that Russia could no longer
fight, the latter would have to draw the appropriate conclusions for his
diplomacy. Verkhovsky's plan and that of his partisans in the committees obviously rested on this logical connection between the speeches.
Verkhovsky decided as a preliminary to prepare the parties for his
speech, and, among others, he requested and received a meeting with several responsible members of the Party of Popular Liberty. He told them
that he did not think it possible to hold the army from collapse by any
other means than by promising a quick peace. In case this were done, he
counted on raising the enthusiasm of the troops and leading them to victory. A change of the troops' mood was also necessary for domestic political reasons. On one occasion he had succeeded in averting a

Bolshevik uprising. But perhaps the next time this would not succeed
. . . . He asked the party members whether they thought it feasible to
raise the question of peace with the Allies at the conference, to which
he proposed to go as the representative of the democracy.

Verkhovsky received the answer that raising the enthusiasm of the
troops by means of promising peace was a means that had already been
tested—and it had baneful results. Nothing could guarantee that, instead
of an increase in enthusiasm, the promise of peace would not cause a
new epidemic of desertions from the front, only this time the epidemic
might be worse than the last. That was why it would be difficult to induce our Allies by such means to accept "democratic" proposals. Those
who nevertheless wanted to insist on them [the "democratic" propos-
als]—and at the same time spoke about the conclusion of a "general"
peace—fell into self-contradiction. The Allies would not accept an end
to the war that amounted to a draw or that favored Germany; even if we
were to refuse to fight any longer, that would not force them [the Al-
lies] to make peace. They would continue the war in any case, but, now
liberated from any obligations to us, they would not hesitate if necessary to end the war by making concessions at our expense. Thus, the
"democratic" way of posing the question of peace at the Allied conference was fruitless and hopeless, and for us it would be humiliating and
harmful. It would be harmful because, having once spoken loudly about
peace, we could not quit the war without achieving peace. Instead of a
"general" peace, we would be forced by the complete collapse of the army to speak about a "separate" peace. A separate peace was the last
word of the so-called "democratic tactics."[6]

Verkhovsky had the look of one shaken and embarrassed by these objections. He bowed and took his leave. But the evening session of October 21 showed that the Constitutional Democrats' objections had not
compelled him to repudiate the plan of his campaign. In his speech he
operated on the basis of very loose calculations. The Minister of Food
Supply would undertake to feed only five million, but we had seven million soldiers at the front. Consequently, it was impossible to fight on.
Furthermore, the decline in the productivity of the factories made impossible the supply of the army at the same level as before: this led him to
the same conclusion.[7] Verkhovsky's entire argument before the committees, many members of which were accustomed to serious and specialized
work, was in this vein. At the conclusion of his speech Verkhovsky introduced the proposal he had worked out earlier: to listen immediately to
the speech of the Minister of Foreign Affairs, and then to open a debate
on both speeches. The members of the Party of Popular Liberty opposed this—and won support not only from among the cooperatives,

but also from among the leftist members of the committees. They indicated that one could not regard the conclusions of the War Minister as final and absolute, and before opening a debate on foreign policy, which was fundamentally dependent on these conclusions, it would be necessary first to try to verify the conclusions.

When this proposition was accepted and the debate on it was opened, the first opponent of Verkhovsky to speak, to the complete surprise of the committees, was Minister of Foreign Affairs, M.I. Tereshchenko. He asked three questions. Did the War Minister believe the data on which his [Verkhovsky's] analysis was based to be reliable? Was it possible to draw conclusions about the current level of supply without knowing the past levels and without having the opportunity to draw a parallel between present and past? And, finally, did the War Minister not suppose that to set out on the path indicated by him was tantamount to betrayal and treason? M.I. Tereshchenko also informed the audience that within the Provisional Government the questions touched on here had not been discussed, and that he had heard Verkhovsky's opinions for the first time tonight. After this sensational statement, the members of the Party of Popular Liberty introduced a new proposal: to terminate the discussion altogether until such time as the commission heard the opinion of the *entire* government, not just that of individual ministers, and to place on the agenda of the following joint committee session special reports on the comparative level of army supply in 1916 and in this year, in order to clarify how hopeless was the current situation. Other voices associated themselves with the voices of the Constitutional Democrats—after which the War Minister, in his confused and confusing answers to Tereshchenko's questions, touched anew on a matter that had escaped unnoticed in his speech to the Soviet of the Republic: the question of the necessity to concentrate power in the hands of someone who could manage the armed forces and who could, in case of need, resort to coercive measures. Just before this Verkhovsky's order to the troops of October 17 had appeared in the press. In this order, in very sharp language, Verkhovsky stated that "the disintegration and anarchy of the reserves are ruining the nation," and he "demanded that all commanders, in a close alliance with the commissars and the army committees, take the most decisive steps, including the use of armed force to suppress anarchy," since "until now, there have been more words than deeds." When the minister repeated these ideas in the committee, he was asked from the left: Was not this power about which he had spoken called "dictatorship"? "If you wish, you may call it by this name," was Verkhovsky's reponse.

The echoes of this debate found their way into the press in the next several days, and they produced the same impression as they had in the committee. *Den* [Day] wrote: "Has the nation entrusted its fate to a man in whom narrow-mindedness or adventurism exceeds a sense of duty and loyalty? . . . Adventurism smelling of the Black Hundreds, drunken fascination with the possibility of a dictatorship that now affects so many people, and internationalist phraseology are surprisingly combined in a person who occupies one of the most responsible positions in the state." *Russkoe Slovo* [Russian Word] said: "Having come forward at a time of a new assertiveness on the part of the 'Soviet' dictatorship and of increased Bolshevik strength, General Verkhovsky at once adopted the appropriate tone and began to speculate on the 'Kornilovshchina' and on the 'salvation of the revolution,' and thus he leapt onto the back of Comrade Trotsky's chariot." Of course, if General Verkhovsky had been a born 'comrade,' then his revolutionary career would not have ended with his dismissal, and we would have seen him in the role of a real general of the revolution, at the head of regiments sworn to obey Comrade Trotsky and victoriously conquering . . . Petrograd. But General Verkhovsky was only a "grandee for an instant."

The talk about "dictatorship," in connection with the impending uprising of the Bolsheviks, finally made an impression even on Kerensky. He decided to part with the War Minister. Verkhovsky's careless speech before the joint committees turned out to be the orange peel on which the War Minister slipped, even in the opinion of the leftists. The question of Verkhovsky's dismissal was raised by M.I. Tereshchenko, who went straight from the committee session to the Winter Palace to see Kerensky. Tereshchenko pointed out the impropriety of a separate speech by a minister, without warning to the government, on a question of such enormous importance and of such significance in principle. Verkhovsky admitted his guilt in this respect. Tereshchenko also stressed the insupportability of Verkhovsky's claims and the difficulties that would confront the Minister of Foreign Affairs in the conduct of foreign policy if these [Verkhovsky's] views should be adopted [as government policy].

After this, Verkhovsky could only tender his resignation. He was permitted to do this in the form of a "leave for reasons of health, and a release from the responsibility of being the War Minister". He was also required immediately to leave Petrograd, in order to end any rumors about his possible role in the event of a Bolshevik uprising. The official announcement of this resignation was drawn up, following Kerensky's usual vacillations, only on October 23 and was published on October 24. On the eve of this decision, on the 22nd, Burtsev's newspaper

Obshchee Delo [Common Cause] was closed for printing the foolish dispatch that "in a session of the committee on defense the War Minister proposed to conclude peace with the Germans in secret from the Allies." The chairmen of the committee, Skobelev and Znamensky, testified in print that Verkhovsky had made "no such proposal" in the committee on defense or in the joint session. The Allied ambassadors received from M.I. Tereshchenko the appropriate assurances. Tereshchenko proclaimed his victory by inviting M.V. Alexeev and P.N. Miliukov to be delegates who would accompany the ministers to the Paris conference. Alexeev provided a checklist of measures to restore the fighting capacity of the army, and for the fourth time insisted on the consistent and rapid implementation of the program that had been approved in June, in July, and in August and September. Miliukov spoke about the interests of Russia in the Far East, about our tasks in Armenia and in the Straits.

Such was the situation when the debate on foreign policy was reopened at the October 23 session of the Soviet of the Republic. The delegates were even less interested in foreign policy on that day than they had been earlier. In the meeting hall scarcely one hundred members remained, and they did not listen to the speakers. The session opened at 12 o'clock after a long delay, and was shortened even more by a break, during which, as also occurred during the debates, rumors were circulated in the lobby about the impending Bolshevik uprising, and representatives of the parties conducted unsuccessful negotiations about a transition formula in foreign policy that might gather a majority behind it. The only real purpose of the debates at this point was to reconcile Tereshchenko with the "democracy." This ought to have been accomplished by the speech of M. I. Skobelev, on the one hand, and by Tereshchenko's "explanation" of the misunderstandings that his speech had elicited among the "democracy." Of course, the minister had been "insufficiently energetic" in changing the course of Russian foreign policy. Nevertheless, "he did not manifest Miliukov's stubbornness."

Skobelev said that the "tragedy of Russian democracy" was that it had been forced simultaneously to obtain a swift peace and to strive for the democratic resolution of problems raised by the war. Concerning individual issues he provided consoling news. "The Belgian ambassador was satisfied by the explanations of the Executive Committee." "In the Alsace-Lorraine question there is no longer a disagreement between the Russian and the French democracies." The Poles, Armenians, and Serbs had been given promises that had satisfied them. With Lithuania and Latvia we would somehow reach a "brotherly" agreement about the preservation "of a great political-economic organism," in which "the democracies of all nationalities inhabiting [former] tsarist Russia, will have an equal stake." Concerning the harm to Russia from the neutralization of the Straits without complete disarmament, Skobelev said: "Let the Russian democracy take care lest the final disposition, toward which it strives in the field of international relations, become a means of its [Russia's] enserfment." In any case, the "Instruction" had served a purpose: "It had served as a litmus paper, immediately showing the pole of war and the pole of peace." There was nothing to fear where the army was concerned: "The representatives of the political current which chose to remain outside this auditorium [that is, the Bolsheviks] will at the decisive moment lay down their lives on the altar of their motherland. There are problems in the other armies as well: these problems can be explained as consequences of the length of the war." The delegation to the conference, of course, should be united, for "this [delegation] expresses the united will of a united revolutionary country." However, "a difference in views on particular concrete questions between members of the delegation is permissible." "The next immediate step of the Provisional Government should be *to propose to the Allies that they declare the goals* that will compel them to continue to wage war and in the absence of which [after the achievement of which?—PNM] they would be prepared tomorrow to lay down their arms, and *by this means transform the old treaties into historical artifacts*; finally, the government must move from the passive policy of silence toward vigorous public measures and it must make a *public proposal to the opposing side on behalf of all the Allies to enter immediately into a discussion of the condi-tions of peace.*"

M.I. Tereshchenko's response contained no new concessions to the "democracy," but it did contain several reproaches to the "democracy." The "zig-zags" in foreign policy, for which the minister had been criticized, had not occurred, but in domestic policy the "growing anarchy had lead to very serious zig-zags in the work of the government." "We have not abandoned the positions we took in May," said the minister, "but certain organizations have done so, if one compares their statements in March with those that they issue now." "The ministry cannot give up pursuit of the basic aims which constitute the national-political interests of Russia." His task at the conference was "to harmonize our views on the issue of peace as closely as possible with the views of the other side;" "the other side must agree to a peace without annexations." But there were two essential preconditions to this. First, that no one say of the [Russian] army that it consists only of men wearing soldiers' uniforms, but that everyone work to revitalize the army. Second, "that those who go abroad, . . . feel that behind them is a nation, that there are people who care for Russia and support and will create a united nation," just as our Allies had done.

"If this does not occur, then, whether there is one set of representatives or two, whether there is a controller and a minister or a controller alone, nothing will come of it."

At this statement the debate on foreign policy in the Soviet of the Republic was terminated. For the Soviet there remained two days to live—and these two days were filled with debates not about a worthy representation for Russia abroad, but rather about how to deal with the newly-arrived domestic hurricane that threatened to submerge everything: the leaders and the executives, and the very ship of state which was steering the nation toward the Promised Land of the Constituent Assembly. Before we return to these decisive days of struggle and to the role during them of the Soviet of the Republic, let us stop and examine where the danger really lay.

CHAPTER VII

THE BOLSHEVIKS PREPARE

Shortly before the Bolshevik Revolution the Bolsheviks' leader, Lenin himself, formulated the revolution's ideological justification in his brochure "Can the Bolsheviks Retain State Power?" This way of posing the question was the result of the then almost universal conviction of the press of the various factions that the Bolsheviks either would decide not to take power because they had no hope of retaining it, or they would seize power but would be able to hold onto it for only a short period. Among moderates some even found a Bolshevik seizure of power to be quite desirable, for "it will cure Russia forever of Bolshevism." From this perspective the Party of Popular Liberty was often showered with the criticism that, in opposing the triumph of Bolshevism, the party only delayed the inevitable revolutionary process and the disorganization of the nation connected with this process.

Experience demonstrated that this thoughtless self-assurance [of the moderates] was a profound mistake. The Bolsheviks took power and they retained it for a sufficiently long period as to deal not only to the possessing classes, but also to the entire nation irreparable blows, and to have squandered irrevocable opportunities in the inexorable competition of international forces. Thus, now [in 1918—ed.] one can with greater objectivity attend to what Lenin was planning to do, can assess what was true in his predictions about the future—a truth that won for the Bolsheviks the trust of the masses, that inspired them with that courage of "daring" that Kerensky lacked, and a truth that justified, through the success of Bolshevik actions, Lenin's preliminary predictions and calculations. We are not speaking here about success in the building of a social republic, but rather about the political victory of a party group which covered itself with the flag of a social republic.

Lenin took as his point of departure a statement of *Novaia Zhizn* in the issue of September 23.[1] "Is it necessary to demonstrate that the proletariat, (1) is isolated not only from the other classes of the nation, but also (2) from the genuinely vital forces of the bourgeoisie, that it cannot (3) technically manage to control the state apparatus, and (4) set this apparatus into motion, in (5) exceptionally complicated circumstances, or that it (6) will be unable to withstand the tremendous

pressure of inimical forces, which will sweep away not only the dictatorship of the proletariat, but also the entire revolution?" One after another
Lenin refuted all six points of this assertion.

Of course, the proletariat was "isolated" from the bourgeoisie, because the proletariat was fighting against the bourgeoisie. But in Russia, the proletariat was isolated from the *petty* bourgeoisie to a lesser extent than elsewhere. The Executive Committees of the peasant deputies
to the Petrograd conference spoke on behalf of 23 provinces and four armies against a coalition with the bourgeoisie in the government, when
only three provinces and two armies spoke in favor of a coalition *without the Constitutional Democrats,* and only four industrial and wealthy
provinces favored a coalition without limitations. Furthermore, the nationalities represented at the conference opposed a coalition by a vote of
40 to 15. Hence, Lenin stated: "The nationality and the agrarian questions are the root issues for the petty-bourgeois masses of the population of Russia at the present time: and on both questions the proletariat
is not 'isolated' at all. It has behind it the majority of the people . . . It
alone is capable of pursuing a decisive, genuinely 'revolutionary-democratic' policy on both questions, and in particular, of carrying out 'immediate and revolutionary measures against the landowners, the immediate
restoration of complete liberty to Finland, the Ukraine, Belorussia, the
Muslims, and so on.'" What of "the question of peace, that cardinal question of all contemporary life"? The proletariat would act here, in truth,
as the representative of all nations, . . . for only the proletariat, having
attained power, would at once propose a just peace to all the warring nations, only the proletariat would embark on genuinely revolutionary
measures (the publication of secret treaties), in order to obtain, as quickly as possible, as just a peace as possible. Thus, "this precondition for
the retention of state power by the Bolsheviks already exists."

Furthermore, it was not true that the proletariat was "isolated from
the vital forces of the democracy." The Kadets, Breshkovskaia, Plekhanov, Kerensky and Co. were "dead forces." The "living forces," "connected with the masses," were the left wing of the SRs and of the Mensheviks, and the strengthening of this left wing after the "July counter-revolution" was "one of the most reliable objective signs that the proletariat
is not isolated." A portion of the masses now following the Mensheviks and the SRs would support a purely Bolshevik government.

That the proletariat "cannot technically manage to control the state
appartus," the army, police and bureaucracy, this was very likely true in
the sense that this was "one of the most serious, most difficult tasks facing the victorious proletariat." But "Marx taught, on the basis of the experience of the Paris Commune," that the proletariat must not simply

manage to control the state machine, but must destroy it and replace it with a new one. "This state machine was created by the Paris Commune, and the Russian Soviets of Workers' Soldiers', and Peasants' Deputies are the same type of state apparatus [as the Paris Commune]." This was the Soviets' main *raison d'être*, their justification for existence. The Soviets, as a "new state apparatus," were invaluable: (1) because they provided an armed force of workers and peasants closely connected with the masses; (2) because this connection was easily accessible to examination and renewal; (3) precisly because this was an apparatus that was more democratic, and alien to bureaucratism; (4) because this apparatus "will provide a connection with various professions, thus facilitating by this means various reforms of the most profound character;" (5) because the new state apparatus would provide "a form of organization of the vanguard" of the oppressed classes, which "can raise up this gigantic mass;" and (6) because the new state apparatus "will provide the opportunity *to combine the benefits of parliamentarism with the benefits of unmediated and direct democracy*—that is, to combine through the elected representatives of the people, both the legislative function and the execution of the laws"—"a step forward, which has a universal-historical significance." "*If the popular creativity* of the revolutionary classes *had not created the Soviets, then the proletarian revolution in Russia would have been a hopeless cause*, for there is no question that the proletariat could not retain state power with the old apparatus." "The SR and Menshevik leaders prostituted the Soviets, made them play the role of talking-shops, of an appendage of conciliatory policy. . . . The Soviets can recover fully the use of their appendages and of their capacities only by taking all state power."

What was the purpose of this seizure of power? Lenin responded: "The state is a tool of class domination." If there was to be the domination of the "proletariat," then the proletariat would have to take into its hands "workers' control" over production and distribution, not "state control," as the Kadets and Mensheviks had agreed to do; in their mouths, it was simply a bourgeois-reformist phrase, but [what was needed was] "nation-wide workers' control" as an apparatus "of socialist revolution." In order to carry out this task, there existed in the modern state "besides the oppressive apparatus of the army, police and bureaucracy, a bookkeeping-notarial apparatus. It is neither wise nor necessary to destroy this apparatus; it is necessary to detach it from subservience to the capitalists, to sever from it, to cut away the capitalists' threads of influence from it, to subordinate it to the proletarian Soviets, . . . basing oneself on the achievements already attained by large capitalism." "Capitalism created the apparatuses of accounting, such as the banks, syndicates, post offices, consumers' cooperatives, employees' unions.*Without large banks socialism would be infeasible* . . . . A single state bank, the largest of all the large banks, with its branches in every volost, every factory—this is *nine-tenths of the socialist apparatus.*" The most humble employees, those engaged in the factual work of bookkeeping, control, registration, inventory, and billing, would probably submit to the Soviet, but with the "handful" of higher employees and capitalists it would be necessary to "act with severity." "These Mr. So and Sos we know by name: it is enough to take the names of the directors, board members, large stockholders, and so on. There are several hundred of them, or at most several thousand in the whole of Russia; for each one of them the proletarian state . . . can appoint tens, or hundreds of controllers." The heart of the matter was not the confiscation of the capitalists' property: in confiscation there was no element of organization, of accounting, of proper distribution. Confiscation could easily be replaced by the collection of a *just* tax ("if only at the Shingarev rates").

Would the proletariat be able "to set into motion" the new state apparatus? For this purpose there was a means "more powerful than the laws of the Convention and of its guillotine." "The guillotine only smashed active resistance: this is not enough for us: . . . we must also smash passive resistance, the more harmful kind of resistance . . . ." It was "insufficient" to "sweep away" the capitalists; it was necessary to "enlist them in state service." This would be achieved through a bread monopoly, a bread card, and a universal labor obligation. "He who does not work, must not eat." "The Soviets will introduce a work book for the rich." Those who were especially stubborn would be punished by confiscation of all their property and by prison.

But that was still not all. The state apparatus of old Russia had "set into motion" 130,000 landowners. Would the 240,000 members of the Bolshevik party, who represented not less than one million of the adult population, really be unable to govern Russia? We could "increase by tenfold this apparatus" by involving *the poor* "in the everyday work of administration." Did they have enough skills? Yes, if they would be charged with carrying out "revolutionary measures, such as the distribution of housing in the interests of the poor [which practice became known later as "the packing of apartments"], the distribution of food products, of clothing, of footwear in the cities, of land in the countryside." "Of course, mistakes are inevitable, but . . . can there be another way to teach the people to govern themselves, other than practice?" "The main thing is to inculcate in the oppressed and in the workers faith in their own strength, to show them in practice, that they *can* and should take upon themselves the proper, strict, ordered, organized distribution of bread, of all food, of milk, of apartments and so on, in the interests of the poor."

The fifth argument was that the Bolsheviks could not retain power, because of the "complicated circumstances," . . . but when had circumstances not been complicated during genuine revolutions? "A revolution is the sharpest, the most violent, the most desperate class struggle and civil war. Not a single revolution has succeeded without a civil war."

The sixth and last argument was that the victory of the proletariat would provoke hostile forces to smash both the proletariat and the revolution. Lenin responded: "Do not be afraid." "We have seen these hostile forces and this pressure in the Kornilovshchina." There would not be a civil war, but at most a futile rebellion of a small groups of Kornilovites, who would drive the people into a frenzy, and "provoke the people into a repetition on a grand scale of what occurred in Vyborg." "We have not yet seen the strength of resistance of the proletariat and the poorest peasants . . . . Only then, when tens of millions of people, who have been oppressed by want and capitalist slavery, see for themselves, sense that power in the state has been won by the oppressed classes—only then will manifest itself what Engels called 'hidden socialism:' for each ten thousand of publicly-known socialists there will appear a million new fighters, who until that time will have been politically asleep." "A starving person cannot distinguish a republic of capitalists and landowners from a monarchy," and so apathy and indifference ruled the people. "But here, where the last unskilled worker, or unemployed person, every cook, every ruined peasant can see—not from the newspapers, but with his own eyes—that the proletarian government is not grovelling before wealth, but is aiding the poor, . . . that it is taking surplus products from parasites and is aiding the hungry, that it uses force to install the homeless in the apartments of the rich, that it forces the rich to pay for milk, but does not give them a single drop of milk until the children of the poor are fed, that the land is being transferred to the laboring peasants, the factories and banks are under the control of workers, that swift and serious punishment awaits the millionaires who conceal their wealth—when he will see and feel this, *then* no force of the capitalists and kulaks [rich peasants] . . . will be able to defeat the popular revolution, but, on the contrary, the revolution will conquer the entire world, for in all nations the socialists' revolution is at hand."

The final utopian refrain did not of course deprive all these arguments of a very realistic content. Naturally, this was not socialism. But it was demagoguery, and very effective demagoguery, especially given the weakness and amorphousness of the Russian class superstructure and given the susceptibility of the unprepared masses to any experiment. Until the masses had become disillusioned as a result of these experiments, Lenin's assumption of the masses' support was quite correct. But afterwards? In the interim the "new state apparatus" would be created. Although Lenin proposed to rename his party the "communist" party, he was a poor believer in the federation of communes from the bottom up. In socialism he was more a Saint Simonist than a Fourierist, and he was completely alien to anarchist arguments. He was a centralist and a statist—and he counted first and foremost on measures of direct state compulsion. In objecting to the "reformist" Bazarov, he said: "The state, kind people, is a machine of violent coercion of one class over another. As long as it is a machine for bourgeois coercion of the proletariat, the proletarian slogan must be only this: the destruction of that state. But when the state becomes a proletarian state, when it becomes a machine for proletarian coercion of the bourgeoisie, then we shall certainly be wholeheartedly in favor of strong government and centralism." And then, in the interests of the proletariat and of the poor, the new state apparatus of violent coercion would be able to discipline and to tighten control on the poor as well.

In the "postscript" to the brochure Lenin quite pointedly explained why in July and earlier the Bolsheviks did not want to govern and why in October they did not intend to follow the "unimaginative" advice of *Novaia Zhizn*—to remain "invincible, occupying a defensive position in the civil war" and not assuming the burdens of "the attacker." Lenin's response could also serve as an answer to those who contended that it would have been better to allow the Bolsheviks to take power earlier, when they were less organized and still did not have the masses on their side. "Then [i.e. in July and before] we would not have proceeded with the experiment." "If the revolutionary party does not have a majority in the vanguard of the revolutionary classes and in the nation, then there can be no question of an uprising. In addition, an uprising requires: (1) the growth of the revolution on a country-wide scale; (2) the complete moral and political failure of the old—for example, the "coalition" government; (3) serious vacillations in the camp of the intermediate elements—that is, those who are not wholeheartedly for the government, although yesterday they might have been wholeheartedly in its favor." While looking for these signs, the Bolsheviks on July 3-5 "restrained the few elements who wanted a civil war" and "did not set our sights on an uprising." "It was only long after July 1917 that the Bolsheviks won a majority in the Petrograd and Moscow Soviets and in the nation." It was precisely after July 3-5, precisely in connection with

Tsereteli's followers' revelations of their July policy, precisely in connection with the masses' perception of the Bolsheviks as the most progressive fighters, and with the perception of the socialist bloc as traitors [to the cause], that the downfall of the SRs and Mensheviks began.

Even before the Kornilovshchina this decline was illustrated clearly by the elections of August 20 in Petrograd, which gave a victory to the Bolsheviks and dealt a devastating blow to the "socialist bloc." (The percentage of votes for the Bolsheviks rose from 20 to 33 percent, while the absolute number of votes in their favor fell only 10 percent; the percentage of votes for all the "moderates" fell from 58 to 44 percent, while their absolute number of votes fell 60 percent.)

The disintegration of the SRs and Mensheviks after the July Days and before the Kornilov affair was also demonstrated by the growth of the "left" wing in both parties, for the leftists reached 40 percent of party membership. Thus, "after the proletarian party had won a gigantic victory," it became necessary to give that party different advice than the advice *Novaia Zhizn* was providing: "Do not separate yourself from the excited masses by stepping toward the 'Molchalin democracy'" and "if you organize an uprising, then *go to the attack* while the enemy's forces are disorganized." "Catch the enemy unawares," Marx himself had said, quoting the words of the "great master of revolutionary tactics, Danton: boldness, boldness, and again boldness." The workers and soldiers would not tolerate Kerensky's government for a single day, for a single hour, if they knew that a Soviet government would make an immediate proposal of a just peace to all belligerents, and, consequently, that it would, in all probability, achieve an immediate cease-fire and a quick peace. "The soldiers of our peasant army will not tolerate for a single day, a single hour the survival of Kerensky's government against the will of the Soviets, for this government suppresses the peasant uprising by military measures."

"If objective conditions make civil war inevitable, or even highly probable, then how can one attribute paramount importance to the Congress of Soviets or the Constituent Assembly?" "Will the hungry agree to wait two months? . . . Or will the history of the Russian Revolution, which from February 27 to September 30 moved forward tempestuously and with unprecedented rapidity, now move from October 1 to October 29 [the day of the scheduled opening of Constituent Assembly], in a very calm, peaceful, and legally-balanced fashion," and thus provide an opportunity to place paramount importance on peaceful, legal-constitutional tactics, on the "simple" things of the legal and parliamentary sort, such as . . . the Constituent Assembly? "But this would be simply ludicrous, gentlemen; this is a sheer insult to Marxism and to logic in general."

There was no doubt that the logic of events was on Lenin's side. "Clearly seeing, sensing palpably and emotionally the presence of a condition of civil war," he gave the signal. Calling the just-formed coalition "a government of civil war," Trotsky obviously meant this: not that the coalition would begin a civil war, but that under this coalition the "objective circumstances of the moment" had brought about the "inevitability" of a civil war with incomparably greater chances for the victory of the "proletariat" than there existed on July 3-5.

Lenin's brochure was dated October 1, and it quite rightly emphasized that conditions favorable to a victorious uprising by the Bolsheviks had come into existence even before the "Kornilov days." We know that already on August 29 an armed uprising by Bolsheviks was supposed to occur. The uprising was anticipated by Kornilov, who sent, in accordance with the desire of the government and with his own plans, troops which were to arrive in the capital on the day scheduled for the Bolshevik rebellion. Of course, the Bolsheviks had every reason to think that Kornilov would not spare them, and that, given the change in the government's course that would inevitably occur in case of Kornilov's victory, they would find it difficult to continue their activity. And they preferred to avoid the blow directed at them, so they cancelled the scheduled uprising and thus placed Kornilov in the unfavorable position of attacking not the Bolsheviks, but the Provisional Government itself. This was very clever, and it showed a very competent leadership. In any case, the Bolsheviks did not cancel altogether, but rather delayed the realization of their plan. As soon as the Kornilov movement had been suppressed and there had commenced, in addition, a prolonged governmental crisis, they undertook serious preparations for the decisive battle. During the period of the government's greatest weakness, a document was written which cast a bright light behind the scenes of this preparation. Just as in the days preceding July 3-5, there was solid German assistance [to the Bolsheviks] in the form of money and weapons.

According to a telegram from the representative of the Diskonto-Gesellschaft to a certain Mr. Farzen in Kronstadt, Lenin received on August 29 the sum of 207,000 marks through certain persons indicated by Farzen in Stockholm. We do not know to what use the money was put. But on September 8 (23), according to a special telegram from the chairman of the Rhein-Westphalia coal and industrial syndicate, Kirdoff—that is, by special order from the chief source whence came the German subsidies, the office of the banking house W. Warburg created a new open account *for the use of Comrade Trotsky.* A certain lawyer (intelligence assumed that this was the well-known activist, Jonas Kastren) purchased weapons with this money, and no less famous an intermediary of the Bolsheviks in Stockholm than Fürstenberg-Hanecki got in touch with a "comrade" in Haparand, in order to prepare the shipment of these weapons and of the "sums demanded by Comrade Trotsky" to Russia. Eleven days later, on September 19 (October 2), Fürstenberg informed Antonov (this was probably the same person who was victorious with the future Bolshevik supreme commander in the attack against Rostov) in Haparand that "the instruction of Comrade Trotsky has been carried out: from the accounts of the syndicate and the ministry [probably, the Ministry of Foreign Affairs in Berlin] 400,000 krons have been taken and transferred to Comrade Sen [Sumensen], who simultaneously will visit [Antonov] and give you the above sum."[2]

Obviously, this serious preparation explained the attitude which the Bolsheviks adopted at this time *vis-à-vis* the "government of civil war," as Trotsky had earlier called the government of the third coalition, and toward all those "socialists" who cooperated in the creation of this coalition and of the Soviet of the Republic. For the sake of the impending uprising it was necessary to preserve the absolute purity and clarity of the position which in the working class and soldiers' milieu of Petrograd ultimately discredited all socialists, except the "left wing" of the Soviet of Workers' and Soldiers' Deputies, as "traitors" who did not wish immediately to give the people bread and peace. We saw the beginning of this campaign in the resolutions of the Petrograd Soviet of Workers' and Soldiers' Deputies during the negotiations over the coalition. Now it remains for us to follow how this campaign developed during the month of October, in parallel with the final preparations to enact on the streets of the capital "Comrade Trotsky's enterprise."

On October 9, that is, just after the Bolsheviks walked out of the Soviet of the Republic, there took place in Smolny Institute, under Kamenev's chairmanship, a plenary session of the Petrograd Soviet of Workers' and Soldiers' Deputies, in which the respective tactical positions of moderate and extremist socialism were articulated and clarified. Trotsky, in his report on the Pre-Parliament, stated that it was an unnecessary institution that only played into the hands of the imperalistic bourgeoisie, who were using the Pre-Parliament to implement their counter-revolutionary demands. He concluded his speech with an appeal to "*everyone to be prepared for the struggle to seize power*, since only the Soviets can save the nation and end the war through a genuine democratic peace." Liber futilely argued on behalf of the Mensheviks that the Bolsheviks "are ridiculously oversimplifying the issue of power," that "after two weeks they will discover that power does not generate bread," and that "having thought about it conscientiously, they will understand that it is one thing to take power into one's own hands, and another thing to keep it there." Liber added that "conscience had prevented the Mensheviks and SRs from taking power into their own hands, for they were not demagogues, and they knew that promises, once given to the people, would have to be fulfilled and that the people must not be deceived." The conclusion to be drawn from this was that one must never issue promises that cannot be kept, whether or not one is in power.

But here lay the difficulty of the intermediate position of the Mensheviks: for while they did not refuse to make promises, they did refuse to put themselves into a position in which they would have been forced either to keep the promises, or to refuse formally to keep them. The Bolsheviks leapt across the line of convention into demagoguery—and they attracted to their side the majority [of the Petrograd Soviet]. Against the votes of 169 Mensheviks and SRs the overwhelming majority of the Petrograd Soviet supported a resolution proposed by Kollontai,[3] which resolution said that the Pre-Parliament had been created to strengthen the power of the bourgeoisie, to bypass the All-Russia Congress of Soviets, and that the "Kornilovite" Kerensky needed the Pre-Parliament to advance his "Bonapartist plans."

The same kind of defeat awaited the SRs when the defensist Kaplan demanded from the Executive Committee of the Soviet emergency measures to defend the capital and cooperation in calling out the Petrograd garrison to meet the enemy. This last measure, on which the command of the Northern Front had insisted, was, of course, unpopular in Petrograd. An officer, a certain Pavlovsky, introduced a resolution demanding the immediate dismissal of the new government, the seizure of power, the arming of the workers, and a prohibition of the calling out of the Petrograd garrison. "The counter-revolutionary command must be replaced by a new, revolutionary 'committee of defense,' to which must be transferred all authority for the defense of the 'revolutionary people.'" This resolution of the Bolsheviks was also adopted by the Petrograd Soviet. At this session the army was represented by 36 delegates from the Romanian Front who stated that the soldiers were demanding an immediate conclusion of peace and the transfer of power to the Soviet; otherwise, the army itself would conclude peace and lay down arms. Chairman Kamenev greeted this statement by expressing pleasure that Bolshevik slogans had finally been assimilated, and he promised attentively to study the delegates' desires and to arrive at solutions satisfactory [to them].

On October 11 the experience was repeated at a still larger meeting of the representatives of the Soviets of the Northern Region, in which representatives of Moscow, the Baltic Fleet, and Petrograd Soviet took part, and which was chaired by Ensign Krylenko.[4] After a sharply-worded resolution having to do with 37 Bolshevik prisoners who remained in the Crosses Prison, a resolution that was proposed by Antonov and approved by the congress, Trotsky again demanded the transfer of power to the Soviets. The sailor Dybenko,[5] acting as the representative of the Finland regional committee, stated that the committee was conducting a constant struggle against the government. The representative of the Baltic Fleet said that the fleet was carrying out only those military orders which were countersigned by the commissars of the Soviet, and if the government did not conclude peace, then the Baltic Fleet itself would take steps to conclude it. The representative of the Volynsky Regiment, as if to underline the decision of the preceding meeting, stated that the regiment would not leave Petrograd in response to a mere command of "the counter-revolutionary government." In the subsequent session of the congress the delegates adopted an appeal to the peasants, which spoke "about the nearness of the decisive battle of the workers, soldiers, and peasants for land, for freedom, for peace." The representative of the Latvian Soviet of Workers' and Soldiers' Deputies claimed that 40,000 Latvian Sharpshooters were at the disposal of the congress. The only means of struggle against these resolutions of the congress available to the moderate majority of the Executive Committee of the Soviet of Workers' and Soldiers' Deputies was the statement that the congress was merely "a private meeting of individual Soviets, and not a congress with full authority."

For the Bolsheviks the "congress with full authority" would have to be the All-Russia Congress of Soviets, scheduled for October 20. According to the sense of their resolution (see Kollontai's resolution above), they wanted to appeal to this future congress over the decision of the Democratic Conference and of the agencies charged by the Democratic Conference with creating the coalition government. The Bolsheviks also decided to time their uprising, together with the demand to transfer all power to the Soviets, to coincide with October 20. The government learned about this as early as October 10, and on October 12 the issue of the maintenance of order in Petrograd was raised in Kerensky's meeting with his chief-of-staff, the War and Navy Ministers, Generals Cheremisov and Baranovsky.[6] Evidently, at that time the task of keeping order was thought to be simple and the tranquility of the capital to be well protected. The ambiguous attitude of the socialist part of the government toward the Bolsheviks continued, despite the impending threat from the Bolsheviks. At this same time Minister of Justice Maliantovich, acceding to the demands of the regional congress, deemed it possible to continue to release from prison Bolsheviks arrested after the uprising of July 3-5, even those such as Kozlovsky and Raskolnikov, or the ring leaders of the machine-gun regiment, the soldiers Semtsovye and Sakharov. Maliantovich found that these Bolsheviks could not be prosecuted under article 108 for "rendering aid to the enemy," just as one could not have prosecuted Leo Tolstoy. In vain did one of the assistant ministers object that it was impossible not to classify as "rendering aid to the enemy" such actions of the Bolsheviks as their refusal to obey their military commander, the confiscation of rifles from those wishing to go to the front, the explosions in defense factories, the detention at stations of trains loaded with artillery ammunition, and so on. (*Russkoe Slovo,* October 14)[7]

Also in vain military counterintelligence issued to all citizens a special appeal, reminding them that the work of German agents had intensified significantly in the past days, and that "the goals of the secret German agency and *of its allies in Russia* are to weaken our fighting strength, ultimately to undermine our economic strength, and *to exhaust the morale of the population by exacerbating the political struggle and inducing it to take the forms of pogroms and anarchy.*" (*Russkie Vedomosti,* October 15)

The first to draw attention to the seriousness of the approaching danger was the leadership of the moderate majority of the "revolutionary democracy." They had received reports about the energetic agitation which the Bolsheviks were conducting in the factories of the capital and among the soldiers of the Petrograd garrison. The Executive Committee of the Soviet of Peasants' Deputies was the first to condemn the plans of the Bolsheviks in a resolution, adopted on October 15 by a vote of 32 to 3, with 7 abstentions. "Having heard a report concerning the All-Russia Congress of Soviets of Workers', Soldiers' and Peasants' Deputies that is to meet on October 20, and at which it is proposed to carry out the demand for the transfer of all power to the Soviets, the All-Russia Congress of Peasants' Deputies considers it necessary categorically to state that, at present, such an act may have profoundly deleterious results for the nation and for the revolution, for it may lead to civil war, which will be advantageous to the foreign enemy that penetrates ever further onto our native soil, and also to the opponents of laboring people. Only the Constituent Assembly can decide finally the issue of power . . . . A decision on this issue on the eve of the Constituent Assembly, which is to be summoned in only a month-and-a-half, will be not only harmful, but also a criminal act, disastrous to the motherland and to the revolution."

On the following day, October 14,[8] the same issue was raised in the joint session of both Executive Committees [of the Soviet of Workers'

and Soldiers' Deputies and of the Soviet of Peasants' Deputies] in connection with the question of the defense of Petrograd. "In these days of
danger," said the speaker, Dan, "one of the factions of the revolutionary
democracy is conducting agitation in order to turn from words to action.
To what action? To what will this agitation lead?" Riazanov shouted
from his place: "To peace and to land!" "But the army," Dan continued,
"understands the agitation as an appeal not to carry out strategic orders.
The workers understand it as an appeal for an immediate uprising. Some
name the 16th, others the 20th [of October]. The Bolsheviks must answer as to whether they are being correctly or incorrectly understood;
they must say if they are telling the masses that an uprising will be accompanied by a bloody war, by a pogrom. Workers and soldiers are coming to us, the Central Executive Committee, and they say that they do
not know whether they should participate [in the uprising] or not. On
one hand, they should, on the other, it seems they should not. Let the
Bolsheviks directly, honestly, and publicly say here: yes or no?"

The Bolsheviks answered only with protests and commotion, trying
to drown out the speaker and break up the meeting. When they did not
succeed, they demanded an hour's adjournment to discuss Dan's resolution. When the assembly resumed its meeting, Piatakov delivered a
sharply-worded, demagogic speech, and introduced a resolution concerning the transfer of power to the Soviets. After prolonged debate everyone, except the protesting Bolsheviks and the Left SRs, voted for the
following resolution introduced by Dan. "Taking into account the precar-
ious military position of Petrograd, which is threatened by enemy attack and by the pogromist agitation being conducted by the counter-revolution, . . . the Central Executive Committee of the Soviets of Workers' and Soldiers' Deputies and of Peasants' Deputies, appeals to all
workers, soldiers, and peasants and to all the inhabitants of Petrograd to
preserve complete calm . . . and it considers impermissible under the circumstances any form of uprising, which can only provoke the pogromist movement and lead to the destruction of the revolution."

The non-socialist part of the government also directed attention to
the impending danger. A. I. Konovalov more than once insisted before
Kerensky on the adoption of real preventive measures against the event
of an uprising, on a precise explanation of which units of the military
would support the Provisional Government, and on the drafting of an appropriate plan of defense. These discussions were conducted on October
13 and 14. Kerensky's responses were evasive: measures had been tak-
en, there was nothing to fear, the military would provide sufficient
means of defense in case of need. On October 14 Konovalov insisted
that a report be heard from the Chief-of-Staff of the Petrograd Military

Region, General Bagratuni—the only man with any competence on the military regional staff—and Bagratuni's impression was that no measures had been taken, there was no plan, and that an uprising would certainly take the government by surprise.

On the evening of October 14, Kerensky departed the capital for Stavka, and returned only toward evening on October 17, and he still planned to depart again soon—this time for a long period—to the lower Volga, to Saratov, and to other cities, "to become acquainted with the mood of the people," as he put it. Konovalov continued categorically to protest against this plan.   Being unhappy over these repeated admonitions, Kerensky began simply to avoid conversation and to avoid giving direct answers to direct questions. The only steps taken in these days were orders issued by the chief commander of the Petrograd military district, Colonel Polkovnikov,[9] a typical representative of the new "revolutionary" command, promoted to his post not because of the value of his professional experience, but because of his revolutionary loyalty.   There was no lack of strong words in these orders of October 17. "Anyone capable of calling the masses to civil war at present," said the orders, "is either a blind fool or a person consciously acting in favor of Emperor Wilhelm." The orders mentioned the strict prohibition by the Provisional Government "of any sort of meeting, assembly, or procession, whoever arranges them," and finally there was a threat "to suppress by the most extreme measures any sort of attempt to violate order." Petrograd, Kronstadt, and Finland with all their troops were under the direct command of the Commander-in-Chief of the Northern Front (Cheremisov), and, in order to lay to rest the delicate issue of calling the Petrograd garrison out of the capital, Cheremisov called a meeting of military representatives in Pskov.

To these paper measures and formal directives the Bolsheviks responded with practical steps. The first such step was taken at the October 16 session of the Petrograd Soviet of Workers' and Soldiers' Deputies. On Trotsky's suggestion, the Soviet created the military headquarters of the impending uprising, under the title of the Military Revolutionary Committee. Trotsky made the usual demagogic arguments: "It is necessary to defend Petrograd against . . . the bourgeoisie, who want to rely on Wilhelm's troops against the revolutionary democracy." "Having learned a lesson from the experience of the Kornilovshchina, we cannot subordinate ourselves to the orders of agencies which have not yet been purged of counter-revolutionary elements. We must create our own agency, in order conscientiously to go forth to fight and to die." The Menshevik-Defensists protested "against adventures disastrous to the revolution." The Menshevik-Internationalists spoke against a mass uprising at present; but the majority voted to adopt the plan to create a

Military Revolutionary Committee, and Trotsky gave his benediction to this agency and sent it forth to do "urgent and fruitful work."

Indeed, the work did turn out to be urgent. There already existed an entire plan for an insurrection on the night of October 17. The masses were supposed to move toward the center of the city from three directions: from Okhta, from Narva Gate, and from Novaia Derevnia. A military detachment was supposed to seize the bridges across the Neva and to occupy Peter and Paul Fortress. Another detachment was supposed to seize the palaces. On this pretext the Provisional Government hurriedly met at two o'clock in the morning, and listened to Kerensky's, Verkhovsky's, and Nikitin's reports on countermeasures. After 4 A.M. the meeting continued in Kerensky's office with the high command of the military district; and steps were even taken to strengthen the defense of the Winter Palace. For this purpose cadet-artillerymen and two schools of ensigns were invited from Oranienbaum, although Polkovnikov continued even now to assure everyone that the majority of the garrison was opposed to the uprising.

At the final moment the Bolsheviks cancelled their preparations. Why they did this is not clear. Verkhovsky, as we have seen, gave himself the credit for having delayed the Bolshevik insurrection, and he explained their decision as being a result of their becoming alarmed over the impression caused by news of their plans among troops of the Northern Front. Like Kornilov, Verkhovsky had threatened to move frontline soldiers to Petrograd. Nevertheless, the threat turned out to be without foundation. True, the new candidate for Kornilov's role abandoned his post in the interim. It is possible that, in view of the measures taken by the government that night, that the Bolsheviks wanted to check their forces again. Finally, the Congress of Soviets, with whose meeting the insurrection had been planned to coincide, was delayed by the Central Executive Committee of the Soviet of Workers' and Soldiers' Deputies from October 20 to October 25. In connection with this, the entire disposition of the battle might have been altered. But the battle was merely delayed. The Bolsheviks now said, in essence, that they would not designate the day of their uprising at all.

The Bolsheviks took advantage of the delay in their uprising to strengthen their positions among the Petrograd workers and soldiers. Trotsky appeared at meetings in various units of the Petrograd garrison. The impression he created was typically such that, for example, Skobelev and Gots who were to speak after Trotsky in the Semenovsky Regiment were not allowed to speak by the soldiers. Trotsky advanced the slogan to wait for the instructions of the All-Russia Congress of Soviets. On October 19 there was a closed meeting of the regimental and company committees, called by the Military Section of the Petrograd Soviet. The delegates who were present turned out to be inclined toward the Bolsheviks, and the only difference in their statements was that not everyone was aware of the attitude toward the insurrections taken by the Central Executive Committee of the Petrograd Soviet, and in certain units the issue of the insurrection had not yet been formally discussed. Thus, the representative of the Izmailovsky Regiment said that his units trusted only the Soviet of Workers' and Soldiers' Deputies, and they would rise up at the Soviet's first call *against* the Provisional Government. The delegate of the Egersky Regiment stated that the regiment would rise up on the order of the Petrograd Soviet to *overthrow* the government and to transfer all power to the Soviets. The representative of the Volynsky Regiment said that soldiers of his regiment would *not carry out the orders* of the government. The delegate of the Pavlovsky Regiment said that his regiment recognized neither the government nor the Central Executive Committee, but that it had not discussed the issue of insurrection. The representative of the Keksgolmsky Regiment came with a prepared resolution calling for an immediate convocation of the Congress of Soviets, which would adopt measures to end the war. The representative of the XX Rifle Regiment indicated that the regiment demanded the immediate termination of the war and the transfer of land to the land committees. The representative of the Guard and of the Fleet Company stated that sailors did not trust the government, that they were waiting for an order from Tsentroflot, and they demanded an end to conciliatory politics. The Grenadier Regiment and the representative of the 2nd Oranienbaum School of Ensigns (the one posted in the Winter Palace) stated that they would come out *in support of the government only on the order of the Executive Committee of the Soviet*. The cavalrymen said they would remain neutral, although there were several Cossack squadrons and shock battalions that *sympathized* with the Provisional Government.

After all these reports Trotsky spoke, and he indicated directly the purpose of the meeting. "We have [made] no decision as to the time of the insurrection," he affirmed; "but the government wants to enter into an open battle against us, and we shall accept the battle; the Petrograd garrison will oppose the transfer of troops to the front." Then a series of resolutions of the Petrograd Soviet was read, proclaiming the unbreakable connection between it and all units of the garrison. Provisions were also made for the appointment of special commissars of the Petrograd Soviet for all military units, for duty at field telephones, and for the communication each day of the plans of the Military Revolutionary Committee, which had just been elected. In a word, the details of relations with the garrison were taken care of in expectation of an immediate insurrection.

Concerning the general situation in the city, correspondents of *Russkie Vedomosti* reported the following facts on October 20. "On the outskirts of the city, in the Petrograd factories such as the Nevsky, the Obukhovsky, and the Putilovsky, Bolshevik agitation for an insurrection is continuous. The mood of the working masses is such that they are prepared to move at any moment. Petrograd has witnessed recently an unprecedented flood of deserters. The entire railroad station is overflowing with them. At the Warsaw Station you cannot pass, for soldiers of a suspicious appearance, with blazing eyes and excited faces [bar the way]. All the outlying areas of the city produce a terrifying impression in this respect. On the embankment of the Obvodny Canal a crowd of drunken sailors moves about aimlessly . . . . There are reports about the arrival in Petrograd of entire gangs of thieves, who sense the chance to make a killing. Dark forces are organizing themselves, and they overflow the teahouses and lower haunts [*pritony*] . . . . A commissar of the Narva subdistrict informed the police about the appearance at the Baltiisky Factory of a large group of sailors . . . . In connection with the expected Bolshevik insurrection, private credit establishments report a strong demand by clients of their banks for the valuables belonging to the clients." This was a result "of the conviction of the broad masses of the populace that the insurrectionary Bolsheviks will turn first to the destruction of private commercial banks."

The days of October 20, 21 and 22 passed in this tense state of expectation. Patrols walked the streets; now and then there appeared mysterious automobiles with men in soldiers' uniforms who shot into the air with revolvers and rifles. Near the Winter Palace stood armored cars, light artillery and rifles. The approaches to the palace and to military headquarters were guarded by sentries. On Sunday, October 22, the feast of the Divine Mother of Kazan, Cossacks scheduled a religious procession, but the Bolsheviks announced the "day of the Petrograd Soviet." At a general meeting of regimental committees in Smolny Trotsky announced that there would be a "showing of our revolutionary forces." However, in view of the Cossack demonstration, the Petrograd garrison introduced a resolution which invited the "brother Cossacks" to "tomorrow's meetings," which explained the goal of the "day of the Soviet" as "the collection of funds for the revolutionary press," and which warned against the "provocation of our common enemies," Kornilov and the bourgeoisie.

The "day of the Petrograd Soviet," October 22, passed more tranquilly than had been expected.[10] The frightened populace stayed home or kept to the side. Meetings were not attended by large crowds, and the Bolshevik orators who spoke at them did not win the unanimous sympathy of the audience. Although the Cossack religious procession was cancelled nevertheless, a crowd of demonstrators that was unaware of this cancellation gathered at St. Isaac's Cathedral and formed a rather inspiring procession to the Kazan Cathedral. Toward evening the crowd dispersed, and the day ended peacefully. Yet simultaneously the last preparatory steps toward the decisive insurrection were being taken, and perhaps that was the explanation for the moderate tone of the Bolshevik speakers, who invited their partisans to hold back from an insurrection and to gather strength for the moment when the Petrograd Soviet would give the signal to seize power.

At the center of the impending insurrection stood the Military Revolutionary Committee, organized on October 20, and ordained to replace the headquarters of the Petrograd military district as leader of the Petrograd garrison. On the night of October 21/22, the committee began to put its plan into action.[11]   Members of the Military Revolutionary Committee appeared at military headquarters and demanded to be admitted into the control of all orders issued from headquarters and to have the right of decision over them. Colonel Polkovnikov responded to the demand with a categorical refusal. Military headquarters already had one "revolutionary institution:" that was the special conference of representatives of the Central Executive Committee of the Soviet of Workers' and Soldiers' Deputies and of the Soldiers' Section of the Petrograd Soviet. But now there was a struggle between the Central Executive Committee and the Petrograd Soviet, and the latter had decided directly to take revolutionary power over the military headquarters into the hands of its own committee. After Polkovnikov's refusal one of the members of the special conference in the headquarters, a member of the Soldiers' Section, the soldier Ogurtsovsky, stated that under such conditions he could not work with headquarters. Then Polkovnikov adopted a compromise measure: he appealed by telephonograms to all the regimental committees of the Petrograd garrison by inviting all of them to send their representatives to military headquarters.

Given the inclination that the garrison had shown toward the Military Revolutionary Committee, one might have foreseen what would be the outcome. The representatives of the regimental committees were elected, but, on the proposal of the Military Revolutionary Committee, they were sent not to military headquarters to see Polkovnikov, but to Smolny, "to work out coordinated tactics and to adopt a resolution on their relationship to district military headquarters." After prolonged debate at this meeting (on October 23) it was decided to a send a telephonogram to all units of the Petrograd garrison, which telephonogram was to say that the district military headquarters, having refused to recognize the authority of the Military Revolutionary Committee, by this act had broken with the Petrograd Soviet, and had become "the direct tool of counter-revolutionary forces." The telephonogram also contained the following directives: "No orders to the garrison are valid without the signature of the Military Revolutionary Committee. All orders of the Petrograd Soviet pertaining to tomorrow remain in force. All soldiers of the garrison are responsible for showing vigilance, self-possession, and military discipline. The revolution is in danger. Long live the revolutionary garrison!" A delegation of six men was supposed to go to district military headquarters and to announce there that, from now on, headquarters could communicate with the garrison only through the Military Revolutionary Committee.

As these decisions were being elaborated in Smolny, at district military headquarters there was a meeting of the garrison and brigade committees together with representatives of the Executive Committee of the Soviet of Workers' and Soldiers' Deputies, the Executive Committee of the Soviet of Peasants' Deputies, and of the Petrograd Soviet. Members of the Petrograd Soviet stated that they were present only to gather information, but a member of the Soviet, Second Lieutenant Dashkevich, presented a demand that all orders issued by military headquarters be countersigned by the Military Revolutionary Committee. Representatives of military headquarters explained that they could not accept the commissar of the Military Revolutionary Committee because they already had a commissar—the representative of the Central Executive Committee, Malevich, and before the appointment of another commissar they would have to await the resolution of the conflict between the Central Executive Committee and the Petrograd Soviet.

The government could not, of course, fail to direct attention to the activity of the Bolsheviks, which the longer it remained unpunished, the more unceremonious and aggressive it became. At the insistence of A. I. Konovalov, Kerensky summoned the ministers to the Winter Palace on October 23 for a discussion of the current situation. They unanimously found that the unauthorized formation of the Military Revolutionary Committee should be considered a criminal act—all the more so because it had occurred in the theater of military activity. Attention was directed to the indecisiveness of Polkovnikov's actions and to the need to concentrate the defense of the capital and of the government in the hands of another and more experienced leader.

We have already noted A.F. Kerensky's mood in these last days of the existence of the Provisional Government and his constant hesitations to adopt swift and decisive measures, when needed. Kerensky's mood certainly affected his response to the political crisis at hand. In his later article, entitled "Gatchina" (*Sovremennye Zapiski*) [Contemporary Notes], Book X, 1922), Kerensky refused to accept the responsibility [for the failure of his government]. He placed this responsibility partly on the shoulders of his fellow party members: "Around October 20 [we have seen that this had begun much earlier] the Bolsheviks began to put into action in St. Petersburg their plan of armed insurrection to overthrow the Provisional Government. This preparation went rather successfully, particularly because the remaining socialist parties and Soviet groups, who regarded all reports about the impending events as 'counter-revolutionary fabrications,' did not even try at the time to mobilize their forces, which were capable at the crucial moment of resisting the Bolshevik conspiracy from within the revolutionary democracy itself." We have seen the internal causes of the paralysis of the "remaining socialist parties." But A.F. Kerensky himself also regarded very lightly the impending insurrection. In response to the statements of the ministers, he said that he was very glad of this insurrection, for it was the best means to effect a final separation from the Bolsheviks.

To achieve this objective, the government nevertheless had to ready its forces. A.F. Kerensky wrote in the above-mentioned article: "For its part the government was preparing to suppress the mutiny, but, not being able to rely on the St. Petersburg garrison which had been demoralized completely by the Kornilov uprising, the government sought other means of resistance. On my order troops were to be sent at once from the front to St. Petersburg, and the first echelons from the Northern Front were supposed to appear in the capital on October 24. At the same time [that is, after the 20th, or even after the 23rd] Colonel Polkovnikov, the commander of troops in the St. Petersburg military district, received an order to work out a detailed plan for suppressing the mutiny. He was told at that time to identify and to organize all reliable units of the garrison." We have seen how far from these glib expressions was the real state of affairs in which Polkovnikov was forced to work. According to Kerensky, Polkovnikov "reported personally to me every morning; he constantly reported that among the troops under his command, the units that the government had at its disposal were 'fully sufficient,' to deal with the impending uprising." We have just seen that at the very time when Kerensky was issuing orders to Polkovnikov and listening to his reports, the ministers were demanding the replacement of Polkovnikov by a more energetic and experienced man. In the article "Gatchina," Kerensky admitted that these observations were well-founded, but again he spread the responsibility from himself to the entire government. It was very unfortunate, he said, "that *we, the members of the government,* learned too late that Polkovnikov himself, as well as part of his staff, played in these fateful days a *double game,* and that they were affiliated with that section of the officer corps in whose plans entered the overthrow of the Provisional Government by the Bolsheviks." Indeed, there was such a disposition, and not only among the officers. But to accuse Polkovnikov of a conscious "double game" obviously was going too far.

For its part the Military Revolutionary Committee was full of activity. In a crowded meeting of the Petrograd Soviet on October 23, in the presence of the numerous public, committee member Antonov reported on the first two days of activity of the Military Revolutionary Committee.[12] "Almost all units of the garrison have already recognized the authority of the committee and its commissars," said Antonov. "Various institutions in the capital have also turned to the committee. Typesetters of one printing plant have asked the committee whether they must fulfill orders which they believe to be inspired by the 'Black Hundreds';[13] and the committee directed that the printing plant not fill a single suspicious order without its sanction. Workers of the Kronverksky Arsenal compained that, on orders from military headquarters, a significant number of rifles were to be issued from the arsenal. The committee sent its commissar to the arsenal, and the commissar detained ten thousand rifles, scheduled to be sent to Novocherkassk. The committee directed in general that workers should not issue weapons from the warehouses or plants without its order."

Furthermore, Antonov stated that the Military Revolutionary Committee was not only informed of the measures which the government was taking against the event of an uprising, such as summoning troops from the front and from various cities, but it had also taken its own measures. Thus, an infantry unit that was headed for Petrograd had been stopped in Pskov. An infantry division and two regiments in Venden had refused to go to Petrograd. The committee did not yet know what had happened with respect to the detachment of cadets that had been summoned from Kiev, or to the shock battalions, but it would soon receive information. Antonov noted incidentally in his report, that, despite the threats of military headquarters and of the Central Executive Committee, the commissars of the Military Revolutionary Committee had not yet been arrested. "And, what is more, they will not dare to arrest [the commissars]," he added to thunderous applause.

Indeed, having heard that evening Polkovnikov's report,[14] the government discussed the question of whether immediately to arrest the Military Revolutionary Committee, but . . . it decided to await further developments! In the meantime, Kerensky discussed with Maliantovich the possibility of mounting judicial investigations against the committee's members . . . . The physiognomy of the city, under the impact of the government's inactivity and of the failure to punish criminal actions, changed noticeably. The Red Guards began unauthorized searches; shooting could be heard in several places. At emergency meetings the soldiers, sailors, and workers appealed to the populace to accept Bolshevik slogans.

On October 24 the newspapers published an appeal from the Petrograd Soviet to the citizens, soldiers, and populace of the capital. The papers repeated that the military headquarters "had broken with the revolutionary garrison and with the Petrograd Soviet," had become a "direct tool of the counter-revolutionary forces," and that "the Military Revolutionary Committee declines any responsibility for the actions of the Petrograd military district." The soldiers were told that "no orders to the garrison are valid without the signature of the Military Revolutionary Committee." The populace was informed that in all military units and in "all especially important points of the capital and its peripheries," commissars had been appointed, and that resistance to them was "resistance to the Soviet of Workers' and Soldiers' Deputies" (the announcement did not mention which Soviet) and that without the confirmation of the Soviet no orders or directives should be carried out. Citizens were invited to render to their commissars "the utmost support."

For his part, the military commissar of the Central Executive Committee at military headquarters, Malevsky, directed to the committees of the Petrograd garrison a counterappeal, in which he called for the preservation of calm and reminded everyone that "any insurrection will provoke a civil war, which will be favorable to the enemies of the revolution." Thus, the conflict became public and open. All the optimistic information which reached the Winter Palace in the depths of the night, information to the effect that the conflict had been resolved successfully, "in a quite painless manner," turned out to be untrue. The Military Revolutionary Committee not only did not recognize the Central Executive Committee, but did not even express the desire to subordinate itself to the Petrograd Soviet, if the Soviet should move toward a compromise. The Muscovite *Sotsial-Demokrat* [Social-Democrat] stated with complete candor that same day: "A civil war has begun. War has been declared and military maneuvers have commenced. We must say this

quite firmly. Kerensky and his agents are our public enemies: no negotiations with them. One does not talk with enemies, one strikes them."

Given this situation, the government could no longer keep its silence. Finally, Kerensky spoke out. He spoke on that same day, October 24, at a session of the Soviet of the Republic; it was, alas, his last
speech. He narrated the history not of his preparations, but of his negotiations, which had lasted for as long as the enemy had required in order
to prepare itself [for insurrection]. "Despite a whole series of statements, attempts at persuasion and proposals, which have come from a
whole series of public organizations," Kerensky said, "and in particular,
despite a very moving statement, which was made yesterday by the representatives of all the delegates that have arrived here from the front, we
have not received in this period a statement cancelling the directives issued by the Military Revolutionary Committee. We only received a
statement at 3 A.M. that, in principle, all points, which were presented
as an ultimatum from the military authorities, were accepted." Thus, Kerensky thought it necessary to add, "the organizers of the insurrection
had been compelled formally to state that they had committed an im-
proper act, which they now repudiated." It was this, obviously, that the
government had considered a "painless end" of the uprising. From the
audience people exclaimed: "That is original!" "But," Kerensky continued, "as *I had expected and was certain on the basis of all the preceding
tactics of these people, this was simply a delaying tactic and a conscious deception.* By now an entire day has elapsed, and we do not have
the statement that was supposed to be posted in all the regiments; but
we do have evidence of the opposite—that there is now occurring the
voluntary issuing of cartridges and weapons, and also that two companies have been called out to assist the revolutionary headquarters. Thus,
I must affirm before this Temporary Soviet of the Republic that . . . a
certain portion of the populace of Petersburg is in a *state of insurrection.*"

Kerensky pronounced these words in the satisfied tone of a lawyer
who had finally succeeded in establishing the guilt of his adversary—just as he had established the guilt of Kornilov—a guilt in something which the adversary had been carefully and skillfully concealing.
Even at this moment he cared above all about the "juridical classifica-
tion" [of the Bolsheviks' conduct], as he expressed it here. But from the
audience was heard the ironic comment: "They have been waiting [for
this]." And Kerensky, amidst increased commotion on the extreme left,
added: "I have proposed immediately to begin an appropriate judicial investigation, and have ordered the appropriate arrests." . . . The arrests
of whom? An order for Lenin's arrest had been issued several days

earlier, but Kerensky himself noted—he thought acidly—that "ringleaders have the custom and the great capability of hiding themselves," so "none of the terrible consequences of an insurrection" threatened them.

Those were all the steps that the government claimed it had taken. And Kerensky's entire speech, which was lacking its usual deliberate ornateness, and which grew more anxious and confused every minute, was intended not to suppress the insurrection, but to exculpate Kerensky in the eyes of the left, and even in the eyes of the insurrectionaries. In order to demonstrate that they were really criminals, he established Lenin's guilt by quotations from the Bolshevik newspapers *Rabochy Put* [Workers' Path] and *Soldat* [Soldier]. But, so as to soften even this attack, Kerensky even at such a time refused to renounce his usual approach—to balance a blow to the left with a blow to the right. He stated that propaganda against the government (from the audience people exclaimed: "in favor of a strong government") was also being conducted by *Novaia Rus* [New Russia], *Zhivoe Slovo* [Living Word], and *Obshchee Delo* (Burtsev's paper), and that these papers, on his order, "were also closed tonight." He also considered it "extremely important to note for his own sake," that "the organizers of the insurrection themselves," "Lenin himself," had given to him, Kerensky, "a usurper, who had sold himself to the bourgeoisie," evidence that under his government "the best-situated proletarian internationalists in the world" could organize their rebellion without being punished at all. He returned again and again to this notion in the course of his speech. "The government can be reproached for weakness and for its extraordinary patience, but, in any case, no one has the right to say that the Provisional Government, during the entire period *when I stood as its leader* and even before, resorted to any measures of forcible pressure whatsoever *before there was a direct threat to the state's survival.* I also ask those members of the Soviet of the Republic, who are shouting that the government's actions were not in time and that we did not act at all, to remember . . . that regardless of anything else, we had to try to govern so that the new regime, the regime of liberty, would be as free as possible of reproaches that it had engaged unnecessarily in repressions and cruelties." "No one can possibly suspect that the measures we are adopting have any other purpose than the necessity to save the state."[15]

During his speech Kerensky received a copy of a document which the Military Revolutinary Committee was just issuing to the troops: "The Petrograd Soviet of Workers' and Soldiers' Deputies is in danger. I order the regiment to be brought to full battle readiness and to await further directives. Any delay or nonfulfillment of this order will be considered a betrayal of the revolution. For Chairman Podvoisky, Secretary

Antonov."[16] This was the language of authority. . . . Kerensky, reading the document to the assembly, repeated that there was a "state of insurrection," and continued by condemning the "mob," by appealing to
"reason, conscience, and the honor of the populace of the capital," and
by frightening it not only with a breach in the front, with a new military catastrophe, but with a new "attempt" at counter-revolution, "perhaps more serious than Kornilov's attempt."[17] Kerensky declined responsibility in advance and placed it on the shoulders of others, and he
testified to the government's innocence and to his own personal innocence. From the left they shouted in response: "They are guilty, who behind the back of the democracy prolonged the war."

As the rest of the audience applauded, the left stubbornly sat in silence. But it was toward them that Kerensky continued to direct his arguments, and, at the conclusion of his speech, he even made new advances
to them. The Bolsheviks—a party that would soon be destroyed—"promises to the people land and peace." But the government
was also prepared to offer the same. It was now "discussing in final
form the question of temporarily transferring land, *before* the Constituent Assembly, to the disposition and administration of land committees." The government also "proposed in the coming days to send its delegation to the Paris conference in order that there, in accordance with its
convictions and its program, among any number of other issues, it
could raise the question of and draw the Allies' attention to the necessity
of defining precisely and concretely the tasks and goals of war, that is
the question of peace." These statements, based on agreements reached
in the Central Executive Committee of the Soviet, obviously were intended to strengthen the latter and weaken the Bolsheviks among the
masses. In fact, they only deprived the government in this final moment of its own clear and concrete position, and took away the last defenders on whom it might have relied. To defend the government—yes,
of course! But. . . to defend Kerensky? The Kerensky, who two months
ago had had the chance to crush the Bolsheviks, but who even now, in
the face of obvious danger, justified himself before them? The Kerensky, who himself disorganized his own defense, who did not wish to rely on the honest Kornilov, and who did not dare to trust the intriguer,
Verkhovsky? That was the thinking even among those circles which
could have rendered real support to Kerensky at that juncture.

But Kerensky's attention had been diverted in another direction. He
demanded on that very day, in the afternoon session, that the Soviet of
the Republic answer his question, "Can the Provisional Government
carry out its duty with an assurance of the support of this high
assembly?" Having made advances to the "revolutionary democracy,"

he assumed that, at least the moderate section of the democracy, the democracy of the Executive Committee which was locked in a fierce struggle with the Military Revolutionary Committee, would cast aside all its doubts and scruples and would support the government unconditionally and wholeheartedly. About the elements of the assembly who understood the principle of the state, he, of course, did not have to worry: whatever they might have thought of Kerensky, they understood at that moment that all partisan calculations and disagreements had to be put aside and that the government would have to be supported, no matter what.

After his speech, Kerensky, in his own words, "not expecting a vote, returned to the military headquarters, to the interrupted urgent work, thinking that not an hour would pass before he would hear news about all the decisions and practical undertakings of the Soviet of the Republic to assist the government." It was not clear what "practical undertakings" Kerensky had in mind here. These undertakings were the business of the government, and with them, as we have seen, the government was terribly late. Of course, the Soviet of the Republic could and should have offered to the government its moral support. Truth to tell, under the circumstances its support was not worth very much. Yet, if the Soviet of the Republic had rendered support to the government, then at the very least, regardless of the course of events, it would have justified its own existence.

Kerensky attributed too much importance to the Soviet of the Republic, but he had his own reasons for doing so. His hopes—and his last reproaches—were related not to the supreme representative institution as a whole, but to those political allies for whom the support of a fellow member and a "comrade" was a special obligation. As we shall now see, Kerensky's reproach that the Soviet of the Republic "wasted that entire day and entire evening on endless and useless arguments and more arguments," applied only to the socialist section of the Soviet.

Incidentally, the preeminence that Kerensky then attributed to the socialist elements in the Soviet had its effect on a plan which was never implemented, but which certainly existed and whose meaning was very symptomatic.

Among the elements of the "revolutionary democracy" who then were seeking a "united front" with the extreme left wing, there circulated the idea of excluding from the Soviet of the Republic the entire rightist section, of augmenting the Soviet of the Republic with Bolsheviks, and of turning the institution into the "Convention" of the republic. Much later one newspaper even reported that Kerensky himself was involved in negotiations over a possible change of course and that his "close friend V.K." had "already managed to make preliminary steps toward negotiations with the responsible leaders of the socialist parties" on the subject of forming an exclusively socialist government that would include the Bolsheviks. Although "a political figure close to the Bolsheviks, Mr. E" had responded that "the time for unification of the socialist democracy including the Bolsheviks probably has passed," he did not refuse "in the event of an official proposal from Kerensky to convey such a plan to the responsible leaders of the Bolshevik party."[18] Of course, for such a proposal "the time had passed," when at the October 24 session of the Soviet of the Republic Kerensky had called these leaders "traitors and betrayers" and had ordered their arrest. But nevertheless, these rumors, which were not altogether implausible, explain to us the mood within the "democracy" at this moment, when it was forced to make a decisive choice and "courageously to stand on one side or on the other," as Kerensky himself had demanded when he condemned forevermore "the people who never make up their minds to speak the truth courageously."

The adjournment announced after Kerensky's speech in order to permit the parties to meet in caucuses lasted until 6 P.M. The opinion of the rightist elements of the Soviet was quite clear and unanimous: there was no point in debates at the moment; it was necessary immediately, without debate, to carry out, if possible by a large majority, the decisive vote requested by the government to condemn the insurrection and to support the government. The leaders of this section of the Soviet decided to restrain themselves from making any speeches. On the other hand, among the parties of the "revolutionary democracy" the mood was more confused. Regardless even of the strong pull of the left which we noted above, the center would have to take refuge behind a justification that would be more or less acceptable to the Congress of Soviets which was to open its first meeting the next day, October 25, and where there loomed the prospect of a bitter struggle against the Bolsheviks' proposal to transfer all power to the Soviets. Therefore, the formula drawn up by the socialist parties offered the government only conditional support. The socialists promised to support the government in the event that it would adopt the following proposals (which were already mentioned, as we have seen, in Kerensky's speech): (1) All privately-owned lands must be transferred to the jurisdiction of the land committees; (2) the Provisional Government must take decisive steps in foreign policy—namely, immediately to publish secret treaties and to send to the Allies a demand to publish their war aims. Since there was very little reason to think that the entire membership of the current government would accept these conditions, their adoption by the Soviet of the Republic meant a new governmental crisis at the height of the insurrection. The negotiations for an exclusively socialist government must also be understood against this background.

Given the distribution of votes on the preceding roll calls over issues of principle, one could already foresee that the Soviet of the Republic would be unable to reach a consensus even on an issue that for the Soviet of the Republic itself as well as for the government was a matter of life and death. But if the *support* of the Soviet at this point had no great positive significance, a *refusal* of support would undoubtedly have a very great *negative* impact. In this case the government would be deprived of its last moral support. While this would not have any practical effect on the outcome of the struggle in Petrograd, it was very important for the army and for people in the provinces what position the Soviet of the Republic might adopt in the conflict [with the Petrograd Soviet]. Everyone understood this, even the intermediate elements such as the cooperatives and the Popular Socialists on whose attitude the outcome of the vote in the given assembly hinged. But, while they understood this, they did not wish, on the other hand, to sunder themselves completely from the socialist front. Once this front moved to the left, then the most they could resolve to do was to abstain from voting for the leftist formula. But at the same time they had agreed to vote for the formula of the rightists and, in case the vote on the rightist formula should come first, then perhaps they might have given the government the majority it had demanded. An accidental chain of circumstances led to a vote on the leftist formula before the vote on the rightist one; the cooperatives and Popular Socialists did not understand that, given such a sequence of voting, their abstention was tantamount to rejecting the formula that they wanted to vote for. Unfortunately, the more influential figures in their midst, such as E.D. Kuskova, were absent from this part of the meeting, and the sequence of voting caught the entire group by surprise. It recovered only when its abstention had thrown the balance in favor of the leftist formula. After that, the rightist formula was a dead letter and was not even put to a vote.

Thus, in this decisive moment, the Soviet of the Republic again manifested that basic trait which we have encountered constantly: the commitment of its centrist leadership to abstract ideologies, which led to its victimization by leftist demagoguery, and, thence led to indecisiveness and confusion on fundamental issues requiring a quick and clear decision. On this occasion this trait showed itself especially clearly, since the issue at hand was not the complex matters of military affairs and diplomacy, but the most simple and elemental question: whether to support the principle of the state and the government during an open in-surrection against it. Even at such a moment, when there was a mutiny on hand, a mutiny which wrote on its banner utopian slogans and which so obviously threatened to forfeit the war and to deliver Russia to the mercies of the victor, to dismember Russia, to enslave it economi-cally, even then a majority of the assembly was not to be found that would express the national will; and if the Soviet of the Republic re-flected the real opinion of the nation in this matter, then in such an event it was obvious that Russia had no other way forward into the hoped-for future than the way of terrible ordeals and learning by bitter experience.

The Provisional Government, taken as a whole, could not interpret the decision of the Soviet of the Republic except as a vote of no con-fidence—and especially, of no confidence in the non-socialist part of the cabinet. Under normal circumstances, the result of the vote would have been the final collapse of the coalition and the formation of an ex-clusively socialist government. But how can one walk out on the eve of an insurrection, even though the struggle against the insurrection ap-pears hopeless? This was a question that the representatives of the Con-stitutional Democrats and of the propertied elements in the government had to put to themselves. They received the formal right to step down. A sense of duty to the motherland forced them to remain and to share in Kerensky's lost game. As far as Kerensky was concerned, at 11 P.M. he and several members of the government held a meeting with the lead-ers of the socialist majority of the Soviet democracy who supported the cabinet—Avksentiev, Gots, Dan, and Skobelev.

From the beginning Kerensky told the delegation of the socialist groups that he was angry about the "resolution they had adopted," that "the government, after such a resolution, would resign tomorrow morning," and that "those who voted for it must accept the entire re-sponsibility for events, although, apparently, they had very little notion of those events." "To this, my angry philippic," wrote Kerensky in "Gatchina," "Dan calmly and rationally responded—Dan who was at that time not only a leader of the Mensheviks, but also a chairman of the All-Russia Central Executive Committee . . . . First, Dan said to me, that they were informed much better than I was [about events], and that I exaggerated events under the influence of reports from my 'reac-tionary military headquarters.' Then he told me that the resolution of the left majority of the Soviet of the Republic 'that the government finds so unpleasant' is extremely useful and important for 'changing the masses' mood,' 'that its [the resolution's] effect is already being felt,' and that from now on the influence of Bolshevik propaganda would 'quickly decline.' On the other hand, in his [Dan's] words, the Bolsheviks themselves in negotiations with the leaders of the Soviet majority had expressed the willingness 'to subordinate themselves to the will of the majority of the Soviet;' they said they were prepared 'tomorrow to undertake all measures to quell the insurrection,' which had 'ignited itself independently of their desires, without their sanction.' In conclusion," Kerensky said, "Dan, having mentioned that 'tomorrow' [it is always tomorrow] the Bolsheviks would disband their military headquarters, said to me that all the steps I had taken to suppress the uprising were only 'irritating the masses' and that, in general, I by my 'interference' only 'hinder the representatives of the majority of the Soviet from successfully conducting negotiations with the Bolsheviks to end the insurrection.' To complete the picture, I must add that precisely during the time when this significant report was being made to me, the armed detachments of the 'Red Guard' were occupying one government building after another."

Dan's statements were the best illustration of the attitudes that determined the behavior of the left wing of the Soviet of the Republic on the eve of the Bolshevik victory. Springing from a profound misunderstanding of the real circumstances, these attitudes tied the hands of the government and deprived it of any possibility to act decisively. However, it would be a mistake sharply to demarcate the attitude of the socialist elements in the government itself from the attitude of those political circles which supported the government. In his most recent explanations Kerensky has begun to understand more clearly that which he did not understand during his tenure in the government, and he has shown the inclination to place the responsibility for not understanding on those representatives of the "revolutionary democracy" whom the Bolsheviks, in this decisive moment, "not without success were trying to force to look, but not see, to listen, but not to hear."

The non-socialist elements of the government saw Kerensky's own behavior in the same light. The difference, was, of course, in the *degree* of blindness of the "leaders" of the socialist parties—and of the blindness of the members of the government that had been put forward by these parties, against the will of the more farsighted. But the snare of the ideology that entangled both the one and the other and forced them "to look, but not to see, to listen, but not to hear" was one and the same. Having just encountered in earnest the practical consequences of their wrongheaded doctrinairism, the "leaders" at the last minute, in complete self-contradiction, changed—not their principles, but the practical conclusions to be drawn from these principles. And so, having seen that the "pride of the government" had been wounded by the resolution

of the socialist majority of the Soviet, that the government would have
to resign, the "leaders" told Kerensky that, in adopting their formula of
transition, they did not intend to express a lack of confidence in the
government and that the issue of the government's resignation or of
changing its composition had not yet been posed.[19]

The leaders of the Bolsheviks had triumphed, and they did not hide
their triumph. On the evening of October 24 in a session of the City
Duma, V.D. Nabokov took note of this triumph in the joyous smiles
which Lunacharsky could not conceal during his speech. The city
mayor, Shreider, protested against the interference of the commissars of
the Military Revolutionary Committee in the affairs of municipal self-
government, and the City Duma adopted an SR resolution supported by
the Kadets, that protested against any violent armed insurrection, that invited the populace to unite around the Duma as the plenipotentiary representative agency, in order to subordinate naked force to the law and to
proclaim the precedence of civilian government the only legitimate representative of which was the City Duma. Moreover, the City Duma also adopted a proposal to form a Committee of Public Safety, consisting
of 21 representatives of the revolutionary organizations, 20 representatives of the City Duma, 17 from the regional Dumas, and one from
military headquarters, from the government commissars and from the
procurator's office. This belated attempt to juxtapose to the Military
Revolutionary Committee an agency of more moderate groups could
not, of course, have succeeded.

After Smolny's silent rejection of the district military headquarter's
ultimatum, calling on Smolny to cancel the order not to obey directives
of the military authorities, detachments of Red Guards, automobiles and
trucks girded themselves tightly around Smolny throughout the day and
the evening, and live ammunition was distributed. At the emergency
session of the Petrograd Soviet which met that evening, Trotsky delivered a speech in which he took note of the Military Revolutionary Committee's previous steps, described the complete impotence of the government and the first successes of the new revolution. He predicted that Kerensky's government had but 24 or 48 hours to live. "We have half a
government," he said about the government, which "the people do not
trust and which has no faith in itself, for it is dead within. This half-
government awaits the sweep of the historical broom, which will clear
a place for a genuine government of the revolutionary people." However, Trotsky was still wary of speaking openly about the insurrection.
He took the position that the Petrograd Soviet was only defending itself
against the "plotters" and "counter-revolutionaries." "The Military Revolutionary Committee arose, not as an agency of insurrection, but for the

purpose of the self-defense of the revolution." It was in this same sense that he answered the delegation from the City Duma that appeared in Smolny at 2 o'clock. "Our slogan is all power to the Soviets. This slogan must be realized in the coming period, the period of the All-Russia Congress of Soviets. Whether it will lead to an 'insurrection' or an 'uprising' depends not so much on the Soviets as on those who, despite the unanimous will of the people, hold state power in their hands."

Probably that was Trotsky's original plan: having prepared for battle, to confront the old government with the "unanimous will of the people" as articulated by the Congress of Soviets, and thus to give the new government the appearance of legitimacy.[20] But the old government turned out to be weaker than he had anticipated, and it fell of its own weight into his hands before the congress had managed to meet and express itself. And on the same evening of October 24 Trotsky no longer concealed that "the will of the people will be the only sanction of the revolution which has already begun—and begun successfully." "Yesterday the government closed two newspapers which have an enormous influence on the Petrograd proletariat and on the garrison. This is a direct attack, a direct counter-revolutionary insurrection, and we shall repel it decisively." "We have said that we cannot tolerate the smothering of the free word, and we have decided to restore the operation of these newspapers, after having given the honor of guarding the presses of the revolutionary newspapers to the valiant soldiers of the Litovsky Regiment and to the 6th Reserve Engineers Battalion." Indeed, at 11 A.M. on that day the sealed presses of *Rabochy Put* and *Soldat* were opened by the above-named units of the garrison, printed issues of the papers were distributed, and at 2 P.M. the Military Revolutionary Committee sent an order in which, after the justification given above by Trotsky, there were directives to open the newspapers, to continue their publication, and to give the "honor of guarding the revolutionary papers against counter-revolutionary acts" to the above-named military units.

Furthermore, Trotsky cited another victory by the insurrection over the government. "When the government began to mobilize the cadets, it simultaneously ordered the cruiser *'Aurora'* to move away from the capital. . . .The problem was the sailors to whom Skobelev had come with hat in hand during the Kornilov days to beg that they defend the Winter Palace from the Kornilovites. The sailors of the *'Aurora'* fulfilled Skobelev's request at that time. But now the government is trying to send them away [in the Winter Palace the sailor sentries had, in fact, been replaced by cadet sentries]. But the sailors inquired with the

Military Revolutionary Committee: and today the *'Aurora'* stands where it stood last night."

So far as prospects for the immediate future were concerned, Trotsky summarized them on that evening of October 24 as follows. "Tomorrow the Congress of Soviets will commence. The task of the garrison and of the proletariat is to place at the disposal of the congress the accumulated force, which governmental provocations are intended to destroy. Our task is to make sure that this force reaches the congress intact and undamaged. When the congress announces that it is organizing a government, then it will complete the work which has been performed across the entire country. This will signify that the people, which has liberated itself from the power of the counter-revolutionary government, calls its own congress and will create its own government. If the sham government makes a sudden attempt to revive its own corpse, the popular masses, organized and armed, will rebuff this attempt decisively, and the strength of this rebuff will be the greater, the greater is the attack from the government. If the government tries to make use of the twenty-four or forty-eight hours which remain at its disposal in order to plunge a dagger into the back of the revolution, then we declare that the vanguard of the revolution will return blow for blow, iron for steel."

The actual intentions of the leaders of the revolution far outstripped these official statements of Trotsky. As we have already noted, the Congress of Soviets was supposed to be presented with a *fait accompli*. And already on the morning of October 25 the Military Revolutionary Committee, anticipating the outcome of the measures it had taken, published the following resolution "to the citizens of Russia," dated 10 A.M.

"The Provisional Government has been overthrown. State power has passed into the hands of an agency of the Petrograd Soviet of Workers' and Soldiers' Deputies, the Military Revolutionary Committee, which stands at the head of the Petrograd proletariat and garrison. The cause for which the people has struggled—the immediate proposal of a democratic peace, the abolition of landlords' property in land, workers' control over production, the creation of a Soviet government—this cause is now secure. Long live the revolution of workers, soldiers, and peasants!"

What had occurred on that night that had given the headquarters of the insurrection the right to issue such a report? In the evening the government's situation still had not seemed entirely hopeless. Tsentroflot had spoken against the insurrection, saying that "any armed uprising is disastrous to the interests of the revolution." A delegation from the

Cossack Host and from the 1st, 4th, and 14th Cossack regiments had appeared at 12:30 A.M. at the Winter Palace. Kerensky had just finished his "strormy explanation" with the delegates of the socialist groups. We have seen that, instead of support, he had received from them only reproaches that his directives were interfering with their efforts to reach an agreement with the Bolsheviks to end the insurrection by peaceful means. Now from the other flank of society support was offered to him, but also conditionally. The Cossacks, according to Kerensky himself, wanted to know what forces he had in his disposal for the suppression of the uprising, and they demanded a personal directive from Kerensky and a personal guarantee that this time Cossack blood "will not be shed in vain" as it had been in early July. Kerensky responded with a call to carry out their duty, and with the explanations that he had been at the front from July 3-6, but that he had taken stern measures on his return. He received from the Cossacks a pledge to "carry out their duty" and he signed an order to the Cossacks to carry out the instructions of the military district headquarters. According to other reports, however, the Cossacks demanded that Kerensky liquidiate the Bolshevik organizations and arrest the Bolshevik leaders as state criminals, but Kerensky answered that he had decided not to arrest Trotsky, who was in the Soviet of Workers' and Soldiers' Deputies. Instead of an arrest, the Minister of Justice[21] had been permitted to propose that the procurator's office invite Trotsky and other Bolsheviks because of their subversive speeches to a meeting in the Peter and Paul Fortress.

Evidently, the Cossacks were dissatisfied after their conversation with Kerensky, since the result of the meeting was that the Cossack Soviet, which was in session the entire night, decided not to intervene in the dispute between the Provisional Government and the Bolsheviks. On the other hand, the socialist delegation passed the night in negotiations with the Bolshevik leaders. The whole night, Kerensky complained, "these past masters spent on endless arguments over various formulas, which would supposedly become the basis for reconciliation and for ending the insurrection. By this method of negotiating the Bolsheviks gained an enormous amount of time. And during this time the fighting forces of the SRs and the Mensheviks were not mobilized." On neither flank of Russian society was there a firm resolve to defend Kerensky's government.

However, it would be incorrect to conclude that nothing was done during the night to defend the government.

The military telegraphers and the main committee of the Union of Postal Workers and Telegraphers declared themselves against the Bolsheviks' enterprise and in favor of the Central Executive Committee.

The Bolsheviks who had arrived in the middle of the night at the main telegraph office, left after negotiations with the representatives of the Union of Postal Workers and Telegraphers; the Bolsheviks left behind only one comrade in the equipment room to observe the course of work. When district military headquarters learned that the Bolsheviks had decided to seize the electric lighting and telephone stations that night, it immediately strengthened the guards at these stations by adding cadets. On the directive of district military headquarters, the bridges over the Neva River were raised, with the exception of the Palace Bridge on which an armed guard was stationed. True, the city government refused to take responsibility for raising the bridges, and several of the bridges were lowered again that night. On orders from the district military headquarters, all commissars of the Military Revolutionary Committee were "dismissed," their "illegal actions" were cancelled, "independent demonstrations" by units of the garrison were prohibited without orders from the district military headquarters; it was categorically forbidden to carry out orders issued by certain organizations, and in the event of "unauthorized armed demonstrations and of soldiers coming out onto the streets," officers were ordered to remain in their barracks, under penalty of "court martial for armed mutiny."

All of these orders, of course, were several days late and, being published at a time when the insurrection had already begun, they naturally remained paper orders only.

A. F. Kerensky recalled that in the final nocturnal session of the government, after his conversation with the delegations of the socialists and the Cossacks, "several of the members of the government very severely criticized the 'indecisiveness' and 'passivity' of the high military authorities." Kerensky reproached these members for completely forgetting that "we were forced to act the entire time, while being caught between the sledge-hammer of the right and the anvil of the leftist Bolsheviks." However, the criticisms levelled by the non-socialist members of the government were intended precisely to point out that Kerensky's own tactics had placed him—and along with him the entire Provisional Government—in this position of pitiful helplessness. Moreover, as we have shown above, this criticism was no news to Kerensky. Having ignored these observations and not having adopted in time the decisive measures on which the non-socialist members of the government had insisted, Kerensky, now face to face with impending catastrophe, was prepared to see danger even where there was none. At the end of the meeting of the government, after 1 A.M., he heard a proposal of the infantry commander and of the chief-of-staff to organize at once an expedition to seize Smolny Institute—the Bolsheviks' headquarters.

Kerensky said that he approved the plan on the spot, and he added: "During this conversation I followed with great attention the strange and ambiguous behavior of Colonel Polkovnikov, and observed with great care the crying contradiction between his very optimistic and consoling reports and the sad reality of which I was aware."

"This psychological method of observation," which reflected more on the observer than on the observed, is already familiar to us from the Kornilov episode. As Kerensky's own anxiety increased, he listened the more keenly to the accidental reports of "loyal and honorable officers," and he quickly concluded that, in fact, "what is occurring cannot be classified except as betrayal." He hurried along with Konovalov and his assistants to military district headquarters across Palace Square, administered a new examination to Colonel Polkovnikov and reached the conclusion: "It is necessary immediately to take the command into my own hands." He gathered "in military headquarters itself several senior officers" "whom he could trust with his eyes closed," and he summoned "by telephone those whose presence seemed to him especially necessary." He decided to "involve the party military organizations, in particular, the large number of these organizations connected with the SR party" [about which he had just given a very unsatisfactory appraisal]. Obviously, this last-minute appeal to what were actually small and disorganized partisan elements would merely alienate from him the more rightist elements, who already viewed him with hostility, and would ultimately disorganize the government's defense. Kerensky himself made the following observation on this subject: "The officers, who had gathered in a large number in military headquarters, behaved themselves with respect to the government, and in particular with respect to me, ever more defiantly. I later learned that among them, on the initiative of Colonel Polkovnikov, there was agitation for my arrest. At first they whispered about this, but toward morning they began to speak loudly, almost not restraining themselves in the presence of strangers."

Kerensky did not mention that his own account betokened not so much a betrayal as a shift in the center of the last hopes for the preservation of the principle of the state, especially as it was revealed in the course of the night how disorganized were the government's actions. "Without Kerensky it might be easier to deal with the Bolsheviks; one might be able, without difficulties, to put an end to 'this so-called strong government.'" That was how Kerensky formulated the idea of the officers, which idea he classified as "senseless." He said: "There is absolutely no doubt that all that night Colonel Polkovnikov and several other officers of the military district headquarters were in constant communication with anti-governmental rightist organizations, which at that

time acted with increased strength in the city—for example, with the Soviet of the Cossack Union, the Union of the Knights of St. George, the
St. Petersburg branch of the Union of Officers, and other military and civilian organizations of the same type."

Subsequent historians will clarify whether the subject of these negotiations was an insidious plan to overthrow Kerensky by relying on the
Bolsheviks, as Kerensky suspected, or a last attempt to organize a defense. The author of these lines finds it more probable that a readiness
to defend the government was not lacking in these rightist circles, but
that this readiness diminished significantly during the night, after the officers were in fact pushed aside from the organization of the capital's defense by Kerensky's directives. Kerensky himself testified to this change
in mood, when he said that already from the evening on, the cadets,
whose mood had been excellent at the beginning, began to lose their
pluck; later the commanders of the armored cars started to show anxiety;
every extra minute of futile waiting for reinforcements diminished even
more the "battle-readiness" of the cadets and automobile commanders.
Naturally, neither the cadets, nor the automobile commanders, nor the
Cossacks wanted to find themselves in isolation. From now on the decision rested on the attitude toward the defense of the Provisional Government taken by the Northern Front and the echelons summoned from it.

While waiting for these reinforcements, Kerensky and Konovalov,
who had remained alone in the Winter Palace, experienced anxious
hours. Kerensky recalled that "the long hours of that night dragged on
torturously. From every quarter we awaited reinforcements which, however, stubbornly did not arrive. There were uninterrupted telephone negotiations with the Cossack regiments. Under various pretexts the Cossacks stubbornly sat in their barracks, and in 15 or 20 minutes they
would 'explain everything' and 'begin to saddle the horses.' On the other hand, the party fighting forces not only had not appeared at military
headquarters, but had done nothing at all in the city. This at first sight
mysterious fact has a very simple explanation. The party centers, distracted by the endless negotiations with Smolny, counted much more
on the authority of a "resolution' than on the force of bayonets, and did
not manage to issue the appropriate directives in time." It is the duty of
Kerensky to his socialist followers to explain precisely what "fighting
forces" they might have had at their disposal at that time and what sort
of orders they failed to issue. According to his own political scheme,
Kerensky divided all public circles into three groups: "Bolsheviks of the
left;" "Bolsheviks of the right;" and "circles genuinely dedicated to the
revolution and whose fate was bound to the fate of the Provisional Government." Kerensky dismissed the first two groups as hostile, and, in

the final analysis, he placed all the responsibility on the third group, among whom "there reigned some sort of inexplicable assurance that 'everything will shape itself,' that there was absolutely no reason to be especially fearful or to resort to heroic measures to save the government." The only person to evade even partial responsibility was Kerensky himself. It only remains for the historian to repeat that throughout the period before October 24 the head of the government shared the psychology he attributed to his political allies . . . .

The night of October 24/25 passed in these anxieties and mutual accusations. "At 7 A.M.," Kerensky recalled, "having spoken again by direct wire with the Commander-in-Chief of the Northern Front about expediting the sending of reliable troops to St. Petersburg, and without waiting for the Cossacks, who were still 'saddling their horses,' Konovalov and I, downcast by the impressions of that night and exhausted, returned [from military headquarters] to the Winter Palace in order to get a little sleep."

Not an hour had passed when Kerensky, who had fallen asleep on a couch, was awakened by a special courier, who brought upsetting news. The Bolsheviks had seized the central telephone exchange and all the palace's telephone connections with the city had been cut. The Palace Bridge, under the windows of Kerensky's room, was occupied by pickets of sailors—Bolshevik sailors. The Palace Square was empty and deserted.

Indeed, the Bolsheviks had continued to work energetically through the night. After nightfall they had begun to occupy all the most important points in the capital in accordance with the plan mentioned above. At 9 P.M. there had appeared at the Baltic Station a commissar of the Military Revolutionary Committee and also a company of the Izmailovsky Guards Regiment. The commissar, dressed in an ensign's uniform, stated to the station commander that, on instructions from the committee, he [the commissar] was assuming the authority for supervision of train traffic. At 5 A.M. a detachment of sailors occupied the State Bank building on the Ekaterinsky Canal and placed it under guard "on behalf of the government." Early in the morning a commissar from the committee appeared at the Crosses Prison, where the arrested Bolsheviks were being detained, and presented to the sentries from the Volynsky Regiment an order from the regimental committee to free the Bolsheviks whose names were listed by the Petrograd Soviet. On this list were the former editor of *Okopnaia Pravda* [Frontline Pravda], the famous Lieutenant Khaustov, the no less famous figure from Kronstadt, "Doctor Roshal" and others. After futile attempts to negotiate with Minister Maliantovich, who gave an evasive answer, the prison inspector bowed to the commissar's demand. On that same night a significant number of ships of the Baltic Fleet in battle order entered the Neva River; several of these ships went as far as Nikolaevsky Bridge, which was occupied by detachments of the insurrectionaries.

The hour of the decisive confrontation was near. The awakened Kerensky, Konovalov, and their adjutants rushed at 9 A.M. to the district military headquarters, and there they already found the traces of the Bolsheviks. The cadets who were guarding the palace had received from the Bolsheviks an ultimatum to abandon the palace under the threat of merciless repressions. The palace's armored cars had been stripped of certain parts and rendered useless for defense. It had become clear that it was now impossible to defend the Winter Palace. "Having consulted with Ministers Konovalov and Kishkin, who had rushed over at the time, and having talked with several officers of the military district headquarters who had remained loyal to their oath," Kerensky decided "to go, losing not a moment, to meet the echelons that had become bogged down somewhere near Gatchina." He left at the Winter Palace a helpless government.

At 9 A.M. two officers rang at the house of V. D. Nabokov, who was eating his breakfast. In an agitated tone they told him: "You probably know that the insurrection has begun. The post office, telegraph, telephone, arsenal, and train stations have been seized; all the main points are in the hands of the Bolsheviks. The troops are going over to their side; there is no resistance; the cause of the Provisional Government is lost. Our task is to save Kerensky, to drive him away as fast as possible by automobile to meet the troops that are still loyal to the Provisional Government and are moving toward Luga. All our cars have either been seized or sabotaged." They asked V. D. Nabokov to obtain for them two "covered automobiles." Not having received what they requested, they repeated the attempt with the secretary of the American embassy, Whitehouse. The American ambassador David Francis gave an account of this in his book.[22] "Secretary Whitehouse rushed in in great excitement and told me that his automobile, on which he carried an American flag, had been followed to his residence by a Russian officer, who said that Kerensky wanted it to go to the front. Whitehouse and his brother-in-law, Baron Ramsai, who was with him, accompanied the officer to General Headquarters in order to confirm his authority for making this amazing request. There they found Kerensky . . . . Everyone seemed to be in a high tension of excitement and all was confusion. Kerensky confirmed the officer's statement that he wanted Whitehouse's car to go to the front. Whitehouse asserted: 'This car is my personal property and you have (pointing across the square to the Winter Palace) thirty or more automobiles in front of the Palace.' Kerensky replied: 'Those were put out of commission during the night and the Bolsheviks now command all the troops in Petrograd except some who claim to be neutral and refuse to obey my orders.' Whitehouse and Ramsai, after a hurried conference, came to the very proper conclusion that as the car had virtually been commandeered they could offer no further objection. After they had left the Headquarters Whitehouse remembered the American flag, and returning, told the officer who had originally asked for the car that he must remove the flag before using the car. He objected to doing this and, after some argument, Whitehouse had to be content with registering a protest against Kerensky's use of the flag . . . . I approved Whitehouse's action, but gave orders that no mention should be made of the occurrence to anyone . . . . A rumor reached me later that Kerensky had left the city in an American Embassy automobile under the American flag."[23]

The last was not quite true. Kerensky travelled in his own automobile, but the American car, which in Kerensky's expression "just happened to be there," followed him "at a respectable distance," but nonetheless "under an American flag" and obviously not out of simple courtesy to "our Allies' wishes." Kerensky emphasized in his narrative that he had decided "to act quite openly" and in a manner that followed to the letter "the usual external appearance of his daily travels." But perhaps the American flag did play a roll in the "confusion of the patrols and the Red Guards" mentioned by Kerensky. However this may have been, on his passage through crowded places in the capital, despite being recognized by many passing soldiers, Kerensky was not stopped. "Within a second after my passage," he noted, "not one of us could explain to himself how it had happened that this 'counter-revolutionary', and 'enemy of the people' had not only been permitted to pass, but had even been given an honor." This passage clearly captured the mood of the fleeing Kerensky and the psychology of an uprising that was beginning to understand but was not yet fully conscious of its goals.

"Heading into the working class quarters and nearing the Moscow Gate," Kerensky continued, "we started to pick up speed, and finally, we were moving with head-spinning velocity. I remember that at the very edge of town, the Red Guards, who were standing on sentry duty and were envying our automobile, began to run onto the highway from both sides of the road. But we passed through, and they not only did not attempt to stop us, they did not even manage to identify us." For Kerensky the danger had passed.

But let us return to what was happening in Petrograd on the fateful day of October 25. The chief attention of the insurrectionaries, of course, was directed to the ministers and to the Soviet of the Republic.

Having been summoned to a morning meeting, the ministers gathered at the Winter Palace. The square between the palace and the military headquarters building, and also the adjoining section of the Nevsky Prospect up to the Moika were still free of the insurrectionaries. Further up on the Nevsky Prospect armored cars of the Military Revolutionary Committee had already appeared that morning. Behind the bridge across the Moika the workers constructed barricades and set machine guns. Detachments of insurrectionaries also approached the Winter Palace from Millionnaia Street. S. N. Prokopovich and E. D. Kuskova, who were coming from this direction to the ministers' meeting at the Winter Palace, were arrested. Kuskova was set free. Later, at the Millionnaia Street exit there stood armored cars, which, in accordance with the decision of the armored car battalion, were maintaining "neutrality" between the government and Lenin.

Around the Mariinsky Palace all surrounding streets were occupied little by little. The members of the presidium of the Soviet of the Republic, who had met early at the invitation of the chairman Avksentiev, discussed the current situation. Other members were still arriving at the palace when the building was cordoned off. Soldiers were positioned in a line on the Grand Staircase, which led from the lower vestibule to the palace's first floor. At approximately 1 P.M. the members of the presidium were interrupted by a demand immediately to disperse; otherwise, shooting would begin within half an hour. They had no choice but to submit to force. A council of the senior statesmen protested against the violence, and charged their chairman to convoke the Soviet of the Republic at the first opportunity A few members who had gathered in the almost empty hall of the palace were informed of this decision. There was no attempt, such as the one made by the City Duma, to leave an organized agency or group of members to react to events. This reflected the general awareness of the impotence of this ephemeral institution [the Soviet of the Republic] and its inability, after the resolution it had adopted on the eve of the revolution, to undertake any collective action whatsoever. One after another the members of the Soviet of the Republic walked down the staircase and through the relaxing soldiers, who looked on them indifferently or angrily. At the bottom, near the stairs, the soldiers examined the documents of the departing members and permitted them to go out onto the square one by one. The members thought that the soldiers were looking for someone, and that arrests would be made. But the revolutionary headquarters had other concerns. The members of the Soviet of the Republic were all let through except for V. A. Obolensky, whose short detention was, apparently, provoked by his title.[24] The Mariinsky Palace was now empty.

After Kerensky's departure, the man who had to discharge the duties of the prime minister was A. I. Konovalov, and the duties of carrying out the military defense of Petrograd fell to N. M. Kishkin. Over Konovalov's signature an appeal was issued to the army beginning with the words: "In Petrograd grave events are occurring." The appeal presented the history of these events. "Immediately after the order to the troops of the Petrograd garrison to go to the front to defend the captial from the attacking foe, intense agitation commenced in the regiments and in the factories." Then there occurred the "unauthorized convocation" of the Military Revolutionary Committee, which threatened by its actions to paralyze the defense of the capital. The government took measures against it, but, "in view of the instability and indecisiveness of part of the Petrograd garrison, not all the directives of the Provisional Government were obeyed." As a result, "civil war and anarchy threaten Petrograd; it is also threatened by the cessation of the activity of the government apparatus, an end to diplomatic work intended to bring peace nearer, an end to efforts to summon the Constituent Assembly, an end to the allocation to the army of supplies, clothing, and ammunition . . . . The fighting army cannot permit such a traitorous blow to its back." And Konovalov appealed to the army to "rally around the Provisional Government and the central agencies of the revolutionary democracy."

While waiting for the appeal to reach the front and to have the effect that the government was counting on, it was still necessary to take immediate action in Petrograd itself.

In the military headquarters across from the Winter Palace—the only territory that the government still had at its disposal—there was a discussion about the means to fight against the uprising. There were really no effective means of fighting left, and it was not surprising that the reactions of the military participants of the conference—Bagratuni, Polkovnikov, and General Alexeev, who had been specially invited to participate—were extremely pessimistic. The representatives of the Cossack regiments who had offered the government their support the evening before now stated to the Petrograd Soviet that they would not carry out the government's orders, and that, while standing neutral, they were ready to defend state property and the personal safety of citizens. Regiments of the garrison did not obey the orders of military headquarters, and arrested their own officers.

On the square between the palace and military headquarters there slowly gathered around noon, on the orders of the military headquarters,

cadets from the military schools: from the school of ensigns, from the
engineers' battalion, from the school of ensigns at Oranienbaum and Peterhof, and a platoon from the Konstantinov Artillery Academy. As one
can see from the memoirs of A.P. Sinegub, the attitude of the cadets
was complicated. They vacillated between the necessity of carrying out
their duty—defending the motherland from the enemy of all that they regarded as holy—and a skeptical attitude toward the government, and especially toward its "chief spokeman" Kerensky. In the psychological disposition of the falling government they had seen too much in common
with the force against which they would now have to fight, at the risk
of their lives. Naturally, disagreements surfaced when they discussed the
situation in their "soviets" that morning. During the day these disagreements intensified to the degree that the following became clear to the cadets: the hopelessness of their position and their isolation; the absence
of Kerensky, whose departure they interpreted as flight; the lack of military supplies for holding the palace; and the absence of a united, competent leadership. N. M. Kishkin, who participated in the morning conference at the military headquarters, tried to inspire in the defenders of the
palace a faith in the possibility of defense until the arrival of the units
from the front that Kerensky had gone to obtain. But Kishkin must
have known that the officers of the military district had no such faith.
In anger he dismissed Polkovnikov from the staff, and returned to the
Winter Palace in order to organize from there the resistance. Savinkov
urgently tried to persuade General Alexeev to go to the Cossack Union,
with which he [Alexeev] had good relations at the time and which had
made him [Alexeev] its representative to the Soviet of the Republic.
But it was clear that the leaders of the Cossack Union had very little
control over the Cossack regiments, just as the military headquarters
could not control the garrison. General Alexeev was forced to recognize
that his further participation in a position of leadership was useless, for
there was no one to lead. After this Savinkov departed in search of Kerensky.

At approximately 4 P.M. A.I. Konovalov tried to summon to the
Winter Palace those public figures near to the cabinet, so that they
might discuss the situation with the ministers, who were still in session at the palace. V.D. Nabokov, who had managed reach the Winter
Palace through the lines of soldiers that cordoned the palace off, found
there the following scene. "In the hall one found all the ministers, with
the exception of N.M. Kishkin [at the moment Kishkin was at military
headquarters]. A.I. Konovalov was extremely agitated. The ministers dis-
ported themselves in small groups; some walked back and forth across
the hall, others stood near the window. S.N. Tretiakov sat next to me

on a couch and began with indignation to say that Kerensky had discarded them and betrayed them, that the situation was hopeless. Others said (one recalls that Tereshchenko was in a highly nervous, excited state) that it was necessary to 'hold out' for forty-eight hours, until troops loyal to the government arrived in Petersburg." Nabokov added: "Of course, my presence was quite useless. I could not help to do anything, and when it became clear that the Provisional Government did not intend to undertake anything, but had assumed a passive, waiting posture, I preferred to leave (just after 6 P.M.) . . . . About 15 or 20 minutes after my departure all exits and gates were locked by the Bolsheviks, who no longer allowed anyone to pass through."

The few defenders of the Winter Palace, who remained without leadership, had kept their optimism in the first half of the day by means of rumors. There had suddenly circulated among them the news that "General Krasnov's echelons are in Petrograd and have already taken Nikolaevsky and Tsarskoselsky Stations." Or the shooting that rang out from the direction of the Nevsky Prospect was interpreted as evidence that "the Cossacks are already coming toward the palace from the Nikolaevsky Station." The longer they remained isolated, of course, the less they believed such rumors.

The cadets who had gathered on Alexandrovskaia Square in the morning had already received their assignments, and an attempt was made to use them for offensive purposes. Military headquarters wanted to clean the Bolsheviks out of the telephone exchange on the Morskoi Canal, whence the insurrectionaries had cut all the communications between military headquarters, the palace, and military units. It was also decided to send help to the Soviet of the Republic in the Mariinsky Palace. But the cadets did not succeed in getting through to the Mariinsky Palace. The supervision which the cadets established at the telephone exchange only made clear their complete inability to cope with the Bolsheviks who had taken the exchange. Military commissar Stankevich, who tried to direct these weak attempts at resistance, finally entered into negotiations with the insurrectionary forces and "agreed to lift the siege of the telephone exchange, after receiving safe conduct for his cadets." However, some of the cadets were captured by the Bolsheviks. The rest, after returning to Alexandrovskaia Square about 3 P.M., found there a picture of chaos and an absence of any direction. In the White Hall of the Winter Palace committees of the Oranienbaum and Peterhof schools arranged a conference and summoned a representative of the government to make explanations. Not being satisfied by the explanations of Palchinsky, they arranged a general meeting of the garrison of the Winter Palace, to which members of the government came. The speeches of

Konovalov, Maslov, and Tereshchenko were, according to the cadets' accounts, heard without any "respect." "Ultimately, the cadets nevertheless agreed to stay, provided that there would be activity [forthcoming from the government] and that information about events should prove accurate." The director of the engineering school was appointed commander of the defense of the Winter Palace and all the forces in the palace were placed under his command.

Alas, there were not many of these troops, and the morale of the defenders of the Provisional Government continued to worsen. Soon a plan of defense of the palace was worked out by cadet units. That evening they were joined by a detachment of Cossacks—"old men," who had not agreed with the decisions of their "young" to keep neutral in the struggle that had arisen. Invalids also arrived to help, as did the Knights of St. George and a shock company of the women's death battalion. They began to build barricades out of the firewood that was stacked on the square in front of the palace. But at that moment the artillery platoon from the Konstantinov Artillery School received the order to leave the palace and to take their guns with them. These guns were immediately captured by the Bolsheviks at the exit onto the Nevsky Prospect, and were then aimed at the palace. After the cadets from the Konstantinov School left the palace, so did the Cossacks. Among them there had been agitators who had promised safe passage from the palace on the Winter Canal side, where they had been stationed. As the cadets were organizing the defense of the palace gates, Bolsheviks gained free access into the palace from the direction of Millionnaia Street, and immediately they took advantage of this access to initiate propaganda . . . .

At 7 P.M. envoys from the insurrectionary forces, two soldiers, approached the Provisional Government. They demanded that the government recognize that it had been overthrown. Otherwise, they threatened to open artillery fire on the Winter Palace. The ministers arranged a conference over this proposal. At the conference both representatives of the military, General Manikovsky and Admiral Verderevsky, said that further resistance was hopeless, and it was necessary either to surrender to the victors or to find a way to escape. However, the civilian ministers understood that military defeat would not necessarily end their political role. They were representatives of the legitimate government. They had moral authority on their side, and if they were condemned to leave the stage, they would do so in a fashion that would not destroy, but rather would preserve for the future the idea that they represented. Among the ministers there were also those who still believed in the possibility that, by delaying the denouement, they might still be able to hold out until Kerensky arrived with the promised troops.   For one or another of these reasons, the ministers unanimously decided to stay at their posts and meet steadfastly the fate that awaited them. The government firmly told the envoys that they would surrender power only to the Constituent Assembly. By the time this decision had been reached, the defense of the Winter Palace had already become impossible. The palace was tightly surrounded on all sides.

The armored cars of the Military Revolutionary Committee appeared on the Palace Square, and occupied all entrances and exits. For a certain period there remained a free path on the embankment. But the palace was threatened from the Neva River by the cruiser "*Aurora*." The Peter and Paul Fortress announced its neutrality. Destroyers from Kronstadt patrolled the Neva. Thus, the Winter Palace was completely isolated. The only means by which the government could communicate with the outside world were several telephones in the palace that the Bolsheviks had forgotten to disconnect and which were operative until late at night. The women of the shock company made the only attempt to break through this encirclement. They were sure for some reason that General Alexeev was still in the military headquarters building, and they decided to rescue him, whatever the cost. This attempt only demonstrated that for the bold-spirited to go out from behind the barricades constructed by the cadets onto the Palace Square would mean death. Those among the women who were not killed by bullets and were captured by the Bolsheviks were subjected that evening and night to terrible abuse from the soldiers, to rape, and to execution.

After the government's refusal to surrender the Winter Palace, there began about 8 P.M. the first rifle fire and artillery fire on the palace. The cruiser "*Aurora*" also fired. The ministers were forced to move from one room to another, from front rooms to ones in back in order to save themselves from the bullets. Sailors who had disembarked from their ships near the Nikolaevsky Bridge approached the palace by running from building to building along the embankment. Several sailors climbed up onto the roof of the gallery of the Winter Palace, and, having broken through the roof, threw a bomb into the building. The shock waves from the bomb explosion knocked down one cadet. Palchinsky[25] rushed to the roof, discovered a sailor, and told the sailor that he was under arrest. Simultaneously, the lower floor of the palace next to the drainage canal filled with Bolshevik partisans. Threatening a new bombardment of the palace from the "*Aurora*," the agitators offered free passage and mercy to those who would lay down their arms and leave the palace voluntarily. Some of the cadets from the second Oranienbaum school complied with this request.

The government, however, still kept its spirits high. The person in charge of transportation and communication at Stavka, Lebedev, and Chief-of-Staff Dukhonin reported in detail to the government as to which Cossack units were supposed to arrive to assist the government on October 26 and 27, and they also described the support that the government could count upon. But would the government be able to hold out until help arrived, at the earliest on the morning of the next day? The government continued to hope so. At 10:05 P.M. it sent to the provincial and district commissars the following telegram: "The Petrograd Soviet of Workers' and Soldiers' Deputies has announced the overthrow of the Provisional Government and it has demanded the transfer of power to it, under threat of bombardment of the Winter Palace from cannons of the Peter and Paul Fortress and the cruiser '*Aurora*,' stationed in the Neva. The government can transfer power only to the Constituent Assembly, and for that reason it has decided not to surrender itself and to place itself under the protection of the people and the army, about which it has sent a telegram to Stavka. Stavka responded by sending a detachment. Let the army and the people answer the attempt to raise an insurrection among the reserve units of the fighting army. The first attack on the Winter Palace at 10 P.M. has been repelled."

Alas, the last words were attributable more to the high spirits of those under siege and to their noble conception of their duty than to the actual situation. As we have seen, the territory in the palace that was at the disposal of the government now began to shrink. The telephone in the office where the ministers were located now ceased to work. A.M. Nikitin entered the office of A.I. Konovalov in order to telephone E.D. Kuskova and to inform her of the growing danger. In response, Kuskova informed the minister that a large deputation was headed toward the Winter Palace; the deputation consisted of people from municipal self-government and from various parties. In fact, the city mayor had summoned an emergency session of the City Duma, where it was reported that the Winter Palace was surrounded by troops, that the government had been given a twenty-minute ultimatum to surrender, after which a bombardment would commence. On the suggestion of the SR Bykovsky it was decided that the entire City Duma would go to the Winter Palace to support the government with all the authority of the agency of democratic self-government. The central committees of the SRs and of the United Mensheviks accompanied the City Duma.

Just at that moment a cadet entered the government's quarters. He had been sent by the commander of the palace's defenses with a report that indicated that the situation had become desperate: the main military headquarters had been taken by insurrectionary forces; the Winter Palace was full of agitators. Having heard the report, Konovalov and Tereshchenko thanked the cadets for their steadfastness and expressed the assurance that the barricades would last until morning when troops would come to the rescue. Palchinsky rushed after a cadet who was leaving and told him the good news about the decision of the City Duma, and asked that the cadet convey the news to the barricades. In the imagination of the cadet, the news took on the following form: "Public figures, the merchantry and the people, with the clergy at the head, are coming to the palace; they will soon arrive and liberate the palace from the siege."

In fact, for a short time the news about the procession of the fathers of the city and the clergy boosted the morale of the palace's defenders. Even the cadets from Oranienbaum seemed to pull themselves together. The commander of the defense ordered the platoon of cadets to clear the Bolsheviks out of the section of the palace adjacent to the Hermitage. The belated expedition, in which Palchinsky took part, was full of enthusiasm. The cadets managed to clear several halls, and the cadets whom the Bolsheviks had taken prisoner in these places were set free. But this was the final success. The first patrol, which consisted of sailors, stopped the procession of City Duma members that was moving toward the Winter Palace along Nevsky Prospect. After negotiations with the commissar of the Military Revolutionary Committee the procession was told that it must return immediately; otherwise, it would be fired upon, despite the presence in it of the leaders of revolutionary parties. The participants in the procession had no choice but to return to the City Duma. There they took steps to organize an "All-Russia Committee for the Salvation of the Revolution," which in the next few days entered into communication with the remainder of the Provisional Government, but could act only in a conspiratorial fashion.

N.M. Kishkin did not abandon hope up to the last minute. At 3 A.M. he telephoned his party comrade, Assistant Minister of Finance A.G. Khrushchov, and asked the latter to make it known, wherever possible, that the government needed just a few reinforcements to hold on until morning, when he was certain that Kerensky would arrive with troops. "What kind of party is it," said Kishkin agitatedly and reproachfully, "that cannot send us even three hundred armed men?" This was the last telephone call from the palace.

Finally, it became clear to the defenders of the palace that further resistance to the crowds of insurrectionaries, who had their sympathizers inside the palace and who were infiltrating into the palace more and more new groups, was impossible. The commander of the defense entered into negotiations with the envoys, and surrendered the palace on the condition that the cadets' lives be spared. The envoys refused to make any promises whatsoever concerning the fate of the government. The Oranienbaum cadets finally decided to leave the palace. A group of remaining cadets with rifles continued to guard the Provisional Government. Having received the news of the surrender, the ministers hesitated for a certain time, and Palchinsky insisted on continuing the defense, trying unsuccessfully to rally the remaining cadets. However, it was obvious that it was already too late not only to defend themselves, but even to open formal negotiations about the conditions of surrender. The crowd of Bolsheviks was quickly approaching the last refuge of the ministers. The crowd consisted of sailors, soldiers, and Red Guards.

At the head of the crowd there walked a very short, unattractive man, who was trying to restrain the rows of men pressing forward. His clothes were in disorder, his wide-brimmed hat was tilted to the side, his glasses scarcely rested on his nose, but his small eyes shone with the triumph of the victory and with anger toward the vanquished. This was Antonov: a name that we have encountered more than once before. Antonov, who was accompanied by Palchinsky, was invited by the latter to enter the office that was guarded by the cadets, the office where the ministers were seated.

A.M. Nikitin was no longer among the ministers. Returning from his telephone conversation with E.D. Kuskova, he heard a shout: "Surrender!" Passing through two rooms and coming out into the round hall, he found Red Guards, soldiers, and sailors, who were busy disarming the cadets. Catching sight of Nikitin, the insurrectionaries asked him who he was, and discovering that he was a minister, they arrested him and escorted him to Commissar Chudnovsky, a soldier of the Preobrazhensky Regiment. Nikitin was the first arrested minister, and this arrest gave rise to great excitement among those present. The remaining ministers tried to enter into negotiations with Antonov, but completely in vain. In a hoarse voice Antonov stated that any resistance was futile, and he ordered the ministers to obey unconditionally his future directives and those of the military command.[26] Yielding to force, the government decided to surrender unconditionally, and it suggested that the cadets follow suit. Antonov called into the ministers' quarters twenty-five armed men chosen from the crowd, and charged them with the task of guarding the ministers who had surrendered.

Commissar Chudnovsky drew up a protocol about the arrest of eighteen persons: Konovalov, Kishkin, Verderevsky, Tretiakov, Maslov, Liverovsky, Manikovsky, Gvozdev, Maliantovich, Borisov, Smirnov, Salazkin, Bernatssky, Tereshchenko, Rutenberg, Nikitin and Palchinsky.[27] All the soldiers who had been selected to guard the ministers signed the protocol, but the commissar did not. Then they led the

arrestees out of the palace and down Millionnaia Street, where they
found themselves in the midst of an crowd of armed soldiers and sailors,
some of whom had been drinking; the crowd demanded that Kerensky be
given up to them. Learning that Kerensky was not present, they . . .
prepared to vent their anger on those who were at hand. Somehow, with
great difficulty, the procession moved from the Winter Palace to the
Peter and Paul Fortress. It required three hours to move that short
distance; it was encumbered at every step by angry crowds from the
masses. Here was how one of the participants, Minister A.M. Nikitin,
described the trip:"The crowd threw itself upon us with the cries: 'Shoot
them!' 'Drinkers of our blood!' 'Raise them up on bayonets!' 'To hell
with automobiles!' and so on. The crowd broke through the guard that
surrounded us, and if it had not been for the intervention of Antonov, I
do not doubt that the results would have been awful for us. They led us
on foot down Millionnaia Street in the direction of the Peter and Paul
Fortress. Along the way, Antonov kept hurrying us along, for he feared
vigilante justice. We walked along, surrounded by the angry crowd.
When we went out onto the Troitsky Bridge, we met a new crowd of
soldiers and sailors. The sailors shouted: 'Why treat them with consideration? Throw them into the Neva.' Again we were in danger. Then we
were taken under the arms of our guards and led by them single file. At
that juncture there was intense firing from the other end of the bridge.
The Red Guards were shooting, and so were armed soldiers from an automobile. The crowd accompanying us immediately fled, but this saved
us from vigilante justice. We all lay on the ground next to our guards
[This is not quite accurate: three of the ministers—Liverovsky, Tereshchenko and Tretiakov—quite demonstratively remained standing.].
The shooting lasted for a long while, and only when we sent guards
ahead to explain that they were also with the insurrection did the shooting stop. We rose and were escorted to the fortress."

Now the victory in Petrograd was complete. But the Bolsheviks did
not wait for the arrest of the ministers to announce their triumph. In the
evening newspaper, *Rabochy i Soldat* [Worker and Soldier] on that
same day, October 25, there appeared the following bulletin and appeal:
"All train stations, the telegraph, telephone exchange, and post office
are occupied. The Winter Palace and the military headquarters are cut off
from the telephone network. The State Bank, Winter Palace, military
headquarters and adjacent points are surrounded. The cadets are paralyzed.
Armored cars have gone over to the side of the revolutionary committee. Cossacks have refused to obey the Provisional Government. The
Provisional Government is overthrown. Power has been transferred to

the hands of the revolutionary committee of the Petrograd Soviet of Workers' and Soldiers' Deputies."

The appeal "to the front and to the reserves" read as follows: "In Petrograd power is in the hands of the Military Revolutionary Committee of the Petrograd Soviet. Soldiers and sailors who rose to a man have triumphed without shedding blood. Kerensky's government has been overthrown. The committee appeals to the front and to the reserves not to give in to provocations, but to support the Petrograd Soviet and the new revolutionary government, which will immediately propose a just peace, transfer land to the peasants, and summon the Constituent Assembly. Local power passes into the hands of the Soviets of Workers', Soldiers' and Peasants' Deputies." There followed the signature of the Military Revolutionary Committee.

Later, probably the next day, the committee set a radio telegram "to all army committees of the fighting army, to all Soviets of Soldiers' Deputies," in which the ideology of the revolution was presented in a fuller form. The telegram began by saying that the "Petrograd proletariat and garrison have overthrown the Kerensky government, *which has rebelled against the revolutionary people.*" "The Petrograd Soviets of Workers' and Soldiers' Deputies, triumphantly welcoming the revolution that has occurred, *have recognized, until such time as a government of Soviets will have been created, the government of the Military Revolutionary Committee* . . . . The temporary revolutionary committee calls on revolutionary soldiers vigilantly to observe the behavior of the officer corps. Officers who directly and openly refuse to join in the revolution that has been accomplished must be arrested immediately as enemies of the new government. The Petrograd Soviets see the salvation of the revolution in the immediate proposal of a democratic peace, the immediate transfer of the landlords' land to the peasants, the transfer of all power to the Soviets, and the prompt convocation of the Constituent Assembly. The popular revolutionary army must not permit the dispatch from the front to Petrograd of politically unreliable units, but must act by words and by persuasion to prevent this; where it cannot prevent the dispatch of such units, it must act by ruthlessly applying force . . . . The concealment from the soldier masses of this order is tantamount to a most grave crime against the revolution and it will be punished with all the severity of the revolutionary law. Soldiers, for peace, for land, for popular power."

In theory, the new government ought to have been created by the Congress of Soviets, which was the highest plenipotentiary agency of Soviet representation. But the Bolsheviks were not entirely certain they could trust it, since with the arrival of new deputies their numerical preponderance kept diminishing. By October 25, when it was proposed to open the congress, 560 deputies had arrived, and of them only 250 were Bolshevik party members. True, 69 Left SRs had associated themselves with the Bolsheviks, so together the two groups constituted a majority with 319 members. Of the remainder there were 159 delegates belonging to the Right SRs, 14 to the Menshevik-Internationalists, 3 to the anarchists, and 16 to the Popular Socialist groups. There were 3 nonparty socialists, and 22 delegates with no party affiliation. The party affiliation of the other 24 delegates is unknown.

The membership of the congress had not yet managed to make known its views and the nascent struggle had not yet ended in Bolshevik victory in Petrograd, when the socialist groups who were competing against the Bolsheviks decided to transfer the battle over the Bolshevik seizure of power and over the democratic agencies to the Congress of Soviets itself. In pursuing this goal, the Mensheviks walked out of the presidium of the Petrograd Soviet; their representatives there—Broido, Vainshtein, and Liber—made the following statement on the party's behalf. "The Bolsheviks' party, behind the back of the Soviet and under cover of the Soviet's name, has organized a military conspiracy which threatens disaster to the cause of the revolution and of liberty, the disruption of the Constituent Assembly, and catastrophe at the front. The Menshevik faction, without distinction between its different currents of thought, spoke publicly against this criminal adventure when it was discussed in the meeting of the Soviet, and publicly announced its refusal to participate in the Military Revolutionary Committee, which leads the plot. Now, when this adventure has become a fact, the faction considers itself obligated to wash its hands of any responsibility for the disastrous results of the conspiracy, and with the consent of the Central Committee of the Russian Social Democratic Workers' Party (United) announces its walkout from the Presidium of the Executive Committee of the Petrograd Soviet of Workers' and Soldiers' Deputies, and summons all members of the faction to active party work."

This, however, did not mean that the Mensheviks intended their "active party work" to support the Provisional Government against the "conspiracy" and the "criminal adventure." On the contrary, even here the Mensheviks contrived to occupy an intermediate position that was quite incompatible with the desire "to wash their hands of any responsibility for the disastrous results of the 'conspiracy.'" At a meeting of the United Mensheviks, faction members who had arrived for the congress worked out the following contradictory position to defend at the congress. On one hand, they "condemn the policy of the government, which is provoking the uprising" and offered a "friendly rebuff to the government's attempt to suppress the insurrection by armed force." We have seen, however, that on that day of open armed conflict when there was no place for any kind of neutrality these groups preferred to confine themselves to words of persuasion—that is, they remained simple bystanders, observing events taking place before their eyes. For the future the Mensheviks recognized the "necessity of a complete reconstruction of the government," to be understood as the making of an "exclusively socialist" and "democratic" regime.

Much more concrete, more worthy and more politically literate was the position of the Central Committee of the SR party, which resolved that (1) the Provisional Government was the only lawful government until the Constituent Assembly should meet, (2) that the adventure undertaken by the Bolsheviks must be decisively condemned by the central committee, and (3) in the event that a new Bolshevik-staffed government should take office, not a single SR would enter the government. Equally concrete was the position of the Executive Committee of the Soviet of Peasants' Deputies, which published its appeal to the peasants, soldiers, and workers. "Against the will of the representatives of the all-Russia peasantry and of the representatives of the army, power has been seized by the Petrograd Soviet of Workers' and Soldiers' Deputies. The seizure of power three weeks before the Constituent Assembly is a seizure of power from the entire people . . . . The army has been dealt another blow in the back, its capacity to resist has been weakened. The Petrograd Soviet promises peace, bread, and land. This is a lie. It will give us civil war, anarchy, and slavery. The Provisional Government announced the final draft of a law on the transfer of land to the disposition of land committees and it announced decisive measures to bring about peace. Let the army and peasantry know that, in following the Petrograd Soviet, they will deprive themselves of land and freedom, and will make impossible the convocation of a Constituent Assembly."

The opening of the Congress of Soviets was scheduled for 5 P.M. At that time it was perhaps still possible to transfer the struggle to the arena of parliamentary arguments. But the congress did not actually open until 11 P.M., by which time the fate of the ministry had almost been decided and further resistance in Petrograd had become pointless. Given this circumstance, it was obviously hopeless and psychologically impossible to fight against the accomplished fact of the Bolshevik seizure of power in an assembly where the Bolsheviks had a majority. Even the socialist opposition decided to take another course—the course that it had taken *vis-à-vis* the Northern Regional Congress of Soviets: it decided not to recognize the congress.

But before this decision had been made, the congress opened and constituted itself. Dan, who opened the congress, stated that now was not the time for political speeches, and he suggested the election of a presidium. Fourteen Bolshevik leaders and seven Left SRs were elected to the presidium. Then the Menshevik-Internationalist Martov, raising the question about the order of the day, proposed the adoption of all measures for the peaceful settlement of the current crisis, the election of a delegation to undertake negotiations with the remaining revolutionary democratic organizations, and the adoption of measures to end the bloodshed. This proposal, which had no hope of being implemented, was adopted unanimously. And only after all this did the entire right wing of the congress walk out of the congress. Meanwhile, the Central Executive Committee of the Soviet of Workers' and Soldiers' Deputies sent to all Soviets and army committees the following explanation. "The second All-Russia Congress met at a moment when in the streets of Petrograd the blood of our brothers was already flowing and a civil war had begun, a war caused by the Bolsheviks' seizure of power. The factions of the SRs, the Menshevik Social Democrats, the Internationalists, and Popular Socialists did not think it possible at such a moment to participate in the congress and have walked out of it. As a result of this, the Central Executive Committee calls on the Soviets and army organizations to rally around it for the defense of the revolution. The Central Executive Committee will summon a new Congress of Soviets, as soon as conditions for its proper convocation are created."

This, of course, was the strongest measure at the disposal of the socialist opposition. The Bolsheviks had already announced the transfer of power of the revolutionary committee into the hands of the congress. The announcement that the congress was not properly constituted and that its decisions were illegal deprived the future new government of its source of legitimacy, even according to Bolshevik theory. But, of course, this would not stop the Bolsheviks. At the first rumors about the impending walkout and about the declaration of the Central Executive Committee, the Bolsheviks hastened to issue warnings against this declaration. They had a completely defensible position: once the congress had opened, constituted itself, set an order for the day, and voted on one proposal (Martov's), it was no longer in the power of the secessionists, who had taken part in all these actions, to pronounce the congress invalid. As far as the authority of the Central Executive Committee was concerned, it had expired at the congress. Thus, the congress continued to sit and to make decisions. During the night of October 25/26 it carried out its basic task: to create a government. In distinction from its predecessors, this provisional government of workers, soldiers, and peasants received the title of the "Soviet of People's Commissars." This symbolic change of titles signalled the beginning of a process in which the old governmental apparatus was replaced by a new one, in accordance with Lenin's plan.

The original composition of the Soviet of People's Commissars, appointed on October 26, was the following: the chairman of the Soviet was Lenin-Ulianov; Commissar of Internal Affairs—A. Rykov; of Agriculture—V. Miliutin; of Labor—A. Shliapnikov; of Commerce and Industry—V. Nogin; of Education—A. Lunacharaky; of Finance—I. Skvortsov; of Foreign Affairs—L. Trotsky; of Justice—G. Oppokov; of Food Supply—I. Teodorovich; of Posts and Telegraphs—P. Avilov; of Nationalities—I. Dzhugashvili-Stalin. Military and naval affairs were entrusted to a committee whose membership included V. Ovseenko (Antonov), N. Krylenko, and F. Dybenko; D. Riazanov was later appointed Commissar of Railroads.[28] The subsequent story of this government and of its undertakings belongs to the following period of the Russian Revolution, just as do the history of the attempts to struggle against it by the "Committee for the Salvation of the Motherland and of the Revolution," the history of the "sabotage" of the old governmental apparatus, and the whole history of the civil war, which followed in the center and in other parts of Russia against the unrecognized government of "people's commissars." Below we shall excerpt from this history only those episodes that were most closely related to the liquidation of the overthrown government.

CHAPTER VIII

THE END OF RESISTANCE

Kerensky reaped what he had sown. In the army the attitude toward him had long been sharply negative, and among the elements who understood the principle of the state, elements that he had dismissed as incapable of swiftly assimilating the ideas and phraseology of a "democratized" army, there was even hatred toward him. Yet he did not even find support among those whom he had promoted to take the place of those pushed aside—promotions which were always guided by his clients' reputations as radicals and which created for them unexpectedly brilliant careers. General Verkhovsky was right when he attached to these newly-minted officers of the army and fleet the nickname: "As-the-Wind-Blows." They supported Kerensky so long as the wind was blowing in his direction. Now they were the first to turn their backs on him in the expectation of serving new masters. Thus, it soon became evident that neither Kerensky's enemies nor his friends wanted to defend him. An angry fate determined that at this moment, when it was necessary to gather all forces for the defense of the Russian principle of the state, that this principle should have borne Kerensky's name. To a very considerable extent, the Bolsheviks owed their easy victory to the fact that they had such an adversary as Kerensky in the high post of supreme commander-in-chief.

Scarcely having departed from Petrograd, Kerensky immediately encountered a manifestation of the troops' hostile attitude toward him. Friends of the Bolsheviks learned at once of Kerensky's departure from Petrograd in the direction of Gatchina, and Smolny sent a directive to Gatchina to detain him there. The local military revolutionary committee was supposed to carry out this order. The committee missed him by five minutes. Kerensky, having learned that he was being followed, cancelled the directives he had issued to gather all the necessary supplies for his further journey, immediately got into his automobile, and drove away, abandoning the second automobile with the American flag to the Bolsheviks. "My mind a blank, counting the minutes and shaking from every bump, terrified of nails," Kerensky and his fellow passengers reached Pskov toward evening on October 25.

Alas, here also the local military revolutionary committee had been active, for it too had received a telegram calling for Kerensky's arrest in the event he should appear in Pskov; this telegram was signed by Ensign Krylenko and the sailor Dybenko. Making a precautionary stop at the private apartment of General Quartermaster Baranovsky, Kerensky learned that even the Commander-in-Chief of the Northern Front, Cheremisov, was in touch with the revolutionary committee and was not inclined to compromise himself before the Bolsheviks by defending the Provisional Government.

Already by 6:30 A.M. on October 25—that is, before Kerensky's departure from Petrograd—the headquarters of the III Cavalry Corps, situated in the region of the city Ostrov, had received a ciphered telegram concerning the dispatch of the I Don Division and its artillery to Petrograd. It had also received a confirmation of this directive signed by Kerensky himself and countersigned by Colonel Grekov on behalf of the Cossack Union. Of the 50 squadrons and companies and 23 artillery pieces of the III Corps that were normally at the disposal of the corps commander, there were available at that moment only the eight companies and eight artillery pieces of the Don Division and six companies and ten artillery pieces of the Ussurian Division. The remaining units of the corps were dispersed in various cities from Revel to Vitebsk.

The commander of the III Corps, General Krasnov,[1] who was appointed to replace General Krymov, recounted in detail in his memoirs how this corps, which had been assigned during the Kornilov days to the defense of Petrograd, was gradually atomized and demoralized by Bolshevik agents. Already in late September the corps was moved from Tsarskoe Selo further from Petrograd to the vicinity of Ostrov. Then during October units of the corps were sent to Staraia Russa, Toropets, Ostashkov, Borovichi, Revel, Novgorod and so on. At the moment when Kerensky's order was received, General Krasnov had at hand only 18 companies out of 50.[2]

General Krasnov had immediately issued the order to gather the units of the corps near Luga, from which he proposed to move toward Petrograd by foot so as to avoid the fate of Krymov. But General Cheremisov hastened to cancel Krasnov's order, and thus made impossible immediate movement toward Petrograd. The companies which were on trains ready to move to Luga were ordered by the Commander-in-Chief of the Northern Front to disembark from their trains. At the station an order was received from Cheremisov to dispatch the echelons that were now in Ostrov not to the north toward Petrograd but to the south—toward the Martsen Station.

At approximately 11 P.M.—that is, just at the time when the fate of the Winter Palace was decided—General Krasnov learned about the cancellation of his orders. He decided personally to clarify matters with the Commander-in Chief of the Northern Front, and at midnight of October 26 he set off for Pskov. Having arrived there at 2:15 A.M., Krasnov found Cheremisov occupied; he was taking part in a meeting of the local military revolutionary committee.

By this time Cheremisov had already managed to settle his accounts with Kerensky. Having been summoned by Kerensky to Baranovsky's apartment, Cheremisov "did not hide," in Kerensky's words, that he did not intend in any manner to link his future to the fate of a "doomed" government. Cheremisov admitted that he had already cancelled the order for the sending of troops to Petrograd that had been issued earlier, after the receipt of Kerensky's telegram. He claimed to have no troops that he could send from the front to the capital. He could not even vouch for Kerensky's safety in Pskov. However, Cheremisov was going to a meeting of the local military revolutionary committee where he would find out about the attitude of the troops, and he promised to inform Kerensky of the results.

Cheremisov returned only after midnight, and only to state that he could not offer any assistance whatsoever to the Provisional Government. Kerensky could not stay in Pskov, and if he were determined to resist, he would have to go to Stavka, to Mogilev, to Dukhonin. According to Kerensky, Cheremisov concealed from him that Dukhonin had already twice requested a direct conversation with Kerensky and twice had been refused permission. Kerensky asked Cheremisov to send Krasnov to him, but again received a duplicitous answer: "Krasnov was here and went back to Ostrov."

In fact, Krasnov arrived at Pskov, as we have seen, at 2:15 A.M. and after 3 A.M. he was received very reluctantly by Cheremisov. Cheremisov repeated his order to Krasnov—to dispatch the Ussurian Division to Martsen, and to order the Don Division to disembark and to concentrate in its old quarters near Ostrov. To Krasnov's puzzled question of how to reconcile this order with the order of the supreme commander-in-chief, Cheremisov sluggishly yawned and said: "There is no central government; it has been driven out by the Bolsheviks in Petrograd. The supreme commander-in-chief has gone into hiding, God knows where, and you must obey my orders alone, since I am commander-in-chief." When Krasnov requested that Cheremisov issue this order in writing, Cheremisov responded by shrugging his shoulders, and with a look of pity he parted with Krasnov, giving the latter not an order, but good advice: "Stay in Ostrov and do nothing."

Krasnov did not follow this advice. He set off to find Commissar Voitinsky, and waited for Voitinsky in his apartment until 4 A.M.. Voitinsky told Krasnov in confidence that Kerensky was in Pskov and wanted to see him.

Grudgingly, suppressing in himself "a feeling of disgust and repulsion," Krasnov went to the indicated address. He was going "not for the sake of Kerensky," but for the sake of a motherland "that had not managed to find a leader more capable."

At that moment Kerensky was waiting for an automobile to take him either to Ostrov or to Mogilev. He tried in vain to fall asleep. "In the night silence, it seemed, I could hear the seconds racing by . . . . I had never hated so much this senseless racing of the clock, always forward, forward." A ringing at the front door interrupted this wearisome waiting. In Krasnov was Kerensky's salvation, and Kerensky immediately adopted the imperious tone that left its impression in Krasnov's memoirs. "Where is your corps? Is it coming here? Is it close? Why is it not near Luga?" Krasnov noted: "Despite the imperiousness of the tone and the deliberate brusqueness of manner, there is nothing majestic [about Kerensky]. He is not Napoleon, but he poses as Napoleon.

"I told Kerensky that not only was there no corps, there was not even a division; units were scattered over all northwest Russia, and before they move they must be brought together: to move in small units is madness." Kerensky responded: "This is trivia. The whole army stands behind me; I shall lead it myself, and everyone will follow me." Krasnov began to dictate to Baranovsky which units were located in what positions; both of them [Kerensky and Baranovsky], Krasnov thought, "were simply playing, they were not acting in earnest." "'You will receive all our units,' said Baranovsky. 'Not only the Don, but also the Ussurian Division; also, the 37th Infantry Division, the I Cavalry Division, and the entire XVII Army Corps.'" Krasnov was already working out a plan for the campaign in his mind. Yet he was also plagued by doubt as to whether Kerensky was sure of what he [Kerensky] was saying. Having ended this scene, Kerensky "suddenly sank into his chair, crumpled, his eyes dimmed, his movements those of an old man."

Nevertheless, [despite Krasnov's objections], it was decided to advance on Petrograd with "small units," in the expectation that there would be large reinforcements. Just before dawn Krasnov and Kerensky, submerged in sleep, departed Pskov, and with the pale morning they approached Ostrov. Krasnov's first act was to halt the Don companies which were dispersing to the villages and to inform them that they were going to Petrograd and Kerensky was going with them. Despite the measures taken, Kerensky's name provoked more curiosity than enthusiasm. Several days later, when Krasnov's effort had ended in failure, General Cheremisov told Krasnov by telephone: "The blame for everything [for the resistance to the Bolsheviks] is Kerensky's. When he was in Pskov, I predicted to him how it would end. He didn't listen to me, and this is the result."

This conversation occurred on November 1. But on the night of October 26 General Krasnov wanted to "carry out his oath." And he had answered Kerensky differently than Cheremisov had answered. Krasnov had said: "The I Don Division has excellent morale. True, after the advance [toward Petrograd] on General Kornilov's order and after what happened later, your [Kerensky's] name was not popular in it, but the Cossacks will understand that they are moving not for the sake of a person, but for the sacred cause of liberty against the aggressor. If the infantry moves, so will the Ussurian Division."

This refrain—"your name is not popular"—was repeated constantly in the following days. During the same conversation, in response to Kerensky's proposal "to speak with the Cossack committees," General Krasnov answered with another reminder that "after the Kornilov affair, your [Kerensky's] name is unpopular." When Kerensky nevertheless carried out his intention to speak to the Cossacks, there were cries from the rows of auditors: "You want to choke in our blood . . . you will be walking up to your knees in blood!" On the next day Lieutenant Kartashev, who had been summoned for a report, refused to shake hands with Kerensky, and told the latter: "Excuse me, I cannot offer you my hand. I am a Kornilovite." General Krasnov observed that "nearly half the detachment consisted of such Kornilovites."

Regardless of the obstacles, Cheremisov's resistance was broken. Thanks to the energy of Krasnov, the echelons moved forward. But the railroad employees continued passively to resist. The coupling of cars was delayed; then there was no one to drive the train so a Cossack captain had to take the engineer's place. Finally, around 3 o'clock on October 26 the train moved out. At considerable speed the train passed through Pskov station, where a crowd of several thousand hostile soldiers had assembled. Approaching Gatchina, Kerensky triumphantly congratulated General Krasnov as commander of the army headed for Petrograd. "The commander of an army and two companies," Krasnov sarcastically noted! "A total of 700 horsemen, and if we are forced to dismount, an effective force of 466 men in all."

"Toward evening of that day (October 26)," Kerensky recalled, "in the train near Luga, we received the first news about the capture of the Winter Palace [the news came from Pskov, from General Baranovsky], . . .

This most credible report seemed unbelievable, and the messenger from Pskov struck me as suspicious . . . . Involuntarily I found myself thinking that the tragic news had been fabricated by a Bolshevik agent." Kerensky wanted to believe, despite the evidence, [that the Bolsheviks had not succeeded] for on this belief rested the very possibility of future struggle.

Kerensky regarded matters very lightly, and at the beginning he was certain that the troops could disembark directly at Nikolaevsky Station before the Winter Palace could be taken. General Krasnov disabused Kerensky of this notion by explaining that it would be necessary first to concentrate forces near Gatchina, and from thence to move to Petrograd "following all the rules of the art of war."

According to preliminary information based on orders issued previously, Krasnov was supposed to arrive in Petrograd with "a strong corps, almost an army." In addition to the units of the III Corps, there were orders for the dispatch of the 44th Sharpshooters Division, units of the XVII Army Corps with their artillery, and also certain units of cavalry, which were supposedly coming from Moscow to Dno Station. In reality, not only did these units fail to arrive, for reasons indicated above, but of the squadrons of the Don Cossacks at hand, Cheremisov succeeded at the last minute in detaching three squadrons under the pretext of defending Pskov from the Bolsheviks. At noon on October 27 Krasnov arrived and disembarked at the commercial Gatchina Station with only five and one half squadrons, six machine guns, and eight artillery guns—that is, if one counts 60 Cossacks per squadron, with 330 mounted Cossacks, the equivalent of 220 unmounted troops.

Kerensky continued to send telegrams to the Northern Front concerning the loading and dispatching of various units of infantry, and he stubbornly insisted on the immediate movement of troops from Gatchina to Petrograd. In orders to Krasnov, Kerensky stated that Krasnov was to "take command of all the armed forces of the Russian Republic in the Petrograd district with all the rights of an army commander." When Krasnov noted that his forces were so few that on their arrival in Petrograd they would have to disperse along the streets, and these dispersed units would be "not separate patrol units, but isolated, individual Cossacks," Kerensky promised reinforcements.

Early on the morning of October 27 Krasnov's small detachment disembarked at the commercial station in Gatchina. By this time Bolshevik units from Petrograd, Krasnoe Selo, and Kronstadt had already arrived in Gatchina. But exaggerated rumors of Krasnov's strength were making the rounds. In Petrograd Krasnov's forces were numbered at more than 10,000. The Bolshevik units, not being aware of the situation, one after the other agreed to surrender their rifles and machine guns to Krasnov's Cossacks. Unable to take prisoners, Krasnov dismissed the Bolshevik units, and they either set off wandering or returned to Petrograd. The Gatchina garrison proclaimed itself to be "neutral." From the local school for ensigns and cadets Krasnov's detachment even received a small reinforcement, though only for the purpose of guarding the area of Gatchina itself. From the Cossack units two squadrons of the 10th Don Regiment, two squadrons of the 9th Don Regiment, and half a squadron of the 1st Amur Regiment arrived. The remaining Cossack units were detained by Cheremisov in Pskov and by the garrison commander in Revel. "Neither the 37th Infantry, nor the 1st Cavalry Division, nor units of the XVII Corps were visible on the horizon."

A.F. Kerensky stayed at the Gatchina Palace, in the apartment of the commandant, "which apartment I fortunately had abandoned only two days ago, in a nick of time." According to his own testimony, from the moment of his arrival in Gatchina Kerensky "began to send telegram after telegram demanding the dispatch of troops. From everywhere the response was that the troops had already been sent or were being sent." "Kerensky was certain," according to calculations based on official data, "that the first echelon of infantry should have arrived in Gatchina toward evening on October 27." He summoned Krasnov and insisted that Krasnov continue the march toward Petrograd.

Krasnov, who was better acquainted with the situation, did not share this confidence at all. "To advance on Petrograd with these forces," he noted in his subsequent memoirs, "was not insanely brave, it was simply stupidity." But, recognizing that civil war has its own peculiar principles and counting on the moral effect of a military attack led "not by the tsarist general Kornilov, but by the socialist leader, the democrat Kerensky," Krasnov summoned committees, discussed the situation with them and decided to attack. According to Kerensky, on that day "Krasnov was full of confidence and good spirits." However, the external appearance of "confidence" of both men hardly reflected their real emotions. In the first version of his memoirs Krasnov admitted that already on the evening of October 27 the mood of the Cossacks was not at all "completely satisfactory," as Kerensky wanted to think. Not waiting until the promised arrival of reinforcements late that night, the Cossacks already had begun to grumble early that evening. "This is a deception.... This is the same kind of adventure as in the Kornilov days .... They want to gamble with Cossacks' lives .... They say the infantry is coming, but where is the infantry?" "That evening a deputation of officers from the garrison came to Krasnov and said: "Kerensky is interfering with everything. The troops do not like him and they will not follow him. What would happen if you took responsibility for this work, arrested Kerensky and assumed leadership of the movement?'" According to Krasnov, Savinkov, who had just arrived from a meeting of the Cossack Union, was saying the same thing to him.[3] "Why should you permit Kerensky to be here? Things are going well. The Cossacks will accomplish what you wish. The Cossacks will save Russia from the Bolsheviks, but Kerensky will present himself as the savior, and this unworthy man will become the idol of the crowd."

In saying this, Savinkov not only based himself on his own personal opinions and feelings, but on what he had heard in Petrograd from the officers two days earlier. According to Savinkov,[4] Colonel P., who had arrived from the front, told him that "according to his [Colonel P.'s] information, officers in Petrograd would not support the Provisional Government, for they did not trust Kerensky." Lieutenant N.N., who served in the headquarters of Petrograd military district, "made him aware that among the officers in Petrograd there was so much sentiment against A.F. Kerensky that many of them thought it necessary immediately to arrest him [Kerensky]." According to several officers at headquarters, A.F. Kerensky, by interferring with the orders of the commander of the Petrograd military district, Colonel Polkovnikov, was hindering the successful defense of Petrograd. Perhaps not unrelated to these conversations of Savinkov was the appearance before Krasnov of a deputation of Cossacks who asked for permission to arrest Kerensky. When Krasnov denied them permission on the grounds that "Cossacks have never been traitors," the deputation requested that at the very least Kerensky not be permitted near the detachment. This Krasnov promised, and he "prevailed upon Kerensky, under the pretext that he [Kerensky] should not subject his life to risk, to stay in Gatchina," while Krasnov's detachment moved to Tsarskoe Selo. At 2 A.M. the movement toward Tsarskoe Selo commenced.

The garrison at Tsarskoe Selo consisted of 12-16 thousand soldiers who were not inclined to join in the battle. Krasnov could counter them only with newly formed units—400 mounted Cossacks, or 265 unmounted troops. But the illusion of the strength and numerousness of Krasnov's detachment was still intact. The detachment had not yet become demoralized, and by swiftness of movement Krasnov thought he could compensate to a certain extent for the insufficiency of his actual forces.

The first Bolshevik units, which were encountered on the road even before dawn, surrendered without resistance. At dawn, approaching Tsarskoe Selo, Krasnov's detachment stumbled upon a line of guards who fired sluggishly. Prolonged "conversations" began, as a result of which the marksmen broke into different groups. Part of them joined Krasnov, while another part made an attempt to surround the detachment. At that point Kerensky arrived on the scene; he had become "sick of waiting" for the outcome on the watch tower of the Pulkovo Observatory, where he had settled temporarily. According to Krasnov, Kerensky was "very much overwrought." Despite being asked to return to Gatchina, Kerensky "thrust himself into the crowd of hesitating soldiers"; his "penetrating hysterical voice" rang out. Part of the soldiers were successfully disarmed, but the encirclement by the units which remained faithful to the Bolsheviks continued. The situation was becoming critical. Krasnov convinced Kerensky to return to his observation point.

"During the course of this conversation" Kerensky noted, "General Krasnov somehow comported himself with me differently than before." He "somehow not very logically explained to me that my presence interfered with the operation and bothered the officers." To Kerensky this seemed "very strange, and not really comprehensible." But Savinkov's appearance in the small room of the observatory where Kerensky was sitting "made instantly clear to me the new situation in the detachment." Kerensky attributed the change in the mood of the troops to the appearance of a delegation from the Soviet of the Cossack Union. He recalled later that Savinkov "attempted to speak with an especially mysterious and tragic look on his face; in a particularly minatory tone he asked me whether I intended to offer him some sort of official position with me." Savinkov's manner of presenting himself and of imposing his will on someone else was well captured by Kerensky. Kerensky missed the chance to bring Savinkov over to his own side. "I refused to engage him in serious conversation; we parted," Kerensky noted. We shall soon see the results.

The sun was nearly setting, there had been no decisive attack on Tsarskoe Selo and Kerensky again lost patience. He "no longer doubted that the sudden [?] paralysis that gripped all the units of the III Cavalry Corps was not the result of military-technical considerations, but of political considerations." Krasnov was showered with "written demands for the immediate beginning of military actions against Tsarskoe Selo, for the opening of artillery fire." Kerensky remained "profoundly convinced" even later that it would have been possible, "given the good will of the commanders and the absence of intrigue," to have taken Tsarskoe Selo by morning, a half day earlier. "The deliberate delay on the outskirts of Tsarskoe Selo" he considered "a fatal blow to the entire operation."

However, as we already know, the entire situation was "fatal." Toward evening on October 28 this merely became clearer than it had been earlier. And there is no doubt that Krasnov, who had decided to move on the basis of the peculiar fates governing civil war, understood ever more clearly with each new step that fortune was not on his side. He ordered two rounds of artillery fire, and a crowd of thousands of his opponents rushed at once to the station and demanded to be sent off to Petrograd. Almost without resistance the Cossacks captured the railroad station, the radio station, the telephone exchange. At twilight the Cossacks began to enter the city. But this was not the end of the matter. Krasnov was aware of the small number of his troops, and he knew the tactical danger of entering Tsarskoe Selo. Late that evening he told Kerensky that it would be necessary to pull back the troops and to delay occupying the city until morning. Kerensky vigorously protested and demanded immediate entry into the city. Kerensky was supported by Stankevich,[5] who had just arrived from Petrograd and who conveyed optimistic reports about the mood of the capital. From the morning of October 29 Kerensky was determined to "begin preparations for the liquidation of Petersburg," and he continued to refer to the "movement of squadrons" of troops coming to his assistance. Obeying this order and understanding the significance for morale of capturing Tsarskoe Selo, Krasnov entered into the city that night and occupied the palaces. Kerensky, who was full "of the darkest thoughts," returned to Gatchina to spend the night. However, according to his own account, Kerensky still "hoped to find fresh troops in Gatchina." He found "only . . . telegrams." In his memoirs Kerensky admitted: "After a day of our absence [from Petrograd] the mood among the lower classes had become much worse."

The situation in Tsarskoe Selo was also not auspicious. As Krasnov had foreseen, to maintain a force consisting of a handful of Cossacks in a city of many thousands of people was much more difficult than to maintain the force in Gatchina. There were no cadets in Tsarskoe Selo, and the Obukhovsky battalion, which was favorably disposed to Krasnov, agreed to help only by stationing sentries. The Tsarskoe Selo garrison, which outnumbered by "ten to one" the forces of Krasnov's detachment, remained neutral, but only until such time as it could assess the constellation of forces. It goes without saying that there was no hope for the arrival of the reinforcements promised by Kerensky. On the morning of October 28 the detachment numbered only eight and one half Cossack squadrons—that is, 510 mounted or 340 unmounted Cossacks. On October 28 three additional squadrons of the 1st Amur Cossack Regiment arrived, but, according to Krasnov's testimony, they announced that "they would not take part in a fratricidal war, that they would remain neutral." The Amur squadrons stayed in the countryside outside the city, did not enter Tsarskoe Selo, and even refused to set up pickets to relieve the exhausted Don Cossacks.

From the front there was also disheartening news. General Cheremisov had telegraphed the various units of the front that "the political struggle taking place in Petrograd should not concern the army," and this telegram had an immediate effect on the movement of troops toward Petrograd. Cheremisov's chief-of-staff, General Lukirsky, telegraphed Krasnov that the "Primorsky Dragoon Regiment had refused to board trains for Vitebsk and that only one squadron that had boarded a train had gotten as far as Polotsk." We have seen that Cossack units of the III Corps which had not managed to set off with Krasnov had been detained, and the 13th and 15th Don Cossack Regiments had not been permitted to leave Revel. The squadron of artillerists which was coming from Gatchina to assist Krasnov had been fired upon by Bolsheviks and had retreated to the Izhor Station.

Thus, Krasnov's detachment found itself isolated. Under such circumstances it was obviously impossible to move to Petrograd. General Krasnov decided to quarter his troops during the day of October 29 in Tsarskoe Selo. In the second version of his memoirs, he explained this decision in the following fashion: "The men with me were really exhausted. They had gone two days without sleep, in a state of constant anxiety. The horses had sunk into torpor, because they had not been rested. We simply had to have a breathing space. But my men were not so tired physically as they were exhausted by waiting for help. The committees told me that the Cossacks would not advance until infantry arrived." Krasnov hoped that "someone would arrive the next day" and that, in any case, he might be able to assess the situation more accurately.

On that day of October 29 an unsuccessful uprising of cadets occurred in Petrograd (see below). According to Kerensky, the news of this uprising was received in Tsarskoe Selo "only around 4 o'clock that afternoon, when all was already lost." Kerensky suggested that "if we had been informed in time of events in the capital, we would immediately have hastened to the assistance [of the cadets], however unaware the news of the uprising might have caught us." But we have seen how little influence Kerensky actually had over the course of events, and how it was impossible "immediately to hasten" from Tsarskoe Selo to Petrograd. During the day of October 29, the "situation" became even more unfavorable to the continuation of the march toward Petrograd and to Kerensky personally.

According to Krasnov, "the officers of my detachment, all Kornilovites, were upset over Kerensky's behavior . . . . His popularity fell. He
was nothing in Russia, and it was stupid to support him . . . . We will
march with whomever you wish, only not with Kerensky." Krasnov
guessed that, "under the influence of conversations with the officers and
the Cossacks," Savinkov came to him [Krasnov] and proposed to remove Kerensky, to arrest him [Kerensky], and to assume leadership of
the movement himself. Lieutenant-Colonel Lavrukhin of the 9th Don
Regiment approached Krasnov with the same proposal; he [Lavrukhin]
"almost demanded the immediate removal of Kerensky from the detachment, because the Cossacks did not trust him [Kerensky]. They thought
that he [Kerensky] was at one with the Bolsheviks and would betray
us." It was with this mood in mind that Krasnov persuaded Kerensky
"with great difficulty to go back to Gatchina, where the regimental staff
had been sent and whence it would be possible to communicate with
Stavka. Stankevich and Voitinsky tried unsuccessfully to raise the Cossacks' morale by explaining to them the political import of the struggle
and the necessity of the march on Petrograd. The results of these attempts at persuasion became evident in the appeal which was composed
on October 29 "by a conference of representatives of the entire
detachment."

The detachment "protested vehemently against the slander that the
Cossacks are serving the counter-revolution." The detachment said that
it was going to Petrograd "on the order of the Supreme Commander and
on the order of the central committees of the Soviets of Workers' and
Soldiers' Deputies, of the Kiev Congress of Cossack Frontline Troops,
of the Soviet of the Cossack Union, and of other agencies of the Russian democracy." In order "to purge Petrograd of the Bolsheviks who
had illegally seized power," the detachment "had placed itself at the disposal of those agencies trusted by Russia," namely, the Provisional Soviet of the Republic and the Committee for the Salvation of the Motherland and of the Revolution, which had the right to decide the question of
the reorganization of the government of the republic. The detachment
wished "to guarantee to them [these agencies] the opportunity to resolve this issue without any pressure, regardless of the source." As we
see, this position was tantamount to "neutrality."

In order to counter this appeal, which had no avenues for distribution, the Military Revolutionary Committee broadcast from the Petrograd radio station to all fronts and all armies, to all Russia, a proclamation, which informed them that "the front has refused to come to the aid
of former minister Kerensky, who has been overthrown by the people
and who is trying illegally to resist the legal government elected

by the All-Russia Congress of the Soviets." The radio telegrams falsely
stated that "Moscow has joined the new government," that a whole series of other cities had done so as well, that not a single infantry unit
was moving against the workers' and peasants' government. The radio
telegrams threatened that "if the Cossacks do not arrest Kerensky who
has deceived them, and if they move against Petrograd, then the army of
the revolution will defend by force of arms the precious achievements of
the revolution." The demagoguery went further: the ministries of Kerensky had ruined the food supply system and destroyed order in Petrograd;
"Kerensky is attacking the people on the demand of the nobility, the
landowners, capitalists and speculators, in order to return land to the
landowners, etc.."

In Tsarskoe Selo itself there was no lack of expressions of the same
mood. Representatives of the machine-gun officers of the 14th Don Regiment told Krasnov directly that they were "at one with Lenin," because
"Lenin is for peace." Meetings of the 16,000 soldiers in the Tsarskoe
Selo garrison yielded, at best, a resolution against "fratricidal war" and a
promise of complete neutrality. Krasnov recalled that "the entire day
was spent in fruitless negotiations." During the day his forces were augmented by three squadrons of the 9th Don Regiment, an armored train,
two artillery pieces from the Reserve Cavalry Battery from Pavlovsk of
which one lacked a crew to fire it, a Reserve Squadron of the Orenburg
Combined Cossack Regiment which was armed only with sabres, and
several cadets from Petrograd. Krasnov's detachment, according to the
second version of his memoirs, consisted on the evening of October 29
of nine squadrons or 630 mounted Cossacks (420 unmounted troops).

However, Kerensky, joined by Savinkov and Stankevich, continued
to insist on the attack. Kerensky was certain (see "Gatchina") that "in
the St. Petersburg garrison, both in the regiments and among the special troops, there were enough organized anti-Bolshevik elements prepared at the first propitious moment to come out against the Bolsheviks
with weapons in hand . . . and at the crucial moment to deal a decisive
blow in the rear of the Bolshevik troops, who had taken up positions in
the front line at Pulkovo against my [that is, Krasnov's] detachment."
In Petrograd at that time the thinking was that Krasnov had at least a
thousand troops. Despite the mood of the Cossacks and the committees,
Krasnov persuaded his detachment "to carry out more intensive reconnaissance" in the direction of Pulkovo, in order to "discover the enemy,
find out everything and later to decide," if necessary, "to retreat, defend
themselves, and await help." However, they asked Kerensky to remain
in Gatchina during the course of the battle, whence he intended to sally
forth to "meet the approaching squadron."

Early on the morning of October 30, a gymnasium student who had broken out of Petrograd gave to Krasnov a scrap of paper, on which was printed the letterhead of the Cossack Union. The paper, which bore the signature of the union's chairman Ageev, gave the following report concerning the situation in the capital: "The situation in Petrograd is terrible. The cadets, who are at the moment the sole defenders of the populace, are being attacked with knives and assaulted. The infantry regiments are wavering and stand around, the Cossacks are waiting for the infantry to move. The Soviet of the Cossack Union demands your immediate movement toward Petrograd. Your delay threatens the complete destruction of these children—the cadets. Do not forget that your desire to seize power without shedding blood is a fiction, since here every cadet will be slaughtered."

Krasnov answered, sending his response to the address "of the Committee for the Salvation of the Motherland, at 9:30 A.M.": "I am coming at once to Petrograd." He asked whether the Petrograd garrison could place sentries around the city, and if the 1st, 4th, and 14th Don Regiment could come to meet him. In the original version of his memoirs Krasnov remarked: "It was with courage born of despair, with only eight fighting battalion squadrons—that is, 480 mounted or 320 unmounted troops—that we left Tsarskoe Selo on the Alexandrovskaia-Pulkovo line."

On October 30 the decisive battle was fought near Pulkovo, if one can call a "battle" an encounter of a small group of men consisting of less than 500 soldiers, with an adversary whose number was "15 to 30 times greater," who "were very well trained" and who "moved quite correctly in the field" under the leadership of the German Lieutenant Otto Bauer and whose number included the disciplined Latvian Sharpshooters.

Beyond the ravine through which the river Slavianka flows, one could have seen the slopes of the Pulkovo Mountain, scarred by trenches and darkened by the five to six thousand Red Guards who had occupied it. The thick columns of men were descending the slopes; the Red Guards were moving unevenly into the ravine, now surging forward, now rushing back; sailors keeping to their military formations were positioning themselves in the proper places. The Red Guards occupied the center; the Kronstadt sailors, with their German instructors, skillfully operated on the flanks.

The strength of Krasnov's detachment lay in the artillery and in the armored train: from time to time both masked the small number of his men. However, one cannot defeat an enemy by artillery fire alone, and there were no troops to carry out an attack. It remained to count on the psychological effect on Petrograd of the artillery fire and to hold on, at least until evening. But the only regiment to arrive from Petrograd, the Izmailovsky, was on the side of the Bolsheviks. True, the regiment immediately dispersed after the first round of shrapnel. The ease of this success induced the Orenburg squadron to mount an attack. Crowds of Red Guards ran in disorder. But the sailors, who were stationed in the village Suz, repulsed the attack. The commander of the squadron, 18 Cossacks and 40 horses were killed or wounded. The squadron threw itself into retreat, and this small episode revealed the superiority of the sailors. The battle began to subside.

After 2:00 P.M. the adversary deployed artillery and began an enveloping movement from the flanks. Toward evening the artillery shells and rifle ammunition of the Krasnov detachment had been expended, and the commandant of Tsarskoe Selo categorically refused to issue new ammunition. "The powder magazine was surrounded by a crowd of armed infantrymen. It was necessary to seize the ammunition by force, but there was no force to carry out the action," General Krasnov recalled in his original description of the battle. Gots, who had arrived from Petrograd, stated that "the Cossacks cannot leave the barracks because they are surrounded by Soviet troops." The situation was becoming tragic—or, more precisely, the tragedy of the situation had finally become clear. "If only two battalions of infantry had approached me to offer assistance at that time," wrote Krasnov, (five days earlier the ministers besieged in the Winter Palace had spoken of only 300 soldiers), "matters could have been set right. But assistance never arrived." And Krasnov, who retreated at nightfall, wrote an order to the III Cavalry Corps as he sat in a dacha abandoned by the inhabitants: "The intensified reconnaissance carried out today has made it clear that . . . our forces are insufficient to capture Petrograd . . . . Tsarskoe Selo is being gradually surrounded by sailors and Red Guards. . . . The necessity to await the arrival of the promised reinforcements compels me to retreat to Gatchina, there to establish a defensive position."

But where were these "promised reinforcements"? In his memoirs Kerensky spoke about a "whole pile of telegrams reporting on the approach of various squadrons" and on "approximately 50 military trains, overcoming all obstacles, which had broken through and were heading toward Gatchina from various fronts." Where was the portion of truth, the portion of self-deception and the portion of exaggeration in these statements?

In order to find the answer, we must temporarily leave the theater of military actions between Tsarskoe Selo and Gatchina and look at what was happening during this period at Stavka and at the front. The

historian wishing to answer this question has at his disposal a copy of
the telegraphic tape of the negotiations between Stavka and front headquarters during the October insurrection.[6] From these negotiations we
see how swiftly the attitude of the army and the frontline commanders,
which attitude was initially favorable to the Provisional Government,
changed as soon as the weakness of the government became clear and
the first successes of the Bolsheviks became evident. In October the
same thing happened with the Provisional Government as had happened
with the tsarist government in the February days. An accidental revolutionary explosion in the capital was supported passively by the army,
because the attitude of the officer corps as well as that of the soldiers
had hardened against the one government and then against the other. In
this sense, it would be correct to say that the fate of both revolutions
was, in the final analysis, decided by the army.

At the first rumors of revolution in Petrograd on the night of October 24/25, the attitude of the officer corps was one of complete loyalty
to the government. Having received at 2 A.M. Kerensky's directive "to
send all regiments of the Caucasian Cossack Division, the 23rd Don
Cossack Regiment and all remaining Cossack units located in Finland,
by railroad to the Nikolaevsky Station in Petrograd where they will be
under the command of Polkovnikov," and "in case it should prove impossible to send the troops by railroad, to send them squadron by squadron in marching order," Dukhonin immediately conveyed this directive
to Lukirsky,[7] the chief-of-staff of the Supreme Commander of the Northern Front, Cheremisov. Dukhonin received the reply: "The directive is
already being carried out, railroad transport is being arranged, . . . the
first to arrive in Petrograd will be companies of the bicycle battalion
which are now at the ready in the Batatsky Station." The united army
committee at Stavka gathered that same night for an emergency meeting
and "sharply condemned the uprising" of the Bolsheviks.

During the day of October 25 as events unfolded, this attitude
changed. The Executive Committee of the Romanian Front ("Rumche-
roda") spoke out against "encroachments from the right as well as from
the left." But at the Southwestern, Western, and Northern Fronts committees argued until four o'clock and failed to adopt any resolutions.
The V Army of the Northern Front and the reserve organizations were
inclined to support the Bolsheviks. The bicycle battalions were held up
"by somebody" 70 versts from Petrograd, and the dispatch of the Cossack Division on October 25 was "not carried out." At 10 P.M.
Cheremisov cancelled officially all directives to send military units to
Petrograd. To Dukhonin's anxious questions about why he had done

so, Cheremisov gave a false answer: "This was done with the agreement of the supreme commander [Kerensky], which agreement I received from him personally." When Dukhonin requested permission to negotiate with Kerensky himself, Cheremisov continued to lie: "That is not possible. It is in his [Kerensky's] interests [not to speak with you]." Explaining his volte-face, Cheremisov invented the following justification: "This evening someone—most likely rightist elements—appointed Kishkin Governor-General of Petrograd. Kishkin's adherence to the Kadet party is well known at the front. This appointment caused a sharp change in the attitude of the military organizations of the front—a change not in favor of the Provisional Government." Finally, Cheremisov completed his fabricated explanation with the statement that "Kerensky has resigned from the government and has expressed the desire to transfer to me the duties of the supreme commander." Cheremisov tried to communicate his own attitude to the Commander-in-Chief of the Western Front, Baluev.[8] Cheremisov told Baluev more directly that "according to the latest information, without Kerensky's assent the Kadet Kishkin has been appointed the Governor-General of Petrograd; *in view of this circumstance* the sending of troops to Petrograd *is aimless and even harmful*, since it is obvious that the troops will not take Kishkin's side." In response Cheremisov received from Baluev a sharp reproof: "It is very unfortunate that your troops are taking part in politics. We have sworn allegiance to the Provisional Government, and it is not our business to consider whether Kishkin or somebody else should be Governor-General of Petrograd . . . . I consider it a great misfortune for Russia if power should be seized by such irresponsible parties as the Bolsheviks, since this will mean anarchy and inevitable disaster for Russia . . . . Beside Petrograd there is the vast expanse of Russia, and there is still a question of how Russia will view this." Cheremisov's response was: "We have no right to stay out of politics and not to take into account the political mood of the masses."

As a result of these exchanges, General Baluev did not wish to take part in the unification "even of the two fronts, the Northern and Western," as Cheremisov had ordered. Cheremisov stated that he would wait for further orders from Stavka. Stavka was in a very difficult position. At approximately 1 A.M. it had received the news about the arrest of the ministers. No one knew where Kerensky was. Moreover, the Bolshevik Military Revolutionary Committee had sent to all fronts a demand to inform the soldiers about the events in the capital and to arrest those who were against the revolution. This demand could not be concealed from the army. And so Stavka, before issuing the requested orders, conducted a survey of the front commanders as to whether the front commanders had at their disposal military units which would support unconditionally the Provisional Government.

General Baluev answered this inquiry for the Western Front: "I cannot rely on a single unit. The majority of units certainly do not support the government. Even those units that are around me are good only to stop pogroms and disorders, but they will be of no use as support for the Provisional Government." The Commissar of the Romanian Front, Tizengauzen, responded to the same inquiry as follows: "It is probably not possible to move troops from the front merely for the defense of this government . . . . The membership of the current government is not especially popular with the troops and as such is of little interest to the soldiers." On the contrary, "the defense of the Constituent Assembly is very popular: the whole front would come to the defense of the Constituent Assembly and would resist attempts to break it up." From the Southwestern Front General Makhrov declined to answer; he referred to information communicated to him by Cheremisov that the dispatch of troops had already been halted.

By the morning of October 26 the attitude of the Northern Front had changed under the influence of Kerensky's decision to advance by foot to Petrograd, and as a result of Commissar Voitinsky's report to Cheremisov that the Bolsheviks were isolated, "since the entire organized democracy has come out against them" and their [the Bolsheviks'] victory "is a Pyrrhic victory." Cheremisov then decided to "continue the movement by railroad of units of the III Cavalry Corps and he ordered elimination of the posts of the revolutionary committee." Cheremisov had evidently ceased to insist on his version of events. Dukhonin decided to send a telegram to Kerensky through headquarters of the Northern Front; although he asked the "piece of telegraphic tape to be destroyed," he offered Kerensky a personal opinion. "I consider it essential to send to Petrograd not only the III Corps, but also the other indicated units; of course, it will be necessary to advance by foot, since the railroad workers have passed a resolution not to permit troops through to Petrograd." At 2:00 P.M. on October 26 Stavka received an order from Kerensky which, along with the appeal of five democratic organizations (the SRs, SDs, Tsentroflot, the army organizations in Petrograd, and the Presidium of the Executive Committee of the Soviet of Workers' Deputies), reinforced for a short time the anti-Bolshevik attitude of Stavka. Dukhonin hastened to convey this good news to Baluev on the Western Front, but he heard in reply that Minsk was in the hands of the Soviet of Workers' Deputies, the garrison was unreliable, and Baluev himself had been placed under arrest by the 37th Regiment, which was "entirely at the disposal of the Soviet." The moment of optimism over the "isolation" of the Bolsheviks also had an impact on the Southwestern Front, from which N.I. Iordansky expressed the hope that "the majority is in favor of the Provisional Government and is prepared to send a detachment to Petrograd." Iordansky excused himself for not sending troops, however, on the pretext of Kerensky's order: "I have received the order. One phrase gives rise to misunderstanding: the phrase about the possibility of forming a new government.[9] If this signifies a readiness to compromise with Petrograd, then it is a mistake. The slogan should be the restoration of the government and the summoning of the Constituent Assembly." "The moment for the destruction of Bolshevism has arrived, and we will be forced from our true purposes if the half-measures of July 3-5 are repeated." Thus, the attitudes of the left and the right in the army coincided on a single point: they were equally hostile to Kerensky.

Unfortunately, it was at this moment of optimism that our source—the conversations of Stavka with the fronts by direct wire—was broken off. In order to follow how, over the course of the next two days, October 27 and 28, this optimistic mood was transformed into a pessimistic one, we shall turn to the (unpublished) recollections composed at the request of the author of this book by General Shilling, the commander of the XVII Army Corps, which was to be sent against the Bolsheviks, and also to the recollections of the commissar of the VIII Army (to which the XVII Corps belonged), K.M. Vendziagolsky, who unsuccessfully tried to organize the dispatch of the XVII Corps to Petrograd. Having arrived at Stavka on October 26 and having reported to Dukhonin on the position of the VIII Army, Vendziagolsky learned in the office of the military commissar, which was under the aegis of the supreme commander, that Stavka "proposes to organize a combined detachment under the command of General Vrangel, in order to send part of this detachment to the area near Petrograd, and part to defend the approaches to Stavka."[10] Vendziagolsky spent a day in Mogilev, until midday on October 27, but no detachment was formed. Then, with the permission of his superiors, he decided to travel further to the north, where, in Vitebsk and Pskov provinces, the XVII Corps was stationed. The corps had just been moved there from the Romanian Front and had arrived in the region of Nevel-Gorodok between October 15 and 25, where it was stationed at the disposal of the supreme commander.

"The mood in Nevel and in the units quartered in it (the reserve artillery division, a heavy artillery division from the Riga front, and the Siberian Reserve Engineers Battalion) was Bolshevistic," General Shilling testified. Shilling summoned to the city the politically reliable

"Cossack Death Unit" [*kuren smerti*] which consisted of 700 Ukrainian soldiers, and through them occupied the post office, telegraph office, and railroad station on October 27. From the headquarters of the V Army, where the committee was Bolshevik, there was a shower of telegrams with an appeal to submit to the Bolsheviks. Having broken the telegraphic tie with the V Army, General Shilling decided to communicate directly with Stavka. At 1:00 A.M. on October 28 he was approached by Vendziagolsky, who informed him of the situation prevailing at Stavka. To Shilling's question, why did Stavka issue no orders and pass on no information, he received from Vendziagolsky the answer that "there at Stavka they are not certain whether they can rely on the units of the corps." In order to verify this, on October 28 at 11 A.M. General Shilling gathered representatives of all units of the corps and presented to them his view of Bolshevism. Two hours later he received a response from the chairman of the corps committee, Lieutenant Zotikov, that everyone agreed with him and would follow him. Then Shilling dispatched the chief-of-staff of the corps, Colonel Bronsky, in an automobile to Stavka with a note addressed to Dukhonin and written by Vendziagolsky. General Shilling requested permission to put the corps' troops on trains and immediately to send squadrons in two directions: toward Pskov and Luga and toward Bologoe and Chudovo.

Before this note arrived at Stavka, General Shilling received from Stavka a secret packet, containing an order to occupy the railroad junctions at Dno and Orsha and to equip each battalion with four machine - guns so as "not to permit the Bolsheviks access to Stavka." However, the men detailed by Shilling (from the 140th Zaraisky Regiment) were held up, since "Northern Front headquarters knew of the movement of every military train and apparently Stavka's orders were not being carried out there."

At approximately 11:00 P.M. on October 29 General Shilling received from Stavka an answer to his own request. Stavka ordered Shilling to send from his corps to Petrograd a brigade of soldiers, a motorized division, and a division of light field artillery. General Shilling ordered these units, which were spread out over the surrounding 25 versts, to concentrate at railroad stations where they would embark: thus he hoped to guarantee a trouble-free embarkation. The 11th Pskov Infantry Regiment, the 12th Velikolutsky Regiment, the 17th Motorized Division, and three batteries of the 35th Artillery Brigade were assigned to this duty. "To the great surprise of the officers," General Shilling noted, "the regiments and units arrived for embarkation but there were no trains. The soldiers stood under an open sky, in abominable rainy weather. The officers barely managed *after 10 hours* to obtain two trains for the 12th Velikolutsky Regiment and one train for officers of the 3th Infantry Division. Agitation against embarkation and dispatch of the trains continued throughout this ordeal." As a result of this agitation, on the evening of October 29 Shilling was forced to cancel the embarkation of the propagandized 3rd Division and to replace it with the reliable 35th. The officers of the 3rd Division and the units of the 12th already aboard trains were ordered to disembark. In their place—but only on October 30 and 31, the embarkation of the 137th Nezhinsky and 140th Zaraisky Regiments commenced. Here again the story repeated itself. "The trains were provided very slowly. It happened that a train would be provided, an entire squadron would climb aboard, but *engines* to pull the train *were not provided for 24 hours*, and the soldiers were sitting in cars that were neither equipped with heaters nor for passengers." However, "on this occasion the mood of the soldiers was courageous and cheerful . . . . Everyone was eager to go, despite the fact that the Bolsheviks were swarming all around them."

The movement of the entrained squadrons toward Petrograd finally had begun, but on the way to Petrograd the trains encountered every manner of obstacle. "According to the reports of the commander of the 137th Nezhinsky Infantry Regiment, of the corps commissar, and also of the head of the 35th Division," General Shilling stated, "it became clear that everywhere at the stations the squadrons suffered delays, were not provided with engines, and that in the seizure of power by the Bolsheviks Vikzhel played a most despicable role." Only by using force did the first of the squadrons succeed in breaking past Pskov and arriving at Luga, where "the entire garrison—6 or 7 thousand men—immediately surrendered without a fight. All the sentry positions were occupied by soldiers of the Nezhinsky Regiment, and the artillerists located in Luga went to the battalion commander and surrendered the locks from their guns." Having threatened to return and to bombard Pskov, this first squadron brought in its wake the mortar battery of the 17th Division. A deputation of Bolsheviks that included the sailor Dybenko, which came to Luga to dissuade the advanced elements that had arrived there, left without success. The corps commissar Zotikov even decided to go to Petrograd, to Smolny, and he returned from thence successfully, having threatened the Bolsheviks with the Luga troops. But, alas, these partial successes came too late. The endless delays of the soldiers, for which delays the railroad workers were responsible, achieved their purpose. We know that already on October 30 Krasnov's detachment, lacking reinforcements, had lost the decisive battle near Pulkovo and had been forced to retreat. And subsequently rumors reached Luga about negotiations between Krasnov and the Bolsheviks, while on November 2 Dukhonin's order was received—and this time it was effective and final—to halt the movement of squadrons toward Petrograd. The Nezhinsky Regiment did not believe this order really had been issued, and it sent representatives to Stavka to find out. There the order was confirmed, so the units "began to return to their former posts . . . . Of course, this time they were not in the same mood as they had been earlier," noted General Shilling. "The poison of Bolshevism had begun to penetrate even their milieu."

What was the cause of Dukhonin's decision? We shall discover it if we return to Gatchina to the Krasnov detachment and to Kerensky. Vendziagolsky also was headed through Pskov after reaching agreement with General Shilling about the attack.

Having arrived in Gatchina two days before the Pulkovo "battle" and having had an audience with A.F. Kerensky, Vendziagolsky discovered the complete confusion of the supreme commander-in-chief and the disagreements that swirled around his person. "To my horror I noticed that neither the supreme commander nor anyone around him [Krasnov's staff was not there] had even the slightest notion about the disposition of the troops of the Northern Front . . . . The news about the possibility of the arrival of 'an entire corps' fell upon everyone as an unexpected good fortune. It remained to await the arrival of the corps, but there was no possibility, given the absence of communications, of following its progress. In the staff quarters of the supreme commander what struck one was the general bustle, the running about, the machine guns in the dining room, the tinned goods in the yard, the endless roaming about, and the complete absence of serviceable communications, the almost complete isolation from all Russia. Commissar Voitinsky and Semenov, the retainers of A.F. Kerensky, 'appointed' me commissar of an armored train, which was assigned to capture a railroad station by October 29." "Later Voitinsky cancelled this appointment when Vendziagolsky told him that the armored train would be able to hold Nikolaevsky Station only by raining devastation and terror on the Bolsheviks." "In the view of this good-hearted man," Vendziagolsky noted, "an armored train ought to be more a means of moral suasion . . . ." "Within a short time they asked me to go as commissar to some squadron in Valk or somewhere else, and later they appointed me an agitator in certain shaky units with the program: 'If they are too far to the right, step on their tails' (Voitinsky's expression) . . . ."

The appointments and commissions rained down all night and all morning on October 29 from those rushing about A.F. Kerensky—

from Stankevich, Voitinsky, Semenov, the three adjutants, from the head of the civil chancellary, and from many other people with various titles whom Vendziagolsky could not remember. Soon all these people sensed that Vendziagolsky was their enemy, especially when Savinkov appeared in Tsarskoe Selo and in Gatchina. Savinkov had several unpleasant discussions with Kerensky in which he indicated that the Cossacks had no faith in Kerensky, that they feared a repetition of the history of July 3-5, and that Kerensky's speeches to them were having an unfavorable impact. The mood of Kerensky's retainers was expressed in Voitinsky's conversation with Savinkov, in which the Commissar of the Northern Front "expressed the fear that 'counter-revolutionaries' would take advantage of the Bolshevik uprising to achieve their own counter-revolutionary ends." Savinkov added that "it seemed to me that he [Voitinsky] trusted neither the Cossacks nor me." And in fact on the evening of that same October 29 Semenov took from Vendziagolsky a formal "deposition concerning rumors of an allegedly impending coup d'etat, the arrest of Kerensky and so on." The trembling lips of Commissar Semenov pronounced the "dread" word: "Savinkov." "Being frightened of their defenders, the retainers of Kerensky and Kerensky himself had already thought up [or, more accurely, had continued to discuss—see above] a new political combination."

According to Vendziagolsky, in Kerensky's office there was a struggle: the idea of conciliation was born. Stankevich and the other commissars said something. Chernov and others turned up in the Gatchina palace. Rumors began to circulate about the formation at Stavka (in Mogilev) of an exclusively socialist government. Avksentiev and Chernov were named to it. Even during the Pulkovo battle Savinkov learned from a certain member of the Committee for the Salvation of the Motherland, that A.F. Kerensky intended to depart Gatchina for Stavka. Reasoning that such a departure would "be considered as desertion during the time of battle" Savinkov considered it necessary to return to Gatchina to dissuade Kerensky from this course. Savinkov recalled that "Stankevich argued with me, but Kerensky, after consulting with the Cossack captain that had accompanied me, agreed with my reasoning." On the evening of that same day, October 30, Savinkov had a new conversation with Kerensky about his appointment as commissar to Krasnov's battalion. "I told Kerensky that I did not share and do not now share his politics, that his tenure in government had for a long time seemed to me to be ruinous for Russia, that I had fought against him by all legal means, and that I was prepared to fight him by illegal means, for I consider him one of those guilty for the Bolsheviks' uprising, against which he [Kerensky] had not taken any measures at the proper time."

After this candid conversation, Kerensky, "in view of the exceptional circumstances," confirmed Savinkov in the office which Krasnov's officers had asked him [Savinkov] to assume.

Among the leadership there were disagreements; among the government's defenders there was constant political agitation. "The Bolsheviks openly incited the soldiers and Cossacks to rebellion," noted Vendziagolsky. "Agitators darted everywhere . . . . The inhabitants of Tsarskoe Selo were grumbling: what kind of order is it, what kind of war, if the enemy infiltrates the troops without impediment, if there are meetings on the streets, shooting in the city, and Kerensky howls away in speech after speech?" Savinkov confirmed that "Bolshevik agitators tried to prove to the Cossacks that Bolsheviks and Cossacks were brothers and were pursuing the same end—for both wanted above all for Kerensky to resign from office. . . . It was impossible to fight against this propaganda. In Tsarskoe Selo there was a garrison of several thousand men; in this armed crowd the handful of Cossacks of General Krasnov was swallowed up." The fruits of the agitation were also evident on the field of military battle. While the Bolsheviks "looked at us as we looked at the Germans, while they fought cruelly and stubbornly, while they mutilated corpses," wrote General Krasnov, "the Cossacks could not break away from the view inculcated in them by the agitators that the Bolsheviks were 'their own,' that they were 'brothers,' that this was a 'fratricidal' war, and, where possible, the Cossacks spared them [the Bolsheviks]. The Cossacks were often led into self-deception; they permitted military scouts and spies who had penetrated into their midst to 'argue' with and to 'confront' them."

Kerensky was completely in agreement with Savinkov's and Vendziagolsky's description, but Kerensky placed the blame for the defeat of the Krasnov detachment on Krasnov himself. "There were no measures taken to guard, to isolate the troops from the rest of the populace, or even to preserve the external appearances of order. Everywhere, in the tree-lined alleys of the park, in the streets, at the gates of the barracks, meetings were conducted, small groups met, agitators darted in and out and appealed to our Cossacks. As before, the crux of the propaganda was a comparison of my going [to Petrograd] with Kornilov's. Krasnov more and more removed the mask of his 'loyalty' [to the government]." In a word, in this atmosphere of intrigue the signs of betrayal were clearly visible.

The retreat from Tsarskoe Selo on the evening of October 30 was the signal for the open manifestation of all these attitudes, which had been poorly hidden behind the thin facade of military discipline. At Gatchina the first rumors of the retreat, according to Kerensky, "provoked panic in some, and doubled the energy and audacity of others." Before the actual return of Krasnov, at 10 P.M., Kerensky met with a delegation from Vikzhel, which presented the following ultimatum: to enter into immediate negotiations with the Bolsheviks or face the threat of a railroad strike. When Kerensky later asked Krasnov how the general would react to this proposal, Krasnov responded that, in order to gain time, it was necessary to begin negotiations for a cease-fire; that this would somewhat pacify the Cossacks, who were looking ever more warily at their officers; and that it would provide a chance for reinforcements to arrive.

In fact, the Cossacks no longer believed in any "piles of telegrams about the movement of squadrons," for Krasnov's detachment returned to Gatchina completely demoralized. On the morning of October 31 the 9th Don Regiment refused to set up sentries and did not take its rifle ammunition; the regiment stated that it did not wish to take part in a fratricidal war. Sentry duty had to be done by two companies of the 10th Don Regiment that had recently arrived from Petrograd. Even Kerensky had begun to lose hope in the arrival of auxiliary troops from the front. At that time, according to the testimony of his adjutants, he "was in direct communication with Stavka and the Northern Front, and from this direct line he learned that in certain areas the front had gone over openly to the side of the Bolsheviks; that at certain points, such as Vinnits, Kiev and Moscow the Bolshevik uprising had spread; that the Latvian regiments had abandoned the front and had moved to the rear, having destroyed Venden and Iuriev. Thus, for Kerensky the situation seemed such that further delaying and dragging out of operations was impossible."

How the change in circumstances affected Kerensky was apparent from his directive on the evening of October 30. A few days earlier he had attempted to leave Gatchina "to meet arriving squadrons" and was stopped by the vigorous statement of the Cossack delegation that the Cossacks had linked their fate with his and would not permit him to depart. Now, "having taken advantage of a new group of friends who had arrived from Petrograd," Kerensky "had conveyed through them a letter addressed to Avksentiev, which letter entrusted to the Chairman of the Soviet of the Republic the rights and obligations of the prime minister and proposed the immediate addition of new members to the government." Afterwards, in response to the demand of the officers' council at Gatchina, Kerensky appointed to the position of commander of the city's defense Savinkov, whom Kerensky considered, as we have already seen, one of his most dangerous enemies. "At that time we already sensed," wrote Kerensky, "that we were swiftly approaching the inevitable" and that "our own fate seemed to us to be very problematic." Late that night, Kerensky released from his service one of his assistants, a married man, and "entered a fraternal alliance" with another, who did not wish to leave his [Kerensky's] service.

At 11 A.M. on October 31 A F. Kerensky approached General Krasnov and invited the general to meet with representatives of the political parties and the commissars concerning Vikzhel's proposal. Vikzhel's telegram, which was sent "to everyone," had presented a "categorical demand immediately to stop the civil war and to meet in order to form an exclusively revolutionary socialist government." In case this demand was not carried out, the railroad union promised to "halt all movement on the rails" starting at midnight on October 30. This threat, of course, did not apply to the Bolshevik troops who were attacking from Petrograd, but it was a genuine hindrance to the movement of squadrons assigned to come to the assistance of Krasnov's detachment. This was the "strict neutrality," which Vikzhel claimed in the same telegram "was incumbent on it at the beginning of a civil conflict." In addition to Kerensky and Krasnov, those who took part in the discussion were the representatives of the Cossack Union, Savinkov and Anikeev, Commissar Stankevich, Captain Kozmin, Lieutenant Colonel Popov and Captain Azhogin.[11] We shall take our description of this meeting from the original version of General Krasnov's memoirs.

"We sat in the palace drawing room, at a round table. A.F. Kerensky sat at a slight distance from the others. He was obviously very agitated. He informed the participants of Vikzhel's proposal and he asked us, the representatives of the detachment, to indicate to what extent the proposal was acceptable at present.

"I described the current situation to Kerensky. The promised reinforcements were not arriving. The Cossacks had no faith that the reinforcements would arrive; there was considerable debate among them about what to do. Today they had already refused to submit to orders. If significant infantry forces did not approach soon, it would be pointless to fight."

"What do you propose to do?" asked Kerensky.

"If there had been no proposal from Vikzhel, our situation would be desperate. We would have to try to break through to the south, where there are troops loyal to the government; we would have to go by foot and to endure all the tortures of hunger. Now, since we did not issue this proposal and since Soviet forces experienced in yesterday's battle the strength of Cossack resistance and incurred heavy losses, we can dictate very favorable conditions and can bring an end to the civil war, which is difficult and distasteful for everyone."

Krasnov said that "Lieutenant Colonel Popov and Captain Azhogin supported me. To Savinkov's question of how many Cossacks remained reliable, Captain Azhogin courageously reported that the demoralization would pass quickly, that it was intensified by the consciousness of one's isolation, weakness, of being abandoned by everyone. To fight under such circumstances was not possible. I added that we might be left with a few officers and two or three dozen Cossacks."

"Well, does this mean we are forced to surrender to the Bolsheviks?" Kerensky asked bitterly.

"No," I answered. "We should take advantage of Vikzhel's proposal and enter into negotiations."

"Savinkov began to speak. He spoke with great bitterness and with a genuine and strong patriotism. He vividly sketched the difficult, unbearable situation into which Russia would fall if the Bolsheviks should enter the government. He said that he could be party to an agreement only if there would be no Bolsheviks in the government. Because if one Bolshevik should enter the government, that Bolshevik would be able to ruin all the ministries. Savinkov said that we should struggle to the end and save Russia.

"Captain Kozmin spoke with the same zeal as Savinkov. He nevertheless thought the Bolsheviks' military forces to be weak, and he thought that they could be beaten even now. He asked me how long did I plan to linger here."

Krasnov responded: "I consider our position in Gatchina beyond the Izhora River very favorable. During this cold autumnal period I seriously doubt that Soviet troops will try to ford the river. Even in the summer, because of the swampiness of the banks, it is a difficult river to cross. But I need troops, and I don't have any. In the place of defensive pickets, I have mere observers. I cannot vouch for our safety even for a single night, because they [our forces] will not hold out under good pressure from the enemy."

Krasnov indicated that "Stankevich stood on our side. He tried to show that an agreement with the Bolsheviks was inevitable.[12] One could not deny their strong influence, and so one would have to take them into account. His opinion was that we should work out the conditions for negotiations and that someone should go to Smolny, after messengers had been sent there.

"And so in favor of negotiations were Stankevich and the three of us, the representatives of the military detachment; against negotiations were Savinkov, Anikeev and Kozmin. Savinkov said: 'I conceive of negotiations only as a clever military maneuver to gain time. Troops will come to us, Russian society will sober up, and we shall again march on Petrograd: indeed, there they will await us as saviors.'

"After long contemplation, A.F. Kerensky half-decided to enter into negotiations,[13] Captian Kozmin and to a certain extent Anikeev agreed that it was impossible to fight on. Only Savinkov honorably and zealously, like a youth, stubbornly held out, searching for the means to help his much beloved motherland.

"Everyone rose. We walked about the room, and exchanged disconnected phrases.

"Savinkov said: 'We have the Polish troops. The Poles will understand that the Bolsheviks will lead them to disaster. I shall go at once to the Polish Corps and shall lead it here.'

"This did not seem feasible to us. Did the Poles really want to interfere in our internal affairs? And when would the Polish Corps arrive? In the final analysis, the adherence of the Poles would not have any effect on the Cossacks and would not induce them to fight.

"More than two hours had passed since our meeting had begun. The time was passing in conversation, but it was necessary to act. I reminded everyone of this. We began to draft the text of a communique, which we decided to send by telephone and via messengers both to Smolny and to the military headquarters of the Soviet troop detachment at Krasnoe Selo."

According to the second version of Krasnov's memoirs, "During the meeting of the leadership, another meeting was taking place involving the army committees. The sailor-envoys who had arrived from Smolny shamelessly flattered the Cossacks and lured them by promising the immediate dispatch of special trains to take the Cossacks straight to the Don. The sailor-envoys stated that they would not make peace with the generals, but that they wished to make peace over the heads of the generals with a genuine democracy, with the Cossacks themselves." The Cossacks came to Krasnov later, and he gave them the text of the agreement on which they ought to have insisted, but he did not mention the author of the agreement. According to this proposal, "the Bolsheviks shall end all fighting in Petrograd and shall grant a full amnesty to the officers and cadets who had fought against them, and shall withdraw their [Bolshevik] troops to Chetyre Ruki; Ligovo and Pulkovo will be neutral. Our cavalry shall occupy, only for purposes of keeping order, Tsarskoe Selo, Pavlovsk and Peterhof. Before the conclusion of the negotiations neither side shall cross the line of demarcation. In case negotiations are broken off, 24 hours advanced notice shall be given before crossing the line." Late on the evening of October 31 this proposal was sent via an officer and two Cossacks to Krasnoe Selo.

Kozmin drafted another statement and sent it to the "Committee for the Salvation of the Motherland" in response to Vikzhel's telegram. The statement expressed a willingness to stop the bloodshed, provided that the arrested members of the government and those loyal to the government be released from prison and that there be negotiations with the representatives of the parties about reorganizing the government on the bases of the dominance of the [socialist] majority, the need to continue the defense of the nation, and the calling at the scheduled time of the Constituent Assembly, which alone could decide questions about land and freedom, war and peace.

A third document, composed by Stankevich and signed by Kerensky,[14] was sent with Stankevich to the Soviet of People's Commissars. In addition, in order to make sure that the message got through, at 6 P.M. Kerensky sent another telegram to Vikzhel indicating that a cease-fire had been proposed. Testimony about Kerensky's mood after this meeting was provided by Vendziagolsky, whom Kerensky summoned in order to check once more on the possible approach of the XVII Corps and on the Polish infantry which Savinkov had mentioned at the meeting. Vendziagolsky received a written invitation to: "go to the Polish Corps." "Suddenly Kerensky put his head between his hands and shrieked: 'The Poles will not come; I know they will not come.'" "I thought to myself," noted Vendziagolsky, *"for you* they will probably not come. For Poland, which is bound with the future of Russia, perhaps they will." Vendziagolsky then added a later reference: "This time the minister [Kerensky] was right. The Poles did not come. A good general, Dowbor-Musnicki, turned out to be a blind politician!" Following this digression, Vendziagolsky continued his description. "Kerensky lay down and covered his face with his hands. One sensed the internal weakness of the man. One even began to feel sorry for him. Kerensky's assistants and members of his retinue whispered in the corners. From time to time uncertain advice issued from them. 'You could try this, or maybe you could try that.'"

Savinkov agreed with Vendziagolsky that, given the circumstances surrounding Kerensky, there was nothing that could be done. Savinkov suggested that Kerensky travel to Bykhov and to Minsk. Kerensky agreed and signed an order to load the Polish Division on a train, which order was dated 8 P.M. on October 31. True, immediately afterwards he cancelled this order and directed Savinkov to go to meet the XVII Corps at Nevel, and then Kerensky again changed his mind and ordered both Savinkov and Vendziagolsky to remain in Gatchina.[15] Savinkov and Vendziagolsky ignored this order and "making jibes [about Kerensky], they set off," at 9 P.M. on October 31 for Pskov.

Rumors about the negotiations quickly circulated in Gatchina and further weakened the Cossacks' resolve. The regimental committee of the 9th Don Regiment approached Krasnov around 5 P.M. with a request on behalf of the entire regiment to arrest Kerensky as "a traitor, who had drawn them into a reckless adventure." Krasnov replied: "It is not our responsibility to judge him. The Cossacks, in whom he [Kerensky] placed his trust, must not sink to vigilante justice and betray their superior. The Don would never forgive such an act. As the head of the state, if he [Kerensky] has acted improperly, he will not escape a public trial." The Cossacks answered that Kerensky might flee, and Krasnov was forced to permit them to select a Cossack to keep an eye on Kerensky. In the palace courtyard, which was full of Cossacks, impromptu meetings were held on this matter. Kerensky learned about those meetings and summoned Krasnov, who reassured the minister that, while the "situation is dangerous," he [Krasnov] promised that he would not permit the "surrender" of Kerensky and that he would maintain a reliable guard. Having come from the headquarters of the French General Niessel,[16] Krasnov said the same evening that he "considers the situation hopeless," although one battalion of foreign troops might be able to save him. "Niessel heard [Krasnov's statement], said nothing, and quickly left."

The night of October 31/November 1 passed in great anxiety. The dark corridors of the old Pavlovsky Palace "teemed with suspicious and embittered people." "Officers curled up in one room and slept on the floor without undressing. The Cossacks, who would not be parted from their weapons, lay in the corridors and already did not trust one another." In Kerensky's rooms, which had been overcrowded even yesterday, there was not a soul. Before dawn Kerensky "destroyed all papers and letters which could not be allowed to fall into strangers' hands." Then he "lay down on his bed and dozed off, thinking only one thought: 'Would the reinforcements arrive by morning?'"

At 10:00 A.M. he was suddenly awakened. Instead of securing a cease-fire, the Cossacks who had been sent as messengers to Krasnoe Selo returned with a sailors' delegation, headed by Dybenko. The basic demand of the delegation was Kerensky's unconditional surrender. The Cossacks were prepared to accept this demand.

"An enormous, handsome man, with black tightly-curling hair, shining white teeth, with a ready wit and a smiling visage, a man of great physical strength that gave him the appearance of nobility," Dybenko, according to Krasnov, "charmed for several minutes not only the Cossacks, but many officers as well." "Give us Kerensky, and we will turn Lenin over to you: you can hang him right here in the palace." Krasnov drove away the Cossacks who had brought this proposal to him.

At this point Kerensky decided " . . . to expose as traitor Krasnov himself." Around noon Kerensky summoned Krasnov to his quarters.

"He [Krasnov] entered, and his bearing was correct, but too calm," Kerensky noted. Then, "nervousness, which replaced the superficial calm of the first moments, the darting eyes, the strange smile—all this left no doubt." No doubt of what? Even at that moment Kerensky did not shed his pose of greatness. He spoke with Krasnov as he had spoken with V.N. Lvov and with Krymov. "What is happening down below? How could he [Krasnov] permit a sailor to enter the palace? How could he not send warning, or inform [Kerensky about what was occurring]?" Krasnov gave a long explanation.

Here is how General Krasnov himself related this final conversation with the supreme commander.

"I found Kerensky nervously pacing diagonally across his room and in a state of great agitation. When I entered the room and approached him, he stopped opposite me, almost touching me, and said in an excited voice: 'General, you have betrayed me. Your Cossacks are saying that they are arresting me and will hand me over to the sailors.'"

"Yes," I answered, "that talk is going on, and I know that there is neither sympathy nor trust for you anywhere."

"But the officers are also talking."

"Yes, the officers in particular oppose you."

"What should I do? I have only one choice: to kill myself."

"If you are an honest man and if you love Russia, you must go at once by automobile with a white flag to Petrograd and go to the revolutionary committee, where you will negotiate as the head of the government."

According to Krasnov, "Kerensky thought for a while; then, looking me straight in the eyes, he said: 'Yes, I shall do that, General.'"

"I shall provide you with an armed escort, and I request that a sailor go with you in the automobile."

"No," Kerensky said quickly. "Not with a sailor. You know that Dybenko is here."

Krasnov answered that he did not know who Dybenko was.

"He is my political enemy," Kerensky said.

"What can you do about that?" Krasnov answered. "Anyone occupying such a high position will naturally have enemies as well as friends. You now have much to answer for; but if your conscience is clean, Russia, which loves you, will support you and you will lead it to the Constituent Assembly."

"Good, but I shall depart during the night," Kerensky said thoughtfully.

"I do not advise you to do that," Krasnov objected. "That would look as if you were running away. Go peacefully and openly, as the head of the government."

"Fine, only give me a reliable convoy."

Krasnov left Kerensky's apartment, called the Cossack Russov (who was the man selected to keep watch over Kerensky), and asked Russov to summon reliable people to accompany Kerensky to Petrograd.[17]

The divisional committees were called to meet, and after six hours of negotiations, at 2 P.M. the following conditions for a cease-fire were drafted:

(1) the complete amnesty and release from prison of all the cadets, officers, and other persons who had taken part in the struggle [against the Bolsheviks], except for those persons who were accused for good reason of treason against the government; (2) the release from prison of and the granting of the proper passes to *all members of the Cossack Union;* (3) an end to robberies, assaults, and brutal outrages against peaceful citizens if such were occurring, and a ban on such acts in the future; (4) a free and organized safe-passage for all families of Cossacks now living in Petrograd, with the right to transport necessary property; (5) the establishment of a reliable guard at Gatchina and vicinity after the departure of the Cossacks; (6) a full guarantee of order and normal life in the Gatchina Ensigns School and in the Aviation School; (7) the right to prepare everything for the rail transfer of the Cossack squadron, without the Cossacks being forced to hurry the process; (8) immediately after the end of the negotiations to open all railroads, in order to make possible the supply of food and other necessities; (9) to allow passage through military checkpoints and to establish free communications with the capital. *"Comrades Lenin and Trotsky must not enter a ministerial post nor be part of any national organizations until they have demonstrated their innocence of treason."* On the other hand, it was resolved, based on a speech by representatives of the revolutionary committee, *"to hand Kerensky over to the discretion of the revolutionary committee"* where he would be guarded by three Cossacks, three people selected by the political parties, and three people selected by the sailors, soldiers, and workers of Petrograd "until such time as he could be *brought to trial before a public tribunal."* Both sides gave their word of honor that neither Kerensky nor anyone else would be subjected to any violence or vigilante justice under any circumstances.

As we have seen, Kerensky was correct in thinking that "down below" there was "bargaining over the price of his head." In view of the contents of these resolutions, which are cited here from Krasnov's

original brochure, Krasnov's advice to Kerensky also becomes understandable—namely, that Kerensky should go to Petrograd voluntarily, with a reliable guard escort. In several points of the agreement
one can see traces of Kerensky's cease-fire proposals which had been
sent the day before to Krasnoe Selo. Of course, Krasnov could scarcely
trust the good faith of the proposals by that "ruddy-cheeked, handsome
giant," Dybenko, to trade Kerensky for Lenin.

However, the Cossacks did trust Dybenko. According to the second
variant of Krasnov's memoirs, soon after the adoption of the above-mentioned resolutions, at approximately three o'clock in the afternoon a
committee of the 9th Don Regiment, led by Lieutenant Colonel Lavrukhin, burst into Krasnov's quarters. The Cossacks hysterically demanded the immediate surrender of Kerensky, whom they would transport under their own guard to Smolny. "Nothing will happen to him," they
said. "We will not allow a hair on his head to be disturbed."

After this point there is an important discrepancy between the accounts of Krasnov and Kerensky. Krasnov reported the end of his conversation with the Cossacks as identical to the previously-cited conversation with members of the same delegation of the 9th Don Regiment, a conversation which had occurred (according to the first variant
of Krasnov's memoirs) at five o'clock the preceding afternoon, October
31. One surmises that in the latter version of the memoirs the author became confused, and that the conversation [of October 31] was wrongly
dated to 3 P.M. on November 1. If this is so, then we may presuppose
that the remainder of Krasnov's account also was confused. Krasnov related the following.

"When they [the Cossacks] departed, I went to see Kerensky. I found
him pale as a corpse, in the backroom of his apartment. I told him that
the time had come for him to leave. The courtyard was full of sailors
and Cossacks, but the palace had other exits. I indicated that sentries
stood only at the main entrance. 'However great is your guilt before
Russia,' I said, 'I do not think that I have the right to judge you. I shall
give you a half hour [to depart].' Leaving Kerensky, I arranged things so
that a reliable guard (promised by the deputation of the 9th Regiment)
could not assemble for a long time. When the guard finally appeared and
went to examine the quarters, Kerenesky was not there. He had fled."

In his memoirs Kerensky claimed that "this is nonsense and fabrication," and that he had not had any meeting whatsoever with Krasnov immediately before his flight. Kerensky's claim was substantiated not only
by the suspiciously theatrical tone of address that characterized parts of
the above-cited conversation, but also by the fact that in the original version of Krasnov's memoirs, written when the recollections were fresher,

Krasnov never mentioned this second conversation with Kerensky. In the original memoirs, Krasnov treated Kerensky's flight as something completely unexpected. Krasnov described how, after the above-cited conversation, which had occurred around noon on October 31, he had scarcely managed to receive information about the course of the negotiations with the Cossacks, to send a telegram to Stavka and to summon to the apparatus the Cossack commissar at Stavka, when in the officers' headquarters he ran into confused Cossacks and their officers, who told him that Kerensky had fled. "This report struck me as extremely unlikely," Krasnov said in his original account. "It was broad daylight: the palace corridor [Kerensky's apartment exited onto two corridors; one was guarded, and the other was locked], the palace courtyard and the square in front of the palace were full of Cossacks and soldiers. How would it have been possible to have fled through the crush of people, especially for a person whose appearance was well-known, such as Kerensky?" Through questioning Krasnov established that Kerensky "fled in a sailor's jacket and blue-tinted glasses."

In an obvious attempt to protect himself from the wrath of his superiors, Krasnov telegraphed General Dukhonin at Stavka: "I have ordered the arrest of the supreme commander-in-chief. He has managed to disappear."

There is, of course, a big difference between issuing an arrest order and abetting an escape, and the only way to escape the contradictions in General Krasnov's account is to accept as more reliable Kerensky's account, which coincided with the original testimony of Krasnov. Kerensky related how, after his "final meeting" with Krasnov, summarized above, he [Kerensky] "told the whole truth to those who still remained with him." According to Kerensky, it was decided that he should stay with his assistant in his apartment, but that he would not give himself up alive, and that at the approach of twilight he would leave the palace by an underground passage that had been pointed out to him by one of the palace servants. But sometime after two o'clock there ran into his room "the same soldier who that morning had brought news of Dybenko" and the soldier informed him that a deal had been made and that a mixed commission had been selected to arrest Kerensky and to hand him over to the Bolsheviks. "At any minute the sailors and Cossacks might burst in." "I left the palace," Kerensky wrote, "ten minutes before the traitors broke into my room. I left, not knowing from minute to minute where I was going. I went through the crowd in an absurd disguise, under the noses of enemies and traitors. I was still walking through the streets of Gatchina when the hunt for me began." Later he drove away in an automobile on the highway toward Luga.

Kerensky's assistants later supplied to the press the following official explanation for his disappearance. "At approximately 3 P.M. when the hopelessness of A.F. Kerensky's situation became apparent—the Cossacks' decision to hand him over to the Bolsheviks would, in his opinion, be followed by vigilante justice, and this was the more likely because he had no hope that his case would be tried under the guidelines of a normal political trial—he decided to go temporarily into hiding, in order that later, when passions will have subsided and the mood of society will have become more objective, he may explain to the nation both the circumstances in which he has operated in the recent days and the factors which compelled him to decide on such a step."

At the very moment when Kerensky's flight was discovered Commissar of the Northern Front Voitinsky informed General Krasnov that "an agreement between Krasnov's squadron and the representatives of the Petrograd garrison has been reached on the basis of Kerensky's deposal from power." Voitinsky sent the following telegrams to Pskov and to Stavka. To Pskov: (following the above-cited sentence) "immediately instruct all echelons moving toward Petrograd to halt and cease all actions connected with the formation of a Kerensky squadron." To Stavka: (following the above-cited sentence) "all manifestations of a civil war must be eliminated. In particular, halt the movement of echelons and inform everyone of the cessation of military activities between the contending sides." A third telegram was sent to "Everyone": (following the same introductory phrase) "The form of the government in Russia has not been decided in advance by this agreement, but the agreement has established an absolute prohibition against civil war. Kerensky has abandoned the squadron."

The first order of business was to bring an end to Krasnov's advance. The Cossack commissar at Stavka, Shapkin, still unaware of the agreement and of Kerensky's disappearance, telephoned Krasnov that Cossack units must be brought together and safe-passage to the Don be attained. Meanwhile, Kerensky should not be surrendered—"Cossack honor will not permit it"—but should be "given the chance to go into hiding." A rumor concerning this conversation immediately reached the Cossacks, and the thought of going home finally broke the remnants of discipline among them. The officers were in a state of confusion when a column of soldiers from the Life Guards Finnish Regiment, consisting of several thousand men in tight formation, marched through Cossack military checkpoints and approached the palace. "The Cossacks left me and ran off wherever they would go," Krasnov reported. Behind the Finnish soldiers there marched sailors, and behind the sailors there were Red Guards. From the windows, as far as you could see, everything was

black from the black greatcoats of the sailors and the overcoats of the
Red Guards. Twenty thousand people now filled Gatchina, and into this
dark mass the Cossacks dissolved completely.

The newly-arrived military units knew nothing about the recently
concluded cease-fire, and they thought that they had "captured Gatchina."
Soldiers, sailors, Red Guards, Cossacks—all mingled together. The
mixed crowd filled the corridors, the staircases and rooms of the palace.
They "roamed around the corridors, stole the carpets, the pillows and
mattresses." "Commissars Dybenko and Ensign Raskolnikov (Roshal),[18] who had arrived with the sailors, ran their legs off trying to pacify their unruly troops. Everywhere there was a hubbub of voices, there
were impromptu meetings, and there were arguments which quickly de-
generated into cursing. The sailors reproached the Cossacks for following Kerensky, the Cossacks reproached the sailors for defending Lenin . . . Both sides stubbornly disowned their leaders and shouted until
they were hoarse that they stood for the Constituent Assembly."

At 11 P.M. Krasnov sent a telegram to Stavka in which he reported
on the demoralization of the Cossacks and added: "We are spending the
night surrounded by sentries of the Finns (the Finnish Regiment), who
are mixing with our own men." There followed the anxiety-ridden night
of November 2. At 1 A.M. there appeared the commander-in-chief of
the Petrograd troops, "Lieutenant Colonel Muraviev,[19] and he proclaimed General Krasnov and staff arrested 'in the name of the Provisional Government.'" When he was informed that the government had just
concluded a cease-fire, one of the conditions of which was that the parties refrain from arrests and violence, Muraviev became embarrassed and
apologized. That was the end of the question of arrest, but Muraviev demanded that General Krasnov come to Smolny "for interrogation."[20]
Due to the lateness of the hour the trip was put off until morning. The
next morning a messenger from Smolny arrived at the Gatchina Palace
and assured Krasnov that the interrogation would last "no more than an
hour." Krasnov set off for the capital.

Smolny was filled to overflowing with armed "comrade" sentries and
office girls. Krasnov was shown to a room that already contained other
persons implicated in the defense of the Provisional Government: one
was Kerensky's assistant, another the commandant of the Gatchina Palace, and so on. Several hours later a sailor appeared to inquire of Krasnov, "On what order had he [Krasnov] acted, and how had Kerensky escaped?" Soon, however, the normal course of the investigation was interrupted by the appearance of the entire committee of the 1st Don Division, accompanied by Dybenko. There was an argument between them
and Ensign Krylenko. Krylenko demanded that as the Cossacks set off

for the Don they surrender their artillery. The Cossacks refused and insisted they would keep the weapons. At this point the Bolsheviks, who did not yet consider their victory to be secure, were afraid of the Cossacks. Krylenko asked Krasnov whether it was true that General Kaledin was already at the outskirts of Moscow. Through Krasnov's chief of staff Trotsky gave Krasnov to understand that he [Krasnov] might receive a high post with the Bolsheviks.

In view of Krasnov's clear unwillingness to accept this proposal, he was placed under house arrest and was escorted to his quarters. Krylenko declared that the agreement with the Cossacks had been annulled by the people's commissars, since the first point of the agreement had not been fulfilled—because Kerensky had been released. A member of Krasnov's retinue responded that neither had the last point been fulfilled, for Lenin and Trotsky were not under judicial investigation for treason, but were at the head of the government. There followed negotiations about where the Cossacks would move from Gatchina, whether to allow them to take their artillery or whether to confiscate it, and so on. Thus passed November 2, 3 and 4, and all this time General Krasnov remained under house arrest. In view of the Cossacks' persistence, their demands were finally satisfied; the squadron was directed to Velikie Luki where Krasnov went to join it. On the night of November 10 the 1st Don Cossack Division set off for the Don. Krasnov wrote Kaledin[21] that these units were completely unable to give battle and were thoroughly demoralized, that they should be dispersed to their homes and replaced by young troops. Kaledin responded that he had no authority to make such a decision. Krasnov "understood that the current was flowing irresistably toward the Bolsheviks."

Stavka's attitude toward all these events became evident on the very day of Kerensky's disappearance, November 1. This attitude was illustrated in the following telegram from General Dukhonin, a telegram sent after the receipt of the Voitinsky telegrams cited above. "Today, November 1, a cease-fire was concluded between General Krasnov's troops gathered near Gatchina and the Petrograd garrison, in order to halt the bloodshed of the civil war. According to a report from General Krasnov, Supreme Commander-in-Chief Kerensky has abandoned [Krasnov's] detachment and his whereabouts have not been established.

"Consequently, on the basis of the statute on control of troops in the field, I have temporarily assumed the office of supreme commander-in-chief, and have ordered a halt to the dispatch of troops to Petrograd. At this time there are negotiations between the various political parties in order to form a [new] Provisional Government. In expectation of the resolution of the crisis, I call on troops at the front calmly to carry out their duty to the motherland, in order not to allow the enemy to take advantage of the trouble occurring within our nation and to penetrate still further into the territory of our native land. Dukhonin."

The "negotiations between political parties" mentioned here obviously were occurring not at Stavka, but in Petrograd. In awaiting their conclusion, General Dukhonin took the only possible official line. But in practice, this position was tantamount to a refusal of any further assistance to Kerensky's government. All the efforts of Savinkov and Vendziagolsky, who had left Gatchina with the goal of persuading front-line army units to continue the battle [on behalf of the Provisional Government], were thus doomed to failure. In Pskov, where they had gone on November 1, Savinkov and Vendziagolsky finally discovered that the delay [in the arrival of reinforcements] that had been the cause for the failure of General Krasnov's march was due to General Cheremisov's directives rather than to the Bolshevik orientation of the infantry. The ambiguous position of the Commander-in-Chief of the Northern Front also forced his subordinates to be extremely evasive. The Chief of Staff, General Lukirsky, sat home and did not go to work at the staff headquarters at all. He admitted that Cheremisov's orders were the result of Cheremisov's disinclination to permit movement of infantry units toward Petrograd, but Lukirsky refused further discussion of the reasons, motivations, and consequences of this tactic. General Baranovsky, a relative of Kerensky, told Savinkov and Vendziagolsky: "In my situation it is awkward for me to get mixed up in all that." General Dukhonin, queried by Savinkov over the Hughes apparatus on November 3, responded only that he was inviting the former Assistant Minister of War to come personally to Stavka. On November 4 Savinkov answered this invitation by letter from Luga. He said he could not come to Stavka because "people were looking for him," but that, given uninterrupted movement of troops, 2 to 5 infantry divisions might still be gathered at Luga, and that "with enough artillery and only a few cavalry units," this squadron might "without much difficulty" undertake a march on Petrograd which would "surely be successful." Expecting no answer, Savinkov again went to Pskov and made a futile attempt to persuade the divisional committee and the officer staff that Cheremisov, who had made league with the Bolsheviks, ought to be arrested.

The divisional committee tried "by every means to straighten out the tortuous paths" of the echelons that had been sent off in various directions by Cheremisov. In fact, on November 3 the first echelon of the 35th Division arrived in Pskov. But the other echelons did not follow. Indeed, "discipline is above all." It was decided to appeal again to a higher authority, to General Dukhonin. Savinkov and Vendziagolsky sent him a telegram on November 5, in which they asked him to give an immediate answer as to "whether to concentrate units of the 35th and the 3rd Finnish Division in the region of Luga or to send them off in different directions." They simultaneously telegraphed Cheremisov that "when the legitimate Provisional Government has been restored, they would inform it of his contradictory orders, which might be understood as showing a disinclination to defend the legitimate government at such a crucial time." Units of the 35th Division, which the previous evening had received Cheremisov's order to move back from Luga to Pskov, refused to carry out that order.

These were the final spasms of resistance. On November 5 came Dukhonin's order which upheld Cheremisov's order. The day before, November 4, Dukhonin had repeated his order of November 1 which halted further troop dispatches to Petrograd. The mood in which he did so was apparent from his conversation on the Hughes apparatus with the new superior, Ensign Krylenko. During this period Krylenko was asking Dukhonin directly: "Just what can we expect from you in relationship to the developments that have taken place?" In a telegram on October 27 Dukhonin had assured Kaledin . . ."that we are in close cooperation with the commissars and the army committees, . . . and we shall fight to the limit for the restoration of the Provisional Government and of the Soviet of the Republic." This same Dukhonin could not now admit that he had reached the "limit." Having indicated in fact that this limit had been reached by his directive to halt further troop movements, and, of course, not sharing the stubborn perseverence of Savinkov nor Savinkov's dogged optimism, Dukhonin nevertheless could not bring himself to recognize the new government. He answered Krylenko: "Stavka cannot . . . take part in deciding the question of the legitimacy of the government. I, as temporary supreme commander-in-chief, am prepared to enter into *businesslike* relations with General Manikovsky." In response to Krylenko's repeated statement that this was not the question at issue, and that the problem was whether the movement of troops, which "disturbs the Petrograd garrison," would be halted, Dukhonin responded simply: "My order of November 1 is being carried out." Printing the Hughesgrams of these negotiations, *Izvestiia* added that "only people who do not yet know what they stand for can act in this way," and that General Dukhonin, of course, could not remain at his post since at the critical moment he failed unambiguously to recognize the government of the Soviets. This set the stage for the death agony of Stavka and of Dukhonin's personal tragedy.

Thus, the army's resistance to the Bolshevik coup came to an end after a few timid moves. It remained for Savinkov and Vendziagolsky to

save themselves, which they did after having returned to Pskov with entrained military units. At the moment of their departure, on the morning of November 6, counterintelligence reported that a detachment of
sailors, headed by Dybenko and Roshal, was already at the Luga train
station, and that soldiers were fraternizing with the sailors. In Pskov
General Dukhonin's order had been received to direct all units moving to
Luga in the opposite direction, to Nevel, and thence to their original
points of departure.

In Petrograd the resistance to the Bolsheviks after October 25 was
concentrated in the hands of the "Committee to Save the Motherland
and the Revolution," founded by the City Duma. Simultaneously, a
struggle was led by the military commission of the SR central committee. The connection between the committee and the commission consisted of several members such as Gots, who belonged to both.

Most likely, the Petrograd resistance held the conviction that had
been articulated by Kerensky—namely, that "in the St. Petersburg garrison, both in the regiments and in the special troop units, there were
still enough organized anti-Bolshevik elements prepared at the first convenient occasion to move against the Bolsheviks." We have seen that
between Petrograd and Gatchina communications with the obvious intention of coordinating the struggle against the Bolsheviks had not been
cut off. The news received in Gatchina was alternately optimistic and
pessimistic. One can say that Petrograd placed its hopes on Gatchina,
and Gatchina on Petrograd.

From the testimony of Rakitin-Braun, Krakovetsky and Feit at the
Moscow trial of the SRs in June 1922,[22] it was apparent that the military commission of the SRs had elaborated a plan whose goal was to
capture Smolny and to strike at the rear of the units of the Petrograd garrison which confronted Krasnov's detachment at Gatchina. This plan
was approved at a special meeting in which Avksentiev, Gots, Bogdanov and Colonel Polkovnikov participated. (The suspicions against
Polkovnikov expressed by Kerensky and by several ministers were refuted by Polkovnikov's involvement in this meeting.) The plan's success depended on coordinating it with the movements of Krasnov's detachment, and thus on the quantity of troops taking part in these movements. But units of the Petrograd garrison, despite the calculations of
the SRs and of the Committee to Save the Motherland and the Revolution, declined to take part in the resistance. The only reliable element
of the resistance was the cadets. And here there came into play a circumstance that led to the collapse of the entire enterprise and to a bloody re-
prisal against the cadets. Smolny discovered the SR plan.

Having learned about this event [the discovery of their plan], Rakitin said, "we [the initiators of the plan] decided to force events and, not waiting for Kerensky's arrival in Gatchina [obviously, the detail is inaccurate], to raise a rebellion.

"I [Rakitin] drew up an order which declared that the Bolshevik government had been overthrown and that all members of the Military Revolutionary Committee should be arrested. This order was to be signed by Avksentiev, Gots, myself, and Sinani."

In this instance the initiators obviously went further than the leadership of the military commission. According to Kerensky, "at the meeting of the military council on the evening of October 28 no resolution concerning an immediate uprising was adopted." This occurred later, when the meeting had come to an end and most of its participants had already departed.[23] At that point several soldiers entered the room where the meeting had taken place and they brought news that Kerensky called "very disturbing, but probably not true." The soldiers announced that the "Bolsheviks, having learned of impending events, had decided to begin to destroy all the military schools on the morning of October 29." The remaining members of the military council decided that "there can be no more delay, tomorrow is the day to move."

This course of events explained why, when it was necessary to sign the order drafted by Rakitin, "neither Avksentiev nor Gots was present." Gots claimed at the trial, immediately after Rakitin's testimony, that he had not seen the order and therefore did not sign it. However, this did not stop the initiators of the uprising. As Rakitin said, "we decided to publish the order anyway, with their names affixed to it."[24]

This was hardly a "provocation," as Kerensky claimed. But, in any case, it was extremely imprudent and ill-considered, and it brought in its wake fatal consequences.

On the morning of October 29 there commenced a cannonade, "the origins and purpose of which," according to Kerensky, "remained completely incomprehensible to the majority of the civilian and military leaders of the anti-Bolshevik movement in St. Petersburg." Rakitin testified that the beginning of the uprising was successful, and that it was at this time that he distributed the order he had prepared on behalf of the "Committee to Save the Motherland and the Revolution." But as soon as the extreme inequality of forces became obvious, the reprisals began.

We have the testimony of an eyewitness, I. Kuzmin, printed in the Right SR newspaper *Narod* [People], as to what occurred on October 29 in Petrograd. "At 7 or 8 A.M. the siege of the Vladimir Military School commenced. I was awakened by the firing of the cannons, machine guns and rifles. The cadets and the Women's Shock Battalion returned fire until 2 P.M. and then surrendered. On both sides there were wounded and killed. How many, I don't know. The walls of the school were breached; the doors and windows were broken and smashed . . . From the moment of the surrender a crowd of armed savages, howling wildly, burst into the school and carried out a bloody slaughter. Many were stabbed with bayonets—unarmed people stabbed! Dead bodies were mutilated: heads, arms and legs were cut off. The murderers robbed the dead, removed overcoats and boots from the dead and put these articles of clothing on themselves.

"Those who remained alive were taken in groups under strong guard to Peter and Paul Fortress, and were subjected to mockery, cursing and threats. This was the bloody road to Golgotha. It came to an end here at the fortress. To the question of what should be done with the captives, the directive followed: 'Shoot them.' The command was issued to the first group of cadets: 'Stand in rows.' With pale faces the cadets took their places against the wall.

"However, the soldiers who had been given the commision to fire, threw down their weapons with curses and ran off.

"Who would volunteer to shoot?

"The cadets stood and waited.

"Then came several shots, and they fell.

"Other groups of cadets and of women from the Shock Battalion were escorted to the fortress as well. Obviously, they too were shot, although the eyewitness to the shooting of the first group of cadets did not see the shooting of the other groups: he ran away from the terrible sight, and only from the sound of the firing did he conclude that the others had been shot as well. This occurred in daylight, in the center of the city . . . . The soldier-eyewitness who related to me this evil deed done in Peter and Paul Fortress, covered his face with his hands and, sobbing, moved off to the side."

Another set of testimony was provided in a letter by A.I. Shingarev,[25] and was published in *Russkie Vedomosti*. "The artillery fire not only silenced the Vladimir Military School, but destroyed neighboring homes, killed and wounded children and women; peaceful civilian institutions were fired upon. Cadets at the municipal telephone exchange who gave themselves up were led out onto the street, where they were savagely murdered; those still alive, but wounded by artillery fire, jumped into the Moika Canal, but when they reached the handrail on the enbankment, they were shot. The marauder-murderers cold-bloodedly robbed corpses, took boots, money and valuables. The account of the Admiralty's regional commissar about these events, which he himself witnessed, elicited groans and cries at a meeting of the City Duma.

"From one of the deputies I heard just yesterday a factual account of a search in one of the women's organizations. There was mockery of the women, unbounded impudence and vulgarity, and arrests. During the search valuable objects, silver spoons, clothes, and money were taken. The new gendarmes carried away everything that had any value whatsoever in their own eyes, but they left behind something of their own: on the floor after their departure there lay a German mark."

This was the formal beginning of a civil war in the capital, the beginning of an endless chain of sufferings on the part of the unarmed masses, which sufferings were inflicted by the armed leadership of the organized robbers' bands. In this war the principle of the Russian state perished. The process of the disintegration of the government which we have followed through the course of our presentation here reached its natural, long-foreseen and long-prophesied conclusion. During the course of the destruction the ideology in whose name the destruction was being accomplished essentially receded into the background. The leaders of the new revolution were lured into the same spontaneous process which had opened the way for their victory and which their predecessors had been powerless to stop. This contrast between exalted slogans, which projected the exclusive and unlimited dominance of the state over private interests, and sad reality, in which the group interests of a privileged clique won an unlimited freedom to abuse [the populace] amidst a turbulent ocean of popular passions—this contrast constitutes the subject of the final section of our history.

It remains for us now to relate the final unsuccessful attempt to save the dying government. The Bolshevik capture of Petrograd and of the state apparatus did not decide the issue of whether all Russia would submit to the seizure of power by the soldiers of the Petrograd garrison. Moscow had still to speak.

The Communist party in Moscow was, of course, well aware of what was happening in Petrograd. As in Petrograd, two forces were struggling against each other in Moscow: those in favor of and those opposed to the uprising and immediate seizure of power. Bukharin, Osinsky, Smirnov favored an uprising and accepted Lenin's point of view. Nogin, Rykov, Skvortsov, and Norov opposed it.[26] The week before the October uprising the editorial pages of the Moscow paper *Sotsial-Demokrat* [Social Democrat] discussed Lenin's letter inviting the Moscow party committee to take the initiative in the uprising, if the party central committee and the Petrograd committee did not wish to assume the responsibility. At a party meeting the leader of the military organization, Iaroslavsky, reported that "the overwhelming majority of the soldiers is on the side of the proletariat." The only obstacle was the Soviet of Soldiers' Deputies, where the SRs continued to dominate. For the final resolution of the issue there was convoked in the large auditorium of the Polytechnical Museum a city-wide conference of the Communist party, which, after speeches by Osinsky, Semashko and Smirnov, unanimously supported an uprising.

The day before the October uprising in Petrograd Moscow representatives Rykov and Lomov participated in meetings at Smolny, where Lenin, shaven and wearing a wig, presided. On the day of the uprising Lomov was dispatched to Moscow "to take power there in cooperation with the comrades." The Communist party organizations (the Moscow committee, the district committee, and the Regional Bureau) immediately appointed a central coordinating committee to unify the work of all these organizations in Moscow and to mobilize, "by means of the customary conspiratorial appeal," all party forces in the province and region to aid Moscow.[27]

Before reviewing the results of this activity by the party institutions, let us look at the activity of the anti-Bolshevik camp following the first news of the Petrograd events of October 25. From the beginning the Moscow City Duma was the focal point for the Muscovite opponents of Bolshevism. The city mayor, the SR V. V. Rudnev, immediately called an emergency meeting of the City Duma and proposed that it make a public statement about the uprising. Personally he opposed the uprising, and even if a change in government were to be recognized as essential, he thought the only feasible government to be a coalition, and not an exclusively socialist coalition at that. The revolution in Petrograd was defended by the Bolshevik Skvortsov, who told the assembly that the seizure of power by the Soviets was "well-organized and almost painless." N. I. Astrov,[28] a representative of the Party of Popular Liberty, objected to Skvortsov; he said that the "painlessness" of the revolution had not excluded acts of violence and destruction, and that the clever planning of the revolution was evidence of German involvement. Astrov proposed that the City Duma create an agency to direct the defense of lives and property in Moscow and its environs. Menshevik speakers disagreed among themselves. The SRs supported Rudnev and the Provisional Government. The meeting decided to appeal to the people of Moscow to rally around the City Duma for the defense of the Provisional Government, and to entrust to the board of the City Duma the right to create a Committee of Public Safety, which would include representation from democratic organizations. Efforts to organize this committee began on the morning of October 26.

According to the SRs' conception, the committee was supposed to consist not of representatives of the central committees of the political parties, but of representatives of *institutions*. This prevented interparty squabbles; it also, on the other hand, gave numerical preponderance to those political groups which dominated the institutions represented in the committee. Thus, the Committee of Safety included: the presidium of the City Duma Board—Rudnev and three of his assistants; representatives of the district zemstvo, the presidium of the Soviet of Soldiers' Deputies,[29] the Executive Committee of the Soviet of Peasants' Deputies, representatives of the railroad and postal-telegraphic unions, and representatives from the headquarters of the military district. Representatives of the City Duma party factions—that is, political groups—were admitted only for *informational purposes*.

The committee declared that all directives having the force of law could be published only in its name, and it set as its goal "the defense of law and order" and "minimizing the ordeal facing the populace." In his order on October 26 the commander of the Moscow military district "appealed [to the populace] not to raise a civil war, to preserve national treasures and state institutions, and not to permit any manifestations of dark forces or pogroms."

The committee was limited to the *passive* defense of public security because of the prevailing mood. There was no predilection for an immediate call to battle, and even those who from the beginning saw the inevitability of battle, considered it necessary to lead the populace gradually to the consciousness of this necessity. The City Duma, which had taken upon itself responsibility for directing the defense, was opposed in principle to an appeal to fight a civil war. It merely assumed the peculiar role of a political shield between the army and the rebels. In the words of an SR who played a prominent part in events, this was a "pedantic notion of politics." While not recognizing the Petrograd revolution, the City Duma committee appealed to the nation and to the front: "The decisive voice in the struggle must belong, according to this conception, to the entire Russian democracy and to the active army."

Having received from Minister Nikitin the right to use the telegraphs, the committee appealed the Petrograd decision to the nation. To thousands of telegrams it received hundreds of answers. But these answers came too late, after the denouement. The hope of persevering until the front made itself heard was also misplaced: we have seen that the front itself held back until it could come to the aid of the victors. In Moscow all hope rested on the command of the military district, but the district commander, Colonel Riabtsov,[30] did not attend the first two days of the committee's meetings. He did not receive commands from the committee as a result of the strange "notion" of the committee's role, mentioned above.

For the Bolsheviks, on the contrary, everything was clear. They moved toward their goal without relying on anyone else, and without glancing either to the left or to the right. Simultaneously with the meeting of the City Duma on October 25 there was a meeting of the Soviet of Workers' and Soldiers' Deputies, which adopted resolutions desirable to the Bolsheviks. True, this meeting was preceded by a general agreement of the Soviet parties, and the parties' common platform proposed "to defend order and to fight against the onslaught of counter-revolutionary forces by forming a temporary *general-democratic* revolutionary agency, consisting of representatives of the Soviet of Workers', Soldiers', and Peasants' Deputies, representatives of the city and Zemstvo self-government, of the military district headquarters, and of the All-Russia Railroad Workers' and Postal-Telegraphic Unions."

But the creation of such an agency, whose membership would have coincided with that of the Committee of Safety organized by the City Duma, did not appeal to the Bolsheviks. The Bolsheviks demanded a recess, then introduced their own formula: "The Moscow Soviets of Workers' and Soldiers' Deputies shall elect at today's plenary session a revolutionary committee of seven persons. This revolutionary committee shall be given the right of *coopting* the representatives of other *revolutionary democratic groups*, with the plenum and the soldiers' deputies having the right to confirm these representatives. The elected revolutionary committee shall begin to operate at once, taking as its task the rendering of *all manner of support* to the committee of the Petrograd Soviet of Workers' and Soldiers' Deputies." The SRs resolutely protested against the "creation of organizations intended to seize power." "Renouncing any responsibility for the results of the Bolshevik attempt to seize power," the SRs refused to take part in the voting. The Mensheviks voted against the resolution, but the Bolshevik formula passed by a vote of 394 to 113, with 26 abstentions; the Moscow "Military Revolutionary Committee," which was charged to "support the Petrograd committee," was elected at once. The Bolsheviks had a majority (4 to 7 members) on the committee. The SRs declined to enter the committee. The Mensheviks entered with the proviso that they did so not to cooperate in the seizure of power by the Soviets, but to help the proletariat and the army to endure as painlessly as possible all the results of the Bolshevik leaders' adventurism, and in order to struggle within the committee for its replacement by a common democratic agency. This position was most peculiar in an agency which would certainly force the cannons to speak. It should be added that even the Mensheviks soon realized the impossibility of their remaining members of an agency that wanted nothing to do with them. "In view of the Bolsheviks' clear violation of the principle of collective action and of the desire to crush the will of the minority and to act behind its back, they [the Mensheviks] were forced to leave the committee."[31]

The Bolshevik headquarters for revolution immediately sprang into action. The building housing the Soviet of Workers' and Soldiers' Deputies was a beehive of activity. One of the committee's first moves was to declare a general strike for the next day and to prohibit the printing of "bourgeois" newspapers. Comrade Golenko organized at once an attack on the presses of these newspapers; the first plates for these papers were confiscated, and on the morning of October 26 only *Izvestiia* and *Pravda* appeared. The army troops in Moscow did not know at first whom they should obey and inquired about this at the "counter-revolutionary" Soviet of Soldiers' Deputies; in order to consolidate the soldiers behind [the Bolshevik party], a conference of representatives from all units of the Moscow garrison was called on October 26. By an overwhelming majority of 116 to 18 the conference expressed its loyalty to the Bolshevik Military Revolutionary Committee. Through a proclamation published on October 27 in *Izvestiia*, the Military Revolutionary Committee took power into its hands. "The revolutionary workers and soldiers of Petersburg, led by the Soviet of Workers' and Soldiers' Deputies, have entered a decisive battle with the Provisional Government that betrayed the revolution. The duty of Muscovite soldiers and workers is to support their Petersburg comrades in this struggle. In order to direct the fight, the Moscow Soviet of Workers' and Soldiers' Deputies has elected a Military Revolutionary Committee, which has begun to carry out its duties: The Military Revolutionary Committee proclaims: (1) the entire Moscow garrison must immediately be placed on battle alert. Each military unit must be prepared to come out at the first appeal of the Military Revolutionary Committee; (2) no orders or directives, other than those issued by the Military Revolutionary Committee or bearing its authorization, should be carried out."

The Military Revolutionary Committee, which had assumed these plenary powers, immediately acted to exercise them. The sentries at the Kremlin were from companies of the 56th Regiment, which had sided with the Bolsheviks, but it was decided to reinforce them with companies of the 193rd Regiment. An order to this effect was transmitted by the Bolshevik Iaroslavsky[32] to the Khamovnichesky Barracks on the night of October 27, and was immediately carried out. The commander of the Kremlin arsenal, Lazarev, also submitted to the demand of the Military Revolutionary Committee to surrender the arsenal's weapons. At 10 A.M. 1500 rifles, with ammunition, were handed out. The entrances and exits to the Kremlin were locked. Ensign Berzin was appointed commander of the Kremlin garrison.

Meanwhile, the center of the resistance to the Military Revolutionary Committee, located in the governor's residence on Skobelev Square, was the military schools—particularly the Alexandrov School on Znamenka. There the cadets were joined by officers who wanted to participate in the struggle against the Bolsheviks and also by many idealistic young students. The first strategic task of the resistance was to occupy commanding positions and the most important points in the city: the Kremlin, the post offices, telegraphs, and the telephone. The second task was to surround Skobelev Square where the Soviet was meeting. During the first days of the rebellion it seemed not only feasible, but even easy to carry out these tasks, since the Military Revolutionary Committee had not yet managed to consolidate its forces. But both the Kremlin and the post office were already occupied by companies of the 56th Regiment who sympathized with the uprising. Negotiations were opened between the military district commander Riabtsov and the Military Revolutionary Committee about how to avoid a bloody confrontation.

Colonel Riabtsov found himself in a difficult position between the cadets, the Committee of Public Safety, and the Military Revolutionary Committee. A man who was not strong and who was given to vacillation, he tried to maneuver between the contradictory demands presented to him, and he very quickly lost all authority. Throughout the day of October 27 he conducted fruitless negotiations with the Bolsheviks about removing Bolsheviks from the Kremlin and replacing them with cadets. During this time Riabtsov remained in the Kremlin amongst the rebellious soldiers, while the Kremlin was surrounded by cadets, who allowed no one to pass through the gates. The Bolsheviks demanded that the cadets should leave the manege, which they [the cadets] had occupied, and should permit passage from the Kremlin of the weaponry taken from the arsenal to arm the soldiers and workers. In exchange the Bolsheviks agreed to order from the Kremlin a company of the 196th Regiment, but they insisted on leaving there a company of the 56th Regiment. Riabtsov insisted that the guarding of the Kremlin and the arsenal be entrusted to the cadets, or that at least they should be permitted to enter the Kremlin to guard the regional court. Soldiers of the 56th Regiment in whose midst these negotiations occurred became agitated, demanded Riabtsov's arrest and threatened to kill him. Finally, Riabtsov promised to lead the cadets away from the Kremlin Gates, and issued an order to that effect, which the cadets refused to carry out. By evening on October 27 Riabtsov finally succeeded in extricating himself from the Kremlin and moving to the Moscow City Duma building from which he conducted further negotiations.

Having moved to a place where the Committee of Public Safety had influence, Riabtsov grew bolder. At 7 P.M. he telephoned an ultimatum to the Military Revolutionary Committee: its troops must leave the Kremlin and the Military Revolutionary Committee itself must be dissolved. The response would have to be given in ten minutes, otherwise military activities would commence. The reason behind this decision was that the Military Revolutionary Committee, "despite all its assurances, has not ordered the mutinous unit out of the Kremlin, and has permitted the widespread theft of arms, machine guns, and ammunition from various places and the distribution of them to Bolshevik organizations." A member of the Military Revolutionary Committee, Arosev, later testified that "we experienced serious wavering," after the Riabtsov ultimatum. "My heart never trembled so much as that moment when we had to vote: either to reject the ultimatum or not to." "The comrade chairman counted out votes: the majority favored rejecting Riabtsov's ultimatum. The cold, hard number of the votes for and against ended our wavering."

Indeed, at that moment the Military Revolutionary Committee was not certain on whom it could rely. Two hours after the decision to reject the ultimatum the first soldier's blood was spilled on Red Square. This was the blood of the tiny avant-garde of the revolution: a detachment of "Dvinsty," the Bolshevik soldiers arrested in Dvinsk in August and sent in September to the Butyrka Prison, whence 860 of them had been released on September 1 "on the order of the Moscow Soviet of Workers' Deputies." The "Dvintsy" were the first convinced partisans of the uprising and were its defenders. A detachment of 300 men came forward to "shed blood for the idea of socialism," and "45 of the best comrades lay at the Kremlin walls, under fire from the cadets." The remainder broke away and reached Skobelev Square, where they came to constitute the basic nucleus of the guard of the Military Revolutionary Committee.

Throughout this period, the night and morning of October 28, the Military Revolutionary Committee experienced anxiety. The headquarters at the Soviet was empty: there were only a few people in the building who were concerned with ongoing business. Those who left the building left probably forever. The mood of those who remained approached panic. "There began a flood of bad news," recalled the Bolshevik P. Vinogradskaia. "It was reported that our troops were being pressed, that the cadets were surrounding the Soviet. The connection with the rest of the city was broken. As if in confirmation of these shattering reports, cadets began to show themselves in all the narrow streets leading to the Soviet from Bolshaia Nikitskaia. Enemy artillery started to bombard the Soviet building. We had no means of answering: our artillery had not yet arrived. The influx of reports from the rest of the city halted, and from hour to hour it seemed that we had fallen into a trap, surrounded on all sides and cut off from the outside world . . . . This moment was the most fearful, the most difficult in all the October days."

On the morning of October 28 the Kremlin received information that all Moscow was in Riabtsov's hands, the garrison had surrendered and had been disarmed, the post office had been occupied, along with the telegraph and all the railroad stations. Riabtsov confirmed these reports by telephone: "All troops have been disarmed by me; I demand immediate, unconditional surrender of the Kremlin." Crushed by these reports, the Bolshevik commandant Berzin "decided to submit to the order and to surrender the Kremlin, in order to save his soldiers from being shot." The soldiers did not wish to surrender: "We shall die in any case," they said, but they nevertheless yielded to necessity and disarmed. Officers and cadets entered the Kremlin, arrested Berzin and the members of the Bolshevik committee. There followed the shooting of the soldiers of the arsenal.

The cadets also attacked other points in Moscow. The Bolshevik M. Olminsky[33] recalled that "the entire center of the city except for part of Tverskaia Street, was in the hands of the cadets: they had the railroad stations, the tramway electrical station, the telephone (except for Zamoskvaretsky). The Military Revolutionary Committee was almost cut off from other districts of the city, and the districts, being poorly connected with each other, carried the entire weight of the struggle, without knowing what was happening in the center. The isolation of the center from the districts (a connection was somehow maintained only through Strastnaia Square) meant that the center was subject at any moment to the danger of destruction. Armored cars driven by cadets appeared on Soviet Square itself. There were moments when it seemed that the only option for the center was flight. This took a toll on the mood of the Military Revolutionary Committee: it inclined the committee to negotiate a cease-fire and to make concessions. There was a quite different mood in the other districts of the city."

However, in the ranks of the current victors the mood was far from joyous. The young military personnel that gathered at the Alexandrov School, the cadets, the ensigns, students, mobilized intellectuals—these were crack troops with great determination. But the nature of their determination was not uniform. At the beginning the young looked on with horror at the possibility of participating in a civil war. The conservative officers had a quite different attitude, for they had enlisted from the beginning as defenders of Moscow. But the democratically-minded youth did not trust the rightist officers, and were afraid of the officers' influence upon them. On the other hand, the young were not satisfied with the "pedantic politics" of the Committee of Safety, which desired directly to control the fight and which relied on the district military commander. But the district commander Riabtsov was terribly afraid of taking any step for which he might later be held responsible by one of the agencies of the "revolutionary democracy." He suffered from extreme neurasthenia: he was endlessly talking when he should have been acting; he was absolutely incapable of issuing orders; he did not have the ability to procure food or ammunition when they were needed. The young mistrusted Riabtsov even more than they did the Committee of Safety; they accused him of deliberately disorganizing the defense of the city and of dealing with the Bolsheviks. They complained about the committee, because it did not replace Riabtsov with a more reliable military leader. (Incidentally, Brusilov proposed himself as leader). But the Committee of Safety, as we have seen, opposed on principle involving itself in execution of policy, feared the rightist officers, and finally considered it unwise to change commanders during the heat of battle.

There was still another force which, under different circumstances, might have played a role in the struggle: this force consisted of the representatives of the overthrown Provisional Government. During this period the Bolsheviks' adversaries could not fail to regard these representatives of the Provisional Government as the sole representatives of the legitimate government. S.N. Prokopovich was the only one of the ministers not arrested in the Winter Palace. He was arrested on his way toward the palace at about 10 A.M., and about 5 P.M. he was released from Smolny. On October 26 he chaired a conference of assistant ministers who were in Petersburg. According to Prokopovich, at this meeting he indicated the need, following the loss of Petrograd, to organize resistance in Moscow; he asked for full authority to carry out this task. Having received this authority from the remnants of the government, he arrived in Moscow on the morning of October 27 and went straight from the railroad station to the Moscow City Duma, where the Committee of Public Safety was in session; he was accompanied by his assistants Khizhniakov and Kondratiev. In the City Duma they proposed to "co-opt" the Committee of Public Safety into the Provisional Government. But, as we have seen, the authority of the Provisional Government was not great, and to operate under its aegis in Moscow would not make matters easier for the resistance. S.N. Prokopovich himself recalled that at that time the rightists in Moscow were saying openly: "At least the Bolsheviks overthrew the power of the Provisional Government; this will make it easy to deal with them in Petrograd." "On both the left and the right," Prokopovich added, "I saw at that time almost open rejoicing over the spiritedness of the Bolsheviks."

In such a climate Prokopovich's proposal of "cooptation" got a more than restrained reaction in the City Duma. The full authority granted by the assistant ministers in Petrograd obviously lost its force in Moscow. The idea of Prokopovich and his comrades—to create in Moscow a surrogate Provisional Government—thus could not be implemented.

Another idea of the minister and his comrades was to publish an appeal to the populace, and by means of this appeal to assume the leadership of the struggle. The text of this appeal was quickly drafted with the assistance of members of the Constitutional Democratic Party. On the following day the appeal was supposed to appear in the newspapers and to demonstrate to Moscow that, despite the seizure of the government in the Winter Palace, the legitimate authority of the Provisional Government had not perished, and that in Moscow there were representatives of the government who were prepared to lead Moscow's resistance to the armed attack against the government created by the [February/March] revolution. However, this plan was also doomed to fail. The appeal was not published, and the presence in Moscow of representatives of the legitimate government had no effect on the course of events.

The pushing aside of representatives of the Provisional Government from the leadership of the struggle in Moscow occurred almost automatically, on its own, as an inevitable result of the relationship between the forces engaged in battle. But at the same time the concrete purpose of the struggle was lost from sight. S. N. Prokopovich recounted that on the third or fourth day of the struggle four public figures approached him; they told him that they did not wish to support the Provisional Government, but they were prepared to do so if he would proclaim himself dictator. This fantastic proposal characterized the mood of the rightist circles. In the more influential leftist circles a different notion came to light—a notion that had already been vented during the Petrograd uprising among the representatives of the socialist parties: the formation of a new, exclusively socialist government. But for the majority of the cadets and the officers who were the most active participants in the Moscow fighting this idea made the entire struggle pointless.

In the next several days all these internal contradictions manifested themselves. But even from the very beginning they had an effect in that, instead of creating a united leadership and immediately taking decisive measures, the defenders of the principle of the state were compelled to waste valuable time on negotiations and on thinking up compromises between the various tendencies which had come together in the common struggle.[34]

We have seen that on the evening of October 27 and the morning of October 28 the Bolshevik committee was in a difficult situation, close to panic, and that it showed readiness to compromise and put off a decision by arms. True, this situation changed somewhat during the course of October 28. After midday on the 28th, V. Smirnov, a member of the Military Revolutionary Committee who had been sent to Khodynka to obtain artillery, finally returned to Moscow; he brought with him three artillery pieces, which were immediately set in place and which began to fire along Tverskaia Street from Skobelev Square and also along Kosmodemiansk Lane. The Bolshevik V. Soloviev recalled the impression made on the Military Revolutionary Committee by the arrival of these weapons: "Now they [the adversary] will not take the Soviet with their bare hands, now we shall hold out for a day or two, until the other districts of the city can lend us a hand." Later, delegations of soldiers from the front arrived to find out what was happening in Moscow. The activity in the other districts of the city had intensified. Nevertheless, the Military Revolutionary Committee's inclination to engage in negotiations for a cease-fire had not yet passed; and there was no shortage of intermediaries between them and the Committee of Safety.

The Mensheviks made the first attempt to arrange negotiations between the two belligerent camps. They told the two sides that they wanted "the peaceful liquidation of the civil war," and that they wanted for this reason "to rally a third force which would compel the two belligerents to take it into account." The Mensheviks proposed to transform the Committee of Safety into a "common-democratic agency, independent both of the City Duma and the Soviets." This transformation might be made to occur if representatives of the socialist parties were to join the Committee of Safety. The SRs and Constitutional Democrats who had joined the Committee of Safety did not agree to this proposal; they operated on the basic assumption that the Committee of Safety united not political parties, but institutions and organizations. After this rejection the Mensheviks recalled from the Committee of Safety all members of their party who had joined it as representatives of institutions. Thus they stood outside both belligerent organizations.

A "third force" that was incomparably more powerful and which actually forced the two sides to enter into negotiations was Vikzhel. Vikzhel stated that it would only permit the transportation to Moscow of troops prepared to support the Provisional Government if "the Committee of Safety will agree to create a homogeneous [that is, exclusively socialist] ministry." "It was with great reluctance and the understanding that it was making a heavy sacrifice that the Committee of Safety obeyed the demand of Vikzhel," testified the chief prosecutor, A. F. Staal.

One of the prominent members of the Committee of Safety later told the author of this book the following: "What choice did we have? Among us there was not one advocate of an exclusively socialist ministry. But what would have happened if we had said that we did not accept that slogan? Vikzhel had stopped outside Moscow those troops that had been sent to the city, and had promised to permit the troops to pass only if its demands were fulfilled. The military advised us not to be stubborn and to agree to anything. The committee members, summoned to the Alexandrov School [see below], were polled by name and every member agreed to accept the responsibility for the decision."

On the other hand, however, Vikzhel also presented a series of demands to the Bolsheviks. Since the Bolsheviks did not accept these demands, Vikzhel stated that from that moment the Railroad Workers' Union would actively oppose the Bolsheviks and would permit the passage of troops to Moscow without hindrance. Under these circumstances, the Military Revolutionary Committee decided to ask for a cease-fire. It was concluded, and scheduled to last for one day—from 12 o'clock on October 29 to 12 o'clock on October 30—under the following conditions: (1) the complete disarmament of the White and the Red Guards; (2) the return of all previously distributed weapons; (3) the dissolution of both committees—the Military Revolutionary Committee and the Committee of Public Safety; (4) the bringing of all guilty individuals before the courts for trial; (5) the establishment of neutral zones; (6) a cease-fire for twenty-four hours to work out the technical conditions for the laying down of arms and the dispersal of military units to their barracks; (7) the subordination of the entire garrison to the commander of the Moscow military district, and the establishment of a military Soviet at Moscow military headquarters; (8) the organization of a common-democratic agency.

The Committee of Safety agreed to all the concessions demanded of it, because it was guided by the calculation that it was only the "political shield for military struggle." For strategic reasons military men insisted on quick concessions. The delegates of the committee appeared in the Alexandrov School, where these issues were discussed before a large auditorium of military men. On the recommendations of the military men of Moscow the cease-fire and conditions outlined above were approved.[35]

During the night of October 29/30 a special "commission of reconciliation" worked out the military-technical questions of the cease-fire and established a "neutral zone" on a line where deputies from Vikzhel would be able to prevent confrontations between the belligerents. A ring of Bolshevik troops passed through Krymskaia Square, Ostozhenka, the lanes radiating outward from it (up to Eropkinsky) to Povarskaia Street, the continuation of Rzhevsky Lane to the north of Povarskaia Street, Skatertny, Medvezhy, Merzliakovsky, the thoroughfare at the Church of the Ascension between Bolshaia and Malaia Nikitskaia Streets, Spiridonovka, Spiridonievsky Lane, Bolshaia and Malaia Bronnaia Streets, Bogoslovsky Lane, the southwestern section of the city-governor's office, the ends of the lane on Bolshaia Nikitskaia Street, the southwestern section of the Bolshoi Theater building.

The cease-fire occurred only on paper. The Bolsheviks never observed it, and in certain places they were not even aware of it. In agreeing to a cease-fire, the Military Revolutionary Committee had only one purpose: to win time for reinforcements to arrive. The news of the failures of Krasnov's detachment which the Bolshviks received during this interval strengthened the Bolsheviks' resolve to continue the struggle. To a categorical question—did they want an agreement or not—the Bolsheviks answered with obfuscations. In the final analysis, they made demands which they knew to be unacceptable. They rejected even the creation of an exclusively socialist ministry and they returned to their purist slogan of "all power to the Soviets." Moreover, they demanded a majority in an advisory agency that was supposed to function until the Constituent Assembly; they insisted that officers and cadets be disarmed, while Bolshevik troops should retain their weapons.

Thus, it became clear that all the concessions made heretofore were in vain. If the military men had connived, so had the Bolsheviks, trying to gain time for "strategic" purposes. But only the Bolsheviks really profitted by the delay.

After the exit of the Bolshevik envoys who had been sent to present the above-mentioned conditions, there occurred in the City Duma building the last meeting of the Committee of Safety with representatives of the military units, the presidium of the Soviet of Soldiers' Deputies who had fled from the Governor-General's house, and "all the voluntary and involuntary inhabitants of the City Duma building," including the Constitutional-Democrat Iurenev and the City Duma employees. At this meeting the mayor of Moscow Rudnev proclaimed the "bad faith of the Bolsheviks, who had taken advantage of the cease-fire to reposition and reinforce their units," and he placed "the entire blame for the inevitable continuation of the struggle exclusively on the Bolsheviks."

The subsequent debate was conducted in a tone of self-justification, until a loss of electricity in the building reminded those present who were the real masters of the situation.

On the next day, October 31, there appeared an appeal by the Committee of Public Safety "To Citizens and Comrades," in which the committee explained its points of disagreement with the Military Revolutionary Committee. The Committee of Safety considered that the only conditions under which military activity could be stopped were the liquidation of the Military Revolutionary Committee, the evacuation of the Military Revolutionary Committee's detachments from points occupied by them, and the return of Moscow to normalcy. To a "victory of might" the committee juxtaposed, on the basis of an agreement with Vikzhel, "the organization of a Provisional Government on the basis of the *responsibility of the new government to the agencies of the revolutionary democracy and also* on the basis of *this government's socialist composition.*"

Like the conditions of the cease-fire, this formula was accepted with the consent of the military men in the Alexandrov School, to which certain representatives of the Committee of Safety had been summoned; these representatives were forced to agree to the formula of a socialist ministry and to take upon themselves responsibility for this step. (These representatives were Rudnev, Filatiev, Buryshkin, Studenetsky, the representatives of the Postal Workers and Telegraphers Union, and of the Zemstvo board.) But, as was indicated earlier, the Bolsheviks were not satisfied even by this concession.

At 4 A.M. the Bolsheviks responded to the committee with a categorical "demand for unconditional surrender, and the threat of an artillery bombardment of the City Duma." The Committee of Safety could only renew the military struggle under the new and, for it, more disadvantageous conditions. Inviting the populace to show a greater independence in fighting for its own defense, the Committee of Safety encouraged its supporters with the news that "units sent from the front are approaching Moscow to suppress the rebels" and "Kerensky's troops are entering Petrograd." The committee could only repeat here the news that it had received. Indeed, Iordansky and Moiseenko[36] sent to Moscow a report that certain units from the front had been ordered to come to the aid of the defenders of Moscow.

In this connection one must mention the proposal of Staff Captain Sokolov, who had come to Moscow from Kaledin and who reported to a certain meeting of public figures under the chairmanship of N. N. Shchepkin[37] the readiness of the Don Ataman to send help to Moscow. This proposal was recounted by Sokolov himself to a correspondent of the Belgrade paper *Novoe Vremia* [New Times];[38] Sokolov added that "the assistant ministers had rejected this [Cossack] assistance." But even regardless of the fact that Sokolov's proposal did not go beyond the meeting of public figures, the proposal could not have had much impact because events were moving so rapidly. S.N. Prokopovich, incidentally, has denied participating in the above-mentioned meeting.

The night of October 30/31 was a moment when the attitudes of the two belligerents changed radically. Exhausted by their continuous efforts, having lost hope that the first blow would succeed, and insufficiently equipped for a long struggle, the small group of defenders of Moscow and of Russia felt itself more and more isolated both from the rest of Russia and from other public elements. The words "cadet," "officer," "student" became words of abuse, and the heroic impulse of the people who bore these titles now paled before the indifference or even open hostility of the populace to whose defense they had rallied and for whom they were sacrificing their lives. The behavior of the troop commander more and more provoked suspicions. The futile concession made to the idea of an exclusively socialist ministry raised before many of the cadets and officers the question of for what purpose and for what political end they were really fighting, and also the question of what precisely was the difference between "all power to the Soviets" and "responsibility" of an exclusively socialist partisan government to "agencies of the revolutionary democracy." On top of all this, the keenly-awaited approach of troops toward Moscow, for the sake of which Vikzhel's assistance had been purchased at the price of this concession, turned out to be illusory. No troops approached Moscow, and the small detachments of cadets sustained serious losses or, after they had been cut off, fell into Bolshevik captivity.

At the apogee of their strength these cadets detachments had held with difficulty the center of Moscow from the Kremlin to the Nikitskie Gates and from the Theater Square to Zubovsky Boulevard; there were at that moment perhaps five thousand men in these detachments.[39] With surprise and uneasiness this army noticed that it was isolated not only geographically, but also socially; that, defending order and the legitimate government, it at the same time—by a process of elimination and very much against its will—became the representative of certain classes. The name "cadet" began to be pronounced with hatred by the democratic populace of Moscow and to be juxtaposed to the "people." In the newspapers of those days one can find signs of the confusion experienced by people who heroically took part in the ideological struggle but who found themselves in a role quite uncustomary for the Russian intelligentsia. Representatives of the six schools for ensigns, having summoned into their ranks common soldiers, stated in print that there were almost no nobles among them, that the overwhelming majority were veteran soldiers—frontliners, "the genuine representatives of the soldier masses," and that among them were "many true, long-time socialists." Yet a group of Bolshevik students, writing in *Izvestiia*, called the cadets "a disgrace" and "expressed contempt for and a protest against the shameless, anti-democratic movement of a small bourgeois group of students," 600 of whom had joined the ranks of the defenders of Moscow and who had accomplished amazing feats of heroic self-sacrifice.

These five thousand defenders of the city were opposed by tens of thousands of troops from the Moscow garrison, although the latter, it is true, were not consciously taking part in a struggle between "the proletariat and the capitalists." The soldiers of the garrison even began, after several days of fighting, to run away from Moscow. But to replace these indifferent and frightened men there were other thousands from the area around Moscow who were more conscious; artillery, some of it heavy artillery, was hauled into the city and placed for a bombardment of the center of town and the Kremlin; armored cars were mobilized, while the cadets had only two armored vehicles and these were out of commission; trenches were dug, and stores of ammunition prepared.

The attitude of the working masses, like that of the soldiers, was not, however, entirely supportive of the Bolsheviks. Evidence of the mood of the workers can be found in a curious transcript of a telephone conversation, which occurred on the third day of the fighting, between a SR and his party headquarters. Here is this interesting memorial of the days of the Moscow uprising.

"Sushevsky District. Numerous meetings, or rather a crowd of people; nighttime. The soldiers did not stay to listen to the speeches. A worker from the Verein spoke. Voices from the crowd asked: 'What party?' The answer: 'A socialist, Menshevik.' There were shouts of 'Down [with the speaker]!' There was the same attitude toward representatives of the other socialist parties. A resolution [stated] the futility of armed struggle initiated without the prior consent of the proletariat. The demand [of the crowd] was to bring to the trial both organizations and their leaders [that is, the Military Revolutionary Committee and the Committee of Safety]. The attitude toward the SRs was also one of disgust.

"Piatnitsky District (Serpukhovskoi, Alexandrovsky). A large crowd. A meeting. Speakers attack[ed] the revolutionary committee and Rudnev. A Menshevik from the Sytinskaia Factory tried to speak. He was not allowed to talk. There were shouts: 'Down with the socialists. To

hell with them.' I spoke—with the same result. A Kadet speaker enjoyed enormous sympathy. It is evident that there can be no agreement
in the future. It was necessary to hand out pamphlets to inform the
masses [about what is going on]. The SRs, who were distributing the
pamphlets, encountered Bolshevik patrols and were taken away. We urgently need an appeal to the populace *from all parties*."

This was the real mood of the masses, who were undisciplined, ignorant, confused, had stopped believing in yesterday's leaders, instinctively sensed where the truth lay, but were unorganized and unaccustomed
to active participation in the struggle. Only the Bolshevik minority was
active. This minority made its presence felt through fanatical Red
Guards, comprised mainly of the very young workers, and this element
manifested a particular intransigence and cruelty in fighting.

After midnight on October 31, with the end of the cease-fire, the
fighting was renewed with special intensity by the Bolsheviks, who had
been encouraged by an influx of new forces and by the news of the defeat of Kerensky's defenders.[40]

During the course of October 31 and November 1 the Bolsheviks destroyed homes at the ends of Nikitsky and Tverskoy Boulevards, where
the cadets had remained; they seized after a prolonged fusillade the heavi-
ly-damaged telephone exchange at Miliutinsky Lane, where cadets were
forced to surrender; they occupied the Hotel Nationale and the seriously-
damaged Hotel Metropole; then they attacked the City Duma, whose defenders, along with the City Duma delegates and members of the Committee of Safety, were forced by 3 P.M. on November 1 to retire from
the City Duma building to the Historical Museum and the Kremlin,
leaving behind in the City Duma building their wounded and their medi-
cal personnel. Another section of the committee was located in the Alexandrov School. These two centers of resistance were subjected to a cruel
artillery bombardment, which continued to intensify on November 2;
the bombardment became, according to the officers, "*not a bombardment directed by soldiers, but a precision bombardment directed by officers—German officers*." Having captured the Historical Museum, the
Bolsheviks undertook from its turrets to shoot into Red Square, thus
making exit from the Kremlin dangerous and transforming the Kremlin
into a besieged fortress. During these days the Kremlin itself with its
historical treasures was subjected to an intense artillery attack. The damage caused by this attack to the ancient churches of the Kremlin was the
first blow to the religious conscience of the Moscow populace: this
damage even prompted from the ranks of the Bolshevik leadership a
painful cry. Lunacharsky wrote that he could no longer tolerate

Bolshevik horrors and that he was resigning from the "people's commissars"—alas, not for long . . . .

Already on the evening of November 1 representatives of the Committee of Safety, Rudnev and Kovarsky, were invited to the Alexandrov School. The executive committee of the council of officers' deputies and the council of representatives from the troops that had had joined the governmental detachment put nine questions to them. The soldiers asked about the situation at the front, about the attitude of Moscow's populace toward the fighting, about the reasons why the promised reinforcements had not arrived, about the prospects for success in the fighting, and so on. When the Committee of Safety did not give satisfactory answers to all these questions, then the soldiers asked: "What measures must be taken to end the futile fighting?" The Committee of Safety, upholding its line of being a "political shield" that was subordinate to the dictates of military strategy, responded that it was prepared to take upon itself the execution of those measures on which the military defenders of Moscow decided.

Then the committee was given the responsibility of beginning peace negotiations. On the afternoon of November 2 a delegation from the Committee of Safety set off for the Military Revolutionary Committee with a proposal to begin peace negotiations. The delegation set itself the task of winning consent on only two points, which it considered questions of honor. First, it would not agree to recognize in any direct fashion the revolution that had occurred. Second, it won a guarantee of the free departure of soldiers, although this was soon violated by the Bolsheviks.

At 5 P.M. a peace agreement on the basis of the disarming of the "White Guard" was concluded. Cadets who did not wish to accept this condition left Alexandrov School for the Kremlin, and here it was decided "not to surrender, to defend the principle of the state to the end, to break through the Bolshevik ring, to leave the city and to effect a union with troops loyal to the government." At 7 P.M. the cadets left the Kremlin with this intention and went back to the Alexandrov School "in a triumphant mood, although the realization that they would have to pass through a series of streets where they would be fired upon from windows and roofs certainly sobered them." The cadets did not manage, of course, to carry out their decision, for there were no troops "loyal to the government" present outside Moscow, and on November 3 there occurred the sad spectacle of the disarmament of the "White Guard." An eyewitness wrote: "In small detachments of 10-20 men the officers, cadets, and students approached the Alexandrov School. The detachment commanders, amidst the general silence of the crowd gathered at the

scene, reported to the chairman of the commission the title of the detachment and the number of men in it. Cadets took their rifles into the
school building, while officers and students placed their weapons right
there on the sidewalk. By 12 o'clock one could see only armed soldiers
and workers."

The Bolsheviks' victory was complete and final. Their victory in
Moscow predetermined their triumph in the rest of Russia. At that moment everyone still thought that the victory would be short-lived and
that, having seized state power, the Bolsheviks would not be able to retain it. Accordingly, there circulated fantastic rumors about the approach
toward Moscow of Kaledin's troops, and there began a migration to the
Don region by Moscow's badly-defeated defenders of order and of the legitimate Provisional Government.

As the Bolsheviks' dominion commenced, the other political parties
confidently predicted that the Bolshevik government would not be able
to fulfill even one of that party's promises, that it would not give the deceived people peace, or land, or bread, or the "socialization" of industry,
and that the disillusioned populace would not tolerate the dominion of
the violent. The Party of Popular Liberty was then predicting that the
Bolsheviks' victory would entail the loss of the war and the partition of
Russia. But no one, including that party, foresaw that the Bolshevik regime would last many years and would lead Russia to the destruction of
all its national goals—political, economic, and cultural—goals that
were the product of centuries.

NOTES

NOTES TO INTRODUCTION

1. In 1884 Tolstoy told Prince Bernhardt von Bülow that the place of the old regime would be taken by "communism pure and simple, the communism of Mr. Karl Marx of London who has just died and whose theories I have studied with attention and interest." See von Bülow's *Denkwürdigkeiten*, Vol. IV (Berlin, 1931), p. 573. This passage is quoted in Lionel Kochan, *Russia in Revolution, 1890-1918* (New York, 1966), p. xi.

2. There is a vast literature on the events of 1917. The most helpful works on the Provisional Government are the collection of documents by R.P. Browder and A.F. Kerensky, eds., *The Russian Provisional Government of 1917. Documents*, 3 vols. (Stanford, 1961), and the recent multivolume monograph by V.I. Startsev, *Revoliutsiia i vlast'. Petrogradskii sovet i Vremennoe pravitelstvo v marte-aprele 1917 g.* (Moscow, 1978); *idem.*, *Vnutrenniaia politika Vremennogo pravitelstva pervogo sozyva* (Leningrad, 1980); *idem.*, *Krakh Kerenshchiny* (Leningrad, 1982). See also: P.V. Volobuev, *Ekonomicheskaia politika Vremennogo pravitelstva* (Moscow, 1962); and A.M. Andreev, *Mestnye sovety i organy burzhuaznoi vlasti (1917 g.)* (Moscow, 1983). On foreign policy, see A.V. Ignatiev, *Vneshniaia politika Vremennogo pravitelstva* (Moscow, 1974) and Rex A. Wade, *The Russian Search for Peace, February-October 1917* (Stanford, 1969).

3. On the Kadets during the revolution, see William G. Rosenberg, *Liberals in the Russian Revolution. The Constitutional Democratic Party, 1917-1921* (Princeton, 1974). For Miliukov the standard reference is Thomas Riha, *A Russian European. Paul Miliukov in Russian Politics* (Notre Dame, 1969), which is, unfortunately, very sketchy on Miliukov in 1917. Miliukov also left memoirs of 1917, which he was careful to distinguish from his history of the revolution: P.N. Miliukov, *Vospominaniia, 1859-1917*, Vol. 2 (New York, 1955). Nevertheless, the richest primary source on Miliukov and the Kadets in 1917 is the three-volume history, cited below in footnote six, of which the present volume is the final installment. Also worthy of attention is V.D. Nabokov, "Vremennoe pravitelstvo," *Arkhiv russkoi revoliutsii*, I (Berlin, 1922), pp. 9-96.

4. For the SRs the classic work is Oliver H. Radkey, *The Agrarian Foes of Bolshevism. Promise and Default of the Russian Socialist Revolutionaries February to October 1917* (New York, 1958). Also useful as background is Manfred Hildermeier, *Die Sozialrevolutionäre Partei Russlands: Agrarsozialismus und Modernisierung im Zarenreich (1900-1914)* (Köln, 1978). On the Mensheviks in 1917 there is no comprehensive monograph in English. However, much of N.N. Sukhanov's *Zapiski o revoliutsii*, 7 vols. (Berlin, 1920-1923) deals with Menshevism. An abridged translation of Sukhanov has been done by Joel Carmichael, ed., *The Russian Revolution. 1917. A Personal Record by N.N. Sukhanov* (Princeton,

1984). There are good biographies of two leading Mensheviks: W.H. Roobol, *Tsereteli—A Democrat in the Russian Revolution. A Political Biography* (The Hague, 1976), and Israel Getzler, *Martov. A Political Biography of a Russian Social Democrat* (Cambridge, 1967). Also helpful on the Mensheviks in 1917 is Leopold H. Haimson, ed., *The Mensheviks from the Revolution of 1917 to the Second World War* (Chicago, 1974), pp. 1-92, 349-388.

5. Radkey, *Agrarian Foes of Bolshevism*, pp. 465-468.

6. *Istoriia vtoroi russkoi revoliutsii. Tom 1. 3 vypuska* (Sofia, 1921-1924). The first installment was translated by Richard and Tatyana Stites as *The Russian Revolution. Volume 1. The Revolution Divided: Spring, 1917* (Gulf Breeze, 1978). The second installment was translated by G.M. Hamburg as *The Russian Revolution. Volume 2. Kornilov or Lenin?—Summer, 1917* (Gulf Breeze, 1984).

7. On *gosudarstvennost* see Richard Stites' introduction to *The Russian Revolution. Volume 1*, pp. vii-viii.

8. Miliukov claimed that the women captured by the Bolsheviks were executed. In fact, the women were released on the initiative of the British General Knox. See Sir George Buchanan, *My Mission to Russia and Other Diplomatic Memories*, Vol. 2 (Boston, 1923), p. 208.

9. A.S. Izgoev, "Piat let v Sovetskoi Rossii (Otryvki vospominanii i zametki)," *Arkhiv russkoi revoliutsii*, X (Berlin, 1923), p. 20, quoted in W. Bruce Lincoln, *Passage through Armageddon. The Russians in War and Revolution, 1914-1918* (New York, 1986), p. 448.

10. Sukhanov, *Zapiski o revoliutsii*, Vol. 6 (Berlin, 1923), p. 9.

11. Miliukov was struck by this remark and quoted it several times in *Rossiia na perelome. Bolshevistskii period russkoi revoliutsii. Tom 1. Proiskhozhdenie i ukreplenie bolshevistskoi diktatury* (Paris, 1927), p. 57 *et passim*.

12. Alexander Rabinowitch, *The Bolsheviks Come to Power. The Revolution of 1917 in Petrograd* (New York, 1976), pp. 159-162.

13. Rabinowitch, pp. 168-314, gives a nuanced analysis of the nature of these disagreements. A more summary treatment may be found in Marc Ferro, *The Bolshevik Revolution. A Social History of the Russian Revolution* (London, 1980), pp. 238-247. The same question is treated from the perspective of Petrograd workers in David Mandel, *The Petrograd Workers and the Soviet Seizure of Power. From the July Days 1917 to July 1918* (New York, 1984), pp. 323-342.

14. The article, entitled "On Compromises," was written on September 1 but not published until September 6. See Rabinowitch, *The Bolsheviks Come to Power*, pp. 169-173. Lenin explored the same issue in three other articles in early September. See V.I. Startsev, "O nekotorykh rabotakh V.I. Lenina pervoi poloviny sentiabria 1917 g.," in A.L. Fraiman, ed., *V.I. Lenin v oktiabre i v pervye gody sovetskoi vlasti* (Leningrad, 1970), pp. 28-37. Leonard Schapiro took these articles as tactical ploys, rather than as serious expressions of Lenin's views. See Schapiro, *The Russian Revolutions of 1917. The Origins of Modern Communism*

(New York, 1984), p. 123. In general, Schapiro was unimpressed by the evidence of serious disagreements among Bolsheviks over party strategy. He saw Lenin as a harder, more decisive and dictatorial figure than other scholars lately have portrayed, and he saw the party as more monolithic than democratic.

15. Sukhanov, *Zapiski o revoliutsii,* Vol. 7 (Berlin, 1923), pp. 115-116.

16. This critique of Miliukov's portrait of Verkhovsky draws on material in Startsev, *Krakh Kerenshchiny,* especially pp. 76-81, 146-148, 204-220.

17. Verkhovsky wanted military courts to investigate disciplinary offenses and mete out punishment within 48 hours of the offense; if the courts reached no decision in this period the right to impose discipline would revert to the commanding officers. Penal regiments would be created for those units engaging in "collective anarchist activity." Startsev, *Krakh Kerenshchiny,* pp. 147-148. Verkhovsky did not, to my knowledge, demand the reinstitution of the death penalty at the front. Therefore, Startsev is too hard on Verkhovsky when charging that "while condemning verbally the counter-revolutionary mutiny of General Kornilov, Verkhovsky in his speech [to the Pre-Parliament] essentially defended Kornilovite methods to control the soldiers' movement."

18. Quoted by Startsev, *Krakh Kerenshchiny,* pp. 212-213; original in *Byloe,* 1918, no. 12, p. 36.

19. Startsev, *Krakh Kerenshchiny,* pp. 210, 212. On page 212 Startsev writes: "It [Verkhovsky's plan for an immediate invitation to peace negotiations] was a desperate stroke, unlikely to succeed, although it would have placed serious difficulties in the way of a Bolshevik uprising. Verkhovsky's plan was risky, but had possibilities." For a Soviet historian this statement is remarkably bold.

20. Startsev, *Krakh Kerenshchiny,* p. 216.

21. Sir George Buchanan, *My Mission to Russia,* Vol. 2 (Boston, 1923), p. 201.

22. Buchanan, *My Mission to Russia,* Vol. 2, p. 216.

23. For price data compared to workers' wages see Z.V. Stepanov, *Rabochie Petrograda v period podgotovki i provedeniia okriabrskogo vooruzhennogo vosstaniia* (Moscow, 1965), pp. 53-55; S.G. Strumilin, *Zarabatnaia plata i proizvoditelnost truda v promyshlennosti* (Moscow, 1923), p. 25; S.A. Smith, *Red Petrograd. Revolution in the Factories, 1917-1918* (Cambridge, 1983), pp. 116-117. See also Ferro, *The Bolshevik Revolution,* pp. 159-166.

24. The monthly number of strikers in Russia increased from 35,000 in April, to 1.1 million in September and 1.2 million in October. Smith, *Red Petrograd,* p. 116. However, in Petrograd itself the incidence of major strikes actually decreased in September and October. See Mandel, *Petrograd Workers and the Soviet Seizure of Power,* pp. 284-285, and Stepanov, *Rabochie Petrograda,* p. 130.

25. Verkhovsky believed that there would be enough food for an army of seven million, whereas in October 1917 there were aproximately 10.2

million Russians under arms. Startsev, *Krakh Kerenshchiny*, p. 208. In a detailed study based on Russian military archives, M. Frenkin has shown the devastating impact of the nation's economic collapse on the army's food and materiel supply. See Frenkin, *Russkaia armiia i revoliutsiia 1917-1918* (Munich, 1978), pp. 449-497. Frenkin believes that even Verkhovsky's estimates were optimistic: "The Ministry of Food Supply agreed in October to 'feed' only a seven-million-man army, while Stavka insisted on food supplies for nine million soldiers, in order 'preserve the front.' However, this argument was senseless. As we have already seen, the food supply for the front units did not exceed 20-26 percent of the projected norms, and was sometimes less than that." *Ibid.*, p. 488. The psychological result of the economic crisis on the army was "to increase the anger that led to disturbances and to spontaneous, bestial acts of revenge against the officer corps." *Ibid.*, p. 497.

26. Smith sees the organization of factory committees as arising from workers' desires to maintain production and to defend jobs in a time of rising unemployment. From limited surveillance of management, who, workers believed, actively "sabotaged" production, the factory committees soon moved to inspection of every aspect of company affairs. Smith, *Red Petrograd*, p. 258. The struggle in factories between workers and management also is treated in Mandel, *Petrograd Workers and the Soviet Seizure of Power*, pp. 264-286.

27. It can be argued that by October 1917 local centers of power much more radical than Petrograd already existed in Latvia and Kronstadt. If one thinks of Latvia, Kronstadt and Petrograd as a "red triangle," the last angle to go "red" was the capital. Such a view places Petrograd's revolutionary movement in a different perspective: it was neither the first Soviet effectively to emancipate itself from the Provisional Government, nor was it necessarily the most "advanced" ideologically among the Soviets. On the revolution in Latvia see Andrew Ezergailis, *The 1917 Revolution in Latvia* (Boulder, 1974), and *idem.*, *The Latvian Impact on the Bolshevik Revolution. The First Phase: September 1917 to April 1918* (Boulder, 1983). For Kronstadt see Norman E. Saul, *Sailors in Revolt. The Russian Baltic Fleet in 1917* (Lawrence, 1978), and Israel Getzler, *Kronstadt 1917-1921: The Fate of a Soviet Democracy* (Cambridge, 1983).

28. On the Red Guards see Ferro, *The Bolshevik Revolution*, pp. 197-199, and V.I. Startsev, *Ocherki po istorii Petrogradskoi krasnoi gvardii i rabochei militsii* (Moscow, Leningrad, 1965). See also Rex A. Wade, *Red Guards and Workers Militias in the Russian Revolution* (Stanford, 1984).

29. There is an enormous literature on Soviets outside the capital. For a recent survey by a Soviet historian, see Andreev, *Mestnye sovety i organy burzhuaznoi vlasti*. For two recent monographic studies in English of the revolutionary situation outside Petrograd, see Diane Koenker, *Moscow Workers and the 1917 Revolution* (Princeton, 1981), especially pp. 143-268 and 329-367, and Donald J. Raleigh, *Revolution on the Volga. 1917 in Saratov* (Ithaca, 1986). For a broader English-language treatment see John L.H. Keep, *The Russian Revolution. A Study in Mass Mobilization* (New York, 1976), pp 113-152 and 339-381.

30. The best short treatment of the creation of the Military Revolutionary Committee is Rabinowitch, *The Bolsheviks Come to Power*, pp. 224-236. See also E.D. Orekhova, "K izucheniiu istochnikov o sozdanii Petrogradskogo voenno-revoliutsionnogo komiteta," in D.A. Chugaev, ed., *Istochnikovedenie istorii sovetskogo obshchestva*, Vypusk 2 (Moscow, 1968), pp. 9-55.

31. The "defensive" or "reactive" element in the October Revolution is an important part of Robert Daniels' explanation of the Bolshevik victory. See Robert V. Daniels, *Red October* (New York, 1967).

32. Leon Trotsky, *History of the Russian Revolution*, Vol. 3 (Ann Arbor, 1960), p. 232. Quoted in Lincoln, *Passage through Armageddon*, p. 442.

33. T.N. Granovsky, *Polnoe sobranie sochinenii*, Vol. 1 (St. Petersburg, 1905), p. 158. Quoted in Priscilla R. Roosevelt, "Granovskii at the Lectern: A Conservative Liberal's Vision of History," *Forschungen zur Osteuropäischen Geschichte*, Band 29 (Berlin, 1981), p. 138.

34. B.N. Chicherin, "Sovremennye zadachi russkoi zhizni," *Golosa iz Rossii*, Vypusk 4 (London, 1857), pp. 56-57. The reference to the dominion recognized on one occasion long ago probably had to do with the passage in the *Povest vremennykh let* [Tale of Bygone Years] in which the Varangians were invited to come rule the Russian lands.

35. Chicherin, "Sovremennye zadachi," pp. 64-65.

36. P.N. Miliukov, *Ocherki istorii russkoi kultury*, 5-e izdanie (St. Petersburg, 1904), Chast 1, pp. 1-2.

37. P.N. Miliukov, *Ocherki istorii russkoi kultury*, p. 17.

38. For an impressive essay on Miliukov as historian see A.N. Tsamutali, *Borba napravlenii v russkoi istoriografii v period imperializma. Istoriograficheskie ocherki* (Leningrad, 1986) pp. 155-204; here pp. 180-185.

39. V. Chernov, *The Great Russian Revolution* (New York, 1936), p. 172. Quoted in Riha, *A Russian European*, p. 329.

40. Paul Miliukov, *Bolshevism: An International Danger. Its Doctrine and Its Practice through War and Revolution* (London, 1920), pp. 5-6. It is likely that this book grew out of what was originally planned as the fourth installment of *Istoriia vtoroi russkoi revoliutsii*. In the "Postscript" to the present installment of the history—a section not included in the translation above—Miliukov mentioned that he planned a fourth installment that would "contain a description of the internal collapse of Russia between March and October and also a history of the struggle for peace in the international arena." *Bolshevism: An International Danger* deals with the struggle for peace in the context of the Zimmerwald program that informed so much of socialist activism on the international front.

41. Miliukov, *Bolshevism: An International Danger*, p.30.

42. Miliukov, *Rossiia na perelome*, vol. 1, p. 128.

43. Miliukov, *Rossiia na perelome*, vol. 1, p. 129.

44. Miliukov, *Rossiia na perelome*, vol. 1, p. 132.

45. Miliukov, *Rossiia na perelome*, vol. 1, pp. 126, 133 *et passim*.

46. Miliukov, *Rossiia na perelome,* vol. 1, pp. 40-41.
47. Miliukov, *Rossiia na perelome,* vol. 1, pp. 37-38.

CHAPTER I

1. General L.G. Kornilov—Commander of troops on Southwestern Front in July 1917. Appointed by Kerensky as Supreme Commander-in-Chief of the Russian army on 10 July 1917, a position he held until his dismissal less than two months later. He was leader of a movement which intended to displace the currently existing Provisional Government and to substitute for it a "strong government" that would restore army discipline and the army's fighting capacity, as well as curb the political influence of the Soviets. Kornilov and his followers were defeated in late August/early September 1917. Having been compromised politically, Kornilov was confined for purposes of investigating his "counter-revolutionary" conduct. The term "Kornilovshchina" was employed principally by the radical left as a label that encompassed all those directly involved in Kornilov's movement, as well as all those who indirectly associated themselves with Kornilov's "counter-revolutionary" agenda. See Volume 2 of this work for Miliukov's account.

2. I.G. Tsereteli (1881-1959)—Georgian-born Menshevik leader whose references to the Soviets as the "revolutionary democracy" introduced the term into Russian political currency. Leader of the Social Democratic faction in the Second Duma. Member of the Presidium of the first All-Russia Central Executive Committee. Minister of Posts and Telegraphs, May-July 1917. Minister of Internal Affairs, July. Participated in the Moscow State Conference in August, but poor health forced his virtual withdrawal from politics several months thereafter.

3. Platform of August 14—Political program drafted by moderate socialists and presented to the Moscow State Conference in August 1917. It was an attempt to win support from the "democratic elements" within the bourgeoisie for what Miliukov regarded as the fundamentally socialist principles pursued by the moderate socialist leadership of the Soviet. See the discussion in Volume 2 of this work, pp. 92-94.

4. Moscow State Conference—Public meeting of 2000 representatives, drawn from the various Soviets, the membership of the four State Dumas, and various economic and public organizations. It convened in Moscow in August 1917 in a tense political atmosphere. It was an opportunity for public debate over Russia's immediate political future, and gave Kornilov and Kerensky a chance to assay their political support.

5. A.A. Bublikov—Progressist. Member of the Fourth Duma. Member of Council, Congress of Representatives of Industry and Trade. Chairman, director of Achinsk-Minusinsk Railroad. His handshake with Tsereteli at the Moscow State Conference was an attempt to reconcile the industrialists with moderate socialists, but it weakened Tsereteli's position in the socialist camp.

6. General Verkhovsky's speech to the soldiers of the Petrograd garrison on September 12, as reported in *Russkoe Slovo* [Russian Word] on October 13. [PNM]
General M.V. Alexeev (1857-1918)—Russian army officer. Chief of Staff of the Southwestern Front, 1914-1915. Chief of Staff of Supreme Headquarters, 1915-1917. Supreme commander, March-May 1917. A candidate for head of state in August 1917 and would-be intermediary between Kerensky and Kornilov. Escaped after Bolshevik Revolution. One of the organizers of the Volunteer Army, and its commander after Kornilov's death.
A.I. Verkhovsky (1886-1938)—Major general. Commander of Moscow military district in summer 1917. Became Minister of War in last two months of Provisional Government, but resigned under pressure from other ministers just before Bolshevik Revolution. Fought in Red Army, 1919-1920. Later taught tactics at Soviet Military Academy.
7. V.N. Lvov—Octobrist. Deputy in the Third and Fourth Dumas. Chief Procurator of the Holy Synod, March-July 1917. Extensively involved in the Kornilov affair. Lvov's conversation with Kerensky on August 26 provided Kerensky with the legal evidence needed to prove that Kornilov was intending a coup d'etat. In order to fight Kornilov, Kerensky demanded that he be given full power to direct the struggle against Kornilov and to form a new cabinet.
8. The terms "directors" and "directory" were borrowed from the moderate phase of the French Revolution between the fall of Robespierre in 1794 and the triumph of Napoleon in 1799. The notion of "directory" was emblematic of political stability, wisdom, and moderation in a dangerously polarized environment.
N.V. Nekrasov (1879-1940)—Transport specialist, professor at Tomsk Technical Institute. Left Kadet deputy in Third and Fourth Dumas. Deputy Chairman of the State Duma, 1916-1917. Minister of Transport, March-July 1917. Joined the Russian Radical Democratic Party in July. Assistant prime minister and Minister of Finance, July-August. Governor-General of Finland, September-October.
M.I. Tereshchenko (1886-1956)—Large landowner, capitalist, sugar manufacturer. Progressivist delegate to Fourth Duma. Chairman of Kiev province War Industry Committee, 1915-1917. Minister of Finance, March-May 1917. Minister of Foreign Affairs, May-October.
B.V. Savinkov (1879-1943)—Prominent populist. Member of the SR Fighting Organization and involved in a sumber of spectacular assassinations in 1905 revolutionary period. Author of novel about terrorism called *Pale Horse*. Assistant Minister of War, July-August 1917. Heavily involved in the Kornilov affair.
N.M. Kishkin (1864-1930)—Physician and Kadet leader. Member of Moscow City Duma and of the All-Russian Union of Towns. Member of the Kadet central committee. Provisional Government Commissar for Moscow, February-August 1917. Minister of State of Charities, September-October.

9. V.M. Chernov (1876-1952)—One of the founders of the SR party, a member of its central committee, and its leading theoretician. Participated in Zimmerwald Conference and Kienthal Conference during war. Editor of SR newspaper *Delo Naroda*. Minister of Agriculture, May-August 1917. Chairman of the Constitutent Assembly, January 1918.

10. M.I. Skobelev (1885-1938)—Menshevik leader. Member of the Petrograd Soviet Executive Committee. Minister of Labor, May-September 1917.

11. See the text of this order in Volume 2 of this work. [PNM]

12. F.F. Kokoshkin (1871-1918)—Attorney, professor law at Moscow University. Prominent Kadet. Kadet deputy in First Duma. State Comptroller, July-August 1917. Elected to Constituent Assembly, but arrested beforehand for anti-Soviet activities. Murdered by Red sailors, 1 January 1918.

P.P. Iurenev—Engineer. Member of Kadet central committee. Minister of Transport, July-August 1917.

13. General A.M. Krymov—Lieutenant general. Involved in the plot of a palace coup against Nicholas II in January 1917. In August commander of III Cavalry Corps. Committed suicide in wake of Kornilov affair.

A.V. Kartashev—Former professor at St. Petersburg Theological Academy. Kadet. Chief Procurator of the Holy Synod, July-August 1917. Author of two-volume history of the Russian church.

14. D.N. Verderevsky (1873-1946)—Rear admiral of tsarist navy. In May 1917 appointed commander of the Baltic Fleet. Resisted revolution in Baltic Fleet. After Kornilov affair appointed Navy Minister. Fled to England and America after Bolshevik Revolution.

S.A Smirnov—Kadet. Appointed State Comptroller in September 1917.

S.N. Tretiakov—Leader in Moscow commercial-industrial circles. President of the Moscow Stock Exchange. Chairman of the Economic Council, 1917 and member of last cabinet of Provisional Government, September-October.

15. N.D. Avksentiev (1878-1943)— Right SR leader. Imprisoned or in exile, 1906-1917. Minister of Internal Affairs, July-August 1917. Chairman of the Democratic Conference. President of the Soviet of the Republic. Leading figure in Soviet of Peasants' Deputies.

16. A.M. Kaledin (1861-1918)— Major general and commander of XII Corps, 1914. Commander of VIII Army, 1916. Ataman of Don Cossacks, 1917. Later an important figure in the formation of the Volunteer Army.

17. L.B. Kamenev (1883-1936) (Real name Rozenfeld)—Joined Bolshevik faction practically at its inception and became a close associate of Lenin in emigration before 1914. In 1917 he was elected to Bolshevik Central Committee where he opposed the October insurrection and was against party's attitude toward the war. He favored a peaceful and "legal" path to power and power-sharing in a broad coalition of socialists. After Bolshevik Revolution he was chairman of Soviets' Central Executive

Committee, and later a member of party Politburo. He later fell victim to Stalin and was executed after a show trial in 1936.

Iu. M. Steklov (1873-1941) (real name Nakhamkis)—Member of Bolshevik faction shortly after 1903. Publicist in prerevolutionary period, member of Fourth State Duma. In February 1917 he was elected member of the Executive Committee of Petrograd Soviet. He defended politics of revolutionary defensism until eve of October Revolution. After October 1917 he was editor of newspaper *Izvestiia* until 1925, and an active historian.

18. A.R. Gots (1882-1940)—One of the founders of SR party. Participated in SR Fighting Organization, 1906-1907. Member of SR central committee. Member of Petrograd Soviet Executive Committee. Member of the first All Russia Central Executive Committee.

V.M. Zenzinov (1881-?)—An SR party leader. Became a revolutionary in 1903, participated in December 1905 uprising in Moscow. In 1909 elected to SR central committee. In 1917 elected member of Executive Committee of Petrograd Soviet. Editor of SR paper, *Delo Naroda*. After October Revolution took party in various anti-Bolshevik activity.

19. B.O. Bogdanov (1884-1956)—Menshevik. Elected to Central War Industry Committee in Petrograd, 1915-1917. In 1917 elected to Executive Committee of Petrograd Soviet. A disciple of Tsereteli and a proponent of defensism, political moderation.

The Committee of Popular Struggle Against Counter-Revolution was an organization dominated by militant opponents of Kornilov and the "counter-revolutionary bourgeoisie." It carried out arrests of suspected "counter-revolutionaries," closed down politically anti-revolutionary papers, and conducted searches for evidence of counter-revolutionary activity. Bogdanov made his speech to the Petrograd Soviet on August 31. See Volume 2 of Miliukov's history.

20. N.S. Chkheidze (1864-1926)—Georgian-born Menshevik. Deputy in the Third and Fourth Dumas. Leader of the Menshevik faction in the Fourth Duma. Chairman of the Petrograd Soviet Executive Committee, February-August 1917. Chairman of the first All-Russia Central Executive Committee.

21. Iu. O. Martov (1873-1923) (real name Tsederbaum)—Menshevik Internationalist leader, closely associated with the founding of the Russian Social Democratic Workers' Party. Participated in Zimmerwald Conference and Kienthal Conference during war. Member of Petrograd Soviet Executive Committee.

V. Volodarsky (1891-1918) (real name M.M. Goldshtein)—Joined revolutionary movement as Bundist, later became Menshevik. In 1917 a Mezhraionets, then Bolshevik. Member of Petrograd Committee of Bolshevik party. In September 1917 elected to presidium of Petrograd Soviet. In 1918 was assassinated by an SR.

Rozanov—Miliukov's reference to Rozanov is mistaken. He surely meant to refer to D.B. Riazanov (1870-1938). Riazanov was a Social Democrat who tried to remain independent of the Bolsheviks and Mensheviks. In 1917 he was a Mezhraionets, chairman of the Central Bureau of

Petrograd Trade Unions and member of the All-Russia Central Council of Trade Unions. He joined the Bolshevik faction after the merger with the Mezhraiontsy, but distanced himself from many of Lenin's policies. After 1917 he became a distinguished Marxist historian. He died in the purges of 1938.

22. V.A. Anisimov (1878-1938)—Menshevik. Member of Second State Duma. In 1917 a member of the Executive Committee of Petrograd Soviet. An SR propagandist during the civil war and member of the Far Eastern government.

F.I. Dan (1871-1947) (real name Gurvich)—Long-time Social Democrat, member of the Menshevik faction and its central committee. Close associate of Tsereteli and Chkheidze, and supporter of coalition government. Member of the Petrograd Soviet Executive Committee and of the first All-Russia Central Executive Committe.

23. A.V. Lunacharsky (1875-1933)—Social Democrat who associated himself variously with the Bolsheviks, the Bogdanov-Gorky *Vpered* circle, and the Mezhraionka. Active worker for Military Revolutionary Committee. From 1917-1929 Commissar for Enlightenment.

N.P. Avilov (1887-1942)—Bolshevik since 1904. In 1917 on Executive Committee of All-Russia Trade Union Council. Candidate member of Bolshevik central committee, April 1917. After October Revolution, Commissar of Posts and Telegraphs. Arrested in Stalinst purges and died in prison.

24. N.I. Rakitnikov (1864-?)—Member of SR central committee. From May-September 1917 worked in Ministry of Agriculture.

25. The conferences of August 30 were attended by the "reduced" membership of the cabinet, that is, the membership minus Chernov, Kokoshkin, Iurenev, Oldenburg, Peshekhonov. After August 31 Nekrasov did not participate either. Those present were Kerensky, Avksentiev, Skobelev, Zarudny, Prokopovich, Tereshchenko, Kartashev, Efremov.[PNM]

26. A.M. Nikitin—Menshevik. Minister of Posts and Telegraphs, July-August 1917. Minister of Internal Affairs, September-October 1917.

27. Prince G.E. Lvov (1861-1925)—Former tsarist official and Zemstvo activst. Kadet deputy to the First Duma. Member of the Moscow City Duma. Chairman of the All-Russian Union of Zemstvos, 1914-1917. As a nonparty liberal, chairman of the Council of Ministers and Minister of Internal Affairs, March-July 1917.

28. P.A. Kropotkin (1842-1921)—One of Russia's great anarchist theoreticians. Invited to join the Provisional Government in 1917, but refused to do so. At the Moscow State Conference he defended continuation of war, called for establishment of a Russian republic. After the October Revolution he was a critic of Bolshevik centralized government and arbitrariness. His Federalist League was suppressed in 1918.

29. A.S. Zarudny—Prominent Popular Socialist. Assistant Minister of Justice, May-July 1917. Minister of Justice, July-August.

30. P.N. Maliantovich—Menshevik. Appointed Minister of Justice in September 1917.

S.S. Salazkin—Appointed Minister of Education in September 1917.

31. *Perekrashivalos v zashchitny tsvet*—literally "painted itself a defensive color." Perekrashit'sia means, figuratively, "to become a turncoat." Miliukov's choice of words hints, not so subtly, at the government's treason.

CHAPTER II

1. S.N. Prokopovich (1871-1955)—Moderate Social Democrat. Minister of Commerce and Industry, July-August, 1917. Minister of Supply, September-October.
   E.D. Kuskova (1869-1958)—Began her political career as a socialist of the revisionist, Bernsteinian type. In 1905 member of the Union of Liberation and thereafter associated with the left wing of the Constitutional Democratic Party. Critic of Bolsheviks in 1917 and to the end of her life. Banished from USSR in 1922.
2. G.E. Zinoviev (1883-1936)—Old Bolshevik. Associated with A.A. Bogdanov's *Vpered* and with illegal publication of *Sotsial-Demokrat*. Long-time associate of Lenin in emigration. In 1917 became a member of the Bolshevik central committee. From July to October was underground, avoiding arrest. After the October Revolution, which he had opposed, he became an important political figure in the Soviet regime and for a time was even considered a possible successor to Lenin. Eventually, he fell from political grace, lost his governmental and party positions, and finally was purged.
3. The final composition of the Democratic Conference was as follows. The Soviet of Workers' and Soldiers' Deputies—230 members; the Soviet of Peasants' Deputies—230 members; cities—300 members; Zemstvos—200 members; postal and telegraphic workers—201 members; trade unions—100 members; central cooperatives—120 members; workers' cooperatives (which had separated from the central cooperative at the Cooperatives' Congress)—38 members; army organizations—83 members; commissars—22 members; Cossacks—35 members; army peasant sections—18 members; officers—4 members; veterans (uvechnye voiny)—6 members; the front—15 members; economic groups—33 members; commercial-industrial employees—33 members; food supply organizations and committees—20 members; the Peasant Union—10 members; teachers—15 members; feldshers—5 members; Union of Orthodox Clergy and Laity—1 member; the press—1 member; Ukrainian Rada—15 members; Muslim Soviet—?; Soviet of National Minority Socialist Parties—10 members; Georgian Inter-Party Alliance—5 members; Poles—2 members; Jews—1 member. [PNM]
4. This was Aladin, who then turned to Prince G.E. Lvov. See Volume 2 of this work. [PNM]
5. A.V. Peshekhonov (1867-1933)—Statistician, publicist, Zemstvo activist. A liberal populist, and one of the founders of the Party of Popular Socialists in 1906. Publisher of the party's newspaper *Narodnoe Slovo*. Member of the Petrograd Soviet Executive Committee. Member of

286 NOTES TO CHAPTER III

the Main Land Committee. Mininster of Supply, May-August 1917. Deputy Chairman of the Pre-Parliament.

6. A.I. Shingarev (1869-1918)—Physician, Zemstvo activist, publicist. Member of the Kadet central committee. Kadet deputy in the Second, Third, and Fourth Dumas. One of the authors of the Kadet agrarian program. Minister of Agriculture, March-May 1917. Minister of Finance, May-July. Member of Pre-Parliament. Elected to Constituent Assembly but arrested before it met for anti-Soviet activities. Murdered by Red sailors, January 1918.

7. A.I. Chkhenkeli (1874-1959)—Georgian Menshevik, deputy of Fourth State Duma. In 1917 commissar of the Provisional Government in Transcaucasus. In 1918 confirmed as head of Transcaucasus Provisional Government. Later foreign minister of Menshevik Georgian government and its ambassador to France.

8. E.K. Breshkovskaia (1844-1934)—"Grandmother of the Russian Revolution." Involved in the Populist movement from 1870. Spent many years in prison and Siberian exile. Toured the United States, 1904-1905, arousing much sympathy for the revolutionary cause. An honored celebrity in 1917 at least among moderate socialists, but with little or no real political influence.

9. M.A. Spiridonova (1884-1941)—SR terrorist. A leader of the Left SRs between 1917 and 1921. In 1917 mayor of Chita. Editor of *Nash Put*, August 1917. Member of Petrograd Soviet and of Central Executive Committee of All-Russia Soviet of Peasants' Deputies.

CHAPTER III

1. A.I. Konovalov (1875-1948)—Deputy of Fourth State Duma. Progressist who joined Kadets in 1917. Member of Council of Congresses of Representatives of Industry and Trade. Founder of All-Russia Union of Industry and Trade. Minister of Commerce and Industry in the first two cabinets of the Provisional Government. Kerensky's assistant in last coalition.

2. V.S. Voitinksy—Economist. Social Democrat and former Bolshevik. In October 1917 commissar of the Provisional Government on Northern Front.

3. G.I. Shreider—SR mayor of Petrograd in 1917.

V.V. Rudnev (1874-1940)—SR mayor of Moscow in 1917. Emigrated from Russia after October Revolution and became editor of journal *Sovremennye Zapiski*.

A.M. Berkengeim (1880-1932)—SR who joined cooperative movement. Appointed to board of Central Union of Consumers. In 1917 chairman of Moscow Food Committee. Later left SRs and worked for Soviet Union of Consumers.

M.S. Adzhemov—Kadet. Member of central committee of Kadet party.

4. Bulygin Duma—Institution named after tsarist statesman A.G. Bulygin (1851-1919). The Bulygin Duma was promised by the manifesto of August 6, 1905. It provided for an assembly to be elected on a very limited franchise, and to have consultative (not legislative) powers. The term "Bulygin Duma" came to symbolize weak and half-hearted efforts to reconcile elements of democratic rule with autocratic government.

5. G.V. Plekhanov (1856-1918)—Father of Russian Marxism. Sided with Lenin in congress of 1903 on most questions, but soon developed significant political differences with the Bolsheviks. In 1914 he created the "Edinstvo" (Unity) group of Mensheviks. In 1917 he supported the Provisional Government on the grounds that the revolution in Russia was a bourgeois revolution.

6. M. Gorky (1868-1936) (real name A.M. Peshkov)—Russian writer who considered himself a Social Democrat. He was close at various times to Lenin, A. Bogdanov, Lunacharsky. In 1917 he edited *Novaia Zhizn*, which opposed the Bolshevik notion of proletarian rule. After the October Revolution he had an alternately intimate and distant (even hostile) relationship with the Soviet regime. He became a champion of "socialist realism," but died under mysterious circumstances, perhaps the victim of the regime.

N.N. Sukhanov (1882-?) (real name Gimmer)—Began revolutionary career as an SR, but became attracted to Marxism. In 1917 associated with Menshevik Internationalists and wrote for Gorky's *Novaia Zhizn*. Member of Executive Committee of Petrograd Soviet. After the revolution he wrote seven-volume *Notes on the Revolution*, a classic contribution to historiography. He served the Soviet regime as an economic planner, but in 1931 was arrested and brought to trial in the so-called "Trial of the Mensheviks."

7. A.V. Kartashev (1875-1960)—Former professor at St. Petersburg Theological Academy. Kadet. Chief Procurator of the Holy Synod, July-August 1917. Author of a two-volume history of the Russian church.

8. N.V. Chaikovsky (1850-1926)—Venerable revolutionary whose revolutionary career began in the 1870s. After the turn of the century joined the SRs. In 1915 became vice-chairman of the All-Russia Union of Cooperatives and President of the Free Economic Society. In 1917 he was elected to the Executive Committee of the Petrograd Soviet. In May 1917 elected to the All-Russia Congress of Peasants' Deputies. During the civil war an outspoken opponent of Bolshevism, a member of the "directory" in Ufa.

9. M.M. Vinaver (1863-1926)—Member of Kadet central committee. Deputy to First Duma. After the October Revolution became the Foreign Minister of the White government in Crimea.

10. In his memoirs (*Arkhiv russkoi revoliutsii*, v. 1) V.D. Nabokov recalled these daily meetings, at 6 P.M., in A.G. Khrushchev's apartment on the Admiralty Embankment. Nabokov provided information concerning Kerensky's mood during this period, which information completely coincides with what has been said in my narrative. It should be born in mind that the intermediary between our meetings and A.F. Kerensky was,

of course, the assistant prime minister, A.I. Konovalov. In our meetings Konovalov always had a very depressed look and it seemed that he had lost all hope. Kerensky particularly depressed him. At that time Konovalov finally was becoming disillusioned with Kerensky and was losing all trust in him. The main thing that drove Konovalov to despair was Kerensky's inconstancy, the complete impossibility of depending on Kerensky's words, Kerensky's susceptibility to every form of influence and pressure from the outside, even of the accidental variety. "Everywhere, nearly every day this is the way it is," Konovalov said. "You talk about everything, insist on one or another measure, and, at last, you win agreement. 'So, that's it, A.F.? Now things are decided once and for all. There won't be any changes, will there?' You receive categorical assurances. You walk out of his study and within a few hours you learn about a quite different decision that has already taken effect, or . . . the crucial measure that was supposed to be adopted right now, to-day, has been delayed again. New events have occurred, or old circumstances have appeared again, though one expected they would not. And so it goes, day in and day out, the same old thing over and over again." [PNM]

11. "Savinkovshchina"—A term derived from the name of B.V. Savin-kov (1879-1925), a former SR terrorist who in 1917 became Assistant Minister of War and who had close ties with Kornilov. Here "Savinkov-shchina" means the active agitation for a "strong government" and oppo-sition to Bolshevik rule.

12. In V.D. Nabokov's memoirs, published in Volume 1 of *Arkhiv rus-skoi revoliutsii*, I find authoritative confirmation of the characterization, which I committed to writing, like the rest of the basic text of my histo-ry, in late 1917 and early 1918. During my month-long absence, V.D. Nabokov "was de facto head of the central committee," and conducted the negotiations over the third coalition government. Tsereteli, "who played a most prominent role in the negotiations," departed for the Caucasus and told Nabokov that he [Nabokov] should deal with F. Dan (Gurvich) in future negotiations. "When the work of selecting the future members of the Soviet of the Republic had been completed," Nabokov wrote, "Ad-zhemov and I agreed with Gots, Dan and Skobelev and decided to meet (at Adzhemov's apartment) to work out a future plan of action and formulate a tactical plan. If I am not mistaken, we met twice at Adzhemov's and I vividly recall the feeling of hopelessness and irritation, which seized me during these conversations . . . . Dan's attitude to the situation had very little in common with Tsereteli's. To our [Nabokov's and Adzhemov's] assertion that the main task of the newly created Soviet we thought was the creation of an atmosphere of public trust toward the Provisional Gov-ernment and of support for the government in its struggle against the Bolsheviks, Dan responded that he and his friends were not inclined to promise their loyalty and support in advance, that everything would de-pend on the form of activity the government chooses, and that in particu-lar they did not see the possibility of engaging the Bolsheviks in strug-gle, regardless of circumstances . . . . 'But this was the whole point of our agreement,' we objected, 'while your current attitude is again, as it

was before, ambiguous, hesitant support [for the government] to the extent that it satisfies you, which does not help the government and does not facilitate its activities.' Dan evaded direct answer, vacillated and engaged in some sort of Talmudic polemic. . . . We left in a downcast mood, with the realization that the same old story was beginning all over again, that our 'leftist friends' were incorrigible, and that all our efforts, which had been aimed at winning agreement and supporting the government in its struggle against anarchy and rebelliousness, would probably not   bear fruit." Nabokov's pessimism was, as is apparent, partly due to extravagant hopes that had led him to the agreement with Tsereteli, whose role we have described previously. However, as a result of the negotiations, Nabokov and Adzhemov took a conciliatory position, about which see below. [PNM]

13. B.B. Veselovsky (1880-1954)—Historian of the Zemstvos.   In 1915-1917 scholarly secretary of the Free Economic Society.   Generally a sympathizer with Kadet ideology.   See *Russkoe Slovo*, October 8, 1917, for Veselovsky's calculations.

14. N.K. Mikhailovsky (1842-1904)—Sociologist, journalist, and one of the chief theoreticians of Russian Populism.

N.F. Annensky (1843-1912)—Zemstvo statistician, economist, journalist, and one of the founding members of the Popular Socialist party.

15. V.A. Miakotin (1867-1937)—Historian, journalist, one of the founders of the Popular Socialist Party.

16. L.M. Bramson (1869-?)—Jewish lawyer, member of the Union of Unions. Elected deputy to the First Duma.   One of the founders of the Trudoviks.   In 1917 a member of the Executive Committee of the Petrograd Soviet.

CHAPTER IV

1. M.A. Stakhovich (1862-?)—Former Orel province marshal of nobility. Deputy to Duma. Governor-General of Finland in early 1917.

2. Kullervo Manner (1880-1937)—Social Democrat. In 1917 speaker of the Finnish Diet. In 1918 head of the Red Council of People's Plenipotentiaries in Finland.

3. The representative of Lapland symbolized the demand made by the Finns rather long ago—to grant Finland the areas from the village of Kure to the castle Petsalo, and the shore of the Arctic Ocean from the Norwegian border to Fisherman's Peninsula. [PNM]

4. Yrjo Mäkelin (1875-1923)—Socialist. Advocate of Finnish independence.

5. B.E. Nolde (1876-1948)—Specialist in international law. Professor at St. Petersburg Polytechnic Institute. In 1914 legal consultant to the Ministry of Foreign Affairs. Member of the Kadet party. Coauthor of Nicholas II's abdication papers. After the October Revolution a distinguished historian.

N.I. Lazarevsky—Chairman of the Juridicial Council under the Provisional Government.

D.D. Grimm—Member of the central committee of the Kadet party. Member, Juridicial Council and Council on Defense.

A. Ia. Galpern—Member, Judicial Council of the Provisional Government.

6. Lauri Ingman (1868-1934)—Theologian. Professor at Helsinki University. In November 1918 became Finnish Minister of Foreign Affairs.

Sateri Alkio (1862-1930)—One of the founders of the Agrarian Alliance. Deputy to the Finnish Diet 1907-1922. In 1919-1920 Minister of Social Affairs.

7. Carl Enckell (1876-1959)—Young Finn. Became Finland's representative in Russia after March Revolution. Later represented Finland at the Paris Peace Conference.

8. V.K. Vinnichenko, *Vidrodzhennia natsii,* Chapter II (Kiev-Viden, 1920). [PNM]

9. Mykhailo Hrushevskyi (1866-1934)—Eminent historian of the Ukraine. Before 1914 Professor of History at Lviw (Lvov) and head of the Shevchenko Society. In 1917 president of the Central Rada. He continued his scholarly work until his death. He was recognized as dean of Ukrainian historians.

10. S.V. Petliura (1879-1926)—Founding member of the Ukrainian Revolutionary Party in 1900 and the Ukrainian Social Democratic Party in 1907. In 1917-1918 was an important figure in the Rada, and in 1919 one of the dominant figures in the directory. His chief fame thereafter rested on his military exploits in attempts to establish an independent socialist Ukraine.

11. Dmitro Doroshenko—Historian. Member of the Society of Ukrainian Progressives. Member of the Social Federalist Party. In 1917 an official of the Rada. Generally in favor of Ukrainian national autonomy in a federal structure. Within the Ukraine he was regarded as a political moderate.

12. Nikolai Porsh—Member of the Revolutionary Ukrainian Party, and a rival within it of Vinnichenko. In November 1917 became Ukrainian Secretary of Justice.

13. Other points of the "Instruction" presented a demand for an exclusively socialist ministry "to be responsible to the democracy of all nationalities of Russia;" for state and regional control over production and distribution of goods; for the abolition of secret treaties and the opening of peace negotiations without waiting for the Allies, etc.. The point in the "Instruction" about the authority of local agencies was expressed more strongly in the "Instruction" than by Porsh in the assembly. The "Instruction" demanded transfer of all power in the Ukraine to the Rada and the Secretariat on the basis of the statute that had been rejected by the Provisional Government during the writing of the "Instruction." [PNM]

14. A. Shulgin—Member of the Society of Ukrainian Progressives, a left-liberal body. Secretary of Nationality Affairs in the Rada's General Secretariat. Unofficial Secretary of Foreign Affairs, late 1917-early 1918. Member of the Ukrainian delegation to the Paris Peace Conference.

A. Zarubin—Russian Socialist Revolutionary. Secretary of Post and Telegraphs in the Rada's General Secretariat.

I. Steshenko—Ukrainian Social Democrat. Secretary of Education in the Rada's General Secretariat.

A. Lotoskii—Member of the Society of Ukrainian Progressives. Advocated that federal ties with Russia be maintained for as long as possible.

Savchenko-Belsky—SR sympathizer. Secretary of Agriculture in September 1917.

Peter Stebnitsky—Moderate interested in a federated Ukraine. In September 1917 representative to Petrograd from the Ukraine.

15. As is appparent from Vinnichenko's book (*Vidrodzhennia natsii*, II, p. 59), the Ukrainian leaders expected more ruthless measures from the Provisional Government. They were certain that they would be called to Petrograd to be arrested there, and that in Kiev the Central Rada would be dispersed by a swift and decisive attack. Vinnichenko added that "neither the Central Rada nor the General Secretariat knew anything about these plans. Only later did it become clear there were cells already prepared for the members of the Secretariat in Petrograd prisons." More generally, these anxieties testified to the mood of the delegates, particularly the mood of Vinnichenko himself, who did not travel with the other delegates. The delegation arrived "on the very day when the Bolsheviks were already bombarding the Winter Palace." [PNM]

16. P.P. Iurenev—Engineer. Member of the Kadet central committee. Minister of Transport, July-August 1917.

17. K.A. Gvozdev—Menshevik. Assistant Minister of Labor. From mid-October 1917 until the October Revolution the Minister of Labor.

18. V.A. Razvozov (1879-1920)—Appointed Commander-in-Chief of the Black Sea Fleet, July 1917. After the October Revolution he was arrested and died in prison.

CHAPTER V

1. V.N. Figner (1852-1942)—Revolutionary veteran. Member of the Executive Committee of the People's Will, the Populist terrorist organization of the late 1870s and early 1880s. Imprisoned 1884-1904. Briefly joined the SRs in 1908, but resigned after the Azef affair.

2. P.P. Riabushinksy (1871-1924)—Textile manufacturer. For a time in 1905 close to the Octobrists, he joined the Party of Peaceful Renewal. In the Fourth Duma he was Progressist. He founded All-Russia Union of Industry and Trade. What he actually warned was that the "bony hand of hunger and national destitution [would] seize the throats of the false friends of the people."

3. N.N. Dukhonin (1876-1917)—Before March 1917 Quartermaster General on the Southwestern Front. In 1917 member of the General Staff. After Kornilov affair while Kerensky was nominally supreme

commander-in-chief, Dukhonin actually discharged the military duties of that post. After the fall of the Winter Palace in October Dukhonin worked hard to support Kerensky and the Provisional Government, at least until that option was no longer viable.

4. A.A. Brusilov (1853-1926)—Russian army officer. At the beginning of World War I, commander of VIII Army. As commander of the Southwestern Front in 1916, he executed one of Russia's most successful offensives of the war. Supreme commander-in chief, May-July 1917. After the October Revolution recognized the Soviet government; helped direct the war against Poland in 1920, and when he retired in 1924 was Inspector of Cavalry.

N.V. Ruzsky (1854-1918)—At the beginning of World War I, commander of III Army. Commander-in-chief of the Northwestern Front 1914-1915. Commander of VI Army, 1915. Commander-in-chief of the Northern Front, 1915-1916. Retired because of illness, April 1917.

5. M.M. Vinaver (1862 or 1863-1926)—Attorney, publicist, Jewish leader. A founding member of the Kadet party. Member of the Kadet central committee, 1905-1921. Deputy in the First Duma. Elected to the Constituent Assembly.

6. I.Z. Shteinberg—Chairman of Left SRs and after the October Revolution Commissar of Justice.

7. M.I. Liber (1880-1937)—One of the leaders of the Bund, and closely associated with the founding of the Russian Social Democratic Workers' Party. Menshevik leader. Member of the Petrograd Soviet Executive Committee. Member of the presidium of the first All-Russia Central Executive Committee.

8. See the passage cited above in V.D. Nabokov's memoirs. [PNM]

9. P.I. Novgorodtsev (1886-1924)—Jurist. Professor of philosophy at Moscow University. Kadet deputy in the First Duma and signer of the Vyborg Manifesto. Withdrew from active role in politics, 1907-1917. Elected to the Kadet central committee, May 1917.

10. P.B. Struve (1870-1944)—One of the founders of the Russian Social Democratic Workers' Party, he broke with Marxism. In 1905 joined Kadets and became member of Kadet central committee until 1915. Deputy of Second Duma. In 1917 worked as head of the Economic Department in the Ministry of Foreign Affairs. After the revolution in October 1917 became a major figure in emigre politics.

CHAPTER VI

1. Pope Benedict XV (1851-1922; Pope from 1914-1922)—Throughout the war he pursued a policy of strict neutrality, and tried to eliminate unnecessary suffering. His most elaborate peace proposal was that of August 1917, but it came to naught, partly because the disposition of the European belligerents was not positive with respect to it, and partly because American intervention changed the strategic and diplomatic calculus of the European governments.

2. V.A. Maklakov (1869-1957)—Member of the Kadet central committee, 1905. Member of the Second and Third Dumas. In 1917 a leader of the right wing of the Kadet party. From July 1917 Russian ambassador to France.

3. As is well known, a week after the victory of the Bolsheviks Lenin published the Decree of November 15 on the right of self-determination of nationalities "up to secession," and on November 29 German Chancellor Hertling stated in the Reichstag that he "respects the right of Poland, Courland and Lithuania autonomously to decide their own fate." [PNM]

4. A.I. Guchkov (1862-1936)—Organizer and leader of the Octobrist faction. Member of the Third and Fourth Dumas. Duma chairman, 1910. Member of the State Council, 1915. Leader in the palace conspiracy against Nicholas II, 1916. Minister of War, March 1917. With Putilov an organizer of the Society for Economic Rebirth of Russia, which provided funds to the Kornilov effort.

5. The reference to the "nobleman Lenin" was, of course, meant to be ironic, since Lenin was ostensibly the head of a working class party. Nevertheless, Miliukov was correct that Lenin was the son of a tsarist official who rose to the status of hereditary nobility. The nobleman Kireevsky was I.V. Kireevsky (1806-1856), one of the principal ideologists of Russian Slavophilism.

6. In his memoirs V.D. Nabokov recounted his personal vacillations on the question of continuing the war and on attempts of B.E. Nolde and M.S. Adzhemov to champion the appropriate view in the Kadet central committee (where a decision of the issue was delayed until my return from the Crimea) and in the private conference at Prince G.N. Trubetskoi's (which conference, as in the central committee, found a majority to oppose the exertion of pressure on the Allies). The conversation with Verkhovsky occurred in Nabokov's apartment on the afternoon of October 20; Shingarev and Kokoshkin were present. Most of the speaking, unfortunately, was done by me. Only from Nabokov's memoirs did I discover that he kept quiet for "psychological reasons," and did not essentially share our view. But the circumstance that made our view unexceptionable was that the only alternative was a separate peace—for to hope to convince the Allies was naive, and no one wanted to resort to a separate peace at that time, as it was not clear that the only way to cut the hopelessly confused knot was to leave the war.

From Verkhovsky's note it was clear that the thoughts he expressed were his own serious convictions. Yet to put them into practice without associating himself with Bolshevik slogans was impossible. In this lay the tragedy of those who, like Verkhovsky, were forced to defend the "democratization" of the army. [PNM]

7. Verkhovsky's speech was recorded in his book, *Rossiia na Golgofe* (Leningrad, 1918). [PNM]

8. V.L. Burtsev (1861-1942)—Populist publicist close to the Kadets and to moderate SR circles. Well-known historian of the revolutionary movement, and an inveterate exposer of provocateurs and police agents.

CHAPTER VII

1. The brochure was written in the last week of September 1917. Lenin himself recalled that he had been developing ideas of the brochure since the day of his arrival in Russia on April 4. [PNM]

2. These data have beeen taken from documents probably gathered by Russian intelligence and foreign intelligence services, and obtained by the American Sisson in late 1917. At that point these documents were sent to Novocherkassk, where I first became acquainted with them. In Sisson's well-known brochure, *The Bolshevist Conspiracy*, this series of documents was printed in small print, as an appendix. Obviously, the most sensational documents, sent by the American in originals or photographic copies, had to do with the collaboration of the Bolsheviks with German officers even after their victory. But even during the period when the documents were being collected there were rumors about their fabrication by persons who sold them to Sisson. Sisson's brochure became the subject of a special investigation by a commission of American scholars, which rejected the accusation of fabrication and pronounced the documents authentic. But, of course, this was not final proof. The Allied governments suggested that there were reasons for doubt [as to the documents' authenticity], and so people have ceased to cite the documents. The belief in their dubiousness has become very widespread. However, this belief may not be well founded. The history of the collection of the documents in Bolshevik institutions for Sisson was recounted by E.P. Semenov (Kogan) in *Posledniia Novosti*. From another source I had the occasion to learn that at least several of the documents gathered by Sisson are genuine. It is quite likely that Semenov's agents, eager for money, turned from the gathering of documents to their fabrication on Soviet letterheads. I have no precise criteria for judging. But the documents cited in the text, I repeat, fall into a completely different category: as I see it, they were gathered by foreign and Russian intelligence. [PNM]

The authenticity of the Sisson documents was a matter of debate for nearly forty years. George F. Kennan finally established that all the documents having to do with German control over the Bolsheviks *after* the October Revolution were forgeries. Kennan could not pronounce final judgment on the documents pertaining to German aid to the Bolsheviks *before* October 1917, but they produced "a distinctly unreliable impression" on him. See George F. Kennan, "The Sisson Documents," *Journal of Modern History*, XXVIII, No. 2 (June 1956), pp. 130-154. There is independent evidence of German financial support for the Bolsheviks before the October Revolution, based on unimpeachable documentary sources in German Foreign Ministry Archives. See Z.A.B. Zeman, *Germany and the Revolution in Russia* (London, 1958).

3. A.M. Kollontai (1872-1952)—Joined the Social Democrtic Party in the foundation period. Became one of the most remarkable theoreticians in the party, mainly as advocate of the liberation of women. By

1917 Kollontai was associated with the central committee of the Bolshevik party, was an early supporter of Lenin's position in favor of proletarian seizure of power. After the October Revolution was the most prominent woman in the party apparatus. For a short time she served as Commissar of Welfare and as ambassador to two countries.

4. N.V. Krylenko (1885-1938)—Ensign, member of the Military Revolutionary Committee. Member, Central Executive Committee of Soviet. In November 1917 was named Commissar for Military Affairs. From 1918-1931 he was government prosecutor in many trials of alleged "anti-Soviets."

5. P.E. Dybenko (1889-1938)—Bolshevik. Chairman of Tsentrobalt. In July 1917 elected to the central committee of the Bolshevik party. In October 1917 appointed commissar of the Red Navy. He fell victim to Stalin's purges and was executed in 1938.

6. V.A. Cheremisov (1871-?)—General. Commander of army corps in June 1917 offensive. Commander of VIII Army, July-September 1917. Commander-in-chief of Northern Front, September-October 1917. Refused to support Kerensky's effort to combat the Bolshevik seizure of power in October. Resigned from the army, November 1917.

V.L. Baranovsky—Major general. General Quartermaster of the Staff of the Northern Front.

7. After this all three assistant ministers—Balts, Skariatin, and Demianov—turned in their resignations and remained only when Maliantovich admitted the wrongness of his actions. The external side of this episode was recounted in the memoirs of Demianov in Volume 4 of *Arkhiv russkoi revoliutsii*. [PNM]

8. The confusion about the dates is Miliukov's.

9. G.P. Polkovnikov—Colonel. Chief commander of Petrograd military district. Dismissed from his post on the very day of the siege of the Winter Palace.

10. Miliukov's text wrongly dates the day of the Petrograd Soviet as Sunday, October 23. I have given the correct date.

11. Miliukov's text misdated the confrontation of Polkovnikov and the Military Revolutionary Committee. The Russian text gives the date as "the night of October 22/23," when it should have read "the night of October 21/22." I have supplied the correct date in the English edition.

12. V.A. Antonov-Ovseenko (1884-1938)—Social Democrat. Veteran of 1905 revolution. Before the Great War associated mostly with the Menshevik faction. In 1917 became member of the Bolshevik central committee. Arrested in July Days. Prominent member of the Military Revolutionary Committee involved in directing the siege of the Winter Palace. After October Revolution served on the Committee for Military and Naval Affairs, as Commissar for Military Affairs in the Ukraine, and in a variety of ambassadorships. Arrested in 1937 and executed.

13. "Black Hundreds"—Originally the term referred to ultra-rightist, anti-Semitic groups involved in anti-Jewish pogroms of 1905. By 1917

it was sometimes used to refer to anyone known to disagree with the extreme left.

14. Polkovnikov's report to the government on October 23 clearly was not so optimistic as Kerensky claimed in characterizing the reports made to him personally. [PNM]

15. In the article, "Gatchina," Kerensky summarized in a different fashion this, his last, speech: "I stated that all possible measures for the suppression of the uprising had been taken and were being taken by the Provisional Government; that [the government] would struggle to the end against the traitors to the motherland and to the revolution; that it would resort without any hesitation to military force, but, in order to succeed in the struggle, the government needed the immediate assistance of all parties and groups." [PNM]

16. N.I. Podvoisky (1880-1948)—Bolshevik. Editor of *Soldatskaia Pravda*. One of the inspirers of the July insurrection. He was a key figure in the Bolshevik Military Organization, an organizer of the Red Guards, and played an important role in the Military Revolutionary Committee in October 1917. After the October Revolution he commanded Petrograd military district and was head of the Commissariat for Military Affairs.

17. A.F. Kerensky later appropriated this viewpoint as a way of justifying himself before posterity. In his article "Gatchina," cited above, he presented the view that the Bolshevik uprising could at most be called the fruit of a new conspiracy by "Kornilovites." "The public groups who had supported the 'dictator' and who had connections with him *resolved* not to render the government any support in case of a showdown with the Bolsheviks. *Their strategic plan* was not to hinder the success of the Bolshevik armed uprising at the beginning, but later, after the fall of the hated Provisional Government, swiftly to suppress the Bolshevist 'rebellion.' By this means they would finally attain the goals of the Kornilov uprising. The military and civilian strategists, the authors of this remarkable plan, were firmly convinced that the Bolshevik triumph would not present any serious danger and that in 3 or 4 weeks the 'healthy elements' of the Russian people would deal with the rebellious masses and establish in Russia a 'strong government.'" Of course, there were rumors of this sort, and the "counter-revolutionaries" were not the only ones in Russia who longed for a "strong government." But Kerensky could hardly have been correct when he claimed that on this mood, which was hostile to Kerensky and which gripped ever broader circles, was based an entire "strategic plan" and that there was even a "resolution" to allow the overthrow of the government by the Bolsheviks. The part of Kerensky's calculations that was reliable may be found in the text of this book, written in 1918. [PNM]

18. *Novoe Slovo*, April 2 (March 20) 1918. The article "Pravitelstvo Kerenskogo nakanune perevorota." [PNM]

19. In his account of events ("Gatchina") A.F. Kerensky generally attributed to the decision of the Soviet of the Republic a more fateful significance than it actually had among the series of factors leading to the Bolshevik success. He was prepared to admit that to a considerable extent the success of the party could be explained by the fact that the

remaining socialist parties and Soviet groups, who regarded all reports of the impending events as "counter-revolutionary fabrications" (that is, in essence, very close to the view taken then by Kerensky himself), did not even try at the time to mobilize their own forces, which were capable at the crucial moment of resisting the Bolshevik plots from within the revolutionary democracy. We have seen that the basic reason for this was the desire to maintain a "united front" of the "revolutionary democracy" (This time the quotation marks are Kerensky's) with the Bolsheviks against the nonsocialist portion of the democracy. *In retrospect* Kerensky desired to shift part of the blame to the "Bolsheviks from the right," "who could not overcome their burning hatred for the government of the March Revolution," and to blame the entire membership of the Soviet "which was rent by internal disagreements and by irreconcilable contradictions of opinion." We have seen that the entire right half of the Soviet was prepared to render immediate assistance to the government, and, consequently, Kerensky's indictment applied only to the left wing because of whose behavior, as we noted above, the entire day was lost in fruitless debate. [PNM]

20. It was probably for this reason that the Bolsheviks negotiated with the other socialist parties. Dan had spoken to Kerensky about these negotiations (see above). [PNM]

21. P.N. Maliantovich even at this decisive moment showed indecisiveness and insisted on the cancellation of an order for the immediate arrest of the members of the Military Revolutionary Committee. He stated that it was necessary first to investigate who were the authors of the appeal to the populace and to the garrison, what was the purpose of the appeal, and only then to carry out the arrests. In the meantime, it would be enough to start a judicial investigation against the members of the Military Revolutionary Committee. On the other hand, however, Maliantovich agreed to resort to arrest as a method of crime prevention applying to those Bolsheviks who, after they had been released on recognizance, had agitated among the troops and the populace (Trotsky, Kollontai, and others). [PNM]

22. David R. Francis, *Russia from the American Embassy* (New York, 1921), pp. 179-180.

23. In the article "Gatchina" Kerensky presented this episode differently. "I don't know how, but the news of my departure spread to the Allied embassies. At the moment of my departure [when Kerensky already had 'ordered his excellent open roadster' with 'the couragious and loyal soldier-chauffeur'] I was approached by representatives of the English and, if I remember rightly, the American embassy who stated that representatives of the Allied powers desired that an automobile with an American flag should accompany me on the road. Although it was more obvious that, in case it should prove impossible to break away, the American flag could not save me or my fellow travellers, but quite the contrary, that during our passage through the city it might attract to us unnecessary attention, I nevertheless accepted this proposal with gratitude as proof of the Allies' regard for the Provisional Government and of their solidarity with

us." It is likely that the Allies' consideration could not have gone so far, that there was no such "proposal" from them, and that, at best, the Americans decided to look askance at the seizure of their automobile, under the condition that their flag not be used. This example demonstrates how Kerensky's attitude influenced his presentation of the facts. [PNM]

24. V.A. Obolensky was a prince (kniaz), and was perhaps suspected of being connected with the royal family.

25. P.A. Palchinsky (1878-1929)—Served on the Military Industry Committee and the Military Commission of Fourth Duma. In 1917 Assistant Minister of Trade, President of Special Council on Defense. After the Kornilov affair he was Governor-General of Petrograd. After the October Revolution and his arrest, he served as an advisor to the State Planning Commission.

26. The account of S.N. Tretiakov in the Peter and Paul Fortress on 7 January. See F.V. Vinberg, *V plenu u "obezian"*, pp. 39-40. [PNM]

27. Only seventeen names were listed in Miliukov's Russian text.

28. A.I. Rykov (1881-1938)—Member of the Bolshevik central committee after the Third Party Congress. In 1917 member of the Executive Committee of Moscow Soviet, and later elected to its presidium. After the October Revolution served as head of the Supreme Economic Council and in the 1920s was a champion of NEP. Tried in the Show Trial of 1938 and shot.

V.P. Miliutin (1884-1938)—Long-time Social Democrat. At first attached to Menshevism, but in 1910 became a Bolshevik. In 1917 chairman of the Saratov Soviet. Became Commissar of Agriculture. Later deputy chairman of Gosplan.

A.G. Shliapnikov (1884-1937)—Bolshevik labor leader, who was head of the central committee's Russian Bureau in February 1917. In 1917 head of the All-Russia Union of Metalworkers. Between 1917 and 1921 a spokesman for workers' interests and a key figure in the so-called "Workers' Opposition." Wrote an important history of 1917.

V.P. Nogin (1878-1924)—Member of the Bolshevik central committee in 1903. In 1917 deputy chairman, then chairman of the Moscow Soviet. Member of the Central Executive Committee of All-Russia Soviet. After the October Revolution he worked in various capacities as Soviet economic manager.

I.I. Skvortsov (1870-1928)—Bolshevik, at points a close associate of A.A. Bogdanov. In 1917 member of the Moscow Soviet. Editor of *Izvestiia* and *Sotsial-Demokrat*. Member of the Moscow Military Revolutionary Committee. After the October Revolution a journalist and economic administrator.

G.I. Lomov-Oppokov (1888-1938)—Bolshevik, associated with Vperedist faction in 1911. In 1917 member of the Moscow Oblast Committee of the Bolshevik party and member of the Moscow Soviet. After the October Revolution he was active in economic affairs, especially in the Supreme Economic Council. Arrested in 1938 and executed.

I.A. Teodorovich (1875-1937)—Old Bolshevik. Member of the central committee in 1907. In 1917 deputy chairman of the Moscow Duma. After the October Revolution a manager of peasant affairs and agriculture. Arrested and died in prison during the purges of the 1930s.

CHAPTER VIII

1. P.N. Krasnov (1869-1947)—General. Commander of III Army Corps, August-October 1917. During the civil war commander of Cossack brigade, then Cossack division. Military ataman of the Don, May 1918.

2. In the following pages I used the account of General Krasnov in two versions. The earlier version was printed by General Krasnov in Velikie Luki in 1917 under the title, "Opisanie deistvii 3-go konnogo korpusa pod Petrogradom protiv sovetskikh voisk." A copy of this "Description" was given to me by the author in the town of Rostov in fall 1918. I used it in composing the first draft of the text of this history, but left the document in Kiev during the departure for Jassy in November 1918. Unfortunately, this copy, according to General Krasnov, was the only extant copy. Another version, more detailed and colorful, but less accurate was published by General Krasnov in *Arkhiv russkoi revoliutsii*. In the text of this history I have used the first version of the "Opisanie," but I have added certain details from the later version, published in *Arkhiv*. [PNM]

3. According to the second version of Krasnov's memoir, he met Savinkov only at dawn on October 28. [PNM]

4. B.V. Savinkov's memoirs of these days are summarized in his article, "K vystupleniiu bolshevikov," published in *Russkie Vedomosti* on November 21. [PNM]

5. V.V. Stankevich—Commissar of the Provisional Government on the Northern Front.

6. Two notebooks, containing copies of the telegraph ribbons of October 25 and 26, copied apparently on orders from Dukhonin at Stavka, were seized by the Volunteer Army after the capture of Kiev in fall 1919, and were published in Volume VII of *Arkhiv russkoi revoliutsii*. [PNM]

7. S.G. Lukirsky—General. Chief of Staff of the Northern Front in October 1917.

8. P.S. Baluev—General. Commander-in-chief of the Western Front, August-October, 1917.

9. The text of the order, which was signed by Kerensky in Pskov, was the following: "The current disorder, which has been provoked by the Bolsheviks' insanity, has brought our nation to the brink of destruction; each person must show his courage and discharge his duty [if the state is to survive]. *If the Provisional Government survives, it will soon announce a new cabinet*; thus each person must remain at his post and must do his duty for the sake of the suffering motherland. It should be rem

remembered that any violation whatsoever of the existing army organization may cause irremediable disasters by exposing the front to a new blow from the enemy. Therefore, it is essential to preserve, at whatever cost, the army's fighting capacity, to maintain complete order, and thus to save the army from new difficulties and not to shake the mutual trust between officers and their subordinates. For the sake of the motherland I order all officers and commissars to retain their posts, just as I shall retain my post of Supreme Commander-in-Chief *until the will of the Provisional Government of the Republic has been made known.* This order should be read to all companies, commands, squadrons, and batteries, to all military courts and to all engineering units. A. Kerensky." [PNM]

10. P.N. Vrangel (1878-1928)—General who commanded cavalry corps in the Great War. In 1919 commander of the Volunteer Army and in 1920 commander of all White forces in Russia.

11. A.I. Anikeev—Cossack *esaul* (ensign). Chairman of the Cossack Soviet in Petrograd.

A.I. Kozmin—Captain. Assistant commander of Petrograd military district in October 1917.

12. According to Savinkov's memoirs, Stankevich even claimed that "he did not look on the Bolsheviks as traitors, and that he thought it possible to appoint Ensign Krylenko as his assistant . . . . The state's interests demanded an immediate agreement with the Bolsheviks and the formation of a new cabinet based on that agreement." In *Arkhiv russkoi revoliutsii* Krasnov also reported that "Stankevich believed that it was nonetheless possible to reach an agreement with the Bolsheviks." [PNM]

13. In his memoirs in the article "Gatchina" Kerensky said that he "endorsed the opinion of the majority," since there were no other solution in sight. "It was necessary to play for time" and "he could not allow Krasnov and his staff to be in a position to tell the Cossacks: 'We were for peace, but Kerensky ordered us to fight.'" [PNM]

14. According to the memoirs of Kerensky, who knew only this paper but did not remember the text, Stankevich was sent to "survey the situation" even in the Committee for the Salvation of the Motherland and the Revolution. "Two of my preconditions I have not forgotten," Kerensky added: "First, the Bolsheviks must immediately lay down their weapons and submit to a newly-organized national Provisional Government; second, the composition and program of this government should be established by agreement of the existing Provisional Government with the representatives of all political parties and with the Committee for the Salvation of the Motherland and the Revolution." Kerensky quite rightly noted that "in any case, these preconditions were not acceptable to the Bolsheviks." Stankevich departed around 4 o'clock for Petrograd. [PNM]

15. In his memoirs Kerensky spoke only about the first order, the one sending Savinkov to Stavka. Kerensky added ironically: "The wise

foresight of Savinkov gave only a rough idea of the atmosphere surrounding me." [PNM]

16. Henri Albert Niessel—French general. Chief of the French military mission to Russia, 1917-1918.

17. I cite this conversation from Krasnov's original account. In the memoirs printed in *Arkhiv russkoi revoliutsii*, Krasnov related the entire conversation up to Kerensky's request to replace the Cossack sentry at the door with a cadet sentry. However, in his own memoirs, Kerensky recalled his "last meeting" with Krasnov more fully, and, not knowing of the original brochure of Krasnov, presented certain features of the conversation in a fashion similar to Krasnov's original account. I shall cite Kerensky's account for comparison: "Krasnov began to explain at great length that the meeting with the sailors had no particular importance, that he was carefully following what was going on there through reliable sources, and that he even considered these negotiations an event extremely favorable for us. Let them talk there, he reasoned: the day will pass in conversations and arguments, and toward evening the situation will clarify itself. The infantry will arrive and we will change the tone. [This was, in fact, Krasnov's customary tactic.] As far as my surrender was concerned, he [Krasnov] would not accept anything of the sort. I could be quite certain of that. But it seemed to him that perhaps it would be useful if I personally—naturally, accompanied by a reliable escort, which he would provide—should go to St. Petersburg directly to agree with the parties and even with Smolny. Yes, that enterprise was very risky, but was it not worth it to save the state [from destruction]?" What was really happening "below" among the sailors and Cossacks? The newly-arrived sailors, Dybenko and Tushin, stated at once that they had no intention of talking with the officers and would talk directly with the [men of the] detachment. [PNM]

18. S.G. Roshal (1896-1917)—Social Democrat. Originally a Menshevik, but by 1914 a Bolshevik. In 1917 one of chief organizers of the Bolshevik group at Kronstadt. Arrested in the wake of the July Days and released only on October 25. He immediately involved himself in efforts to defend the revolution militarily, and perished in Romania—one of the first victims of the civil war. Miliukov mistakenly identified him as Raskolnikov, another organizer at Kronstadt.

19. M.A. Muraviev (1880-1918)—Lieutenant General. Left SR. After 25 October 1917 appointed head of the Petrograd garrison. He was an important figure in early period of the civil war, especially in the Ukraine, but he changed his allegiance from the government after the Left SRs went into opposition in 1918.

20. In *Arkhiv russkoi revoliutsii* Krasnov said that he was called to Smolny that night by Dybenko, Tarasov, and Rodionov "for conversations about what to do with the Cossacks," and he gave his word of honor to return.[PNM]

21. A.M. Kaledin (1861-1918)—Major general and commander of XII Corps, 1914. Commander of VIII Army, 1916, and the Ataman of the

Don Cossacks, 1917. Later an important figure in the formation of the Volunteer Army.

22. A.I. Feit (1864-1926)—Physician. Member of the SR central committee. Witness at the show trial of 1921.

A.A. Krakovetsky (1884-?)—SR. Witness at the 1921 show trial.

23. Avksentiev also endorsed this account in a conversation with the author of this text. He did not take part in the military deliberations under discussion, but, as chairman of the Soviet of Peasants' Deputies, he was in the same building in which the deliberations occurred. At the end of the meeting late at night he left the building with Gots, and Gots told him that nothing had been decided for the next day and the day would pass peacefully. [PNM]

24. "Three days after the supression of the uprising," added Rakitin, "the press carried a letter of Avksentiev, Gots and Sinani with the statement that they had not signed the order referred to above." [PNM]

25. A.I. Shingarev (1869-1918)—Physician. Zemstvo activist and publicist. Member of the Kadet central committee. Deputy in the Second, Third and Fourth Dumas. One of the authors of the Kadet agrarian program. Minister of Agriculture, March-May 1917. Minister of Finance, May-July. Member of the Pre-Parliament. Elected to the Constituent Assembly, but arrested in November for "anti-Soviet" activities. Murdered by Red sailors in January 1918.

26. N.I. Bukharin (1888-1938)—Bolshevik theorist and politician. Member of the Moscow party organization. In the 1920s a major advocate of NEP and "Right Communism." Purged in the 1930s in famous show trial.

N. Osinsky (V.V. Obolensky) (1887-1938)—Bolshevik. In 1917 on Moscow Oblast Bureau and the editorial staff of *Sotsial-Demokrat*. After October 1917 head of the State Bank and first chairman of the Supreme Economic Council.

A.P. Smirnov (1877-1938)—Old Bolshevik. In 1917 member of the presidium of the Moscow province Soviet. After October 1917 appointed Assistant Commissar of Internal Affairs. He was active in economic management, particularly in agriculture. Died in prison.

27. The activity of communists in the Moscow uprising has been summarized in the memoirs of the participants, printed in Moscow communist newspapers of 1917 and 1918, and reprinted in the collection, *Moskva v oktiabre 1917 g.. Illiustrirovanny sbornik zametok i vospominanii uchastnikov dvizheniia.* Pod redaktsiei i so vstupitelnoi statei N. Ovsianikova (Moscow, 1919). [PNM]

28. N.I. Astrov—Attorney. Zemstvo activst and Kadet. Member of the Moscow City Duma and of the All-Russia Union of Towns. Member of the Kadet central committee. Member of the editorial staff of *Russkie Vedomosti.*

29. In addition, the Bolsheviks refused to send a representative. [PNM]

30. K.A. Riabtsov—Colonel. Right SR. Commander of Moscow military district in October 1917.

31. This justification was given in the *Vecherny kurier* on 7 November 1917 in the article entitled "Letopis krovavoi nedeli." [PNM]

32. E.M. Iaroslavsky—Bolshevik. Member of the Moscow party committee and of the editorial board of *Sotsial-Demokrat*.

33. M.S. Olminsky (1863-1933)—Journalist, historian. Old Bolshevik. Member of the Moscow party committee and of the editorial board of *Sotsial-Demokrat*. After the October Revolution he formed the Society of Old Bolsheviks and published many articles on party history.

34. In a letter to the editor of the Berlin newspaper *Rul* on 1 August 1922, a letter intended to answer *Novoe Vremia*, S.N. Prokopovich himself contradicted certain aspects of the above conclusion. Prokopovich summarized his own role in the capture of the Kremlin as follows: "Having studied the situation [in the Committee of Safety, to which he came directly from the train station on the morning of October 27], I summoned to the City Duma the military commander, the late Riabtsov, and asked him how he could have permitted the Kremlin to be captured. Riabtsov answered me that he, as a military man, could only carry out the orders of the civilian authorities. Neither the Provisional Government nor the Committee of Public Safety in Moscow had given him direct orders to engage the Bolsheviks in battle. Then I, basing myself on the plenary powers granted to me by the meeting of the assistant ministers, gave him an order to occupy the Kremlin. Riabtsov obeyed the order, and the Kremlin was occupied by us." S.N. Prokopovich's account of his statement to Riabtsov coincided in part with the evidence concerning the "pedantic politics" of the committee cited above from the testimony of influential committee members. Prokopovich's account also coincided with our description of Riabtsov's personality: Riabtsov was terribly afraid of assuming the responsibility for an independent decision, was prepared to protect himself by allowing someone else to decide things for him, or to shift responsibility entirely to someone else—the Bolsheviks, the City Duma committee, or the Provisional Government. But from my previous remarks it is evident, on the one hand, that the struggle over the Kremlin was already underway when Prokopovich arrived and that the elements of the struggle became clear gradually; on the other hand, the capture of the Kremlin was a complicated task which Riabtsov set himself only on the evening of October 27, when he succeeded in extricating himself from Bolshevik semi-captivity. It was a task accomplished only in the course of the following day, not so much by the use of force as by taking advantage of the panic of the Bolshevik commander inside the Kremlin. The decision to occupy the Kremlin made on the evening of October 27 was not so much the result of the morning "order" by Prokopovich as it was the result of a demand by the Committee of Public Safety that Riabtsov finally should change his point of view on events. [PNM]

35. This and certain other information was conveyed to me by leading members of the Committee of Public Safety. [PNM]

36. N.I. Iordansky—Journalist. Menshevik. Commissar of the Provisional Government on the Southwestern Front.
37. N.N. Shchepkin (1854-1919)—Member of the Third and Fourth Dumas. Vice-mayor of Moscow, 1917. Prominent Kadet.
38. *Novoe Vremia*, 1922. No. 387. Letter from Paris by Mr. P-ev. [PNM]
39. N. Muralov defined as follows the number of forces on both sides: "By my reckoning, our enemy had forces numbering 10,000 men, not counting the officers. On their side were: cadets of the Alexandrov and Alexeev Military Academies, all the Ensigns' Schools, and the District Headquarters; the Committee of Public Safety, the soldiers' section of the SRs and Mensheviks, university students and gymnasium students. We had: all the Moscow infantry regiments, the I Reserve Artillery Brigade, the Bicyclists Battalion, the officers of the *Dvintsy*, the regimental section of the Pavlovskaia Sloboda from Kostroma, from Serpukhova about 25,000 reserve inactives; about 3,000 armed workers, six batteries of three-inch field guns and several heavy weapons, some without gun crews and others with inexperienced gun crews. Two Cossack squadrons who several days later accepted my resolution remained neutral. The militia was also neutral at that time." [PNM]
40. The Bolsheviks accused the cadets of violating the cease-fire. M. Olminsky wrote concerning this: "The counter-revolutionaries hoped to win time for reinforcements to arrive. Cossack regiments approached from the South, and shock brigades moved along the Briansk Railroad. Several hours after the beginning of the cease-fire the first detachment of the shock brigades arrived at the Briansk Station. The cadets grew bold and mounted an attack near the Nikitskie Gates." [PNM]

Additional information on personalities and topics found in the text and notes is available in Joseph L. Wieczynski, ed., *The Modern Encyclopedia of Russian and Soviet History* (MERSH); Harry B. Weber, ed., *The Modern Encyclopedia of Russian and Soviet Literatures (Including Non-Russian and Emigre Literatures)* (MERSL); and David R. Jones, ed., *The Military-Naval Encyclopedia of Russian and the Soviet Union* (MERSU), all published by Academic International Press

INDEX

Abramov (Bolshevik), 102-104
Adzhemov, M.S., 54, 56, 68, 84, 118, 129-130, 286n, 288n-289n, 293n
Afanasiev (Vikzhel), 99
Airola (Finnish nationalist), 81
Aladin, A.F., 285n
Alexeev, M.V., 3, 6, 9-10, 15, 21, 24, 117, 123-126, 130, 134, 156, 200-201, 204, 281n
Alkio, Sateri, 85, 290n
Anikeev, A.I., 239-241, 300n
Anisimov, V.A., 14, 131, 284n
Annensky, N.F., 76, 289n
Antonov-Ovseenko, V.A., xv, 167, 179, 183, 207, 213, 295n
Argunov (Right Socialist), 41
Asquith, H.H., 144
Astrov, N.I., 257, 302n
Aurora (ship), 190-191, 204-205
Avilov, N.P., 15, 213, 284n
Avksentiev, N.D., 11, 14, 16-18, 51, 54, 56, 64-65, 69, 77, 104, 111-113, 119, 187, 199, 253-254, 282n, 302n
Axelrod, L.B., 128
Azhogin (Captain), 239-240

Bagratuni (General), 172, 200
Bakanchinov (Vikzhel), 99
Baltic Fleet, 31, 42, 121-123, 169, 197
Baluev, P.S., 230-231, 299n
Baranovsky, V.L., 169, 217-218, 251, 295n
Baratashvili (Georgian nationalist), 89
Bauer, Otto, 227
Benedict XV, Pope, 133, 292n
Berkengeim, A.M., 43, 56, 73, 286n
Bernatssky, M.B., 66, 207
Berzin (Ensign), 260, 263
Black Hundreds, 295n-296n
Black Sea Fleet, xiii, 91, 93-94, 104
Bogdanov, B.O., 12, 36, 41, 108, 253, 283n
Boldyrev, S.R., 13
Bolshevik Party, viii-x, xiv-xxii, xxiv, xxvi, 1, 5-6, 11-13, 22-23, 26-27, 31, 34-35, 40, 43, 46-47, 50-53, 59, 64, 70-73,

78, 94-95, 108, 110, 112-113, 126, 152, 159-215, 219-220, 224, 227-230, 232, 234-235, 237, 240, 248, 250, 253-254, 257-261, 264-266, 268, 270-272, 274, 296n-297n
Borisov, 207
Bramson, L.M., 77, 289n
Breshkovskaia, E.K., 41, 63-64, 111, 160, 286n
Broido (Menshevik), 210
Bronsky (Colonel), 233
Brusilov, A.A., 117, 264, 292n
Bublikov, A.A., 2, 280n
Buchanan, George, xx
Bukharin, N.I., 256, 302n
Bülow, Prince Bernhardt von, 275n
Bulygin Duma, 287n
Burtsev, V.L., 293n
Buryshkin, P.A., 10, 12, 45, 269
Bykovsky (SR), 205

Central Association of Flax Producers, 28
Central Executive Committee of All-Russia Soviets, ix, xvii, xix, xxii, 4-7, 15-18, 21-24, 29-30, 33, 81, 104-105, 108, 115-116, 134, 169, 171, 173, 177, 179, 183-184, 192, 212, 231
Central Rada of Ukraine, xiii, 92-94, 291n
Chaikovsky, N.V., 63, 127, 130, 287n
Char, A.Ia., 99, 101
Cheremisov, P.E., xvi, 169, 172, 215, 216, 218-219, 224, 229-231, 251-252, 295n
Chernov, V.N., xxiv, 5-6, 8, 14, 36-37, 41, 48, 64-65, 69, 77, 149-151, 236, 282n
Chetverikov, S.M., 45
Chicherin, B.N., xxiii
Chkheidze, N.S., 13-14, 23-24, 27, 31-32, 54, 58, 101, 283n
Chkhenkeli, A.I., 39-40, 43, 47, 286n
Chudnovsky (Commissar), 207

ACADEMIC INTERNATIONAL PRESS

THE RUSSIAN SERIES

1 S.F. Platonov *History of Russia* Out of Print
2 *The Nicky-Sunny Letters, Correspondence of Nicholas and Alexandra, 1914-1917*
3 Ken Shen Weigh *Russo-Chinese Diplomacy, 1689-1924* Out of Print
4 Gaston Cahen *Relations of Russia with China . . . 1689-1730* Out of Print
5 M.N. Pokrovsky *Brief History of Russia* 2 Volumes Out of Print
6 M.N. Pokrovsky *History of Russia from Earliest Times . . .* Out of Print
7 Robert J. Kerner *Bohemia in the Eighteenth Century*
8 *Memoirs of Prince Adam Czartoryski and His Correspondence with Alexander I* 2 vols.
9 S.F. Platonov *Moscow and the West*
10 S.F. Platonov *Boris Godunov*
11 Boris Nikolajewsky *Aseff the Spy*
12 Francis Dvornik *Les Legendes de Constantin et de Methode vues de Byzance*
13 Francis Dvornik *Les Slaves, Byzance et Rome au XIe Siecle*
14 A. Leroy-Beaulieu *Un Homme d'Etat Russe (Nicolas Miliutine) . . .*
15 Nicholas Berdyaev *Leontiev* (In English)
16 V.O. Kliuchevskii *Istoriia soslovii v Rossii*
17 *Tehran Yalta Potsdam. The Soviet Protocols*
18 *The Chronicle of Novgorod*
19 Paul N. Miliukov *Outlines of Russian Culture* Vol. III (2 vols.)
20 P.A. Zaionchkovsky *The Abolition of Serfdom in Russia*
21 V.V. Vinogradov *Russkii iazyk. Grammaticheskoe uchenie o slove*
22 P.A. Zaionchkovsky *The Russian Autocracy under Alexander III*
23 A.E. Presniakov *Emperor Nicholas I of Russia. The Apogee of Autocracy*
24 V.I. Semevskii *Krestianskii vopros v Rossii v XVIII i pervoi polovine XIX veka* Out of Print
25 S.S. Oldenburg *Last Tsar! Nicholas II, His Reign and His Russia* 4 volumes
26 Carl von Clausewitz *The Campaign of 1812 in Russia*
27 M,K. Liubavskii *Obrazovanie osnovnoi gosudarstvennoi territorii velikorusskoi narodnosti. Zaselenie i obedinenie tsentra*
28 S.F. Platonov *Ivan the Terrible* Paper
29 Paul N. Miliukov *Iz istorii russkoi intelligentsii. Sbornik Statei i etiudov*
30 A.E. Presniakov *The Tsardom of Muscovy* Paper
31 M. Gorky, J. Stalin et al., *History of the Civil War in Russia* 2 vols. Out of Print
32 R.G. Skrynnikov *Ivan the Terrible*
33 P.A. Zaionchkovsky *The Russian Autocracy in Crisis, 1878-1882*
34 Joseph T. Fuhrmann *Tsar Alexis. His Reign and His Russia*
35 R.G. Skrynnikov *Boris Godunov*
43 Nicholas Zernov *Three Russian Prophets: Khomiakov, Dostoevsky, Soloviev* Out of Print
44 Paul N. Miliukov *The Russian Revolution* 3 vols.
45 Anton I. Denikin *The White Army* Out of Print
55 M.V. Rodzianko *The Reign of Rasputin—An Empire's Collapse. Memoirs* Out of Print
56 *The Memoirs of Alexander Iswolsky*

THE CENTRAL AND EAST EUROPEAN SERIES

1 Louis Eisenmann *Le Compromis Austro-Hongrois de 1867*
3 Francis Dvornik *The Making of Central and Eastern Europe* 2nd edition
4 Feodor F. Zigel *Lectures on Slavonic Law*
10 Doros Alastos *Venizelos—Patriot, Statesman, Revolutionary*
20 Paul Teleki *The Evolution of Hungary and its Place in European History*

FORUM ASIATICA

1 M.I. Sladkovsky *China and Japan—Past and Present*

THE ACADEMIC INTERNATIONAL REFERENCE SERIES

The Modern Encyclopedia of Russian and Soviet History 50 vols. 1976-
The Modern Encyclopedia of Russian and Soviet Literatures 50 vols. 1977-
Soviet Armed Forces Review Annual 1977-
USSR Facts & Figures Annual 1977-
Military-Naval Encyclopedia of Russia and the Soviet Union 50 vols. 1978-
China Facts & Figures Annual 1978-
Encyclopedia USA. The Encyclopedia of the United States of America Past & Present
  50 vols. 1983-
The International Military Encyclopedia 50 vols.
Sports Encyclopedia North America 50 vols. 1985-

SPECIAL WORKS

S.M. Soloviev *History of Russia* 50 vols.
SAFRA Papers 1985-